ONE SOUL WE DIVIDED

One Soul We Divided

A Critical Edition of the
Diary of Michael Field

EDITED BY

Carolyn Dever

PRINCETON UNIVERSITY PRESS
PRINCETON AND OXFORD

Published by Princeton University Press
41 William Street, Princeton, New Jersey 08540
99 Banbury Road, Oxford OX2 6JX

press.princeton.edu

Library of Congress Cataloging-in-Publication Data

Names: Field, Michael, author. | Bradley, Katharine Harris, 1846–1914, author. | Cooper, Edith Emma, 1862–1913, author. | Field, Michael. Diaries. Selections. | Bradley, Katharine Harris, 1846–1914. Diaries. Selections. | Cooper, Edith Emma, 1862–1913. Diaries. Selections. | Dever, Carolyn, editor.
Title: One soul we divided : a critical edition of the diary of Michael Field / edited by Carolyn Dever.
Description: Princeton : Princeton University Press, 2024. | Includes bibliographical references and index.
Identifiers: LCCN 2023010993 (print) | LCCN 2023010994 (ebook) | ISBN 9780691208008 (paperback) | ISBN 9780691208114 (hardback) | ISBN 9780691255903 (ebook)
Subjects: LCSH: Field, Michael—Diaries. | Bradley, Katharine Harris, 1846–1914—Diaries. | Cooper, Edith Emma, 1862–1913—Diaries. | Authors, English—19th century—Diaries. | Women authors, English—Correspondence. | Lesbians—Great Britain—Correspondence. |
BISAC: LITERARY COLLECTIONS / Diaries & Journals | SOCIAL SCIENCE / Gender Studies
Classification: LCC PR4699.F5 O54 2024 (print) | LCC PR4699.F5 (ebook) | DDC 821.8 [B]—dc23/eng/20230622
LC record available at https://lccn.loc.gov/2023010993
LC ebook record available at https://lccn.loc.gov/2023010994

British Library Cataloging-in-Publication Data is available

Editorial: Anne Savarese and James Collier
Production Editorial: Sara Lerner
Cover Design: Chris Ferrante
Production: Lauren Reese
Publicity: Jodi Price, Charlotte Coyne, and William Pagdatoon
Copyeditor: Cathryn Slovensky

Cover images (top to bottom): Excerpt from Michael Field Diary, Add MS 46794, p. 127r British Library, London, UK © British Library Board / Bridgeman Images; William Morris, Larkspur (detail), manufactured by Morris & Company, Purchase, Edward C. Moore Jr. Gift, 1923 / The Metropolitan Museum of Art; Michael Field (Katharine Bradley and Edith Cooper), Mark Samuels Lasner Collection, University of Delaware Library, Museums and Press

This book has been composed in Miller

10 9 8 7 6 5 4 3 2 1

CONTENTS

List of Illustrations   ix
Acknowledgments   xi
A Note on the Text   xiii
Key Figures and Familiar Names   xvii

INTRODUCTION   1

CHAPTER 1. PREHISTORY: THE 1860S DIARIES   17
   The Oxford Diary, 1867–68   18
   The Paris Diary, 1868–69   26

CHAPTER 2. AMBITION AND DESIRE: 1888–93   32
   Works and Days, 1888–89   34
   Works and Days, Jan. 1890–July 1891   50
   Works and Days, 1891   63
   Works and Days, 1892   80
   Works and Days, 1893   108

CHAPTER 3. DOMESTIC NEGOTIATIONS: 1894–99   122
   Works and Days, 1894   124
   Works and Days, Jan.-Oct. 1895   135
   Works and Days, Oct.-Dec. 1895   142
   Works and Days, 1896   146
   Works and Days, 1897   150
   Works and Days, 1898   162
   Works and Days, 1899   175

CHAPTER 4. CRASH: 1900–1907   195
Works and Days, 1900   197
Works and Days, 1901   209
Works and Days, 1902   215
Works and Days, 1903   222
Works and Days, 1904   236
Works and Days, 1905   240
Works and Days, 1906   246
Works and Days, Jan.–Sept. 1907   262
Works and Days, Sept.–Dec. 1907   267

CHAPTER 5. THE LONG DENOUEMENT: 1908–14   271
Works and Days, 1908   273
Works and Days, 1909   277
Works and Days, 1910   279
Works and Days, 1911   292
Works and Days, 1912   300
Works and Days, 1913   308
Works and Days, 1914   319

Published Works by Katharine Bradley and Edith Cooper   323
Further Reading   325
Notes   327
Index   335

ILLUSTRATIONS

FIG. 1. Michael Field (Katharine Bradley and Edith Cooper)   2

FIG. 2. Edith Cooper's first entry in *Works and Days*   36

FIG. 3. Bernard Berenson   59

FIG. 4. Michael Field at odds, 1892   105

FIG. 5. Handbill advertising *A Question of Memory*   116

FIG. 6. Charles Shannon and Charles Ricketts   126

FIG. 7. "The Zermatt Mystery"   157

FIG. 8. *L'Oiseau bleu*, brooch designed by Charles Ricketts   199

FIG. 9. Edith Cooper's final entry in *Works and Days*   316

FIG. 10. Katharine Bradley's final entry in *Works and Days*   322

ACKNOWLEDGMENTS

THIS BOOK CAME TO FRUITION at a moment of remarkable collegiality among generous, brilliant scholars and artists sharing in the work of the Michael Field archive. For their help and support, kindness, good humor, patience, resourcefulness, sharp questions, corrections, and curry, thanks to Sharon Bickle, Joseph Bristow, Dennis Denisoff, Hazel-Dawn Dumpert, Frankie Dytor, Jill Ehnenn, Kate Flint, Heather Freeman, Dustin Friedman, Regenia Gagnier, Sophie Goldrick, Amy Kahrmann Huseby, Sarah Kersh, Holly Laird, Mark Samuels Lasner, Peter Logan, Kristin Mahoney, Elizabeth Meadows, Alex Murray, Yopie Prins, Simon Reader, LeeAnne M. Richardson, Michelle Taylor, Marion Thain, Kate Thomas, Ana Parejo Vadillo, Sally Shuttleworth, Margaret Stetz, Martha Vicinus, and Heather Bozant Witcher. Sharon Bickle and Alex Murray were sharp, thoughtful reviewers for this book in draft form.

Editing a critical edition from a manuscript with no extant authoritative transcription has been a formidable task. Katherine Arrington and Hayden Elrafei, Frances Pool-Crane, Hazel-Dawn Dumpert, and Heather Freeman have been tireless partners in tracking details, down to the last em dash. Thank you so much Kat, Hayden, Frances, Dawn, and Heather for all your help. All responsibility for errors remaining in *One Soul We Divided* is mine.

The students of Dartmouth's fall 2022 Victorian women writers seminar gamely worked their way through this edition as its first readers, teaching me a great deal in the process both about the work and about how to teach it effectively; thank you, students, for helping me see this material with fresh eyes. I am grateful also to Jessica Beckman, George Justice, Ann Kraybill, Amy Long, Douglas Mao, Liz McMillen, and Barbara Kline Pope, and to Paul Christesen for help translating from Ancient Greek. At Princeton University Press I am indebted to Anne Savarese, James Collier, Sara Lerner, Lauren

Reese, Steven Moore, and the extraordinary Cathryn Slovensky for lending their talents in support of this work.

Michael Field made the sage decision to appoint Thomas Sturge Moore as their literary executor, and today's scholarly community has enjoyed the follow-on benefit of stewardship by Sturge Moore's family: executors Leonie Sturge-Moore and Charmian O'Neil. I thank the executors as well as the trustees of the British Library, the Weston Special Collections Library at the Bodleian Library at Oxford University, the Fitzwilliam Museum at Cambridge University, the National Portrait Gallery, and the Mark Samuels Lasner Collection at the University of Delaware for their stewardship of Michael Field materials, and for their permission to reproduce materials here.

To Charlotte Bacon, Colleen Glenney Boggs, Kimberly Christopher, Mona Frederick, Gregg Horowitz, Ellen Levy, Andrea Macdonald, and Susanne Mehrer: thank you, dearest friends.

My extended family has offered a lifetime of love, moral support, and good humor; I love each of you and all of you. My special thanks are overdue to my brother Mark Dever, the best fellow traveler I could ever imagine.

As always, this is for Paul and Noah, and Carter and Franklin.

A NOTE ON THE TEXT

THE DIARY OF MICHAEL FIELD, titled by its authors *Works and Days*, exists in twenty-nine handwritten volumes housed in the British Library. A related volume, a diary kept by the elder of the Michael Field poets at the age of twenty-one, is held in the Bodleian Library at Oxford University.

One Soul We Divided represents the first critical edition of *Works and Days*, following a collection of excerpts edited by its authors' literary executor nearly a century ago, and aims to make accessible to modern readers for the first time the full scope of Michael Field's grand experiment. This volume includes selections from each of the years its authors wrote (Katharine Bradley from 1867–69, Bradley along with Edith Cooper from 1888–1913, and Bradley alone in the final year of her life, 1914) and presents an engaged Michael Field: engaged with each other, with their friends and acquaintances, and with ideas—from ancient and modern folklore to myth, philosophy, poetry, literature, art, religion, politics, and personalities both human and canine. This text centers Michael Field's voices. I have attempted to keep editorial interventions to a minimum while also offering important clarifying and contextual information wherever necessary.

My editorial method has included the following practices:

- *Manuscript information*: The British Library Western Manuscripts collection holds "The 'Michael Field' journals (1868–1914)," comprising twenty-nine volumes from 1868–1914, Add MS 46776–46804. These twenty-nine volumes are available in digital form at MichaelFieldDiary .dartmouth.edu. Creation of that resource was led by Marion Thain in cooperation with a community of scholars. The Bodleian Library at Oxford University holds Katharine Bradley's single-volume diary from 1867–68, MS. Eng. Misc. e. 336, as well as extensive personal and literary papers and letters from Michael Field.

- *Organization of this volume*: *One Soul We Divided* reunites the 1867–68 diary held at the Bodleian with the related twenty-nine volumes held in the British Library as "The 'Michael Field' journals (1868–1914)." Both chronologically and as a matter of authorship, the earliest two volumes in this series differ dramatically from those that followed: they were written thirty years earlier than the rest, and they were written by Katharine Bradley alone. For these reasons, I have paired these two volumes in chapter 1, titled "Prehistory: The 1860s Diaries." Within that section, I refer to the 1867–68 diary as the "Oxford diary" and to the 1868–69 diary as the "Paris diary." The "double diary" kept by Bradley and Cooper together as Michael Field, under the formal title *Works and Days*, commenced in April 1888. As Michael Field, Bradley and Cooper wrote this text until their deaths in 1914 and 1913, respectively. *One Soul We Divided* presents selections from the diaries chronologically, beginning with the two "Prehistory" volumes (1867–69), followed by the *Works and Days* volumes (1888–1914). I refer to individual volumes of *Works and Days* by their year(s) rather than the volume number assigned by the British Library to avoid confusion introduced by the inclusion here of the Oxford volume.
- *Pagination*: Citations for the manuscript texts of Michael Field appear in running endnotes at the back of this volume. Endnotes mark page breaks in the original manuscripts.
- *Textual transcription*: Working from the copy-text manuscripts of Bradley's early diary and *Works and Days*, I have transcribed quotations as closely as possible. I have exercised editorial discretion to standardize variant spellings, paragraph breaks, and elements such as variant punctuation in some instances. My editorial judgments have been guided at all times by the objective of readability for a modern audience. I have inserted "[illeg.]" to mark a word that I cannot decipher. Michael Field make frequent use of "+," which I have silently changed to "and." I note with square brackets ellipses that I have added to quotations, and I let Michael Field's ellipses stand as written. I have standardized underlined titles and other underlined elements using italics. Only when it is helpful to the interpretation of the text have I retained and marked superscript additions or corrections of tense added by the authors.
- *Authorship*. On the manuscript pages of *Works and Days*, attribution of authorship is straightforward because the handwriting of Bradley and Cooper differs dramatically. Here I have noted the authorship of each passage at its head with the indication KB for passages written by Katharine Bradley and EC for passages written by Edith Cooper.

- *Distinguishing between passages*: When passages from *Works and Days* run continuously or close to continuously, I present them continuously. I insert space between passages to signal breaks in the original text.
- *Editorial notes*: In the main text of the diaries, editorial interpolations appear within square brackets in roman type. I have occasionally inserted notes in *italics* where clarifications of place or person are needed.
- *Footnotes*: Footnotes provide basic context for the reader's convenience.
- *Names and titles*: I have provided information about Michael Field's close family and friends in the front matter following. Bradley and Cooper's published works are listed in the back matter of this edition.

Key Figures

Katharine Harris Bradley (1846–1914)

} Michael Field.

Edith Emma Cooper (1862–1913)

Amy Katharine Cooper Ryan (1863–1910): Younger sister of Edith Cooper, niece of Katharine Bradley; married John Ryan in 1899, converted to Catholicism, died in Dublin.

James Robert Cooper (1818–97): Father of Edith Cooper, brother-in-law of Katharine Bradley.

Emma Harris Bradley Cooper (1818–89): Mother of Edith Cooper, older sister of Katharine Bradley.

Amy Bell (1859–1920): Stockbroker, feminist, close friend of Katharine Bradley.

Bernard Berenson (1865–1959): Lithuanian American art historian and art dealer. Bradley and Cooper vary in their spelling of Berenson's first name. Because Berenson himself adopted the spelling "Bernard" later in life, I have regularized Michael Field's spelling accordingly.

Mary Costelloe Berenson (1864–1945): American Quaker, art historian, and dealer in art and antiquities.

Havelock Ellis (1859–1939): Physician, reformer in the science of human sexuality, author of the first medical textbook about homosexuality.

Louisa Eleanor ("Louie") Ellis (1865–1928): Close friend to Michael Field and collaborator in the creation of their dresses; sister to Havelock Ellis.

Charles de Sousy Ricketts (1866–1931): British artist, illustrator, book designer, publisher; partner of Charles Shannon.

Charles Haslewood Shannon (1863–1937): British portraitist; partner of Charles Ricketts.

Thomas Sturge Moore (1870–1944): Poet and woodcutter; literary executor for Michael Field.

John Gray (1866–1934): Poet and Dominican priest; partner of Marc-André Raffalovich.

Familiar Names

For Katharine Bradley: Michael, Mick, Sim, Master, Minnie; together with Edith Cooper, Michael Field; together with Edith Cooper, the Poets (to Ricketts and Shannon).

For Edith Cooper: Field; Henry, Hennie, Heinrich; P.; together with Katharine Bradley, Michael Field; together with Katharine Bradley, the Poets (to Ricketts and Shannon).

For Amy Cooper Ryan: The Puss, Pussy, Little Pickie, Little One.

For Emma Cooper: Sissie, the Mother, the Beloved Mother-One.

For James Cooper: The Father.

For Robert Browning: The Old Gentleman, the Old.

For Bernard Berenson: The Doctrine, the Faun.

For Charles Ricketts: The Painter, the Fairyman, Fay; together with Shannon, the Painters or the Artists.

For Charles Shannon: Together with Ricketts, the Painters or the Artists.

For Thomas Sturge Moore: Tommy.

For Whym Chow: Whym, Whymmie, Chuckles.

For Musico, the basset hound: Music.

ONE SOUL WE DIVIDED

Introduction

A THIRTY-VOLUME DIARY recounting events public and private through the long demise of the Victorian era and the dawn of a thrilling yet frighteningly "modern" new century. A private diary written not by one person but by two. A diary documenting a passionate love story between two women—and their prospective infidelities and artistic ambitions, achievements, and disappointments. The story of the family from which both women came, and from which they never managed to depart. A text delivered in the handwriting of two Victorian women but in the persona of a male Victorian author.

This is the remarkable story of *Works and Days*, the "diary" of "Michael Field." This text—monumental, elegant, humorous, and always movingly human—offers a rich experiment in late-Victorian and early modernist literature. *One Soul We Divided*, the diary's first critical edition, presents Michael Field in their own words, handwritten across ten thousand pages over three decades. Michael Field's magnum opus will be of interest to readers of Victorian literature and history, and to those curious to learn more about women writers, queer writers, the fin de siècle, and the histories of sexualities. But *Works and Days* will not yield its answers readily, nor in expected ways: just as "Michael Field" is not what nor who he seems to be, Michael Field's private diary (private, though intended for publication) is not what it seems to be. Rather, the diary, like the author, unfolds in and as a series of brilliant experiments. From those experiments we can gain new insights into literary and historical ideas of the fin de siècle and also into the flexibility those ideas displayed when challenged or dismantled.[i]

---

i LeeAnne M. Richardson, in *The Forms of Michael Field* (New York: Palgrave McMillan, 2021), argues persuasively that the "Michael Field" signature itself foregrounds challenges of form that continue through the authors' work.

FIG 1. Michael Field (Katharine Bradley, *left*, and Edith Cooper, *right*). Mark Samuels Lasner Collection, University of Delaware Library, Museums and Press.

The Diary and Its Production

"Michael Field" was the name adopted by two British Victorian women, Katharine Harris Bradley and Edith Emma Cooper, as the nom de plume for more than thirty volumes of poetry and lyric drama they published between 1884 and 1914. Though the pseudonym served an important professional purpose, it was personally significant as well. For the women privately, "Michael Field" signified their joined identity, their intimacy, their marriage consecrated in service to poetic beauty.

I have included here selections from the two known diaries Katharine Bradley kept on her own as a young woman. However, the canonical *Works and Days*—the "double diary"—began in April 1888, when Bradley was forty-one and her niece, coauthor, and romantic partner, Edith Cooper, was twenty-six. From 1888, the diary marched forward in annual volumes until the poets died, Cooper in 1913 and Bradley nine months later, in 1914. Insofar as *Works and Days* stands as a "connected biography," as Bradley described it in her will, its coverage is limited to the last third of Bradley's life and the second half of Cooper's.

Tantalizing questions remain about the biographical prehistory of each woman and of both women together, and about the questions on which the diary remains silent or elliptical. We know a bit about the women's lives before the moment Bradley opened a new notebook and wrote (in red ink, no less) the title *Works and Days*. For instance, we know that Bradley was born on October 26, 1846, near Birmingham, the younger daughter of a manufacturing family with a history of religious nonconformity. In her teenage years, Bradley and her widowed mother joined the household of Bradley's elder sister, Emma, and Emma's husband, James Cooper. Bradley's niece Edith was born on January 12, 1862, twelve weeks after Bradley's fifteenth birthday. A younger niece, Amy Katharine Cooper, followed in 1865.

We know that Bradley showed an early interest in the intellectual world, and that she became a student at the Collège de France in 1868, shortly after her mother's death. Bradley subsequently matriculated at Newnham College, Cambridge, where she studied Greek and eventually joined John Ruskin's Guild of St. George. Ruskin was not encouraging toward Bradley as a fledgling poet—she had published *The New Minnesinger and Other Poems* under the name Arran Leigh in 1875—and her attachment to him soon waned.

Meantime, Bradley's attachment to her elder niece waxed. Edith Cooper was a bright, intellectually inclined girl of seventeen when she and Bradley enrolled at University College Bristol, where Cooper eventually earned a first-class degree in philosophy. This was a heady and worldly period for Bradley and Cooper, full of the energies of feminist and anti-vivisectionist politics, of debates about ideas and art, and of the birth of new shared ambitions realized in 1881 when together, as Arran and Isla Leigh, they published the play *Bellerophôn*. In 1884, together as Michael Field, Bradley and Cooper published a pair of plays, *Callirrhoë* and *Fair Rosamund*, followed in 1888 by *Long Ago*, their first published volume of poetry, based on the lyric fragments of Sappho of Lesbos. Michael Field enjoyed notoriety and a bit of mystery in the late 1880s, until an indiscreet Robert Browning revealed that the exciting new poet was in fact a pair of bourgeois women approaching middle age.

We know that during the Bristol years, Bradley and Cooper became intensely close, intellectually, artistically, and eventually romantically. In her edition of their love letters, Sharon Bickle documents the extensive network of nicknames the women developed for each other, a lifelong practice realized vividly in *Works and Days*. It can read like a private language between the two: Bradley is by turns Michael, Mick, Sim, and, on at least one memorable occasion, Master. Cooper is Field, Henry, Hennie, Little Hennie, and Puss. Robert Browning is "the Old" and Bernard Berenson, "the Doctrine." Edith Cooper's mother is "Sissie" and also "the Beloved Mother-One." Charles Ricketts is "Fairyman," Whym Chow is "Chuckles," and Father Gerald Fitzgibbon is "Goscannon." The ordinary world comes alive in the romance and play of fantastical names; the power to bestow them is the women's gift.

These facts about the lives of Katharine Harris Bradley and Edith Emma Cooper offer us basic coordinates of the women's compelling existence. But they offer us very little in the way of insight about the women's inner lives, neither as individuals nor within the terms of their complex relationship. Among the things we don't know? How the women's intense, passionate union first blossomed. How they resolved for themselves, if they did, what we perceive as an incestuous relationship. How the contours of the dynamic within the Cooper household regarding the connection between aunt and niece were managed (or not), what Bradley described in a letter from 1884 as the "relation torture." How the *Works and Days* project fits within that psychosexual bond, and within the two authors' artistic ambitions.

Victorian ideas about women's sexuality—what does and does not count as incest, for example, or how a primary affective bond between women might be perceived or experienced—do not map neatly onto twenty-first-century sensibilities. *Works and Days* challenges today's readers to distinguish between our beliefs about the historical past and how two late-Victorian women chose to represent themselves and their experiences. What Michael Field take for granted almost always surprises those who are new to this text. For example, readers will find little in the pages that follow suggesting that Bradley, Cooper, their family, and their friends found the poets' same-sex union outrageous, scandalous, or wrong. Readers will find that the poets recognized other same-sex couples when they met them; that they experienced the homophobic humiliation, criminalization, and then death of Oscar Wilde as exquisitely painful; and that they took the deepest private pleasures in their love, marriage, and domestic idyll.

By neither calling out nor attempting to conceal the queer elements of their experience in the diary, Michael Field write a world of unremarkable, even normative, queerness. This is perhaps the remarkable point. Sharon

Marcus has encouraged readers of Victorian women's writing to practice "just reading," to attend to what's manifest on the page rather than to what we expect to find there.[i] Marcus's advice is helpful to keep in mind when reading *Works and Days*: the diary unlocks itself when we "just" read it; when we read what's on the page itself rather than asking the narrative to validate our assumptions about, say, Victorian genders and sexualities and authorship. In the case of *Works and Days*, that page is a mirror revealing an encounter between the fin de siècle and the present. It shows us ourselves, and how our imaginations work when we look to the past.

For Michael Field intended *Works and Days* for us: they left the massive manuscript in the hands of their literary executor, Thomas Sturge Moore, to ensure its safe passage to future readers. Bradley and Cooper were convinced that those future readers—that we—would engage with Michael Field in ways that surpassed those available to their contemporaries. In her will, Bradley instructed Sturge Moore to publish the book under the name "Michael Field." She left all further editorial matters to his discretion, including the complex question of how to portray two women who were one man, aunt and niece, and lovers. Sturge Moore met that challenge by turning the diary's lens away from the women and toward the famous people they knew: his volume of excerpts, published in 1933, focuses on the poets' encounters with literary celebrities of the moment. Fortunately, Sturge Moore was a conscientious literary steward. When he secured the deposit of Michael Field's papers in the British and Bodleian Libraries, he ensured their safe passage to us today.

Katharine Bradley, the elder of the Michael Field poets, was at least a second-generation diarist: the Michael Field papers in the Bodleian Library at Oxford include a daybook kept by Bradley's father as a young man, recording the occasion of his Nonconformist marriage ceremony among other events. The Bradley family's income derived from ownership of a tobacco-product manufacturing company; Bradley herself was quite fond of the "weed." We hear from Bradley first in a diary she kept during the eventful year of her majority, 1867–68. This slim volume, also archived in the Bodleian and included in selections here, recounts Bradley's twenty-first birthday, and the decline of her beloved mother just at that time. Concluding the first volume on the edge of the unknown—"now we have to see what Newton will be without *Grandma*," ventriloquizing her young nieces Edith and Amy— Bradley opened a new volume later in 1868, continuing into 1869. This text

i Sharon Marcus, *Between Women: Friendship, Desire, and Marriage in Victorian England* (Princeton, NJ: Princeton University Press, 2007), 75.

presents the aspiring poet in Paris, a student at the Collège de France. It features extensive passages written in French, on pages running upside down from the end of the book. The English-language 1868–69 volume is Bradley's marriage plot: she recounts her infatuation with a young man, Alfred Gérente, who died tragically just after their first substantial encounter. This, young Bradley declared, was the great love story of her life. Its misfire was equal parts opportunity and tragedy.

Because one early diary landed in the Bodleian and the other in the British Library, it has been difficult for readers to see these two early texts as a linked and indeed continuous pair. When we do consider them a pair, however, and when we further consider the entirety of *Works and Days* as a unified text rather than a series of annual volumes, we quickly see the knowingness that Bradley and later Edith Cooper brought to this work: the literary tropes and formal experiments that situate the text firmly in the context of Victorian and early modernist literary practices.

In 1888, Bradley and Cooper clearly and in earnest commenced their shared work on what became a major, massive, multiplot prose narrative. Bradley wrote first. But only a few pages along, Cooper reveals herself as a silent reader by leaving a note on the back of a page on which Bradley has written. Days later, Cooper speaks again, clearly announcing an idea: "*This has waked my Muse. She is with me." Her asterisk represents the double diary's foundational moment.

Though the two solo-authored 1860s volumes appear anomalous in the context of the full achievement of *Works and Days*, they offer us cues for reading the double diary Bradley and Cooper initiated in 1888. In her early life writing, Bradley organized the narrative of her personal development through conventions familiar from Victorian novels. The focus of the first volume, for example, on her mother's decline and death, establishes young Bradley on the dangerous precipice of womanhood bereft of her most important guide. Her mother's death consigned Bradley to navigate courtship, marriage, babies, wedding linens, and layettes on her own. Bradley's Paris diary also explored the implications of a tragic death, in this case that of Alfred Gérente, for whom Bradley conceived an infatuation on the evening of his sudden and unexpected death. Again, we see Bradley shaping her forward-going identity by means of her loss: if losing her mother has made her a woman, losing her would-be lover has made her something like a widow, having exhausted the excitements of the marriage plot by age twenty-three. There's more than a hint of Gothic precarity in Bradley's early writing.

The losses of her mother and her "lover" serve two seemingly contradictory ends: they frame Bradley within the terms of female convention (daughter, wife) and they exempt her from those very terms. This double maneuver is entirely characteristic of how Victorian novels explore the outer reaches of social identity for women—think Jane Eyre, Becky Sharp, Miss Havisham, Esther Summerson, Lady Audley, Marian Halcombe, Dorothea Brooke, Sibyl Vane—even while maintaining powerful conceits about women as daughters and mothers. From her very earliest experiments in narrative prose, Katharine Bradley writes herself into this tradition. And she does it not once but twice: Bradley repeats the trope in the foundational volume of the double diary. Here Bradley and Cooper frame the narrative through a focus on the decline and death of Edith Cooper's mother, worshipped as "the Beloved Mother-One." The Bodleian diary gives us the orphanage of Katharine Bradley; *Works and Days* the orphanage of Edith Cooper. These are the predicate conditions of Victorian literary womanhood and the framing conditions of narrative voice, first for Bradley, then for Cooper, in *Works and Days*.

Yet in the diary Bradley and Cooper speak in very different voices and, indeed, literary modes. Of the two, Bradley is the more gifted poet, and Cooper (who drafted most of Michael Field's lyric plays) is a truly remarkable prose writer. The distinction between poetry and prose highlights another tension built within the Michael Field relationship. Michael Field, prose author, belongs to a different literary tradition than Michael Field, poet. Michael Field, poet, align themselves squarely within the late-Victorian aesthetic movement. Aestheticism represented a decisive departure from, and critique of, the mid-Victorian linkage of literature and social progress. Consider Bradley's early mentor Ruskin, for example, who offered a vision of art that was both morally and socially attuned. Or Dickens, a writer committed to building empathy for the poor, and presumably empathy's extension into good deeds and the relief of suffering.

Michael Field wanted nothing to do with such a politicization of art. "Dickens—that nightmare literature of a Humanitarian Age," sniffed Cooper in *Works and Days* in 1909. This belies the fact that in their early years both Bradley and Cooper participated in radical causes familiar to educated women of the time, including suffrage and anti-vivisectionist movements. Notwithstanding their history, nor the many socialists of their acquaintance, *Works and Days* expresses no interest in such bread-and-butter Victorian social concerns as poverty or child abandonment, labor, or sexual slavery. Michael Field conspicuously decline models readily available to Victorian women writers. Elizabeth Gaskell, for example, used her gifts as a writer to draw attention to poverty and suffering, and to highlight good works. On the opposite end of the spectrum, New Woman writers shone a spotlight on the lively capacities of independent young women: stenographers and shopgirls on bicycles, loose in the public sphere.

In contrast, Michael Field's literary project had to do with aesthetic beauty as an ideal sufficient unto itself; the aesthetic movement adopted the slogan "l'art pour l'art," or "art for art's sake," from the French poet and novelist Théophile Gautier. Michael Field believed that poetry held the capacity to realize that ideal; thus, beauty itself, realized in poetry, was their guiding principle for art and life. As Richard Dellamora has demonstrated, British aestheticism was distinguished by its associations with male homosexuality, Oscar Wilde being its most famous voice.[i] For a same-sex couple such as Michael Field, the aesthetic literary movement promised a space hospitable to queer identities and expressions, though as women in a men's movement, Michael Field remained socially tangential.

The stringencies of aestheticism are important for understanding the experiment of *Works and Days* because they help make clear what the diary is not: it is not a lyric poem nor a lyric play, and though glorious in itself as a work of art, the diary is not a good example of aestheticism in action. Ideas of beauty suffuse its every page, but the diary is an extended prose narrative that remains relentlessly quotidian, tethered to the calendar and to the "real." Perhaps *Works and Days* gives us a glimpse of aestheticism's backstage, the space where the creaky machinery necessary to the production of poetic beauty grinds away. Perhaps the diary gives us the scullery where beautiful ideas can coexist with the mundane and the grubby, enabling the eventual elevation of a delectable feast. Perhaps the fact that Michael Field were female aesthetes put pressure on them to express the ordinary as well as the extraordinary, because there was no Sarianna (Browning) nor Hester (Pater) to act as helpmeet while the great man wrote. For years, Katharine Bradley enjoyed a pair of beautiful doves and kept them nearby while she wrote. In 1905, those doves died of leprosy, requiring Michael Field to burn the doves' gilded cage. One version of this story is poetic; the other appears in *Works and Days*.

Bradley and Cooper produced *Works and Days* on the cadence of an annual calendar, a structure that supports the impression that the text works as an annual diary. The authors framed each volume by marking New Year's Day and New Year's Eve according to a formula of prospection and retrospection that they established very early in the run. In the context of this calendric frame, Bradley and Cooper scaffolded in additional markers, including

---

i Théophile Gautier (1811–72), *Mademoiselle de Maupin* (1835); Richard Dellamora, *Masculine Desire: The Sexual Politics of Victorian Aestheticism* (Raleigh: University of North Carolina Press, 2011).

their birthdays; the birth, marriage, and death days of various loved ones; Christian holidays, especially the Lenten season and Easter; and the cycles of nature: spring blossoms, midsummer verdancy, the dry cold of winter. Edith Cooper notes that after the women converted to Catholicism in 1907, they exchanged the secular calendar for a Catholic one. They did not, in fact: the difference amounted only to the layering on of Catholic occasions to Michael Field's long-standing annual rituals.

Once they had established the diary's superstructure, Bradley and Cooper seldom departed from the formula. Year after year they purchased the next year's White Book in late autumn. When they traveled, they often left the cumbersome book at home, taking instead a tiny notebook (of which several are housed now in the Bodleian) to make notes and drafts of entries to be written fully in *Works and Days* when they returned. Judging from the neatness and polish of some entries, it seems probable that Michael Field wrote occasional drafts separately before copying them into the White Book. Its very craftedness is an element of the diary's literary claim.

As a poet, Michael Field were concerned to uphold certain myths about how their coauthorship operated in real time. In a letter responding to Havelock Ellis's curiosity about the "how" behind Michael Field's writing practice, Bradley famously wrote: "The work is a perfect mosaic. We cross and interlace like a company of dancing summer flies; if one begins a character, his companion seizes and possesses it; if one conceives a scene or situation, the other corrects, completes, or murderously cuts away. . . . Let no man think he can put asunder what God has joined."[i] Bradley brandishes the twin authorities of the New Testament and the traditional marriage ceremony to certify the Michael Field poetic mosaic. But her brandishing is just that. Michael Field were in fact quite distinctive writers, though linked as thought partners and dedicated to the composite identity of "Michael Field" as the brand for their poetic career.

Bradley and Cooper posit *Works and Days* as a Michael Field creation, but the diary is of course different from the poetry. This is evident not least on its handwritten pages, which give the lie to the claim of "perfect mosaic": two different writers produced this text, in two very different hands, and from two very different perspectives. Further, Michael Field's coauthorship was not systematic: they did not write daily, except when they did. With the exception of a few entries, they did not write directly to each other nor as call and response. They did not take turns. Indeed, the unsystematic nature of their authorship becomes a formal point of the text: their literary discipline heeds the calendar but resists automation.

i Quoted in Emma Donoghue, *We Are Michael Field* (Bath: Absolute Press, 1998), 34.

The women occasionally included newspaper clippings, programs, announcements, photos, postcards, and flowers in the pages of the diary, securing these items with thread or glue. They only occasionally tucked actual letters into the pages of the diary, but they often transcribed some or all of the letters they'd written or received. Periodically we will encounter entries that have been crosshatched in full or in part to make them illegible, or part of a page neatly scissored out. The paper surface of the text bears many traces of the women's physical presence: tearstains and other blots, wrinkles, folds, and lightly penciled notes and corrections. When the emotional temperature rises in times of crisis, the physical presentation of narrative deteriorates; in 1888, for example, around the death of "the Beloved Mother-One," the narrative jumps from voice to voice and date to date. Cooper narrates the death scene itself twice, with variations, first in her transcription of a letter she sent to Robert Browning and second directly. While Bradley and Cooper share the writing of various entries seemingly at random, they each clearly take on narrative ownership of certain events. For Cooper, this includes her mother's death, for example, and the poets' humiliation at the hands of Bernard Berenson in 1892; for Bradley, a first visit to the Paris Morgue and a first encounter with Oscar Wilde. In the final few volumes, Cooper takes over the narrative almost entirely, producing some of the most soaringly ambitious writing of the entire diary. By their lives' ends, the intimacy between Bradley and Cooper had waned. Cooper's more independent narrative voice mirrors this new reality. Bradley's entries following Cooper's death make her awareness of this shift painfully explicit.

Notwithstanding its many elements familiar from the diary mode, *Works and Days* challenges conventions of the diary or journal. Bradley and Cooper use the annual calendar just as Dickens used serial parts: as a platform to build—patiently—long, winding narrative threads. Read as continuous and episodic, Michael Field's text is a bildungsroman, mapping the chronological and psychological development of its protagonists as they overcome adversity and triumph into something like stability. It is a künstlerroman, mapping the development of two talented poets in their relationship to their own craft. It is of course something of the biography Bradley described, and I have suggested elsewhere that the text is novelistic, and specifically vast, multiplot, Victorian-novelistic.[i] When we approach *Works and Days* as a unified literary work, rather than as an episodic index to the lives of its two authors, we gain access to the text's longitudinal dimensions. This is where Bradley and Cooper realized their significant formal and thematic aspirations.

i See Carolyn Dever, *Chains of Love and Beauty: The Diary of Michael Field* (Princeton, NJ: Princeton University Press, 2022).

Just as *Works and Days* gives us a stubbornly unbiographical biography, the diary's relationship to history is similarly, and rather spectacularly, unhinged. As a diary, *Works and Days* honors the pretense of a linear story and hews to conventions of the private history. Michael Field further situate this "reality" among recognizable landmarks: the Victorian fin de siècle, aestheticism, familiar historical events, activities, brands, scandals, deaths.

But when we turn to *Works and Days* to gain insight—or new information—into the historical moment that produced Michael Field, we find that the diary warps concepts of historical time. Take, for example, the deliberately posthumous status of a text that pretends to unroll in real time. Notwithstanding that pretense, our access marks the fact that its narrators are no longer living; they left it to the future in their wills. Consider also Michael Field's intense poetic interest in the past: myths, legends, and events that might have seemed remote to more common imaginations appeal directly, even primarily, to theirs. Robert Browning dubbed them his "dear, Greek women," and the theater critic William Archer accused Michael Field of being unable to write a sentence in a modern idiom. At the same time, Michael Field were fascinated with the looming presence of the "modern," the twentieth century that seemed at first freeing to contemplate but that gave way to the disenchantments of noisy buses, cars, and trains, and literary and social worlds that perplexed them. Throughout *Works and Days*, Michael Field are acutely aware of time, at all times—but they are never entirely at home in the past, present, or future.

Then there are the histories for which Michael Field might be thought to stand, or to which they might be thought to contribute. What of women's history, for example? We have not one but two women writing here, yet they insisted on "Michael Field" as the signature for their biography. Does this call attention to their gender/s or to the patriarchal conscription of the female voice? Or erase both women entirely from the field of vision? The project of situating Michael Field in relation to the concept of women's history recalls how they introduced a female subject in their 1893 sonnet about Leonardo's *Mona Lisa*: with "Historic, side-long, implicating eyes."[i] The eyes of Michael Field are just as historic, sidelong, and implicating as La Gioconda's, suggesting much but revealing little.

When Michael Field were pigeonholed as women writers who were somehow "less than," they expressed their frustration in the diary. Yet they often voiced distaste toward women, whom they typically found silly or irritating. On the other hand, they wrote dozens of plays about powerful women from

---

i Michael Field, "La Gioconda," in *Sight and Song* (London: Elkin Mathews and John Lane, 1892).

the historical past—what my students would call "girl boss" women with sexual agency, bracing intelligence, and words at the ready. Their suffragist zeal of years past was long gone by the time the diary began; Cooper claims in its pages that if she had to choose between poetry and the vote for women, the choice (on behalf of poetry, not the vote) would be easy for her. Though female misogyny is certainly an element of women's history, readers who turn to *Works and Days* to find feminist icons ready for expropriation may be disappointed.

The same is true for Michael Field's relationship to lesbian, queer, and trans histories. These were two women who lived together as a married couple, and who wrote gorgeous love poetry for each other and about the female form. They adopted a male professional persona as a mark of their intimacy. They used male nicknames and pronouns to refer to each other. Their interlocutors—friends and also later critics—vacillate between pronoun types and numbers: he, him, she, her, they? Even so, *Works and Days* gives significant attention to its women authors' supercharged longing for male attention. These dynamics are familial and erotic, to be sure, and they extended even as far as Michael Field's canine Übermensch, their dog, Whym Chow. Bradley and Cooper looked on, shaken, as Oscar Wilde's prosecution for "gross indecency" turned into his imprisonment and later his death. Discussions of their mutual devotion abound in the diary until midway through the first decade of the twentieth century, when "devotion" evolved into claustrophobia for Cooper, its hollow form maintained for the sake of poetry but drained of its erotic power. Throughout *Works and Days*, the Michael Field relationship, whatever that may be, however the diary constructs it, remains elusive.

Michael Field took great—and well-deserved—pride in their standing as a poet, with the short lyric poem and the lyric play at the heart of their artistic practice. Neither of these forms has much to do with the massive, unwieldy text of *Works and Days*, yet even within this massive, unwieldy text, we find the lyric in abundance. I mean this literally, in the sense that Bradley uses pages of the diary as a workspace for poems in progress. I mean it figuratively as well, in the sense that moments of intense meaning, what Wordsworth might have called "spots of time" and what Alex Murray and Sarah Parker have identified as "croquis," or prose poems, pop off the page and command our emotional attention.[i] Indeed, I would suggest that the encapsulation of the lyric within the linear prose narrative of a diary represents

---

i See William Wordsworth, introduction to *Lyrical Ballads*, and Alex Murray and Sarah Parker, introduction to *Michael Field: "For That Moment Only" and Other Prose Works* (Cambridge: Modern Humanities Research Association, 2022), 1–48.

one of Michael Field's more jarring—and thus most interesting—category collisions.

To read *Works and Days* as a unified text, then, as we see it here for the first time, is to notice the depth and range of Michael Field's engagement with literary and philosophical ideas and forms, ancient and modern. As a poet, they are known—again, deservedly—for their serious, sustained engagement with classical myth and literature. The diary, too, is dense with allusions to the Bible; to Greek, Roman, Norse, and Middle Eastern legends; to Celtic and medieval English tales; and to the poetry and prose of the English early modern period. This degree of serious engagement remains true for their own century as well: Matthew Arnold's death is mourned on the first page of the double diary and Robert Browning's on the final pages of that same volume. Wordsworth, Shelley, and Keats emerge as poetic interlocutors, as does Walt Whitman. Ruskin, Pater, and Nietzsche frame Michael Field's artistic horizons in terms both idealistic and pragmatic. Though not feminists politically, by the time they began to write *Works and Days*, Michael Field felt keenly the injustices meted out to women writers; they measured their own genius favorably against the achievements of Austen, the Brontës, George Eliot, Elizabeth Barrett Browning, and Christina Rossetti. Their literary frames of reference were European: their sense of the decadent was directly exported from France, from their reading of Flaubert, Baudelaire, Verlaine, and Huysmans. Tolstoy was extremely important to Cooper's sense of what realist narrative made possible; in brief, "everything." For some time, Michael Field shaped their worldview as a dialectic between Tolstoy and Ibsen.

And then there is the matter of their personal interlocutors, beginning with Ruskin for Katharine Bradley, and for Michael Field, Robert Browning, who died too early to give them the help they'd hoped for. *Works and Days* bristles with encounters with figures who populate the pages of today's literary anthologies and history books: art historian Bernard Berenson; literary writers Oscar Wilde, W. B. Yeats, Walter Pater, George Meredith, Rudyard Kipling, George Moore, (the despised) Vernon Lee, Olive Schreiner, and John Gray; sexologist Havelock Ellis; philosopher George Santayana; and actresses Sarah Bernhardt, Eleonora Duse, and Elizabeth Robins. Later in life, Michael Field hobnobbed with members of the Bloomsbury Group, such as Roger Fry, without betraying in the diary any sense of the Bloomsbury Group's existence.

All this literary and artistic sociality, and much more, saturates the pages of *Works and Days*. But Michael Field were no mere bystanders or onlookers. They lived it and breathed it: to read the diary is to understand Michael

Field's own immersion in the ideas, the habits of mind, of literary, aesthetic, and moral thinkers past, present, and even future. To read the diary is to understand that Michael Field were not dilettantes or casual or facile about their erudition. Rather, ideas were the very air Michael Field breathed, the lens that they used to interpret the world around them.

However, Michael Field's saturation in the world of ideas did not equate to joy in life's simpler pleasures, such as friendships. The women were lonely; they consistently felt isolated from a worldly world they very much wished to join. As an artist, Michael Field were confident in their literary contributions. Yet the world's disregard for Michael Field was devastating, and it became worse when disregard gave way to disdain. "No wonder I regard publication as merely fire insurance," wrote Cooper in 1900. Robert Browning had encouraged the women to "wait fifty years" to find their audience. They did not live for fifty years, nor for anything close to that. But they remained optimistic that their work would eventually find its readers—and here we are. But year after year, throughout their lives, Michael Field grieved their lack of friends and expressed the loneliness they experienced in their life together.

If this diary's subject is Michael Field, it offers us a linear narrative tracking both "his" psychological development and his development as an artist. Of course, Michael Field being Michael Field, it is more complicated than that: the "subject" of the diary is not a male poet; it is two man-loving, often-misogynistic queer women speaking to each other and to us. In some very real sense, the diary's subject is this densely networked world of ideas itself, past, present, and future—except that the world of ideas, as interpreted here, also has to do with lost bags, rugs and bowls, dogs and flowers, uncomfortable train seats, and all the stuff of everyday life. *Works and Days* is where Michael Field document the collision of material and aesthetic demands in their lived experience. This encounter is the most thrilling of all, as both the aesthetic and the material must be judged by how they fare in the tension between the two extremes.

This Edition and Its Production

The copy-texts for this edition of Michael Field's *Works and Days* are the manuscripts of Michael Field's diaries themselves: Katharine Bradley's 1867–68 diary in the Bodleian Library at Oxford, her 1868–69 diary in the British Library, and the subsequent twenty-eight volumes of the double diary Bradley and Cooper titled *Works and Days*, also in the British Library. The digitized page images of *Works and Days*, available at MichaelFieldDiary.dart mouth.edu, are a useful source for cross-checking and validating transcriptions from the manuscripts themselves. They will provide an invaluable resource for readers interested in exploring around and beyond the selections I have provided here.

The established archive of editorial work on Michael Field has been instrumental to the production of this edition, especially Thomas Sturge Moore's 1933 volume of excerpts from *Works and Days*, Mary Sturgeon's 1922 biography *Michael Field*, and Ivor Treby's bibliographical scholarship on Michael Field's poetry and prose. Marion Thain and Ana Parejo Vadillo's *Michael Field: The Poet; Published and Manuscript Materials* has been indispensable, as has Sharon Bickle's *The Fowl and the Pussycat: The Love Letters of Michael Field, 1876–1909*, and the volume by Alex Murray and Sarah Parker, *"For That Moment Only" and Other Prose Works by Michael Field*. Emma Donoghue's brief, excellent biography of the poets, *We Are Michael Field*, offers sharp insights into *Works and Days* as a literary text while also using the diary as source material for the poets' life stories.

One Soul We Divided presents selections from each volume of *Works and Days*. To support its readability, I have divided the text into five chronological chapters. The first offers the prehistory of *Works and Days*, focusing on Bradley's two 1860s diaries, seen here together for the first time. The second chapter, titled "Ambition and Desire," treats volumes written between 1888 and 1893, a time of heady professional ambition for Michael Field, but also a period riddled with challenges, including romantic and professional humiliation. Chapter 3, "Domestic Negotiations," maps discourses of marriage and domesticity for the women between 1894 and 1899. Chapter 4, "Crash," 1900–1907, recounts the reversal of that domestic narrative, the gradual disenchantment of Cooper, the devastating loss of the women's dog Whym Chow, and Michael Field's Catholic conversion, first by Cooper and then by Bradley. Finally, chapter 5, "The Long Denouement," presents tropes of separation and departure that characterize the final years of Michael Field's lives, and of *Works and Days*. Each of these chapters opens with a headnote to map key events and their locations and actors.

This edition of *Works and Days* represents one of several approaches editors might choose to take with this work. My priorities here are clear, so let me make them explicit: I have selected from this massive text a version of Michael Field in relation—in relation to each other and also to others, including family members, mentors, would-be lovers, celebrities, and of course to the idea of "Michael Field" himself. I am fascinated by the personal and artistic networks *Works and Days* writes into being, and I value the new perspectives on literary, gendered, and queer narratives of the fin de siècle these new perspectives offer us. My selections also emphasize the formal experiments Michael Field undertake in *Works and Days,* and particularly those moments when it becomes clear that Bradley and Cooper knew exactly what they were doing in relation to Victorian and emergent modernist literary forms. These editorial choices claim a space for *Works and Days* as a major achievement in the history of women's and queer authorship—even though, or perhaps because, Michael Field do not fit neatly into these categories. I have curated the selections here carefully to present a readable *Works and Days,* through selections comprising less than a fifth of the entire diary; the text has much more to offer. In that spirit, I imagine and hope that future editors will further explore the rich discourses of painting, sculpture, and travel in this text; Bradley's use of the diary as a workspace for poems in progress; and Cooper's careful working-through of her progress on Michael Field's lyric plays. These are several among the many other towpaths here that we have not yet begun to map, nor perhaps to see.

CHAPTER 1

Prehistory

The 1860s Diaries

KATHARINE BRADLEY'S two diaries from the 1860s write a prehistory to *Works and Days*. These early texts focus on Bradley's experience of her mother's decline and death in 1867–68, when Bradley was twenty-one, coupled with the flowering of first love and tragic loss in Paris later in 1868 and into 1869. Though these two diaries differ from the double diary Bradley and Edith Cooper initiated in 1888, Bradley establishes clear formal and thematic principles that Michael Field will follow in future work. Bradley's self-fashioning in this early period partakes of tropes familiar from Victorian novels about how girls develop into women. This pattern offers us a clear example of how Bradley's writing tests the literary tools of the moment.

Almost as soon as the 1867 diary begins, Bradley sets the stage in the most ceremonial and formal terms: the diary begins in the twin context of her own twenty-first birthday and news of her mother's fatal illness. For the remainder of the volume, Bradley grapples with the implications of her mother's death for her own development as a bourgeois woman: How will she establish a married home and have her babies, absent a mother's guidance? The rituals of birthday celebrations mirror the rituals of mourning: both involve the assembly of gifts and tributes, and their detailed enumeration in the text itself offers a kind of love language. We see Bradley's niece, Edith Cooper, in the background of this early diary; she emerges as a precocious five-year-old girl, her doting aunt's clear favorite.

Bradley's Paris diary opens with her arrival in Paris for time at the Collège de France, in the company of a French companion, Miss Gérente. At the center of this text is another death: her companion's brother, Alfred Gérente, died within hours of his first substantive meeting with Bradley. The diary tracks Bradley's sudden, tragically belated recognition that Gérente must have surely been the love of her life. His sudden death means that Bradley's domestic dreams—already precarious given her orphanage—are necessarily dashed. Having checked the box of heterosexual domesticity with this all but imaginary lover, Bradley finds herself at liberty to explore other ways of being an adult woman. The conventionality of the Paris diary is upended, literally, by the fact that Bradley writes a counternarrative within the same book, upside down and backward, as a means of practicing her French.

Bradley's sharply contemplative early diaries reveal the mid-Victorian origins of Michael Field's later experiment in *Works and Days*. Bradley's youthful puzzlement about gender and sexuality occurred at a time of restiveness around issues of gender, class, race, and empire in Great Britain. One approach was that of Queen Victoria herself: her own far more conventionally bourgeois diary, *Leaves from the Journal of Our Life in the Highlands, from 1848 to 1861*, was published in 1868, alongside Bradley's own early authorship. Representing more radical perspectives of womanhood was John Stuart Mill, who published *The Subjection of Women* in 1869. Lydia Becker founded the National Society for Women's Suffrage in 1868, and Josephine Baker and Elizabeth Wolstenholme the Ladies National Association for the Repeal of the Contagious Diseases Acts in 1869. Though votes for women were still a half century in the future, the 1867 Reform Bill expanded the franchise to double the previous number of eligible male voters, including male heads of household. Bradley would have been aware of the contemporary Fenian Rising in Ireland, but unaware that much later in life she would attend the deathbed of her niece Amy in Dublin, nor that the poet W. B. Yeats would appropriate the ideas of Michael Field's play *Deirdre* on behalf of his own play of that title, staged at the Abbey Theatre in 1907.

The Oxford Diary, 1867–68

The extended Bradley-Cooper family were in the process of moving from Birmingham to Newton.
In medias res, 1867.

   KB *Newton, Sunday morning, July 7th.*

   [N]ow my first deep sorrow has fallen, a sorrow that will never wear away, but will scar me to my grave. And in this grief, it will comfort me to write down what happens, and what my Darling says and does in these days, that have become so peculiarly precious to us, that each one of them seems like a pearl of great price,[i] laid in our hands and given to us of God; though night

   i Matthew 13:45–46, parable of Jesus illustrating the great value of heaven.

comes that I lie down beside my Mother, and know that the sweet sleep will soon come to her, the pain and burden be put away; but I praise God from my heart for his mercy;—a mercy I had felt, and blessed him for before, but which is all the more keenly felt now that with the mercy there is something given to bear; just as balm and balsam may be sweet but when we need healing, we learn all its sweetness. She told me, when we first talked of our trouble together that it was very blessed, to feeling oneself in the hands of God; submitting to his[1] will, and trusting in him, and in this blessedness one another lives day by day.

When we came to Newton, and gathered round the tea-table for the first time all together, Edith said, "Now we are all round the table; all of us"; we were, and oh how happy, I thought we should all have been, but for the one dark shadow that hung about her, who was the nearest to us of all; without whom there could be no being all together, no unbroken circle any more on earth. And the next morning at breakfast, she came and kissed us all, and last of all her little grandchild, who clung about her neck and then the tears would come, and we were all still, each knowing what was in our mother's heart.[2]

KB Last night we had a great shock; she had a long talk with my sister; refusing to let her share her grief; yet confessing that the sight that meets her eyes night and morning is very terrible. I wonder we can ever smile or seem happy. I can never settle to anytime again. Everything is subordinate to the one thought; and I grudge the time spent in my music; it seems to be I ought to be always with her. I think she will consent to staying here; while we go to Birmingham and see to the removal. It will be a sore trial to her not to say farewell to all the old friends and places; but it is just this we dread, and for our own sakes, she will bear all. I must go home alone, must leave her but in the sweet country name, that will comfort me.

Her touch is enough to make anything sacred to us; a withered rose leaf even: the garments that she stitches, the books she reads, the trees[3] she loves are all precious.[4]

KB Next Sunday I am 21, but not a woman, even after this great sorrow. I feel a girl all through yet, with unconquerable hope and power of rebound and an elasticity that is amazing to myself.[5] [. . .] I have not much time for birthday thoughts; I am astonished at myself: that I can have any anticipation of a day, round which so many sad thoughts will crowd, but it will be very precious to have her with me—"If I can only live to see both my children reared," she said.—Oh to have had her with me all these years. So young so fair when

I came to her, and now fair with the martyr radiance, fair with a saintly meekness, fair as those ever are over whom the Holy Ghost doth brood. It is *all* to have her with us: to wake her and to wait upon her the livelong day; to make myself look pretty for her sake; to comb out the curls she takes pride again; the curls that have been twined round her fingers and stroked by her loving hand. Now is a blessed time.[6] [. . .]

List of presents received on my 21st Birthday.

1. A brooch of emeralds and pearls, and emerald ring, from my own dear Mother.
2. Gold watch and chain from Uncle.
3. Bunyan's *Pilgrim's Progress* from Fanny and John.[i]
4. Goethe's Complete Works from Elsie.[ii]
5. Memorials of the Prince Consort from Charlie.[iii]
6. A maiden-hair fern, in very pretty pot from the Pop.
7. A jewel-case from Aunt Ann.
8. Poems by the author of John Halifax from Aunt Elmore.[iv]
9. A purse from Uncle Bingham.
10. A Locket from Lizzie and Mary.
11. The first volume of Cowden Clarke's Shakespeare from dear Sissie.[v]
12. A ring of garnets from James.
13. A pincushion from Edith.
14. An emery cushion from Amy.[7]

The Birthday is over and we are all thankful that it is over, and that it was so happily spent. When I went to kiss my Darling, she said, "I hope *you* may have many, many happy birthdays." But it was very sad to hear the way in which she emphasised the *you*, as if the future birthdays must be spent alone, and how can they be happy without her. She lay quiet for some time; and then said bursting into tears, "Well, my earnest wish and prayer to live to see this day has been granted," and we clung to one another, and dare not speak much. Sissie came in and said, "God bless you"; and I sadly missed though I knew what forbade the customary salutation on my birthday.

Mama then gave me a beautiful present—a lovely emerald brooch and ring. She put the ring on my finger. I said to her "Do you know what the em-

i Christian allegory published by John Bunyan (1628–88) in 1678.
ii Johann Wolfgang von Goethe (1749–1832), German author of literary and critical works.
iii Queen Victoria's prince consort, Albert of Saxe-Coburg and Gotha (1819–61), died suddenly from typhoid fever.
iv Dinah Craik (1826–87), English novelist and poet.
v Mary Victoria Cowden Clarke (née Novello, 1809–98) published her concordance to Shakespeare in 1845, and other works on Shakespeare through her long life.

erald means, and why it was chosen?" She said no, and I said, "It means 'Faithfulness'": and she replied that it was emblematic on both sides.[8]

[...] My sorrow has come with my womanhood. I look back to the sunny childhood, and untroubled girlhood God has given to me, and feel that I can trust my future womanhood to him.[9]

KB I feel that selfishness is my ruling sin; self having been for the most part my chief consideration *every day*, until my great sorrow; which has, thank God, taught me to forget myself for one I love; but not for all these around me.[10] [...] Against selfishness, against pride, against evil thought and speech must strive and the graces I most lack are *meekness*, patience, and humility. I have also great need of the habit of order; the love of it I possess. I must also seek to realize that the things that are not seen are eternal; at present, do what I will, the things that are seen are the reality to me. I must learn to be a delightsome and pleasant presence to those around me like a sweet-smelling rose, or a goodly fruit.[11]

Sissie spoke at teatime of her carafe—the first thing she bought for house-keeping and how Mama laughed when she brought it home. I thought of how she had been with Sissie, throughout her engagement, aiding her in all the sewing for the new house, and being ever by her side, when she was choosing her wedding dresses and house linen. I cannot but cry: if ever I know the joys of human love; she will not be there to bless the love. I shall never bring my baby to her—there will be no grandmama for my little ones. And if I am to live all alone always—how shall I bear it—I have seen women bear life pretty cheerfully when they have had kindly[12] loving mothers; but if they have been left all desolate—[13]

KB I love to have a little quiet time to myself. I cannot bear the children about always. I should like to spend several hours by myself every day. Under present circumstances with a heavy sorrow to bear, and all the outer avenues to joy and pleasure stopped, to think, reflect, and shape my thoughts is my sole recreation.[14]

KB Edith told me the other day she loved everyone in the world. I verily believe the child has no unkind or disagreeable feeling connected with any living soul.[15]

KB *Wednesday night, December 10th.* A sad trouble has come to us today. This morning James and I went down to Ashbourne to complete Christmas purchases. It was a wild morning, unfit for us to be out; on our return we found our Darling very comfortable. She had had a very sharp pain in the night. I laid out the bright wools, and pretty doll decorations I had bought, and she seemed pleased and cheerful. After dinner when Sissie was attending to her, I found traces of bleeding. I had just put on a new violet dress, and I felt chidden, as if the return of that dread symptom were a reminder that all these vanities must be put away. Tonight Sissie has read the Christmas number of *All the Year Round*, and we have been glad of the diversion.[i] We are doing all we can to make the coming XMas a happy one, how sad how inexpressibly sad it will be, if we cannot wear even the outer semblance of cheerfulness on Xmas-day.[16]

KB I do not see how I can live without. No one in the world is anything in comparison with her. I see in love there cannot be such a thing as compensation. What can fill up the void in the heart of a desolated mother? Who can be a sacred parent to an orphan child? These relations cannot be filled up— and it is strange that the relation of man to woman which should be the closest and most binding of all, and considered of no account whatever, and the world sees a second bride take the dead wife's place in a twelvemonth, and feels no horror at the faithlessness of man. [. . .] [O]h that the beautiful world *filial* were sexless, love there can be no compensation; but I suppose in matrimonial love there is. How then has Christ chosen it for the image of his divine eternal love? There are so few people with fleshy hearts together. I suppose when two people do get together—both with real hearts, they never do or can forget each[17] other, but having loved one another in the world, they love on to the end. To any human soul, there can be but *one* other truly kindred to it. So rarely do these meet, that the disappointed soul, having tried and failed, must still try again, seeking rest and finding none. So the endless misalliances and miseries that desolate married life.

When I was a very young girl, had *I* been in love, and loved again, I should have married blindly, with no forethought but in very love. Now I see how the wife has to mould her whole nature to her husband's, I should seek an ennobling pattern, by which to remodel myself; and see too whether I had material in my own nature, adequate to, and suitable for the adaptation rather transformation. I should never have thought of sickness, and all the trial that must come before, but now I should ask myself again and again, Will he tend

---

i The Christmas 1867 edition of Dickens's journal *All the Year Round* comprised a story by Dickens (1812–70) and Wilkie Collins (1824–89) titled "No Thoroughfare," released simultaneously as a play.

you in sickness? Will he bear with you in sorrow? Will he cherish you in poverty? Will he love you, when you grow old? Will he be faithful to you, if death should part you from him?[18]

On the day after Emma "Sissie" Bradley Cooper's birthday.
    KB It is sad to see [Mother] look out on the sunshine so longingly. It must have been terrible for her to look back yesterday, on her early motherhood, when she was so young and fair, and had a child so beautiful, when my father used to come and look at them both, till the tears came into his eyes. Now her husband has gone and she is stricken: and the terror of it is more than it is well for us to think of.[19]

KB I have been teaching the chicks. Edith is quiet and reverent. Amy tries to pick fun out of everything she hears. She asked me whether there will be boys in heaven. Yes. Would they have frocks on? I could not tell; I had not been there.[20]

KB I think the difference between me and a true poet is this: a true poet gives out his poetry, it is of him, as much as the fragrance is of the flower; I *suck* a bit of sweetness here and there, and make honey of it, bee-fashion.[21]

KB We have just been trying on our new dresses—the two loveliest we have ever had. My delicate fawn with the blue trimming is beautiful. We did not cry, but seemed occupied with these, while our Darling beamed at us with her warm mother eyes. If I cannot wear my dress *for her*, I will lay it reverently aside in a drawer, and should I ever be married I will wear it on my wedding day. Oh my Darling how thrice precious she is.[22]

KB She heard the children's voices last night and had them called up. She was pleased to look on Amy, but the sight of Edith seemed to bring back all her old tone and look and manner. We bring her a passionflower and a lemon sprig and laid them on the bed.[23]

KB They have been moving her, and I have said passionate things for indeed it seemed to me like murder, and I almost feared she would die from the weariness of it. I cannot bear to see them hurting her; and I feel tonight such a yearning over her, as though I would gladly leave all the rest to be with her. It seems as though the parting would cut away my heartstrings. Sissie's is quite a different nature from mine, higher and more unselfish than mine, but without that terrible intenseness that is almost a bane to me. I can scarcely bear to be out of the room for a moment, but Sis can; there is a doglike cling-ing tenacity about me that she has not. I do not say it is well to have it.

I shall not be the first with anyone on earth now. Sis will have her husband and the children before me, and with her I was the one great thought. She lived to me.

I will not forget how good they all are to me; how James is more than son and brother, how Sissie has been all that it was possible for her to be. But I see that I did unwisely in not[24] quietly insisting in sharing her grief—I know if I had been left alone I could have done all for her and learnt all, though I am deeply grateful that the burden has been taken from me. As it is, as I have not done anything for her immediately, I am considered incapable, and my dearest naturally relies more on Sis. There, it has done me good to write my heart out, but I know I have done wrongfully and admitted Satan into my heart. I will try to get him out soon, though, and to keep my temper sweet and sound for my dear Lord.[25]

KB [. . .] Sissie said, "Look!" I turned and looked and saw death's finger—a faded look had passed across the face. We all knew in a moment what must be. Sissie called James, bidding him come in gently[26] and Sissy, James, Mary[i] and I gathered round the bed, Sissie with a touch of motherly tenderness signed to James who was coming to support her to take care of *me*. The breath came feeble slow and long, the half-opened eyes lowered, the head sunk, there was a little gurgle, one passing spasm, a tear fell from the eyelids, and all was over. James said, "She is gone," but I answered "No, I do not be-lieve you"; we waited but the breath did not come again. We kissed her fore-head and Mary said, "you must come away directly." We came and I cried that I was motherless, but my true sister folded me closely in her arms and prom-ised to be a mother to me always. Then there was a pause, and bitter weeping, and warned by Sissie of the awful change there must be, I went upstairs. I looked towards that little bed, I saw that cold white face something that was not my mother, and with a wild shriek I tore from James's arms and fled away. I did not know how to go far enough. Then we talked of her—Sissie took out the little sleeping necktie she wore and handled it with the passion-ate fondness and we praised her "soft and low."

I went to the poor little children and found them in the garden with white blurred faces. I knew how she would have grieved to see them so; and I folded her precious grandchildren close to my heart. Poor Amy, I think felt sadly[27] neglected, and when I reminded Edith that Grandma had been

---

i Presumably the family's housekeeper or servant.

pleased to hear her sing, she said, "And I sang too." I promised Edie to be (vain promise) what Grandma had been to her, and always to love her dearly, and Amy said, "And you will love me dearly too?"[28]

KB Last night my beloved brother and faithful Mary laid our Darling in her narrow bed. I gathered a heap of early roses, one of her own loved arums, two passionflowers, some fuchsias, and myrtle sprigs to put about her. I had thought through ignorance that the coffin was simply made of boards hard and pitiless, and when I looked on that soft-cushioned[29] cradle-bed my heart was comforted. Sissie went first and laid her love-letters reverently in her right hand. I bought my flowers and put the fair blush roses round that pallid face, the arum for purity and that true woman's heart, and the passionflowers for its love and suffering *underneath*, as consequence and transfixion in the white light of the lily-flower above. We laid the myrtle sprigs, *our* dear warm living love companion wise to that precious dead love the record of which touching her unclasping fingers, close to her left hand. I could not help saying "The myrtle, my Darling"—perhaps she heard me, perhaps she saw us all as we knelt by her coffered form, and I prayed that as I had the hope of beholding her in Christ, I might purify myself, even as he was pure. And the blessed truth of her Resurrection of the body comforted me. Then we rose and Sissie laid a fair white handkerchief over the dear face and over the right hand and we waited to see the lid close overall. I had not been terrified. I had no fear—I was able to say my heart is not troubled, nor afraid. A deep peace washed on my heart. I felt that that coffin lid did not shut away from me my mother. *She was not there.* And all that was[30] there, though corruption for a time should lay cruel hands on it, should be restored, transfigured and glorified when Christ should come. So that neither in body or soul should our Darling perish. [. . .]

In the afternoon her dear hair was brought to us, and we parted the locks, for those who loved her to treasure. I was very fearful that we should not find her love letters: but we at last discovered them in my big desk. We found many letters that we felt we might keep: but the precious little notes we gave to her whose *right* they were. A very noble letter of Papa's signed jointly by them both Sissie read aloud to us. It was only about four days after his marriage a truly filial, reverent, grateful letter; and I thought how few young men, would look beyond this life and crown their heart's wishes with the glorious hope of *immortality*.[31]

KB *Thursday night, June 4th.* Very early this morning we got up, and sat quietly in the bedroom, afar from the too cruel sound. Afterwards in the dark drawing room, we went down and looked at the dark oak coffin. I could not have thought it possible that any coffin could have had so little a ghastly fearful repulsive look. The polished wood, and brass plate with the dear name in Old English, and underneath the triumphant "Resurgam,"[i] gave me a feeling of triumphant pride. I felt all that we could do was done. I shall never forget Sissie's tall figure in her deep mourning dress, bent across that coffin.[32]

The coffin was borne out of sight after the funeral by "rough hands."

KB We felt all of us that we were not parting with what we loved. I kept saying to myself that morning—"But thy spirit mother soars free among the fruitful blest, where the wicked cease from troubling and the weary are at rest."[ii] Mr. Lee was here and looked after us with kind fatherly eyes. We came home very quickly, back to the old threshold, and now we have to see what Newton will be without *Grandma*.[33]

The Paris Diary, 1868–69

KB *Paris. Quai Voiture 21. October 16th.*

The lights of the city showed themselves in the fast-deepening gloom. Two minutes after entering the station I was being kissed by my dear friend on both cheeks. The custom house passed, we drove through the dear bright streets, across the wide Place de Carousel, to our lodgings. From the casement I looked out on the glittering Seine bordered by high poplar-trees, and beyond to the far-stretching Louvre. Light and breadth and airiness such as I never beheld. My first French Amiens fowl and almond pudding and sweet green grapes. The salle à manger bare and comfortless, the chambre à coucher[iii] a complex apartment where we shall live by night and by day. There are two large windows in it, and three good-sized mirrors so that it has a cheery look, but the wind creeps through every crevice and it is bitterly cold.[34]

KB Friday. Madame le Pileur in the morning. In the afternoon I went to the Louvre quite alone, and Miss Gérente went to Quai d'Anjou. At night we went to Madame Bein. All the time I was there I was weighing the advantages and disadvantages. I felt after reflection that I could not be happy there. I love to be free as a bird; and I am too odd a creature to be criticized

---

i "I will rise again."
ii Job 3:17–19.
iii The dining room and the bedroom.

by a family; so we settled to stay at Quai Voltaire, and deep calm possessed me; when to this morning we are threatened by an invasion of young men, with whom we shall be expected to dine. Where to go, what to do we cannot tell. This afternoon we have been to see Mademoiselle Bau. Some years ago she saw a specimen of M. Gérente's[i] talent in Gothic letters, and was seized with frenzy. She could not sleep for the thought of it; and immediately reproduced it. Seeing such wonderful talent, he from time to time aided her, suggesting and giving counsel; now she can produce exact copies of ancient manuscripts, and compose admirably besides. She showed us some illuminated texts that a lady has ordered as an offering to the pope. Also a most elaborate subject, in which the virgin was the central figure, the faces were marvelously delicate, and the colours pure. It is easy to see who is the god of her[35] idolatry; but it is delightful to see her devotion to her art, rising in the summer at half past four to work till night. She is getting old and looks so happy!!! If I am to be an old maid, I would fain, fain to have such a pursuit; but I have not talent for such devotion. I should like though to learn to do the letters.[36]

KB I sat on Alfred's right hand. I told him how much kinder his brothers had been to me than he had, commencing at once to speak English to me: but with his sweet, amused smile he assured me, it was a virtue on his part to speak French. We had the bouillon and "classique" pot-au-feu, then some hare deliciously cooked, pastry and pears. I was quite touched by the delicate and watchful hospitality of my host. He was more like a[37] hostess than a host. He kept supplying me with wine, and last of all with some delicious Muscat. Much against my will, he made me take part of a pear, saying, "Mai si, si, Mademoiselle, tachez d'être obeissante. Tu es toujours très sévère."[ii] I saw, he had been told what I thought of him, and could not help laughing. We all drank wine together. After dinner a rather drowsy time succeeded. Then the merits of the lodgings were discussed; and my list produced. [. . .] When he came to the "Perfect Repose," which I had enumerated as among the advantages of Quai Voltaire, he looked up with such a beautiful smile and said, "that to me would weigh very much." We had tea, and I noticed that he looked quiet and seemed ill. Then we put on our things. In my foolish sly way, I was leaving without shaking hands, but in the passage, he turned to me so pleasantly and said, "Adieu, Mademoiselle; au plaisir de vous revoir."[iii]

---

i Alfred Gérente (1821–68), French sculptor and stained-glass artist; brother of Bradley's companion.

ii "But yes, yes, Miss, try to obey. You are always very strict."

iii "Goodbye, Miss. I will see you again soon."

[. . .] Now I thought[38] I shall really learn to speak French; and oh what pleasant evenings I shall have at Quai d'Anjou. Nevertheless, I felt very sick and tired and on coming home lay on my bed to rest. Miss Gérente brought me some "cressinés," and "Rousillon."[i] I thought, how much kinder she is getting, really like a sister, and I lay musing on the sonnet for my precious mother's birthday, when I heard voices in the adjoining chamber. "Veuz tout de suite, Mademoiselle, venez tout de suite: votre frère est tres malade; il est extrêmement malade."[ii] I rushed after her and got down just in time to reach the car. The bungling messenger, dreading to tell the worst, increased our fears; and made no response to our agonized inquiries. "Est il brûlé? Un accident est arrivé?"[iii] Oh I thought perhaps he is mutilated and disfigured: I did not know what awful sight might be awaiting the eyes of my trembling little friend. "Pray" she said, and when I told her I did pray for her, she added, "Pray *for him*," with a terrible intensity. My dress was caught in the car, and I was detained; as soon as I could I got up the escalier, somehow saw the open bedroom; all stately still and got into the salle à manger where my little friend was. She was crying bitterly; poor Josephine[iv] lamenting and gesticulating. I wondered she did not pass on into the bedroom. I dare not realize—I think I said at last "Est-il mort"; and then they said "Il est parte."[v] [39]

I knelt down by my poor darling and cried, and poor Eugène came in and sobbed like a little child. [. . .] We went into the lady-bedroom and sat down by the fire, the brother and sister went into *the* room together. I longed to follow. I felt as if I should go mad, if they did not let me see him. But soon Miss Gérente returned and we went in afterwards. Miss Gérente and I watched together in the room for a long time, while Josephine was away. "Mon petit" came and purred round us. He seemed disturbed; I dreaded lest he should spring on his master's bed. Poor pussy, we had not the right touch for him. Oh how beautiful that noble head looked in the calm of death. Not one touch of baseness or meanness or littleness; calm strong manhood in perfect repose. There were none of the ghastly English accessories. The glorious dark head looked almost youthful, as it lay on the pillow. The look of untroubled sleep almost made me tremble. [. . .] We went back to the other bedroom, and they brought us bouillon: but I could not take it. I missed the ministering masterhand, and left it untasted. Then the family thronged in. [. . .][40]

---

i By "cressinés," perhaps "cressones," or watercress sandwiches; by "Rousillon," sweet wine.
ii "You are wanted right away, Miss; right away. Your brother is very ill; he is extremely ill."
iii "Is he burned? Has he had an accident?"
iv A servant.
v "Is he dead?" "He is gone."

I think Miss Gérente guessed my secret. This morning she cried very bitterly; and I felt overwhelmed with grief. We went to Quai d'Anjou, and found Madame René, M. Pièquet, and the grandmother. They all went into the room and left me alone. But soon Miss Gérente came; and we went in together. With fresh force the powerfulness of that marvelous beauty came over me. A perfect man lay in great beauty before. A hard-looking, tearless, big-nosed nun was sitting comfortably praying in the room. She seemed like a great black beetle and I longed to brush her out. And all last night she was watching there, where I should have loved to be all alone, learning these glorious lineaments by heart. I cannot give up that beautiful form to corruption; I cannot see that noble head thus in the dust. My heart rebels. At times, I say it was cruel of God to put such love before me; and snatch it out of my grasp, and then think I cannot praise him enough, for so fully answering my prayer that I might know the height and depth of human love. I did now. I have beheld a being higher, nobler, deeper, and better than I have ever seen or *dreamt* of, read of, or conceived. I have often laughed at the abasement of those who were in love have professed to feel: I felt that my love would always make me worthy, and glorify me in my own eyes. But before[41] him, I always felt as a beast. And yet amid my blustering and pride, and shrinking fear for that he should reach my heart, I feel sure that he loved me: that he looked with deep eyes into me, and knew how I could love. There was a quiet inexorableness about him, for which I pretended to be afraid of him; but which I really loved; but he never spoke an ungentle word to me, or gave one impatient look. He seemed so gently tolerant of my nervousness; turning away and waiting quietly while I helped myself at table. He is altogether made of a finer mould than I conceive possible for a man. Perfect ripeness, chastened, purified manhood. I have looked once; I may never be content with any better ideal. Physical suffering, lovely suffering, moral suffering, suffering of the brain and heart, and that most agonizing of our suffering, having every exquisite feeling set on edge, by the constant presence, of coarser, duller minds, all was born almost movingly and with perfect patience. As quite a little boy, he began to love. When age six years old, a beautiful young girl came to teach his sisters music. She afterwards went mad; and threw herself from a window; but perhaps she had caressed the little one. Anyhow he loved her; and kept by him for years after her death, some boxes that had belonged to her. Then there was a schoolfellow of Miss Gérente's, a lovely young English[42] girl: whom he loved passionately. The attachment was returned; but pride came in the way: she wished to make "good connections": he dare not make her an offer, but he always cherished her lovingly in his heart; and though he was devoted to his wife never forgot her. Years after his marriage she married, and once came to see him and brought a little coat for his boy. At nineteen he went to England. He was then surpassingly beautiful; and many people longed for him to mix with society; and many young girls cared for him; but his sole adoration was for his uncle Salt.[i] . . . He followed him everywhere. I think he was in Birmingham eighteen months. His wife was only eighteen when he married her. That was no love-affair; but wishing very much to be married he consulted with his friend M. Lance, and he recommended as advisable, and nice—He and his sister went together to see her. I do not think he was altogether content, but he did not like to retreat. He was most devoted and passionately attached; she was fond of him but exacting and somewhat haughty. She loved her children well. She lost one beautiful little boy, and another one an infant that only lived twelve hours after its birth. Its sufferings were fearful. She died in her confinement. Her husband's grief was excessive and all absorbing. He often said, if sorrow could kill, he should die;[43] [an] unconquerable burst of grief came over him. He only lived for his children.[44]

KB He told his boy how he longed to be proud of him, that it was his only ambition. "C'est ma seule ambition."[ii] And one had read already what his pride was. That his boy should be honourable, upright, subduing what was low and sensual, nothing about getting on the world, or making money. His poor boy. Though fourteen or fifteen, he only looks about eleven or twelve, quite little. It was very touching to see his father's old friend come in and kiss him with such paternal tenderness on the forehead, while he clung sobbing to them. I even relented toward the wild musician, who showed real grief, and did all he could poor fellow. [. . .] Friends kept flocking in yesterday; sobbing women, one delicate and lady-formed; she mourned truly; and after kissing Miss Gérente, at leaving, feeling perhaps astutely that I was grieving with her, she said, "Permettez-moi, Mademoiselle," and gently kissed me too. That was the only sign anyone showed that I had the right to grieve.[45]

As for the other brothers, they treat me as if I were a stranger and foreigner. M. Eugène seems I think always to be wondering what I do there. About yesterday week, after we had been in for the last time, and looked at that glorious head, we left. I turned suddenly at the corner of the street, and I saw a little blue board, on which in white letters was written Quai d'Anjou and I thought, that little board is an epitome of my love. Here I have loved

---

i Perhaps his uncle Nicolas-Auguste Hesse (1759–1869), the renowned painter and stained-glass artist.
    ii "It is my only ambition."

THE PARIS DIARY, 1868-69   31

and lost.[i] [. . .] I feel as if something had been wrenched out of my hand, and I am wounded and amazed, and feel rebellious.[46]

KB Miss Gérente is gone this Monday morning to give her first lesson in English to little Marie. Oh if I can only win that child's love. I love her father more every day. [. . .] I wonder if I shall ever have my picture or one precious lock of hair. I must read Petrarch.[ii] My love will be like his, spiritual, far off, raised above the things of earth.

I can never love any other. May waters quench not love; not even the ice cold waters of the river of Death. My love burns on through them and beyond. I am very happy. To behold such a soul: one might travel from one end of the world to the other unregretfully.[47]

KB *New Year's Day 1869.*

It pains me to write the new date. I say now, *last* year I lost my darling, yes even last year, though not two months ago, Alfred Gérente entered the unseen world. It seems a barrier this new year, between us and our dear ones. In sixty-nine they have no part or lot. They have not[48] breathed its air: it is unconsecrated by the touch of their lives. We begin a new era *alone*. We are full of wonder, as to whether there will be gifts today. Oh if I might have had that *one gift*, perhaps even one reverent new year's greeting, a few precious words in his handwriting, a benediction from his life. "Au plaisir de vous revoir, Mademoiselle."[iii] Yes, not Adieu forevermore—only for a time.[49]

From this point forward, Katharine Bradley's voice as a diarist went silent—as far as we know—until she resumed the practice twenty years later when she undertook the literary experiment she called "Works and Days."

---

i Bradley is thinking of the lines, "'Tis better to have loved and lost / Than never to have loved at all," which Alfred, Lord Tennyson (1809–92) wrote in tribute to his beloved friend Arthur Hallam in "In Memoriam A.H.H.," first published in 1850.

ii Francesco Petrarch (1304–74), Italian poet of unrequited love.

iii "I am looking forward to seeing you again, Miss."

CHAPTER 2

Ambition and Desire

1888–93

BRADLEY AND COOPER first published together in 1881, under the joint pseudonym "Arran and Isla Leigh." In 1884, they cloaked both their collaboration and their gender identities under the nom de plume Michael Field. Over the next several years, they published four verse dramas as Michael Field, attracting critical encouragement. In 1888, in the midst of this literary activity, and while Michael Field was preparing their first volume of poetry, *Long Ago* (1889), for publication, Bradley opened a new diary. After only a few pages, Cooper began to write in the book too. She wrote at first on the blank reverse sides of Bradley's entries but soon entered the running narrative itself.

At the top of the first page of her new diary, Bradley wrote the words *Works and Days* in large letters, using red ink.[i] There's no mistaking her announcement here of a new, and formally organized, literary venture, nor its timing, at a moment of deliberate experimentation. In 1888, Michael Field extended themselves from verse drama to lyric poetry to narrative prose.

Formalizing the venture, Cooper wrote the entry welcoming the new year, 1889, within the same book. Just as we saw in Bradley's diary from 1867–68, the diary's narrative properties cohere when the poets encounter the imminent death of "the Beloved Mother-One"; the crisis gives shape to their narrative of the year 1889. This event of maternal death intervened between two important poetic deaths, those of Matthew Arnold at the very beginning of the book and Robert Browning at its conclusion. This triad of losses frames an identity crisis for Michael Field, to be sure—but also an identity opportunity. Michael Field are devastated. But the occasion al-

---

i Bradley likely borrowed the diary's title from Hesiod's 700 BC poem *Works and Days*, written to his brother; see Dever, *Chains of Love and Beauty*, 214n.

lows them to sharpen their sense of themselves as women, and themself as a poet.

The first epoch in the extended narrative of *Works and Days* takes shape very quickly around these linked questions: those of poetic ambition for Michael Field and those of social and sexual identity for Michael Field's component women. The period from 1888 through 1893 witnessed the moderate critical success of Michael Field's 1889 volume of poetry, *Long Ago*, inspired by Sapphic fragments, and the interest in Michael Field expressed by Robert Browning among others. Notwithstanding his attention, however, Browning also exposed the poet's true identities (and genders), and he counseled his "dear, Greek women" to "wait fifty years" to find sustained critical regard. And then, before he could promote or support Michael Field or even engage in sustained friendship with them, Browning died. Hope and death. Aspiration, humiliation. The pendulum swings from ambition to frustration and back, setting the cadence of Michael Field's career.

In these early years of Michael Field and of *Works and Days*, the poets experienced this dialectic of ambition and frustration not only professionally but also personally and sexually. During this period, when Cooper became gravely ill during a trip to Germany, Bradley looked on when Cooper's nurse in the hospital seemed to lay sexual claim over her lover; Cooper, her hair shorn into short ringlets during her treatment, emerged as a new "boy." Her new names—Heinrich, Henry, Hennie—persisted for the rest of her life, as did Cooper's exploration of romantic and sexual connections outside the Michael Field dyad. Most vivid, and most painful for Cooper, was her attachment to the art connoisseur and critic Bernard Berenson. Her painful, intense love for Berenson would persist until her dying day. In the early 1890s, however, Michael Field sublimated Cooper's extrapoetic attraction through intense engagement with paintings and sculptures in museums all over Europe, under the tutelage—and the abuse and humiliation—of Berenson. At the end of this difficult but exciting period, Michael Field basked in the affirmation of having one of their plays produced at J. T. Grein's Independent Theatre, an occasion that brought London's literary luminaries together for the performance of *A Question of Memory*. The production was an unmitigated disaster. Once again Michael Field realized only humiliation from affirmation. They returned home to attempt to fathom what—or who—life might yet hold for them.

Works and Days in this epoch reads like a who's who of the fin de siècle literary and art worlds, as not only Browning and Berenson but Oscar Wilde, Walter Pater, Havelock Ellis, George Meredith, Beatrix Potter, George Moore, Olive Schreiner, Herbert Spencer, and William Archer wander through its pages. On November 3, 1893—just weeks after the crash and burn of *A Question of Memory*—Edith Cooper locks eyes with Archer and Wilde at a performance of *Measure for Measure* in "a most modern encounter." In the pages of *Works and Days*, Cooper is particularly preoccupied with two contrasting modes of literary modernity, those of Tolstoy and Ibsen. Cooper admires the comprehensiveness Tolstoy achieves in *Anna Karenina* (1877; trans. 1886), the sense of the novel's capacity to hold everything and more. She admires the contrasting sparingness of Ibsen, too: the reduction to its essence of questions of motive in *The Master-Builder* (1892), and the erosion of social facades this new honesty demands. For Cooper, an 1893 argument between her father and Bradley over socialism, which nearly broke up the household, devolved into a Tolstoy versus Ibsen conflict, with Ibsen the winner.

The "modern" emerges for Michael Field in this period as a figure for desire itself, dangled before the poet by Bernard Berenson as a concept to which he has access and they do not. The early 1890s were a period of conspicuous modernization, if not modernity per se; the twentieth century in all its mystery was almost visible over the horizon. Even as the lives of Victorian stalwarts Browning, Arnold, Tennyson, Walt Whitman, and Wilkie Collins ended, "Jack the Ripper" terrorized the East End of London, and the police terrorized male aristocrats engaging in homosexual activities in the Cleveland Street Scandal. Oscar Wilde was flamboyant and ubiquitous, but not yet outed and imprisoned; he published *The Picture of Dorian Gray* first in *Lippincott's Monthly Magazine* in July 1890, followed by *Salomé* (1892), *Lady Windermere's Fan* (1892), and *A Woman of No Importance* (1893). Suddenly it was possible to trespass parts of London on the new Underground, and to send two-way telegraphs. Michael Field made several extended visits to Paris, where the enchantments of the Paris Morgue offered them, on one memorable occasion, an experience to combat a rather squeamish Berenson's ritual humiliation of them.

Works and Days, 1888–89

KB On Sunday, April 15th Matthew Arnold died.[i] We heard of his passing from us on Tuesday morning. On Tuesday afternoon I went alone to Lake Cottage and read some of his poems in the garden, and felt the blessedness of his having entered into the impersonal life.[1]

---

i Matthew Arnold (1822–88), English poet, cultural critic, and school inspector.

KB *In a letter to Browning.*

"Still, it is getting lonely singing in England now that the voices of Rossetti[i] and Matthew Arnold are hushed, and we beg that you will stay with us and help us through the harsh draughty bit of century remaining to us."[2]

KB On Wednesday May 9th we were asked to visit Mr. Browning.[ii] [. . .] We found the drawing room at Palace Gate full of flowers. Under one of "Pen's"[iii] statues, in a pale blue roc's egg,[iv] were our carnations. Mr. Browning came in greeting us as his "two dear, Greek women."[v] He offered τὸ τέκνον a fount of kisses.[vi] Ardently then and afterwards, he spoke of the Sapphics, expressing especial interest in *Tiresias*[vii][3] which he had once himself thought of treating. When I remarked I wished he had treated it, he said "no: it ought to be treated by a woman." He said to Edith he believed the second series of poems even better than the first, and prophesied they would make their mark. But he refuses to write a preface. We must remember we are Michael Field. Again, he said: *wait fifty years.*[4]

EC The slope with level horizon-line at the further end of my valley is a rare tawny-purple, for the brown withered bracken is illuminated by the Tyrian hue of mingled hyacinths, and their brilliant colour is mitigated and diffused by the wintry tints. On the left slope the flowers are close together and uncompromisingly violet, making the cloud-shadows as they pass imperial for a moment. Above are oaks—young oaks—in sunlight, and overall is a blue sky frank with the West Wind.[5]

EC *This has waked my Muse. She is here with me.[6] [The asterisk that appears here signifies a note Cooper wrote on the back of the page.]

i Dante Gabriel Rossetti (1828–82), English poet, illustrator, painter, and translator who was influential to the European symbolists and the aesthetic movement; a founder of the Pre-Raphaelite Brotherhood.

ii Robert Browning (1812–89), English poet and playwright; husband to poet Elizabeth Barrett Browning.

iii "Pen" is the nickname for Robert Wiedemann Barrett Browning (1849–1912), son of Robert and Elizabeth Barrett Browning.

iv In *One Thousand and One Nights*, a "roc" is a mythological bird of prey large and strong enough to lift an elephant. In the case of Browning's foyer, Bradley probably means to indicate a vase. Related, Bradley's own nickname, "Simurgh" or "Sim," derives from Arabic mythology and refers to a large, benevolent female bird.

v Michael Field studied Ancient Greek together. Their collection *Long Ago* (1889), admired by Browning, was closely connected to the poetic fragments of Sappho.

vi From Greek, "to the child." My thanks to Paul Christesen for help with this complex handwritten phrase and its translation.

vii In Greek mythology, the blind prophet who changed genders for seven years.

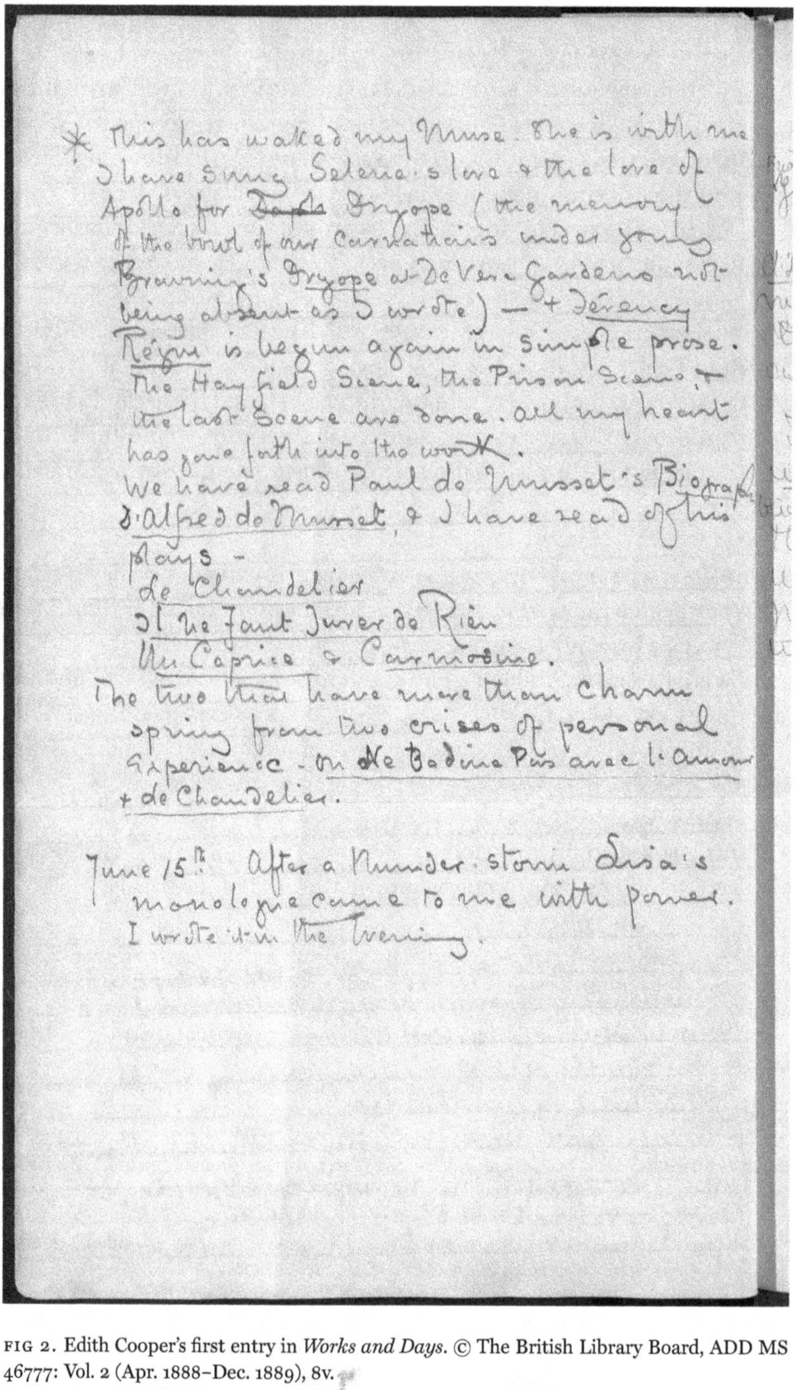

* This has waked my Muse. She is with me
I have sung Selena's love & the love of
Apollo for ~~Daph~~ Dryope (the memory
of the bowl of our carnations under young
Browning's Dryope at DeVere Gardens not
being absent as I wrote) — & Décency
Règne is begun again in simple prose.
The Hayfield Scene, the Prison Scene, &
the last Scene are done. All my heart
has gone forth into the ~~work~~.
We have read Paul de Musset's Biograph
d'Alfred de Musset, & I have read of his
plays —
Le Chandelier
Il ne faut Jurer de Rien
Un Caprice & Carmosine.
The two that have more than charm
spring from two crises of personal
experience - On Ne Badine Pas avec l'Amour
+ de Chandelier.

June 15th. After a thunder-storm Lisa's
monologue came to me with power.
I wrote it in the evening.

FIG 2. Edith Cooper's first entry in *Works and Days*. © The British Library Board, ADD MS 46777: Vol. 2 (Apr. 1888–Dec. 1889), 8v.

KB When [Browning] heard we were writing prose, he said—*"take care you do not derogate."* I asked him what models should be taken for prose comedy. He was not much for models—*"prick it out yourself. Trust yourself."* At last he was forced to go—he hoped we should come again—"under happier auspices." *We could not be so happy again.*[7]

EC *September 25th.*

A great grey wind and rough sea. As we returned from the pier we saw a little dark group of people on the shore and a coast guard standing within the foamy wash of the waves, and keeping faithful ward over a lowly heap covered thinly every now and then by the waters—the body of a young woman. A few nights ago a passenger was missed from the Ostend boat—so probably this was a suicide. She was hidden from sight, but the humiliation of the body socked and tossed by the pitiless sea, lying flat and unowned on the pebbles,[8] could not be hidden—left like seaweed on some sea-creature, the refuse of the great billows that rolled back with the ebb tide of their endless life. Corruption, dishonor, weakness, a natural body! And yet, and yet—there was a look of concern and awe in the men and women around—and the children called for one another with heartless curiosity. And ever the night came down coveringly—each moment nearer to the group and the coast guard with his flying ribbons—and his tall, protective quietude.[9]

KB On March 5th—my little Amy's birthday—I went to the Lyceum [Theatre]. Mrs. Irving and Ellen Terry[i] simply pull a great play to pieces. The next morning, I went to see my vivid old damask rose—dear Miss Swanwick.[ii] We spoke of *Long Ago*—of the Old Gentleman. She told me how once at a dinner-party he said, "I wish you could have known [Elizabeth Barrett Browning]." . . . "It was something for fifteen years to have the society of such a woman; and I valued it, for when we were in Florence, I never left her for an evening." He spoke to Miss Swanwick of the *Sonnets from the Portuguese.*[iii] "It seems to me, if I had written such sonnets, they would have burnt through my desk,"[10] she said. But the poets had been wedded two years before Elizabeth Barrett placed them in her husband's hands. Then had he consulted his own feelings, he would have kept them sacred from the light; but he remembered he was the guardian of his wife's genius, and bade her publish them. Choosing this sublime old maid for this deep confidence of his nuptial life is

---

i Isabel Irving (1871–1944) and Ellen Terry (1847–1928) were noted stage actresses.
ii Anna Swanwick (1813–99), English author, translator, philanthropist, and feminist.
iii The sonnet sequence published by Elizabeth Barrett Browning (1806–61) in 1860.

a sign of the Old Gentleman's fine faculty for selection—the fool, or insensitive person never looks where he is talking.[11]

KB On Sunday afternoon, at Porchester Terrace,[i] a palmer saw my hand. "You will do any large thing well—you see your end, and make straight for it, you have no power over detail. You have an entire lack of fortitude. You cannot rule—never try[12] to—but you have the straight diplomatic little finger— you can wind people around your little finger. You have a rather rebellious hand. You will prove very rusty, if thwarted; but if given your head you will manage your affairs, and fairly well—your impressions are instantaneous— traveling like lightning. You repent their force and vividness—fearing your judgment has been rash, but afterward return to and abide by them. You are rather domineering, i.e., You respect the independence of others too much to interfere with it, but in what concerns yourself you domineer. Never manage your own money affairs—leave Miss Bell to look after those for you. You have an art-hand (this she *repeated*)—more colour than form. Much dramatic— latent and could probably speak in public if trained. You must have had religious troubles—a time of trouble is coming in your life—a malign influence— take care you are not deceived." Something harmful and distressing was hinted at: but when she heard my age—some ten years older than her estimate of my hand—she appeared quite cheered and said—"Oh then that is all passed, and you will have a smooth time." This was a most curious bit of testimony, as when she spoke of a malign influence; there were events in my past to which I felt she probably was referring, and was surprised when she spoke of the evil as imminent. Plenty of imagination, and a rather passionate heart—but very little of the other (sensual) kind of love. My great want she seemed to think was a sustaining, steady, cheerfulness. Great[13] and probably successful ambition (star on Jupiter), much worry over work, self-distrust. Altogether my life evidently gave her the impression of much inward distress, apprehension, and agitation—of nerves and health, with tendency to weak heart.[14]

KB *Monday evening. May 20th.*

[Sissie and I] were alone—we spoke of it. She feels with every morning's light she is ready to go. When she spoke of the earthly side of it and of burial—I begged her to think of providence and the joy she was going to— and she said she did—of God, and Christ—and my father. [. . .] We were *very*

---

i Bradley often visited her friend Amy Bell (1859–1920), British stockbroker and women's suffrage activist, at her home in Porchester Terrace, Bayswater, London.

close. I have been walking twice in the straight top walk—and I shall never forget the kind, almost Motherly look.[15]

EC Mother came to be nursed in our bedroom after quiet, terrible talk with me alone.[16]

KB We cannot possess what we experience.[17]

EC *May 29th.*
We were together while the others were at tea. I read to her Walt Whitman's *Death Carol*: she was silently lulled by it.[i]

Then she asked me for "my Mother's picture that I may kiss it." She looked long and searching at it—then kissed it; I gave her Grandfather's (in the little olive-wood frame) saying "This was your gift to me." It seemed as if her spirit ran to him on a little cry—she looked long, long and proudly at the face, kissed it, and then immediately kissed me with her dear, pallid, firm lips, and breathed "Thus linked—forever! . . . I am as near to my grandfather through you as you are to him . . . These are cords that will never be broken." After tea, in the evening rays—very lovely—[18] She has had the gravity and sovereignty of aspect which Blake gives to the Dead who die in the Lord.[ii] Something of late reticent twilight before the stars, or of early dawn before the spring of light.[19]

May 31. Letters from our beloved "Old" and Sarianna[iii] about our sorrow and *Long Ago* (ah, they are bound together . . . the pain and the joy—like weft and woof). This evening I read them to her—she said, "They could not be more beautiful." [. . .]

June 1. She had a terrible heart attack at three in the dawn—for some time we thought she was dying and gathered on the floor and round her. Through the open window the cuckoo's roving voice wandered[20] to us—far away we heard the coo of a wood pigeon; the world looked beautiful through the flicker of aspens; the day was under promise to come on the enlighted horizon; within all was grave and quiet. Slowly over the face of our Beloved came a darkening like the twilight on mountains, recluse, august, passionless in its unresisted drape: the grey was the very tint of solemnity—the head lowered

i "When Lilacs Last in the Dooryard Bloom'd," elegy to Abraham Lincoln written in 1865 by American poet Walt Whitman (1819–92).

ii William Blake (1757–1827), English poet, printmaker, and painter of the Romantic period, known for his views as a mystic and political radical.

iii Robert Browning and his sister Sarianna (1814–1903).

with the descent of the shadows—the eyes were half-put to rest. Of a sudden the pulse leapt again, and she was given back to Life. She still thought the end was near, and one by one she blessed us, speaking the *God bless you* with a kind of pressure in the voice. A cock crew its lusty signal to daylight; there was a stir of workmen's feet—she said "Man goeth forth to his labour"[i]—it seemed like the quiet comment of a Spirit from the midst of the Rest that Remaineth.[21]

When Alice fetched the Doctor she gathered from the wayside a stem of blue germander—Mother's favourite flower. We laid it on our Darling's knee—she said "How kind!" with a gleam over the wan brow—then added with piercing import "Speed Well!"

This was an ideal deathbed—simple and noble. God seemed to be working like an artist with the divine choiceness of consummation: The issue was a cruel irony—[22]

EC *Next to a pressed flower.*

"Let not your heart be troubled."[ii]

I read to Mother about 10 a.m. The Death Carol of Walt Whitman—she said, "That is scripture too."[23]

June 12. Our darling has been too weak to commune with us, but this evening Sim read to her the beautiful passage on peace and the building of nests in the Sea of Troubles in the Halcyon chapter of the *Eagle's Nest.*[iii] When we were together as she woke, she murmured "He giveth his beloved Sleep."[iv] I spoke softly of sleep and how it was the beginning of fresh life and how fitting it was that we should think of the dead as asleep before they began the immortal life. She said, "I feel it will come gently—no rush: Nature does everything so quietly."

June 13. A letter from George Meredith[v] on *Long Ago* which has given us intense pleasure. This morning when we read it to Mother, her face went tremulous and her eyes were larger and pale with the joy. She said, "Is not that something for a mother and sister to hear!" and added "It must be read to me every day while I live." When I said "now you must go to sleep" she broke into laughter with the sound of tears in it.

i Paraphrase of Psalm 104:34, "Man goeth forth unto his work and to his labour until the evening."

ii John 14:1.

iii John Ruskin published *The Eagle's Nest: Ten Lectures on the Relation of Natural Science to Art* in 1872. The Halcyon chapter, lecture 9 (193), describes the halcyon's ingenuity in building a durable nest fitted exactly to the needs of her offspring.

iv Psalm 127:2.

v George Meredith (1828–1909), English poet and novelist.

June 16—Sunday—In golden sunset-shining I read to her "O sunflower, *weary of time*,"[i] she sighed *Ah!* and wished me to read it twice to her. She spoke of all that Blake's drawings were though it would excite her too much to see them. "I often think of the family in Heaven."[24]

KB *June 20th.* A divine day! Word came in the morning of the last six copies of *Long Ago* being bought . . . Amy broke the news. When we went up there was that warmth in her eyes more perilous than tears . . . She said a little later, with faltering voice—"I call this my Indian summer." And she has bent towards me quite close with divine whisperings from time to time till my heart is filled with honeyed sorrow. "Tell him—Mr. Bell—my sun is setting in glory." "You have my full permission—I mean encouragement, to ask him to come over, if you like." And the blanched face lies still as a tomb, on which the sunlight is playing. She has parted from us, and returns. We grow together: the threads of our lives re-mingle—how can we part?[25]

KB *July 12th. Friday.* [. . .]
Then we went to De Vere Gardens.[ii] I shall never forget the silent grace of our friends' welcome. No crowing chaunt from Sarianna—and the old gentleman behind so still we hardly knew he was in the room—their hearts were as muted bells full of soft rejoicing quieted by perfect sympathy. Afterward, when with tender impatience Mr. Browning said we had enough of that—with reference to the details of illness—at home, and enquired about *the book*—a fine conversation began. We showed him our song-book—pointing out "the fairy-queen Proserpina" and "sweet Suffolk owl."[iii] The last seemed to win him; he would certainly have the book. "Ah Mr. Browning, you will not care so much for the song-book—it is not Greek." "*Try me*" was the emphatic response. [. . .]
When Edith told how I had a friend, who I knew spoke ill of me, yet whom I continued to like, the Poet said, "I do not care[26] what the people say of me—but I don't like them to speak against those I love." His bearing was majestic and animated, the occasion of wonder in me. [. . .] Suddenly from being shut away in our dull bit of Surrey we felt ourselves removed to the

---

i William Blake published the illustrated poem "Ah! Sun-flower" in *Songs of Experience* (1794).

ii Robert and Sarianna Browning resided at 29 De Vere Gardens in Kensington, London, from 1887–89.

iii Perhaps a book of traditional English songs, including the folk song "Sweet Suffolk Owl" and Thomas Campion's song, "The Fairy Queen Proserpina," from the 1613 volume *Two Books of Ayres*.

white central point of London life—to the mid-edge of the intensest passion there. [...]

Mr. Walter Pater[i] hopes we shall be able to call on him about teatime at five o'clock on Monday.[27]

KB *August 31st, Wednesday.*

I must hasten to chronicle our visit to Mr. Pater.

Monday July 22nd. A serious man, quiet—with blue, constantly kind eyes. Sunday half-past twelve.

The rest of the page remains blank.[28]

EC *August 2.*

We arrived at De Vere Gardens about three o'clock: he was out, his slippers announced it to anxious Sarianna. She was indefatigable in talking time down—told of Mrs. Ruskin, her early love of a young officer (who died of a heart broken for her), of the storied marriage with Ruskin, her two hours crying before Church—of old Mrs. Ruskin's coolness—Millais superbly handsome—the desecrating run of it all. Mrs. Millais is fair, tall, Scotch in voice, and she puts on her husband's art the pressure that Lucretia did in Andrea del Sarto's.[ii] We heard about George Eliot—the large lines of her features and the deference of her speech.[iii] Then we saw a photograph from Watts' head of Browning—not conceivably like him—Also one just taken by Groves—his old servant man, once a little plough boy who rang the even bell for Knox Little[iv] two years not forgetting it in work or play—while in service he got artistic hints from "Pen" and in those to become a photographer from Smiles *Self-Help.*[v]

Tea came at 4.30, and the Botticelli table had our two disconsolate cups on it. Then he came—haste about his white hairs, Mr. Orr had promised to drive him home, there had been delay. His love sped to us through movement

i Walter Pater (1839–94), English critic, essayist, and humanist, and a leading philosopher of the aesthetic movement.

ii John Ruskin (1819–1900), English art critic, painter, and writer who was a major influence from Katharine Bradley's youth. His marriage to Effie Gray (1828–97) was annulled (on the grounds that it was never consummated) after she left Ruskin for the Scottish artist and Ruskin protégé John Everett Millais (1829–76). Browning published the poem "Andrea del Sarto" in his volume *Men and Women* (1855).

iii Nom de plume for Mary Ann Evans (1819–80), English novelist, poet, and critic.

iv Ulster-born William John Knox Little (1839–1918), rector of St. Alban's, Manchester.

v George Frederic Watts (1817–1904), British painter and sculptor; William Henry Grove (1848–1937), British portrait photographer. Samuel Smiles (1812–1904) published the popular book *Self-Help* in 1859, advocating for the responsibility of each person to educate himself (or herself).

and words. We told him his picture had been with us. When he heard that Mother would like to see it, although destined for another he gave it to Sim and said zealously, "Then[29] you shall have it."[30]

EC When we happened to speak of returning some books, her brother exclaimed derisively "Are you afraid of Sarianna!" Sim spoke of our tiny house and its turmoils of common sounds—how we thought of him in his great still study. He answers solemnly that he had never been able to say he could have done better if he had had the opportunity. Throughout life he has been blessed with good conditions for work. [. . .]

"I should like to take you two to Venice and show its beauties to you—that would be an inducement." "Pen" and his wife love hospitality. "I am not like that," mused the old poet. "I am not hospitable in their sense. I don't mind dining with thirty or forty people every evening and it's done with. But I do not like to bring them into my inner circle. I like a few people immensely and want to have them with me." [. . .]

N.B. "The Old" likes caraway cake![31]

EC *August 19.*

The great Sculptor Death has been firming the lids and brow and nostrils—he takes each beauty of form and solemnizes it in his great art. The eyes will never open full again—the patient necessity of being closed forever is beginning to press on them. The noble brows bend so dark with another darkness under them—the hollowed gloom that repeats their lovely curves—the forehead is peerless and sacred—not thought, but its solution lies between temple and temple.

There was a young flush in her cheeks—bridal in its welcome of Death. They coloured like peaches under the stimulating frost. All day her eyes had been shrouded and she took food with difficulty and spoke with hard effort. She smiled in the morning when I brought in her rosy autumnal vase of leaves and blooms—a smile of commendation. Sim was with her most of the morning. I read Walt Whitman's heartening Death Carols—Much of the afternoon I slept. She smiled while Amy fed her and was a little better. At night the Shades drew more resolutely round her. The Doctor warned us—He held her hand tenderly, and his *Goodbye* was tender. We got her out of her chair on to the Ilkley Couch[i] (I "clacked" it) by the side of the bed. Sim and I sat by her wiping the dear lips and giving her drops of nourishment. Once I bent

---

i The Ilkley couch was a late-Victorian innovation that allowed invalids to adapt a sofa for their comfort.

over her and said, "The *dear* Mother-One." Out of the obliterating weakness on the beloved face came a smile as if I had touched the deep joy of her being. Once again, I said *Mother*, and again came the smile, the unutterable acceptance of the sweet word in the midst of all of the strangeness of herself. I just caught a *God bless you*, the last[32] benediction she spoke. I felt how beautiful this night-watching was—how close we were to her. She asked, "Is it raining?" Torrents were falling in the darkness with gusts. And there seemed a gradual solemn excitement in her movement, her few words which: we could not understand, her darling face. Father and Amy came, and we knelt round her. She kept looking to the left over the end of the bed with eyes at last undraped—I am sure that she saw death "in a visible shape," the fact which has no parallel—saw it, and realized it in that left direction. Then she turned to us her brilliant eyes full of new experience, awe, astonishment: they had beheld what we knew not and could not know. It was a gaze like that in the wonderful lines "The moon doth with delight / Look round her when the heavens are bare."[i]

Then she let it fall on us each one with the old love, the daily recognition. I looked into her eyes with a smile of good courage, and speaking all the fond names of a lifetime. We discovered that she wanted us to kiss her—one by one we rose—my last kiss found the dear, withered, sunken cheek. I dared not let it fall in its might on the cheek—I said *God bless you* and knelt by her feet again. She wanted my hand. I pressed the loved fingers fearlessly that the passion of my love might be with her a long way on the tract of unconsciousness. When Father said *my Queen* she looked at him with the most confidingly radiant smile. And once when he asked one of us after his old habit "What[33] *The text abruptly stops here to be picked up later.*

EC *August 20.*

Written on Tuesday morning in a letter to "The Old." The beloved Mother died at four o'clock in the dayspring. She recognized us with looks of travelling love till one o'clock. Her beautiful eyes grew large enough to receive death, but love rose up in them instantly and surmounted their great doom. Those looks will live in me like a Second Birth. After she became unconscious, I went apart to read the grand half-chapter of Corinthians, and when I reached the words "For this corruptible must put on incorruption, and this mortal must put on immortality,"[ii] I cried out "O Mother, Mother, come to me, leave that body, and come!" She died on the instant—and

i From Wordsworth's "Ode: Intimations of Immortality from Recollections of Early Childhood" (1807).
ii 1 Corinthians 15:53.

kissed me in her arms—a glorious spirit. I felt her round me and at my lips in an embrace that was like Pentecostal flame—it made me stronger than death. "O thou soul of my soul, I shall meet thee again / And with God be the rest."

Our bond is so deep it seems to go back into my first creation. For a few hours after she was free, I was firm and glad (and able to bring poor father downstairs and light the deathly ashes of the grate into a mocking life). Now I am weak with anguish at missing her dear long-tended body, her humorous, determined little ways, her inciting face—so calm and watchful. O the great moonlight eyes! Defects of course she had—my darling!—but not weaknesses. I could find no speckle of vanity on her womanhood, no jealousy, no love of mere³⁴ details. She rejoiced in the vaults of sky, their larks; in the high-tide sea, and in the least thing that had the universal touch of beauty on it. Oh, I can see her in everything, in each book, each picture: I see her, and then all grows dark in tears.

Sim writes of the sacred end—Roused by some whisper from God, our dearest opened her eyes—those eyes that had never been bright before (always calm and steady) grew luminous and full of excited wonder—to drop from the contemplation of some to us invisible Approach on the low, upturned faces of the children with unspeakable love . . . We are each one happy—though with breaking hearts. I think perhaps the sole road to happiness is by the broken heart. He who brought our peace so teaches us.

When the Blessed one looked forth on death these lines of Wordsworth "The moon doth with delight / Look round her when the heavens are bare" exactly expressed the amplitude and richness of the survey taken by those searching, brilliant, excited eyes.ⁱ³⁵

EC *The deathbed narrative picks up again here.* was that!" The smile became roguish for a moment—the quick of pathos was cut by that kind turn on the dying features. We asked her if she were happy. We heard *yes*—the only thing we could hear, though our ears were in anguish to serve us. She had no nightcap on her silver curving hair. Gradually she sank into unconsciousness; her hand no more responded with dear little finger touches, her eyes were half closed. For a short space there was laboured breathing through the nose. I went into the blue room. I only came back once and then she lay like one of Blake's figures, the head far back on the pillows, the mouth widely opened to the night air, the breath like a child's, and the eyelids impermeable sculpture.

---

i From "Ode: Intimations of Immortality from Recollections of Early Childhood" (1807) by William Wordsworth (1770–1850).

I did not stay; I felt it blasphemy for my imagination to take an overwhelming impress of her mortal end, when she wished me so to remember her living—"You must think of me as I was." So I read Corinthians XV where we read it last together on Easter Day and called her to me from the hindering body. Then she came—just as I turned to the New City of Revelation where there shall "be no more death, neither sorrow nor crying, neither shall there be any more pain: for the former things are passed away"—I felt her press me against the heart of her being and fold me in the immortality we have fed in each other. I threw myself down by the blue bed and thanked God for "the Newly Born"—My darling, my darling. I was strong and almost tearless[36] when the stricken loved ones came away, and dear father who had prayed for strength, and who with gentle service gave back to the mouth its younger loveliness. We went down with a single candle into the comfortless dining-room. I lighted the fire. It was so cold by the grate, but she had kissed me in her immortal life. Mrs. Walters came and the offices of death were quietly and lovingly done. I slipped out, cloaked to please *her*, into the dawn and the rain. I went to the laurel hedge, there, broke a dual bough off of the heavy weeping drops of the rain splashed from the green leaves over me. I brought it in to Sim that She who has conquered Death as a Victor might lie with it on her breast as the Mother and Sister of poets should. Then began the details of mourning, and my force departed.[37]

EC *August 21, Wednesday.*

The telegram came that we might lay her in Gatton Churchyard among the trees and the country sounds. Sim and Father went to choose the spot with the rocky old Sexton, a man of serious nature. The grave will be cut in the clean, hard rock. While they were away, we found the love letters ("Bury them with me") and Amy felt there was something else. At last, we found the letters I have copied—with the poet's inscription from her dear hand. In the morning Mrs. Cadworth brought some of her lovely[38] roses, the roses with delicate hues our Darling loved—Also proof of *Roses and Rue*[i] with his portraits from [. . .]. Little One went into the Garden and from the rue *She* cut for striking [. . .] got two sprays. Our solemn white mother lies in her coffin softly, with her love letters and our letters on her heart, the laurel on her breast, her right hand on her beautiful white copy of *Brutus Ultor* (the most beloved play) and on the original M.S. Copy of the Faun Scene I gave her—the left hand holds a cream sparsely-flushed rose, a deep red one such as she

---

i Michael Field published the poem "She Mingled Me Rue and Roses" in *Underneath the Bough* (1893). Wilde published a poem called "Roses and Rue" in 1885.

loved, and a silver-pink one with a spray of rue and the little poem "From thy Amy Bird" and the fingers close round the little green matchbox with a trail of pimpernel on it, painted by Amy in the happy Sidmouth days, a bit of work Mother was always looking at with joy in its artistic life.

EC The relics laid on her holy, fondled Coffin.

Friday Evening, August 23.

At the head our five volumes (Amy's copies) in their order—*Long Ago* shining on the top—below them our Poet's beautiful letter—on her heart Little One's miniature portrait and Harvey's last letter—full of the prints of the Little One's teaching. To the right, a little lower, our *Song Book* and my copy of *Queen Mary* (the black *Song Book* on the top) then a small bough of Victor's laurel—on the right side of it, Blake's figure of the Creator dividing darkness with a compass of light—on the left my poem which we gave her with the Blake on her silver wedding-day. Under the laurel a photograph of Michelangelo's *Adam* reaching out to the creative finger. Then some Edelweiss sent by Cousin Harriet fresh from the "eternal snows." Then the most cherished bit of father's carving[39] the hart's-tongue and blackberry stand,[i] and last of all at her feet the mignonette Rosa Baker sent so meekly from her own garden—all she had. It was kept livingly in water in the little seaweed glass vase. The portraits of grandfather and grandma were left in each side of our Poet's letter. Next morning the M.S. book of *Carloman* was put under my Blake poem—Sim's pile of paper under the Blake drawing, mine under the laurel, and on the right side halfway up the M.S. books of *Ferencz* and *Clelia Guidascarpe*.[ii] Above Grandma's portrait Sim put her own Bible. At the top of the noble coffin stood our little oak table carrying a pyramid of living flowers and leaves:

> shamrock leaves, a tall Anemone
> Japonica, yellow chrysanthemums and a red gladiolus—

Below white asters, autumn-coloured leaves of Virgina Creeper, green hops, a few cream roses, many red gladioluses (Alice's gift) and Anemone Japoni-

---

i James Cooper was an accomplished woodworker.

ii *Carloman* was published posthumously in 1919 as *In the Name of Time*. *Ferencz* may be an early draft of Michael Field's 1893 play *A Question of Memory*. Yeats published the poem "How Ferencz Renyi Kept Silent," using the same source material, in 1900. *Clelia Guidascarpe* was an unpublished play by Michael Field; it is on deposit at the Bodleian Library. Clelia Guidascarpe is a character in George Meredith's 1867 novel *Vittoria*.

cas and yellow brown-eyed flowers (Rudbeckia) and red geraniums (Sarah's gift) and more little yellow chrysanthemums—such a breathing, hopeful autumn above her.

On the mantel shelf the portraits of Miss Compton, Mr. and Mrs. Dawson—In the centre Blake's *Death's Door*—the portrait of Mr. Browning and at first those of grandfather and grandma—and Blake's *Family in Heaven*. On the chair in the window Blake's *Reunion of Soul and Body*—on the reading stand his Angel blowing the trump into a skeleton, by the cream bookcase on a brown Granwell chair his figures in the tomb.[40]

EC The dear Mother-One told us she would be closer to us after death than in her earthly days—she has fulfilled her promise, and she makes her home and our hearts so fully that we have scarcely felt what mourners call "a void." Her burying was an Easter Feast, for she had built up so goodly a "New Man"—a character so ideal, joyous, and permanent that death left it incorruptible—firm, intact, radiant. On her coffin shone a great laurel bough; and fain flowers in living water, that they should not fade, rose into a festal pyramid in the study where it lay, surrounded by Blake's spiritual drawings and the faces of those who had gone before. So much was her might upon us that we sang aloud to the Eastern Hymn on the return from Gatton Churchyard—a lovely spot where the trees and the "delicate miracle" of the grass are round her. The earthly end was peace—a gentle breath—no more. Three hours before she grew.... well, the wonderful German word *ahnungsvoll*[i] expresses it: the presentiment of Death was strong and close. Her beautiful eyes were lustrous, excited in survey of an unseen Approach, and then fell in warmest love and mellow smiles on us around her. [41]

Friday Evening. Her children were busy all afternoon decking the study for the reception of a sovereign guest. Then we went to tea at the *Recluse*, where Mother was first welcomed to Reigate, sitting on the very green couch that had held her and soothed by the tenderness of our dear friend Mrs. Walters. About eight o'clock we came home to "Keep the feast." The study was lighted with lamp and candle, the faces of dead friends looked down on us from the mantel shelf, but in the centre of the room towered our glorious reliquary flanked by a pyramid of living flowers crimson and white and gold. The dearest tokens lay on our altar. Our household gathered round it and worshipped Corinthians I-XV and the last prayer in the Burial Service. The room grew so sacred that we could not leave it—I made vows deeper than those of marriage—Our joy was without fear.[42]

---

i "Foreboding."

EC *Thursday, October 24.*

Last night on the shore I and my beloved one walked together—she is as close as God when I am worthy of her Companionship. We listened to the continual, pouring voice of the sea. Tawny light was in the sky, wreathed storm and clouds that "dovelike sat brooding."[i] The sand was streamy with the advance of the tide, and over the reflective channels we saw the little ancient city making an horizon of towers; one by one the lighthouses sparkled and the stars rose. It is beautiful to know as one looks at the human lamps on the waters that they are kindled by love, by man's sympathy for man; it makes one feel that the stars are not lighted otherwise. As I thought this the near and far—yea the very far—became indivisible: she and I grew all the closer.[43]

EC *Afternoon.* We went to call on Walter Pater. He was out. We were staidly received by Hester[ii]—she made tea for us with deliberation—"long is art."[iii] She was anxious not to pour into the cups a single drop too much of cream lest the tea should become "white all over." Every now and then an archaic smile tempered her features. The company was interesting, worldly, and the noiseless Hester seemed ashamed of it.[44]

EC *December 12.*

Llannie has just sent us this news of our Poet's illness! Sim is gone through the dark with letters and a telegram. Is this year going to bereave us again—yet again, O God? I should have more hope save for our last meeting; he was so gentle—As autumn is before dropping; presageful, penetrating gentleness, which has somewhat of remembrance about it even when present in the manner and through the look. He said of our *Song Book*, "Try me!" Shall we never hear the caressing voice give judgement and praise? It will half kill our poetry and make all the deep parts of our love memorial, which means more the value of life strikes the ground and is over (at least as the young estimate it).

His kiss comes to my lips again, as I think of him—that seal of his comprehension of one's womanhood—flawless in stamp, tender with knowledge—warm, warm as all action is that is divine and reverent. Perhaps he will die and never think of us. He "dared to believe" last spring that we loved him. As I hoped to have my Mother's smile before she fell asleep—I hope he will think of us. I have always loved him with deep communion of spirit. [. . .]

---

i From book 1 of Milton's *Paradise Lost* (1667).
ii Hester Maria Pater (1837-1922), sister of Walter Pater.
iii From Baudelaire (1821-67), "Le Guignon," in *Les fleurs du mal* (1857).

Prospice![i] He is no longer nearing the place—he is there—It makes me stiff, till I think of the beyond and her breast, that soul of his soul. She was a woman, a poet. His coming will be all gain to her—[45] to him!—can I wish that he should die, as I did for my Darling's blessedness? Perhaps there is a remote strength in me that could say yes—but it is very far away among the hills. He is so great—I am fearless as I write of him—the moment I slip back into myself my tears burn.[46]

KB *December 13 letter to* [. . .]

He is gone evergreen to God—full of courage and energy into that greater world of thought and love. We could not have willed for him a more perfect death—dying on that Thursday for which you were "waiting breathlessly"— able to receive the welcome given of his new book, and passing at the close of its birthday to that resumption of all that is ideal in our past that we call Heaven.

EC. We went with the dark rain on our faces to the Reading Room[ii] just after nine. As I left the house, I recalled the drear, lightless morning after our Darling's death, and felt strange braced. At first we could find no news. Sim went to the *Times*; she said in a slow whisper "it is all over." I read—my breath was quick with pain and tears. I love him as I love my Mother. It was my anticipation to have shown to him her lovely mortal face—God has shown her to him; they have met. A meeting with him was joy at its highest power. Our telegram would reach Venice this morning. No words could contain the shadow of my love[47] for him—they could but bring me to his thoughts, that is all—yes, all love cries forwith intolerable hunger. I hope he thought of us—but such a hope is only a vital kind of despair.[48]

KB We possess a relation with the dead, a vital, influencing relation. The morrow of the death of a great friend one rises impoverished one feels and dwindled in the eye of the world; *in oneself it is as if a great fortune had come to one.* How much more than bequest is this acquisition.[49]

Works and Days, Jan. 1890–July 1891

EC *January 1.*

At the Abbey (yesterday).

Flashes of impression.

---

i Browning published the poem "Prospice," about facing death, in 1864.

ii The Reading Room of the British Library was located in the British Museum from 1857– 1997. The library was then relocated to Euston Road.

The face of Richard, his servant, demure and pondering many things—a face that has met us at our Palace Gate so often or looked helpless at the free energetic entertainment our host gave us at his table. The sight was condensed pain—remembrance in travail of stillborn sobs. [. . .]

At last, the labouring movement of the coffin—so small, octagonal, hung with softest purple, crossed with violets—dark some and some dim; wreaths with sprays of the tender milky lilac of the season. It lay before the golden altar, reverend in stillness—a stillness, which strikes the eyes more than that of the rocks, that may never be moved.

The pall wellnigh brushed us as the coffin was carried past to Poets' Corner.[i] I had never heard "Earth to Earth, ashes to ashes, dust to dust" said over a human body: the voice that so said dropped like sharp gravel, syllable by syllable, on my love—the suffering was torture. All the old days, so brave and fulgent, rose up and[50] seemed to listen to their doom with inexpressible passion. Mortality turns round on mortals outraging its subjects and making what is common to them and it an insult. [. . .][51]

EC Dirges and lulled music ("He giveth his beloved sleep"[ii]) were not for him, who asks to be greeted with a cheer; nor crape-enveloped women, nor old men in their nonage (Canons, vergers, etc.); nor trivial singing boys: still less the row of vivid pressmen under the altar-rail, notebooks in hand—typifying in their very position the sacrilege of the times—its forms and[52] presentment. He would have said once more

"Outside should suffice for evidence:
And whoso desires to penetrate
Deeper must drive by the spirit-sense—
No optics like yours at any rate!"[iii]

In the nave, among the people—the disciples—who should have felt the world less with us, and the Living Risen One nearer. The artists, men of letters, and women of fashion were chill and curious: awe only fell as the bearers carried their freight, "famous, calm, and dead"[iv] under the lantern, where the body rested. The tick of a workman's hammer, on the outside of the Abbey, preceded the organ, when Purcell's music[v] began its exquisite,

i Browning was interred in the Poets' Corner of Westminster Cathedral, alongside Chaucer, Dickens, Hardy, Kipling, and many other writers and artists.

ii A hymn based on Psalm 127:2, also adapted by Elizabeth Barrett Browning as "The Sleep" (1838).

iii Stanza 9 of Browning's poem "House" (1876).

iv From Browning's 1855 poem "A Grammarian's Funeral."

v Henry Purcell (1659–95), English composer of the baroque period.

primordial wail, and the whole standing assembly bent our way—and forward.

We caught an early train home—the mist had risen; Thames looked pleasant. We were unexpected—father asleep, the fire in the study unlighted. I knew the same desolation as when we went downstairs to the ashy grate on August 20.

But the fire soon leapt up, and we had tea by the kind father, who had read the Burial Service at twelve o'clock. The animals warmed their comfortable backs by the study fender. I slept. Then at night, when we read *Asolando*[i] and some of his treasured letters, it seemed as if we were born again. The long-drawn-out anguish (one and three-quarters hours) of the funeral was over and gone. The Unseen was in the deathless places of our hearts. We read the Mother's letters and "Ring out wild bells" and "O living with that shalt endure."[ii] That night I hardly slept—thoughts and suffering had abounded too much—and companionable joy between my Soul and the Dead—the Mother-friend, the poet-friend.[53]

January 2, Thursday.

We got into the train for London at Redhill, as a gentleman was taking possession of a discarded footwarmer. When he sat down, he addressed me, "I can easily push it further that you may share the warmth." I bowed with thanks. Then he became absorbed in a paper. The scales fell from my vision almost instantaneously—it was *George Meredith*. Sim had a suspicion, which she put by as nonsense. Perhaps he became aware of an interest in our looks (I had whispered to Sim *G*.) for every now and then the fulgent eyes swept us in survey. We were reading the *Contemporary Review* (containing the "Lumber-Room," just received by post from Percy Bunting) together.[iii] Sim says my eyes grew sharp as crystal points in their brief search for traits of the person fixed in his portrait by Hollyer.[iv] He drew out letters from Turkey and dropped an envelope under the seat. At Canon St. he got out—our eyes flashed into one another as he passed—easily raising the window at the very moment of descent from the train. He made a step or two on the pavement, and then doubled back a minute's space to throw an uncertain glance into our carriage. I was sure of our man—*why*? I recognized him on the instant—the iron-grey hair and beard, the forward sweep of the moustache, the large beautifully modelled eyelids, the unusual shape of the ear's "porch." Only the

---

i Browning's final volume of poetry, published in 1889.

ii Both from Tennyson's *In Memoriam* (1850).

iii Percy Bunting (1836–1911), editor of the *Contemporary Review* from 1882–1911. Michael Field published "A Lumber-Room" in the *Contemporary Review* 57 (January 1890): 98–102.

iv Frederick Hollyer (1838–1933), English photographer, portraitist, and engraver.

eyes were new, for in the portrait they are covered—quick, much the colour of nuts at Christmastide; yet, with all their rapidity, a certain profound languour emerges and slow recluse[54] smiles, that send their ripple no further than the orbs themselves. Must I confess! I took the envelope (all is fair in war) but it gave no clue, having been evidently enclosed: on it was a list "a few packets of envelopes—a banjo case—a stick of sealing wax" (not in his writing). We still thought that imagination might be fooling us with a mere London man.

On our return, at Canon St., the same figure paused by our carriage, went to the next, and finally returned to ours. His appearance, thus sudden, was so like the portrait I was certain, but the name on a document in his hand made assurance sure. At first this document absorbed all his attention, and I could watch the grave profile. Then I took out my pocket Shakespeare and read *Othello*. He put up his document, took a paper out of his bag, and then seemed to wake to the fact that his travelling companions of the morning were again in the same carriage. He laid the paper on his knees, and his hands on it, and turned full round to watch and receive. I was obliged to read closely, for his eyes were well-prepared for my least look in his direction. Sim, who could only see his hands, says they were folded, determinedly observant. Soon after, she came to sit by me, and we talked vividly each to each. Sometimes his lids covered his eyes as in the portrait; but if we took the moment for a study of his features, the brave lights were upon us, like a tiger's through the jungle.

We actually went on to Reigate to give him a clue to what he, I am sure, more than guessed: it had a strong effect on him. He knows Michael[55] writes from Reigate, and that it is "an addressing of two" when anyone writes back. We read together, Sim and I, our close black bonnets were the same, our faces have a family resemblance.

Shortly, he is fascinating—O strange allure!—all that is Meredithian is in his wonderful glance and the compass of expression in his mustily-hazel eyes: the rest of his face is full of studious wear and unobtrusive dignity. "It could but have happened once and"—we'll hope for a more fortunate sequel than that of "Youth and Art."[i][56]

EC *January 16, Thursday.*

We met [. . .] at the Old Masters. William Sharp came to be introduced to us.[ii] He is comely and ruddy as a David in manhood—with necktie in a

i Browning published the poem "Youth and Art" in 1864.
ii William Sharp (1855–1905), Scottish poet and editor; also published under the pseudonym Fiona Macleod.

vermillion knot. We talked much of George Meredith, whom he was going to visit. He told us of his ways of life. At the end of Flint Cottage Garden is a Chalet, with two rooms—one lined with books is the study, the other the sleeping room. George rises early, often waiting on the sunrise—he comes down to the Cottage for eleven o'clock breakfast, then spends the rest of the morning and the afternoon in rambling or writing. At night he dines with his daughter and listens to music but returns to the Chalet for sleep. It is his habit to work at two novels together, writing one and rewriting the other. He has finished a story (short), "An Amazing Marriage"—and has a longer one, which will be published first, on hand, beside *The Journalist*, which has been announced to appear, but has tarried. He loves wind; with special ardour he loves the Southwester and will throw up an engagement in town when it blows rather than miss it on his hills. He is a firm recluse, coming to London not more than once in three months. Sharp is certain we were mistaken in our travelling companion. He describes George as very handsome and distinguished, endowed with strongest magnetism. He told us how George admired *Long Ago*—adding, "and Mr. Meredith is very hard to please." We expressed our wish to know him.[57]

EC We went to meet Herbert Spencer[i] at lunch, invited by our sweet Miss Baker. He is a character—with a sharp, kindly, positive face. Hazel eyes of extreme intelligence, tarnished hair just over the ears, and under-growing whiskers. But of all faces I find it most difficult to present his in words, even to myself. I cannot fix the characteristics of mouth and nose and look—yet they are not subtle. The brow wholly without artistic or imaginative qualities; but he wore a black silk skullcap which hid what in his portrait is magnificent—his domed,[58] philosophic head. He speaks like a man whose every sentence is connected with a general principle—yet—there is humour and interest in his talk.[59] [. . .] We hear he has a habit of frequently stopping his carriage to feel his pulse; also that he raves at the sight of curly parsley about his dishes. When he is wondering what the millions of sums in the universe can mean, with a religious thrill in his voice, he says in the same breath and tone "There is fluff coming out of that cushion." Once he was expounding his nebulas theory to Miss Rosa, who is rather deaf. She replied about his abstruse subject, while he was saying "I don't think these sausages were sufficiently done this morning. I will have fish tomorrow."[60]

i Herbert Spencer (1820–1903), English philosopher, anthropologist, and biologist who helped advance ideas of social Darwinism; he coined the term "survival of the fittest." He also invented the paperclip.

EC *April 6, Easter Day.*

I read with her in the blue room—she was certainly with me (her countenance as the sun shineth in his strength), for as I sat in the old place and read her chapter out of Corinthians I (XV) to her all my tears were wiped away, and a firm joy given to my being. I could no more cry than I did after she kissed me at the moment when she lived and was dead. I felt no glory like *that*—but a close understanding blessedness, a familiar thrill of union and intercourse.[61] [. . .]

I must put down all I remember of her last[62] Easter. We dressed her and on my arm she came early into the Blue Room, to greet her flowers and pictures. She was in her black dress, her fluffy shawl, and the new nightcap, bought in Bond Street, very white and delicate, in which her silver head was laid to rest at Gatton. She put it on that she might look bright and pretty, for she said she wanted us to remember her last Easter as joyful. Then I read with her, and Amy returned from Meeting—here memory lapses. In the afternoon I can see father sitting with her, as the sun fell on her young leaves and sky-blue squills. Everything she looked at always seems "appareled in celestial light,"[i] for her eyes were illumined by their own vision. After tea we read Wordsworth's *Ode*, and then she was left in quiet with her candle. Later on, I entered her twilight room, with its single taper, to prepare her for returning to her bedroom. She gathered me in her arms, her warm motherly shawl nestling up to me, cheek and neck—I felt the pressure of the motherhood that was deeper than flesh and blood—her kiss was a seal of deathless stamp. She told me she had had one fear and sorrow— that of the parting with us, but that I had made her feel that we should never part and she was *quite happy*. The belief she had planted in me (she always laid me in the gleeds[ii] of immortality from childhood) became her help—blessed was I among daughters. Her victory over death never wavered afterward.[63]

EC *May 4. Sunday.*

The dear Grandmother's wedding day, when, untrammeled by law,[iii] she was made one with her pure young husband.[64]

---

i From Wordsworth's "Immortality Ode."

ii That is, embers, hot coals.

iii Cooper's maternal grandparents (who were Bradley's parents) were wed "without benefit of priestcraft," as followers of the political and religious radical Joseph "Zion" Ward (1781–1837); see Jackie E. M. Latham, "The Bradleys of Birmingham: The Unorthodox Family of 'Michael Field,'" *History Workshop Journal* 55 (2003): 189–91.

EC *Conversation with Miss Heaton about the Brownings and the Rossettis.*

To Dante Gabriel she gave five or six commissions. The first picture he painted for her was *Paolo and Francesca*. Ruskin said, "It was not suitable for a lady," and Miss Heaton weakly made an exchange with him. There is to me a speckled silliness in Ruskin's dealings with women—spite of his chivalry and exaggerated estimate of our sex as Queens.[65] [. . .] Rossetti had a most spontaneous manner. Miss Heaton only saw his wife once—metallic lustre came from her hair—her face was that of *Beata Beatrix* but a little smaller in moulding.[i][66]

KB *Michael Field have gone to Paris.*
Sunday, June 8th. The Morgue.

To the Morgue[ii] this morning quite early in the glowing sunshine. It has been our worship, that temple of death to us the temple of the living God. Liberté, egalité, fraternité[iii]—true *there*—realised the gray, marred faces within laid brotherlike—free from the mesh of life, and equal at last in their destiny-bound all those voyageurs for God. I saw first an old man lying very calm—the whites of his eyes giving the appearance of spectacles, so that he looked like time lying dead in glasses—then a deeply bronzed face full one would say of sin and of experience, finally a rather kindly commonplace fellow, gentle enough in his fixity. It is Michael's church, that little morgue, and he found it quite impossible to remain afterwards in Notre Dame, amid the mumbling and the lights. God has provided for worship in the facts of life. If we will but look deep into birth and death—unflinchingly—accepting all the physical repulsion, tread on through the tether to the indwelling mystery, we shall learn how to conduct ourselves between—under the tricolour, and with the triune gospel written on our hearts.[67]

KB *Yesterday, Monday, July 21.*

We were suddenly summoned to Mrs. Chandler Moulton's last "At home" in Weymouth Street.[iv] The first moments were misery and humiliation. Mrs.

---

i Ellen Heaton (1816–94), benefactor to the Pre-Raphaelite Brotherhood. Rossetti painted *Paolo and Francesca da Rimini* in 1855 as a commission for Heaton. *Beata Beatrix* was an 1870 painting by Rossetti of his late wife, the model and artist Elizabeth Siddall (1829–62). Rossetti had Siddall's grave opened in 1869 to retrieve a manuscript he had buried with her. The exhumed poems were later published in 1870.

ii Opened to the public in 1868, the Paris Morgue had become a popular tourist attraction by the end of the nineteenth century. Michael Field would have been among forty-thousand people, many of them British, who visited daily.

iii Slogan of the French Revolution.

iv Louise Chandler Moulton (1835–1908), American poet, novelist, and critic.

Moulton introduced us as a poet, as Michael Field, and we stood, our wings vibrating in revolt, while hollow, fashionable women lisped their excitement at meeting with us. A moment came when this could be borne no longer; I laid a master hand on the hostess and told her to introduce us by our Christian names. [. . .]

Edith continued the conversation for I, from far, recognized Oscar Wilde,[i] and desiring to make his better acquaintance, found him by my side talking easily.

He has a brown skin of coarse texture, insensitive surface. And no volcanic blood fructifying it from within—powerful features, a firm jaw, and fine head—with hair that one feels was much more beautiful some years ago. It is pathetic when bright hair simply grows dull, instead of turning gray.[68] The whole face wears an aspect of stubborn sense, and the aesthetic is discovered simply by the look of well-being in the body (soul take thine ease!) the soft comfort of the mouth and a lurking kindly laziness in the eye. But the dominant trait of the face is humour—humour that ridicules and gently restrains the willfulness, the hobby-horse passion, the tendency to individualism of the rest of the man. There is an Oscar Wilde smiling ironically at his namesake the aesthete, smiling with almost Socratic doubt.

"There is only one man in this century who can write prose." "You mean Mr. Pater." "Yes—take *Marius the Epicurean*[ii] any page."—We spoke of the difficulties of writing prose—no good tradition—he had almost quarreled with Watts because he wanted to write the language of the god—and Watts sought to win him to prose.[iii]

"French is so wonderfully rich in colour words." We agreed English was poor in such—I instanced *bluish*-grey as a miserable effort, and he dwelt on the full pleasantness and charm of the French colour words ending in âbre bleuâtre[iv] etc. But we should grapple with this colour difficulty.[69] [. . .]

KB We agreed—the whole problem of life turns on pleasure. Pater shows that the hedonist—the perfected hedonist—is the saint. "*One is not always happy when one is good: but one is always good when one is happy.*"[v]

He is writing two articles at present in *The Nineteenth Century* on *The Art of Doing Nothing*.[vi] He is at his best when he is lying on a sofa *thinking*. He

i Oscar Wilde (1854–1900), Anglo-Irish poet, novelist, playwright, and literary celebrity.
ii Pater's novel published in 1885.
iii Theodore Watts-Dunton (1832–1914), English poet and critic.
iv "Bluish tree."
v From Wilde's *The Picture of Dorian Gray*, 1890.
vi Wilde published *The Critic as Artist: With Some Remarks on the Importance of Doing Nothing*, in the *Nineteenth Century*, July and September 1890, and again in 1891.

does not want to do anything; overcome by the maladie de style[i] the effort to bring in delicate cadences to express exactly what he wants to express—he is prostrate after a page of composition. But to think to contemplate . . . Henceforth he is determined to write in a language that will only be understood by minds artistically trained. The writing shall not be obscure—quite clear, but its meaning will be seized only by artists. He once wrote a story of Spain—a story in black and silver—in which he had endeavoured to give something of the dignity and gloom of Spanish life—like heavy, black velvet cushions—and this story when translated[70] into French came out pink and blue. It taught him that after all there were certain dour forces in English—a power of rendering gloom not in French.

He has a theory that it is often genius that spoils a work of art—a work of art that should be so intensely self-conscious. He classed the Brontës, Jane Austen, George Sand, under the head genius.[ii] This was when I said to him there was one sentence of Mr. Pater's which I could not say I would never forgive, because I recognised its justice; but from which I suffered—and which was hard to bear—that in which he speaks of the scholarly conscience as male—adding I did not remember where the passage occurred. "Yes" he said "it is in *Appreciations*, on the essay on style, page seven—left-hand side—at the bottom"—and in all this meaning the one true error was that the page is page eight . . . "Genius," he continued, "killed the Brontës. [Consider] the difference between *Jane Eyre* and *Esmond*. Owing to their imperfect education the only works we had from women are works of genius."[iii]

"What is that pretty book you have in your hand?" "A book from our hostess"—He opened it—and must have seen the inscription to Michael Field. Later on, he said he would send me his fairytales. I gave simply the address Blackberry Lodge, Reigate. I think he understood.

Plato's idea of Heaven is simply one of beautiful moments that enter into immortality of their nature. . . . He, when he gets to heaven, would like to find a number of volumes in vellum that he would be told were his.[71]

What I like about him is the sense of bien-être, of comfort, he conveys to the brain. All that a woman does to man by her presence at the hearth or at

---

i "The sickness of style."

ii The Brontës: three sisters, including Charlotte (1816–55), Emily (1818–48), and Anne (1820–49), known for their poems and novels; Jane Austen (1775–1817), English novelist; George Sand, nom de plume of Amantine Lucile Aurore Dupin de Francueil (1804–76), French novelist and memoirist.

iii Novels by Charlotte Brontë (1847) and William Makepeace Thackeray (1852), respectively. Walter Pater published his *Appreciations, with an Essay on Style* in 1889.

FIG 3. Bernard Berenson, by an unknown photographer. © National Portrait Gallery, London.

a tea-table—he does to the brain—neither lulling nor stimulating—but introducing about it a climate of happiness so that it is twice itself, freed from depression of fragility—a chill . . . We mourned that the English people do not live to art—have indeed no direct contact with it.

His Voice, Edith says, is a barmy one, and this is true. His body is too well tended and looks like a well-kept garden: his spirit one would say was only used to irrigate it. Blustersome torrent passing down its craggy human bed— with him it is conveyed by skilled labour in conduit for the ornamentation of his pleasure ground.[72]

EC A little after four we reached Lady Seton's[i]—no one interesting or companionable was there—the flowers were *artificial* in their vases—conversation and expression followed suit. We were unhappy, until Bernard Berenson[ii] appeared as fresh as a Venetian pink. Much and eagerly we talked about Italian pictures—especially Botticelli's *Spring*.[73] [. . .] When he heard that Mrs. Chandler Moulton was going to a foreign watering-place he shivered and said he would rather be going to die. "I should always prefer death to ennui."[74]

EC *Saturday, August 16.*
A review in the *Academy* of the *T[ragic] M[ary]* by Lionel Johnson of the *Hobby Horse* set.[iii] It is just and many of its comments on unsatisfactory style helpful and distressing. Is there a flaw in our method of dialogue which we seem powerless to detect? Yet we love perfection of style more than the breath of our lives. We must clarify our self-criticism till we overcome this characteristic error. It is not an easy work—we must capture the hundred eyes of Argus.[iv][75]

KB *Quoting from a review of "The Tragic Mary," suggesting that Michael Field has come to the end of a road; their new road should head in the direction of the stage.*

---

i Likely Lady Emma Elizabeth Seton, née Loch (1845–1919).
ii Bernard Berenson (1865–1959), Russian Lithuanian American Jewish art critic, specializing in Italian Renaissance art.
iii Lionel Johnson (1867–1902), English essayist and poet, published the review, "*The Tragic Mary*: By Michael Field," in the *Academy*, August 16, 1890, 123. Johnson, Wilde, and other authors of the fin de siècle contributed to the *Hobby Horse*, a magazine published quarterly by the Century Guild of Artists from 1884–94.
iv Argus Panoptus was the Greek giant pictured with as many as a hundred eyes, some of which always remained awake and alert.

"Let it be admitted at once that *The Tragic Mary* is not so good as some of the other dramas; but even if it were no worse, *The Tragic Mary*, by the very choice of subject, would mark a turning point in the career of this talented writer. To my mind it is as a signpost at the crossing of the roads: so far you have come, and the road has served you well; but you have come to the end of it, and must now, for better or worse, choose a New Road. And whither does the New Road tend? In the direction of the stage? I think so. For in truth there are but two roads open to the talent of Michael Field. In the old Shakespearean form, he has said, and said well, all he has to say. He may return by the road he came, lingering by the wayside, gathering what buds or berries he forgot or could not[76] carry away on his first journey. He may do this; but is this worth doing? Question for him to consider. The other road that is open to Michael Field lies, I think, through a more fruitful country. But before setting out on this new journey a slight reconstruction of his talent, with a view to bringing it into harmony—no, not with Adelphi audiences—let us say with the requirements of some three or four of our leading actors and actresses, is necessary. Mr. Tree talks about special plays to be given on Monday nights—could *William Rufus* be rearranged, I wonder? Could any of Michael Field's plays be given a sufficiently determinate shape? Before giving our opinion, it would be necessary to reread them; but of this at least I am certain—that if Michael Field can reconstruct his talent on a firmer and a more modern basis, the one gem that is missing in the great crown of Victorian poetry will at last have been found."

EC George Moore wrote this—Can it be that on the day when she rose again to life our art will "attain a new life, will partake of Resurrection"?[i] Long have we been feeling the pressure of dissatisfaction with our form, long have we been smitten with the sorrow of indefinite aim. Now a light flashes with renewal through our spirits; we are "im werder"[ii] once more.

Last night the strong sense of *her* freedom and eternal activity wrapped me secure from grief. Her motherhood was active in my soul, her voice ran through me like an oracle of glad tidings of great joy.[77]

As the days go on I long for her more, I love her more passionately. For *myself*—I would give up every pleasure—Italy, friends in Town, recognition of our artwork—everything except the art itself, to have her reknit to my life through the "dear and sweet custom of living together." For her I could not wish a better state than the life of life after death. My glorious Mother, who permeated sickness with joy, who smiles with joy out of the dark place of

i George Moore (1852–1933), Irish novelist, poet, and critic, published his review of *The Tragic Mary* in the *St. James Gazette* on August 18, 1890, 6.
ii "In earnest."

death, who sent down her joy upon us when we could see her no more, whose face visits my memory as a radiance,—will always be her child's ideal, to inspire, raise, support, illumine.

Mother was a joy-bringer, and insofar as I can reach her breast now it is by joy. Sorrow is the shroud we wrap about our Dead to hide them from our souls. We bury them anew every time we grieve for them. By grief we acknowledge we are not able to live near them. How our tears must desolate them!

The beautiful young face on the mantel shelf is bowered in roses and rue (the fulfillment of the little song she so loved—the proof of which came last year just after her death) and a spray of victor-laurel. Her Blake is on the Study Stand, her memory in our hearts, her presence in our Spirits. Blessed among Women would she be—if only we could live purer and more strenuous days to her glory![78]

EC *August 21.*

As of all the objects I saw on my journey I retain with most singular sharpness the faces at the Morgue—so of all the days I have lived I remember these days last year with the most indelible and sensitive exactitude. I remember them as a transformation of agony—the shapes of that agony I recognise and again feel within me the change that wrought them into unimagined forms of gladness. And what was the secret of that change?—The rare dying—"Life uppermost at end of the hard strife."[i] Life alone can alter, can modify—it was her life that moved through the hours and changed them. I was never more happy—save when we read the plays for the first time together, and on some Easter Days.[79]

EC *A visit from George Moore.*

We talked much of the construction of plays for the stage: he made me realise the leading fault of our work—its want of rhythmical progression— the haphazard development of plot which has contented us. The firm yet pliant structure of a work is one of the main requirements of style. And preparation for events and entrances is the true forethought that gives to dramatic art integrity and musical movement.[80]

Christmas Eve.

KB The things of Michael are faring very ill. *The Spectator* has rejected the Elgin Marbles sonnet as "very harsh and unnatural in speech." *The*

i Cooper quotes Michael Field's *Callirrhoë* (1884).

Contemporary has rejected the Ravogli sonnets. Beerbohm Tree has a comedy he will reject.[i] [. . .]

EC After tea we sang carols, and then cheered our maids with blowing out candles blindfolded, taking up potatoes with an egg spoon, paying forfeits, and asking "Who'll buy my goose"—that excellent game with its flavour of the contraband. Truly our ancestors were wise in many things—they knew that Christmas is mournful as the day of a funeral unless all men become children. Late at night, Sim read some scenes from *Pickwick*—the ever young.[ii][81]

Works and Days, 1891

KB *February 23rd.*

During the play we saw Monsieur Berenson, fresh from Italy. When he was asked what the effect of the play had been on him, he said, "Oh, comic, comic." And to us, "It was very jolly!"

On Friday, we went to lunch at the house of his hostess, Mrs. Costelloe.[iii] She is a comely young creature, fresh after much experience of London Society. On Bernard a great change has fallen. Last summer, "There was no doubt in him, no fear." He was a piece of pure, unflawed paganism. . . . Now he wants to make others enjoy. *He is thinking of taking to journalism*—perhaps writing articles on Dosso Dossi[iv] and those artists who have given him[82] such intense pleasure. I admonish, fearing for the magnum opus. After lunch we drive to the National Gallery. Ah *there*, how great, how simple, how happy he is! He persuades one to enter into his experiences as an orator persuades one to enter into his convictions.[83]

In the midst of the Cooper family's move to the house they called Durdans, in Reigate, Surrey.

KB *Friday.*

Alice and Edith toil in secret over the study. How different it is—when at last disclosed—from the old! A simple country parlour of low tone—unmellowed by thought, and passion, and experience. It is *we* who bring the harmonies, not *time*. An uninhabited room would remain crude whatever

---

i That is, the professional fortunes of Michael Field. *The Spectator* and *The Contemporary* were periodicals, quarterly and weekly, respectively. Sir Herbert Beerbohm Tree (1852–1917) was a prominent English theater actor and manager. Bradley was correct about all three rejections.

ii Charles Dickens's first novel, published in 1838.

iii Mary Costelloe (née Whitall Smith, later Berenson) (1864–1945), American art historian.

iv The Italian Renaissance painter Giovanni di Niccolò di Luteri (1489–1542).

happened to the colours. I have not yet taken to this funny little parlour. I like my lair upstairs, where one wakes to find the tulips bulging into blow.

EC—But I have taken to the little place, so generous in promise, so delicately gay in its finished corners. [. . .] What a "grisly" thing a removal is—mortals putting off mortality to put it on again!—All the dust and disjointedness of death and the old life of earth beginning once more.[84]

KB *April 5th. Evening of Census Sunday.*

Such rain! Spring herself coming to us in dripping garments. Amy away beneath the roof of Herbert Spencer. But I would not be away—this marvelous evening when Time mends his pen and writes a few lines, how legible, how impressive, amid his scrawls and miscalculations.

The pathos of the entries!

Father a retired farmer, 72, *widower*. So, the curtain has closed on the tragedy of thy early life; and we see the great figure no more—

And then two dramatists shut up with "the retired farmer." Reading the tiny household chronicle, one falls to speculating on the relations of the playwrights to this aged pastoral faun. And the next Census and the last!

For oneself the one prayer

From decadence Good Lord deliver us!

And for two of the band *togetherness* this time ten years either here, or elsewhere nearer God—if He so will. For little Amy the poesie of the future, and the Rearing of seedlings for the twentieth century.

We for the first time are entered by our new world names. We have [a] place in the Kingdom of Art.[i][85]

EC *Wednesday, May 20.*

Sim and I take an early train to Guildford—then go on by another to Haslemere. A vivid sunlight, often struck out by cloud, moves over the beeches—every tree is yellow and distinct in shape on the wood.

Cowslips grow on the railway banks by hundreds and yet retain their sweet meagerness of growth. In a sodden coppice the King-cups flourish—cuckoo pints[ii] diversify the grass of open fields. Near Godalming great wild strawberries are in flower; and below the underwood bluebells. As we approach Haslemere small oaks gather above the hazels and willows with a

---

i The English government has conducted a decadal census since 1801, listing people by name beginning in 1841. The census is intended to serve as a snapshot of the population on a given day. In the 1891 census, Bradley and Cooper each listed their occupation as "Dramatist," respectively.

ii A form of arum lily, considered toxic.

feminine slimness and grace in their disposition, which is entirely lost when they are older.

At Haslemere Station Mrs. Costelloe flies up to us—a red fez draws her bright hair down on her forehead—there is a gleam of gold in the collar of her black cape, the rainy wind has reddened her cheeks and chin and nose, her eyes smile freshly; she leads us to a little trap outside the station door— and there is Bernie.

The little alien begins at once with his paradoxes, his opinionated rudeness, tempered by the delicacy of perfected senses. I sit by him as if rebuked, shy, observant, in distress. And the old horse[86] trots by green waysides, with aperçus of pine-tufts and clear hills and blue valleys—to a wee garden gate. We find as we enter small shrubs, turf in a slope on which are lots of pleasant-eye narcissus and the straggling stalks of forget-me-nots. The cottage red and scarcely pretty is covered with roses—within, Morris' green willow paper seems to move its branches as if the country wind were in it. From casement and garden there is the choicest view I have ever seen in England—a wider vale, the lines of the Earth differing in level, till the horizon closes them with lovely hills, as in a Venetian picture. Save for the strong greenness of grass and trees one might be looking at Italy.

Gaily Bernie and I stray off together—for I lose shyness as soon as I am in tête-à-tête—and trip through the paths amid the abundant leaves—a gay dampness over everything. We have the sense of the rich depth of life at our side and beyond sight—Springtide! He tells me of the beechwoods of Russia—where he was born—I tell him of Mr. Pater's love of beeches and of how I have discovered that the beech is the tree most sensitive to the ideal influence of the seasons: for it holds the sunlight of May as no other foliage does till it is "more gold than gold," and again in autumn the[87] smouldering passion of the year burns through its red branches into extinction. (Blanche Leppington[i] once said she had watched a beech tree burn itself out for a month.) We speak of Tennyson; we join in delight over Bridges.

By the black stain of a campfire (where the Costelloes and their friends sleep on fine nights), Sim, Mrs. Costelloe, Bernie and I sit in the sun and talk of old age—Even forecasting a time when Bernie is blind and deaf . . . though still left with the joys of smell to vitalise him. We meet Mr. Costelloe (a political Ernest Bell)[ii] and a young woman with rose hues sweeping through her forehead and constant to her cheeks.

i Blanche Leppington (1845–1925), British poet, critic, and activist for conservative social values.

ii Benjamin Francis Conn (Frank) Costelloe (1855–99), barrister and first husband of Mary Costelloe Berenson; Ernest Bell (1851–1933), a writer and animal-rights activist.

All goes wrong after—Sim and I are set in an arbour like idols for fear of the damp, while the natural men and women lie on the grass or on rugs below us tossing about remarks on Socialism. Mrs. Costelloe mixes a salad in the eye of the sun—Bernie lies with his legs raised at the knees, and a cap over his face, from which oracles burst by moments—and one watches the shifting of his limbs like those of a wild creature, and one waits for the flash of happy red when the cap goes aside from mouth or cheeks.[88] [. . .]

Bernie is opposite—I study him in safety for a while. His brow and hair have something deliciously Pagan about them; one could fancy one saw the little horns of Ammon growing out of the ripples on his head—his eyes are as if polished with the activity of their vision and full of the joy their service has made perfect—his lips open like a ripe pomegranate filled with seed—they advance rich and eager to instruct. And yet, with all this, he is a small foreigner, ridiculously happy.

We go [on] a long country walk—There is the sense of the heaviness of green under a blank sky. Mrs. Costelloe and I start forward briskly and discuss *Woman*, a drear and painful subject when the capital letter appears on the lips. [. . .]

Mrs. Costelloe lights the fire with the grace of Diana of the Crossways.[i]

We eat bread and honey, like the Queen in the parlour, and pass out of the wee cottage gate, climb the same pony carriage, and with the same fair company drive to the station—as we left it. We see from the platform the dull red fez on the bright hair, and Bernie in an adoring heap, as the trap remounts the hill—and we wait for the train.

The rural day has made us sad.[89]

EC *Friday, June 5.*

A cloudy morning, but the guests arrive. Bernie admires the study—save for the lavender curtains which he desires to be olive green. He thinks it a delightful working-room. His experience of Italian villas, white and sunlit, makes him an admirer of the house—*this beautiful house*. We walk to the Priory Park; Bernie tells us of his certainty that Religion is a fine Art, between Poetry and Music. He has gone through the discipline of many religions, as he has studied the various schools of art. Once he was a Methodist—he was born a Jew—he has defended Mahomet, he has practiced Buddhism—last spring he entered a monastery as if he were in retreat, and endured the full Lenten rigours: but he is ever Greek and Olympus as real to

i Protagonist of the 1855 novel of the same name by George Meredith.

him as Christ to others. We stroll through the lower path under green oaks; as we retrace the way strong rain gives a vocal freshness to the ground, making a close warmth in the air. During lunch (the table decked with damp buttercups above cherries) the sun comes out. Alice the maid, in her literary fervour, begs to serve coffee on the lawn. While we are waiting for it, Bernie eats the new shoots of the Deodara,[i] like a wildwood creature—his eyebrows sunken; the nose, as we see in fauns; his red lips closing on the verdant tuftlets.[90]

Then we drive forth into the deep country beyond Reigate Heath—Bernie pronounces England "jolly," but abuses the English so doggedly and irascibly from the shining first hour of our Expedition to its end amid smoky blight that the atmosphere of my temper changes also—I am sullen, to my shame, with occasional ice in my tones—I am told I throw unhappiness or constraint over the party. I did not enjoy the drive [. . .] Bernie and Mrs. Costelloe are lacking in affection—they cannot conceive of Love as an integrating, associative power moving through life, even as Inspiration and Instinct do—A power of which we are only conscious when it has acted. Therefore I can never make a *bond* of friendship with either for without cement, we "may cleave but we cannot incorporate." Bernie was waspish—stubborn with annoying rudeness. I am sorry I was the cause of his punishment—not that he was punished sufficiently.[91]

EC *Following one of Berenson's lectures in the National Gallery.*

Here the class broke up, and Bernard disappeared. We stayed to chat with Mrs. Costelloe and were introduced to Mrs. Oscar Wilde.[ii] We had noted her dress—rough sand-gold, cream waistcoat dotted with indigo, black spreading hat with black ribbons and loops of narrow gold and green galloon.[iii] She has earnest eyes, an obstinate manner—a sullen comeliness. She may be shy; she appears haughty. She prayed us to come and see her. She and her husband had so long been interested in our work.[92]

EC *Tuesday, June 17.*

We visit Oscar Wilde—being received by Mrs. Oscar in turquoise blue, white frills and amber stockings. The afternoon goes on in a dull fashion till Oscar enters. He wears a lilac[93] shirt, a heliotrope tie, a great primrose

---

i Cedar.

ii Constance Lloyd Wilde (1858–98), Irish author. After Wilde's conviction, she changed her surname (and their children's) to Holland and moved to Switzerland.

iii A scalloped decorative trim.

pink—very Celtic combination, ma foi! His large presence beams, with the *heiterkeit*[i] of a Greek God that has descended on a fat man of literary habits.

He sat down and told us that in his belief our *Tragic Mary* (Lansdorf volume) and Rossetti's Poems were the two beautiful books (in appearance) of the century—but he was going to surpass us, and would send us an early copy of his *Tales* to make us "very unhappy."[ii] He was delicious on the illustrations, that are not taken from anything in the book, only suggested by it—for he holds that literature is more graphic than art and should therefore never be illustrated in itself, only by what it evokes.[94]

EC In Herbert Spencer's drawing-room, [Miss Beatrix Potter] offered us cigarettes, in manly fashion; after our surprised refusal, she mounted one onto her lips, and soon the gray vapour was softly issuing—the softest thing about this woman, who is not the strong-minded woman of a few years ago, but the self-dissecting, self-prizing, magnetic woman of today. She will not marry till fifty, and then the man must be *devoted* to house and wife.[iii][95]

How heartily I hate the degradation of one sex by the other![96]

EC *Michael Field undertake travel to Dresden via train.*

I watch the painful appearance of things visible—Light is a mere background to a lumpish hill or some hard unamiable tree; it does not mingle with anything. One lies among one's wraps in feverous damp without shame while it is still dawn. The little stations are mere huts, the lines of the horizon come very near to one. There is a revolt in one's gaze against the magnifying illusions of night. The world looks common, and very black—poor little patch as it is! One is hungry—one feels that one's eyes are purple and swollen as if one had fought with an adversary. I look at the Fates—they are two ordinary little Old Maids, dreadful to see in the shiny, heated condition of dishabille, with stray hairs on the cheek and wraps falling from their features. Nothing terrible about them, no dim portentous fascination. Suddenly there is sweetness in the world[97] as one looks out—the Sun himself introduces light to the isolated objects, and it is day. There is the beautiful interpenetration of friendship; there is unity under the sunrise—Earth is born again. Then shame comes, and one hastens to the sponge, the comb, the mirror. One must not remain peculiar now that familiarity is given back to the Universe of which one is a part.

i "Good cheer, joy."

ii Perhaps *A House of Pomegranates*, a book of fairy tales Wilde published in 1891 as a second volume to *The Happy Prince and Other Tales* (1888).

iii Beatrix Potter (1866–1943), English writer, illustrator, scientist, and conservationist.

One begins the comedy of Toilet in the space of a square yard—one reseats oneself curiously reconciled to the view and one's fellow passengers.[98] [. . .]

My nerves are so acute, so fearfully conscious, that I almost scream when Sim touches me in walking, and I feel unemitted screams incubating. The night is synonymous with illness; we are both intolerably, disgracefully ill.[99]

EC Muffled up round my throat, beating on each side as a bird's two wings that flap under a cat's grip, we reach[100] our flat. A mustard plaster[i] or the doctor! The plaster cannot be made, so the doctor is fetched. We wait for him by the supper table, crumbling bits of food. Fraulein in dressing gown now with us, now at the door with a kind suppressed air. The lamp is lighted to be ready for the doctor's use. My throat beats in time to the clock and the clock is ostentatiously audible. It seems like the systole and diastole of phenomenal Life at your ear. Its chipping noise as it throbs is a torture.[101]

EC *Wednesday, August 19th.*

Again a long waiting for the Doctor. I am almost voiceless. At last he comes, looks at my feet, and says that I have got Scarlet fever. . . . There is a pause and I feel that a sentence is gathering against me. I know what it is— You must go to the Hospital. Dismay scatters our fortitude.[102] [. . .]

I get up, as if I were dressing for a great event, with the exaltation of a bride, only I think I am dressing for the last time not as a maiden but mortal. I feel vague, submissive, alarmed, yet very still. I drink Roman Wine—no one comes near to us, not to the door. There is the silence, the sense of flight to far corners that one feels in a house before a coffin is brought out . . . and yet our belongings and my yellow gown and my Love are so familiar in the midst of these Famous appalling circumstances. An officer enters—burly, black, prompt—two men follow in deep-coloured blouses. I am borne through the deserted passages on a chair, and descend, descend—till I come out to piercing grey light and free air. Then I am shut with my beloved in a Coach—very much like a Mourning Coach. We clasp each other with an awful weight of anxiety on our hearts, for they may strive to[103] part us, and we have no German with which to plead. We make a vow, we neither speak, that nothing but death shall sever us. [. . .] I have a feeling, that the dying must have, of external powers taking possession of me and severing me from all I love, all that is familiar, precious, and my own: yet I can do nothing except implore that the carriage may be sent to the door, and we allowed to try at another house, if we can remain together.[104]

i A warm dressing filled with mustard-seed powder, applied to relieve chest congestion and muscle aches.

EC I lie down just as I am, and think how if I came to Die, Amy and father could not reach me. I am conscious of a new, an ideal union with my Love . . . yet she is distracted and as nurse told us after, "said many things." Officialism has fed the sick at 12.30—so it is impossible for me to have anything till six— Even tea and coffee can only be ordered for the next day. Nurse brings a china spoon of wine and gives a drought of each. [. . .]

A great fair official comes, asks questions about my grandparents, and desires to know the exact meaning of "Durdans"—requires money—I know there is a vast deal of fuss; but I am lying at the very centre of heat, satisfied as Demophon when Demeter laid him on the Embers to become immortal.[i]

In the serene light of an August-evening I am fed with fowl-broth . . . Time goes by, the fever burns steadily, and makes me feel less and less mortal. I am delighted to the depths and alive within the circle of the disease. . . . Time goes by . . . Then I see my Love on a little[105] bed by me; I see a table, a shaded lamp, a brown head with flaps of a solemn whiteness bent over a large book. [. . .]

At eight we understand we are to be left alone together for the night—no watching, no feeding. "In the night the sick sleep." Sister's severe form departs. The plain walls remain, some of the beds (some had been removed), the taps and drain, the striped-grey window curtains, and we two, shut in a hospital! How new it seems and strange . . . and that night two years ago our Darling was waking to death and preparing to smite it down in triumph. Her spirit does not come to me. I remember, without feeling that the remembrance is vital—as if it did[106] not belong to my very self, but were in the outskirts of my individuality. I sigh out of the burning fiery furnace of my temperature. "Oh, that I could have a cool little ballet in my hospital-shirt." . . . .[ii]

In early morning light, I open my eyes—Where am I?—in a cabin! I wait for the rocking of the vessel; but the bare walls are stabilised and do not move. Where am I? Suddenly, as the strangest fact that could assail my powers of recognition, I become aware that I am in a hospital, and my Love is by me. What a still, grave, clean place a hospital is! The hot clouds of the night have rolled off my brain . . . I feel a hunger that is a dreadful impotence. The nurse

---

i In Greek mythology, Demophon was a prince burned by Demeter, the goddess of agriculture, in order to transform him into a god.

ii These ellipses appear in the original; as Cooper descends into delirium here, we see her entries become increasingly fragmented and incoherent—even those written after her release from the hospital, as she reconstructs the experience.

at last appears with a tray of white tea-things, a roll, and some "zweibache"—
the latter are soaked;[i] I am raised to the coveted food, and immediately, as if
I were Tantalus[ii] himself, fail to eat a morsel and drop back in a fainting condition. My Love resolves I shall have nourishment in the night—she will fight
with all the weapons of her determination and of her German for the grace.

I am revived by Greek Wine and Sister washes my face, as one would wash
coarse Earthenware.[107] [. . .]

I remember nothing of what passes—

It is twilight; milk is brought and I drink it; then we are left and the lamp
put out. I see my Love by the window—She opens the striped blinds that I
may watch the August full moon, making a poetic daylight throughout the
sky, defining with stern blackness the roof of the near station, and touching
the green of the embowered plane trees till they are magical as an enchant-
ress's role in colour. I feel the outside beauty has an ominous calm about it.
I am fervidly hot; the white beams lie on my brain, and provoke it—They
enter it clear, quiet, precise; they make it vague, distracted, visionary.
They[108] evoke their contraries. I create phantasies that come so fast that
they form an element round me in which I sink, sink—then float along under
them, then sink again. It is a stream the particles of which are impressions
and memories, fortuitously held together, and active as they never have been
and they were never intended to be. My Love, finding how it is with me, lies
on her bed and in a grave low voice recalls the lovely things we enjoyed in
Italy [. . .]

A great dromedary comes along, with red trappings and trophies, in the
midst are set the words *Two weeks at Dresden*!! The ironic beast passes.

Vast Bacchanals rush by, Rubenesque, violent—(Here *Tannhäuser* feeds
the phantasy) [. . .] I am Greek, Roman, Barbarian, Catholic; and this mul-
tiform life[109] sweeps me toward unconsciousness—only the shine through
the blinds tortures me so that I cannot lose myself. I beg my Love to keep a
candle lighted to put out the moon, with all its terrible spectral frilliness—
and to obliterate the white cavern-arch of the door[iii]—Death's Door, that I
keep approaching, that I cannot pass, for as soon as I am near it the brilliant
swirl of images is round me and I am caught back to life. Again and again, I
am magnetically drawn to the grey portal and as often rescued. Then I see
our two straight-beds—they are coffins—we lie near one another in noble
peace. . . . .

i A crisp, sweet biscuit served to babies and the infirm.

ii In Greek mythology, a figure punished by remaining just out of reach of food and drink.

iii By Bacchanals, ecstatic revels; by Rubenesque, voluptuous women in the style of Rubens;
by *Tannhäuser*, Wagner's 1845 opera about the struggle between sacred and profane love.

At last, I am carried away into unconsciousness ... ... I become aware of a figure in a short nightdress—a girl, almost at the other end of the ward, who has leapt to embrace a hero, a dark, magical man in the corner (a cloak stand) who does not respond. In horror at his coldness, she struggles back and falls across the bed half faint. That is how my escapade appears to me—I see that wan creature on the bed. (an ocean of gold pouring down)

I could not tell to moonshine what I would tell to *light* or to *dark*—that is the dilemma. I spring into bed away from it and am saved to consciousness. Then a message arrives from the doctor. I am to have wine. Schwester[i] drenches me—the gold-red wine runs down my nightdress and the sheets ... oblivion ... I fling myself down toward the foot of the bed, half-uncovered ... ... I am covered[110] up by Nurse, turned back on the pillows and again drenched with Mavrodaphne?[ii] ... oblivion ... ... I have my Love close to me and I am telling her about the tones of the light, that is coming in by the window—she says I was wonderful on it, but I do not recall a word I said, nor can she.[111]

EC Sim writes in our White Book—

"It is eight o'clock on Friday night. The good sister sits, praying silently. I fancy, by P. waiting till 'das Mädchen kommt.'[iii] Good, sweet, homely woman;—as a bundle of sweet herbs is her presence in this room.

"It was on Wednesday we were ordered here. How I fought for my young, with how many tongues, and with what agony. Finally, the large room, the bare walls, the carbolic, my beloved laid in a peaceful little *Bett*[iv]—a sense of fresh air, and peace, and religion—a deep gratitude. But the waking yesterday! The horror of imprisonment, the sense of isolation, the strange growing anxiety. Last (Thursday night) was one of delirium and horror, the delicate brain all entangled. I woke to find P. at the other end of the room; she nearly if not quite fainted. This morning there was rich recuperative sleep. [...]

"So strange my part here! For the division in Germany between the quick and the dead is not sharper than between the *gesund* and the *krank*.[v] When I walk about the state garden here,[112] the sick ones from their pale hospital gowns look at my English clothes as the shades at the shadow cast by Dante on the ground. One meets the baskets of bread being bourne along. One sees the little band of delicate, healing children. Large-coated men, like sick wasps, are seen in the further garden through the trees.

i In German, "Sister," used in this case to refer to the nurse.
ii A sweet Greek wine.
iii "The girl is coming."
iv "Bed."
v The healthy and the sick.

"The breeze is carbolic.

"This afternoon a [postcard] from Bernard wanting us to take two tickets for the *Rheingold*.ⁱ

"Now or hereabouts is Durdans in possession of the truth.

"I have not shed a tear—scarcely, through all the biting trouble of this week. But my heart is as thickly inscribed as an Egyptian Tomb. And *Her* day came yesterday in the midst of it. Quietly one had to turn the page. The good, diligent Mädchen is here. Brisk and wakeful are her eyes. How sweet is the life found here—the being with souls in their nakedness—sheltering and blessing them!" [. . .]¹¹³

EC *Sunday, Visitors' Day* [. . .]

I remember Schwester sitting by the further window on this Sunday Morning and saying she had no tie on Earth—nothing but her sick and Christ. She had no relations, no friends. She reproached Sim for too anxiously spending her whole love on me.¹¹⁴ [. . .]

EC Sister had read from the Bible before she left and my whole nature grew elfishly wicked as she read. I determine I will have as much pleasure as I can. I dance at balls, I go to Operas, I am Mars and looking across at Sim's little bed, I realise that she is a goddess, hidden in hair—Venus. Yet I cannot reach her. (I had been writing "Venus and Mars" [National Gallery] just before I left home.) I grew wilder for pleasure and madder against the ugly Mädchen. Sim comes to quiet me and assures me she is "The Little Horse"ⁱⁱ—"You're not the Little Horse (You're not the Little Horse)" I cry out—(the words . . .

*The remainder of this page is redacted.*¹¹⁵

EC Sim continues Monday Morn.

"Last night I received a heartless note from Mrs. Costelloe, with offer of books and no sympathy. I reply:

Dear Mrs. Costelloe,

Thank you for the offer of books. I cannot *now* and *here* read French novels: do not therefore trouble to bring to me the volumes you suggest. The medical report of Edith continues favorable.

Sincerely yours, K. H. Bradley. [. . .]

---

i *Das Rheingold*: The first of a four-part opera comprising Wagner's *Der Ring des Nibelungen* (1876).

ii Perhaps Dürer's 1505 engraving by that title.

"*P's vision*. Written down Tuesday Morn. Aug. 26. A little Love comes to me and lays his little cheek against my heart. He shows me in a vessel his broken wings, his broken bow and arrows, his broken heart. And then he sings . . . In the vessel it looked like a bright, feathered smash."[116]

EC *Berenson and Mrs. Costelloe bring Edith roses.*

(I shall never forget those roses—their beauty nearly stopped my heart. A bright wire basket was filled with moss and set with about twenty blossoms of a fresh, old-fashioned pink such as one sees in eighteenth-century pictures—the colour was soft and a little sad as those fading pinks are, yet over it was the shine of youth, of waterdrops, of silver bloom. In the midst of the flushing pyramid was one single rose of opaline white, the long leaves scarcely severed. I have never had a gift so beautiful, so generous, as a young man's gifts should be. Nurse looked at the smooth and dazzling petals with disapproval, as if the "world were too much with them"[i] . . . but, oh, I lay and gazed intoxicated with the glow, the colour of life itself swelling the buds, fading in the blossoms—with the perfume round me, within me. An insatiable rapture, almost delirium, haunted my eyes and brain.)[117]

EC (On Friday I must have had the locks cut off. [. . .] I was very grave and depressed at the thought of being clipped. While Sim was in the Garden, I got Sister to do it, while I held a glass and directed her scissors from tuft to tuft.—The little white cotton jacket with black and red spots was chosen by Bernie, bought by Mrs. C., and brought on Thursday.)[118]

EC *Transcribing KB.* "Sister kisses her with a kiss that plunged down among the wraps . . . (yes, as the wolf did when he sought the child—O Eros!—in Browning's 'Iàn Ivànovich'[ii]—a fatal kiss!) [. . .]

"My Love and I have our first springtide kisses, shy and brief and full of the future. Pussy feels his cheeks reclaimed by life. Oh, how Love is better than *das Bad*!"[iii]

EC (My love was a little jealous, stormily tearful that Nurse should have forestalled her on my lips . . . but I know whose kisses were vernal—not received for what had been, but for what would be. Still the motherliness in the wonderful passion of Nurse's gave me delight.)[119]

EC *Transcribing KB.* "We take *Kaffee* in Sister's little chamber to which she leads P. 'mid kisses and strange tears." (I remember the narrow bit of a room

---

i Cooper cites Wordsworth's 1801 sonnet "The World Is Too Much with Us," a critique of the industrial materialist's neglect of nature.

ii Published in *Dramatic Idylls* (1879).

iii "The bathroom."

green and close—the bed with its great quilt and dark green silk screen—the little table by it holding the Bible—palm trees with their fans making a canopy—parallel with the bed and the red stove. The great black hair armchair, the wooden table—the bookcase at the foot of the bed—the small washing place by the door.)[120]

EC Sim continues.

"Not soon to be forgotten, the sight of P. and her old Nurse, seated together hand in hand on the balcony. Sister's smile is like the brightness on an apple—the hard fruit, core-sweet, with a serviceable brilliancy that recalls how the September sunlight will forsake it. P. goes back to her white bed and gives me a great kiss like one of the Mother's, when her soul was full of air, or inspiration, or joy."[121]

EC "Poor, old Schwester! She has in her eyes a twofold divineness when she looks at P.—that of the Mother who has done everything for her babe, and that of a Dog who watches for the love of a higher Power."[122]

EC "Pussy wakes from its 'lye' and rings for Schwester, who comes straight to grasp and kiss. She is like one who has been in a desert, who finds an Oasis and simply throws himself down and drinks. The wrinkles of the worn peasant flesh are felt by P. against her cheek—the kisses are almost too rapid to have an aim; her eyes, overfull of love, cannot bear to meet her beloved's—she buries her sight in deep anguish against P.'s face."[123]

EC *Tuesday afternoon.*

"I go into the garden and watch the fish, leaving P. with Schwester, who encloses her with passionate arms and plunges down on her cheeks with kisses. 'Ich bin so hungrig'[i] she said in a stifled sob that came out as a smile of anxious love. P. told her when two nestled together, we called it in English 'ein Love.'[ii] 'Meine Edith giebt mich kein Love'[iii]—she said with jealousy that is jealous of the loved one's receptiveness. P. kissed her cheeks, and then giving a little clap to the round, honest cheek, kissed her lips. 'Danke, danke,'[iv] she said and it was her heart that spoke. Then she kissed P. again and again on her lips—great, spreading kisses."

Wednesday

A cold, sad day till the afternoon.

Schwester took me to her room, and gave me her photograph, with wolf kisses. Through the open door I see the green shadow of the trees and their poignant golden lights. They sound a call in[124] my blood to go out and I am allowed to take a walk between my poet and my nurse to the fish pond.

i "I am so hungry."
ii "A love."
iii "My Edith gives me no love."
iv "Thank you, thank you."

There the light really gambols and the gleeful foam of the fountain leaps up like health; strong, full-coloured reeds; black and golden fish move swift, swift—[125]

EC My Experiences with nurse are painful—she is under the possession of terrible, fleshly love, she does not conceive as such, and as such I will not receive it. Oh, why will Anteros[i][126]

    EC Schwester, while my Love is in the Garden, embraces me bodily and from the outer prescience of language I catch the sound "Eine Machtige Liebe!"[ii]—her hand curls round my heart to feel the life heat and strays. "Die schöne Brust—O das schönes Bauch"[iii]—I don't know the German of the last exclamation! She makes me shiver, but I play with her passion like a child, and she is utterly deceived in it herself—I am her child she has washed and dressed with her piteous, clinging hands, and her honest, stern eyes, altered to a mother hen's belie[127] the welling-up of all her frustrate nature at the touch of first *love* for any mortal . . . [. . .]

    Ausgang[iv] for Sim to get rooms for us at the Belle Vue. I must fight Nurse's unreasonableness. She comes while I am resting, throws herself about me and kisses with the persistency of madness. I manage to make her understand she grieves and fatigues me—instantly with repentance she retires to the armchair, and I pretend deep sleep with anxious ears. She is called away and I slumber. She strives with herself and scarcely ever breaks out after—but the strain makes me dull by the time my Love returns.[128]

EC This seems a little circular bit of my life, shut out by a special, exclusive line from my other days; it is curious how perfectly my imagination has been coming round to the point when this circle began. As soon as convalescence touched me warmly, my thoughts began to revert to the first sensations, the fear, the sadness, the vacancy of "illness"—the splendour of delirium, the still growth of the "machtige Liebe"[v] in Schwester. I see all those things in their completeness as the time comes for me to pass the hospital doors; I am nearer to them when I was passing through them. One cannot know great impressions from one side; one must come on them from the other. The sense of finality in this wonderful orbit makes me feel a cold feeling of survival—a sadness that is awe. A new yearning has been planted in Memory.

i Greek god of requited love and avenger of unrequited love.
ii "A mighty love!"
iii "The beautiful breast—Oh that beautiful belly."
iv "Exit."
v "Mighty love."

(This night Sister kissed me almost as we kiss the Dying—gently, hope-lessly, with dread—realising we shall never see a living face again greet us from their pillow.)[129]

EC *Monday.*

Sister brings the *Kaffee* with a look in her eyes that gives the feeling of an execution. In the midst of uncertain sunlight our clothes are condemned to the *fiery* fire—the dear, apricot dressing gown that mother gave me, her chock-shawl[i]—Sim's Elderflower hat.

While my Love is, by chance, *fort*, Sister assaults me with a great love in bed—kissing me on the lips and breast, gathering my limbs in her arms as if veritably I were a child under its Nurse's or Mother's handling. She would embrace "die ganze Edith."[ii] In this love there is the fearful passion of mere severance—and the still more fearful passion of unsatisfied senses in a strong nature, to whom religion has been an ascetic law. Last of all she lay looking into my eyes—"die helle Augen"[iii]—as if to learn how long they could be true. (How long can they—how long?—and yet I feel my whole being take expres-sion in *immer*!![iv])[130] [. . .]

After dinner we have mortal hours of waiting—the sky unhelpful, grey as when I came to the Krankenhaus, and Sister sits by me pressing my hand, almost as the Beloved did when she was taken into Death. At last—at last, my lace scarf is fastened to my hat and wrapped round me toothache-wise to hide the "crop" of my prison house, the boxes start, I give one look of con-centrated meanings at my little bed and the great, green, simple Ward—a kind of visual comparison, touched with feeling, of first and last impres-sions—then I kiss the moist, powerful lips and look into the brown eyes that bless me and weep for me—I fly, and on Sim's arm, from the stem-filled alley, where I feel mysteriously a stranger, I look back[131] at the little villa in the wood—to see a big, round, grey shape wave a handkerchief, bend, and wave, wave, wave till the dot of white becomes an invisible mathematical point among the trees.[132]

EC From a letter of Schwester Christiane's—written secretly on a small piece of paper in my chosen red ink. I am afraid she is grieving dreadfully; her face looked aged when I visited her on the Wednesday after we left Krankenhaus. She is at rather a critical time in health and I am most unhappy—There's

i A crocheted shawl featuring overlapping square patterns.
ii "The whole Edith."
iii "The bright eyes."
iv "Into always."

something of the mother and of the dumb animal mixed in her intense passion for me.[133]

EC *Wednesday, December 9th.*

The rain it raineth. I am not well and lie in bed, writing of Tura's *Jerome* in a kind of physically realising dream:[i] Sim starts for the National Gallery, where she studies Bellini's *Blood of the Redeemer*,[ii] and meets Mrs. Costelloe. They drive to Mr. Pearsall Smith's (!) for lunch[iii]—Mrs. Costelloe's cook having a broken arm. The old party jests with Sim and gives her apples from Niagara to bring home.

Mrs. Costelloe once dreamt that she was I, and that she enjoyed as I do pictures and beautiful things. She said it was glorious.

I had a dream the other night.

I thought Bernie invited us to drink tea before some kind of celebration in which he was to take part. He was as irritatingly beautiful as he has ever been—I left the room often to escape my admiration. . . . After a while Sim and I were sitting with many others in an open-air walled enclosure, watching curious worshippers and members come in, their heads bound and their robes trailed on the grass. A coffin was carried with stately slowness and laid under an altar—Down the vista of this temple, unoppressed by roof, I saw a scarlet panoply advance, the edges gilded and tasseled. I knew that Dionysus walked underneath and that the part of the young God was taken by Bernie. The assembly rose and sang "O God, our help in ages past, Our hope for years to come."[iv] Sim[134] stepped fearlessly in front of the initiated and said in a voice of stern protest "Edith, don't you sing"—nevertheless I heard my voice like a lark's, high and irrepressible. The vision disappeared, for I was awake.[135]

EC We seek the Bodley Head[v] and came to terms with Elkin.[vi] *Sight and Song* is to be like *Fêtes Galantes*: *Stephania* is to be bound in rich cream, like Oscar Wilde's *House of Pomegranates*, with simple gold lettering. I have since thought that the Head of the "Mariniere de Monstre" by Odilon

---

i Cosimo Tura's *Jerome* (1470).

ii Painting by Giovanni Bellini (1465).

iii Logan Pearsall Smith (1865–1946), American-born British essayist and critic; brother of Mary Costelloe Berenson.

iv Hymn by Isaac Watts (1708).

v London publishing house founded in 1887.

vi Charles Elkin Mathews (1851–1921), Elkin or "The Elk" to Michael Field; British publisher and bookseller.

Redon[i] might be vignetted in gold, like the head of Sappho on *Long Ago*. We increase in liking of Elkin Mathews.

In New Bond Street we seek next the Ladies' University Club[ii] that has just made my Love a special member—hurrah!

It is a modest, refined little London home for us—Morris papers and furniture, excellent magazines, writing cabinet, dressing-room, lunchroom, pleasant housekeeper. We meet Athena Clough, who gives us hearty welcome.[iii] Letters can be sent to our club, and sent on if *wished*—not otherwise for, as the housekeeper discreetly remarked, "it might not be agreeable." What delicious opportunities for crime!!

We end our day at the Paters'. They have changed their receiving day and have not let us know in offence at our nonappearance during the summer and autumn. They were chill for this reason, a blessed, encouraging chilliness; then delightful: all our talk was of pictures. Walter is hard at work on Gaston[iv]—he will be seen on Saturdays, if we will come then. Tottie is very wicked when she returns from Italy [. . .][136]

KB *December 31st, 1891.*

New Year's Eve.

I sit down to keep watch in my little blue bedroom. My Dearest is in bed. I have been nursing her with influenza. Happily, today pains have lessened and she has been very blessed in bed, correcting and preparing the MS of *Sight and Song*.

And now of the past and what it is bearing away.

The first months we were weaving—finding the means to live—offering worship to colour. And we lived light in Spring; and one fair face made the whole world full of exquisite pleasure. Our eyes have learnt much: we have been initiated into the joys of Sight. And the graves in our hearts have sunk— O God—a little deeper. We have walked with God in the very cool of the eventide of death. P. and I are knit up into one living soul. I have learnt perhaps a little patience; and there is the honey of thankfulness in every crevice of my soul. P. is with me—she has spent her holiday in the age of gold. Illness

i Odilon Redon (1840–1916), French symbolist painter and printmaker. Cooper is probably thinking of various images of sea monsters Redon created during the 1890s.

ii Founded in 1883 as the equivalent to men's clubs, providing a space for university women in London.

iii Blanche Athena Clough (1861–1960), advocate for women's education and principal of Newnham College, Cambridge (1920–23).

iv *Gaston de Latour*, Pater's final and unfinished novel, published as *An Unfinished Romance* by Macmillan in 1896.

has made her sweeter, younger, more a child. Heinrich has been born. And the flowers have bloomed and faded in Durdans garden, and I have planted two little sweetbriar trees. Heaven prosper them! I am very happy; giving and receiving perfect love.[137]

Works and Days, 1892

EC *January 12th, 1892.*

My birthday. Golden light over a snowy earth. My love and I breakfast together at the little new table in the study. On the oak table, by the opposite wall, is propped my Love's illustrious present—the largest size Braun photograph of Giorgione's *Venus* mounted on grey felt lining paper and framed in crimson-brown unpolished walnut.[i] It is the largest picture in the house. Its beauty makes one grave; there is such solemn imagination, such noble treatment of line and landscape in it, that one's joy becomes a suppression of the heart.[138] [. . .]

Alice lights the Italian lamp in the study and after tea my Love and I have a great love and talk of the past and of the Beloved Mother-One—of how we miss the greatness of her nature, the dramatic impulse she gave to our work— of how I brought the best of beauty, in literature in Earth to her, as a consecrated minister to her nobleness. Life is so much less worth living since she left us—I would[139] give up Italy, travel, pictures to have her back . . . and yet there is one thing that makes me pause in my passionate desire—she did not understand my need of freedom; she bound and overawed me where I wanted to be free and personal. Such an influence is a crime against me . . . I suffered torments, struggles such as the hermits of the wilderness knew, under my Beloved's construction. She understood an artist's inspiration—she could not understand an artist's temperament. I have so much to bear from this thwarting of the passion in me after liberty from father that I cannot wish to add to the suffering—for me the sympathies of her spirit are with me now she knows.

What a divine blessing it is to me to have my Love, who checks no self-expression, who brings beauty to my eyes, and gladness to my life, who loves me and whom I love with strenuous force, that is half-hidden by our caresses and humorous names, and utter familiarity! Alfred de Musset felt his heart at thirty to see if it still beat[ii]—mine sings out its love to her more loudly than

---

i Adolphe Braun (1812–77), French photographer who produced photographic reproductions of artworks, beginning in 1866.

ii The biographer of Alfred de Musset (1810–57) reported that occasionally de Musset's head ever—it loves art more devotedly, and the South where pictures fill every white town; it loves language with deeper awe and unweariable service . . . Alas, it leaves *Man* much less, and Lads and Causes not at all. And this is Field—his Confession.[140]

EC Our aim in *Sight and Song*.

To render what the lines and colours of certain beloved pictures sing *in themselves* and would express, not so much what they are to us as poets, but rather what poetry they objectively incarnate.

We are longing for proofs—those slender sheets on which fulfillment is as yet a promise are to the author what the coming of swallows is to those who love springtime.[141]

EC *Friday, February 12.*

Sim and I stroll into McLean's Gallery.[i] We are fixing our eyes on the Madonna and Child, painted by Millet for the Church of Notre Dame de Lorette, Paris[ii]—when I feel the flash of other eyes enter mine—I look quickly for the intruding glance, and see a form turned from me, in cape and top hat, that reminds me of Selwyn Image—the peccant Selwyn. And by him is a form like the excited Horne's.[iii] The couple seem determined not to have the discomfort of a meeting—we are determined they shall meet us and make the moment inevitable. Then with frank greeting I shake Selwyn's hand—with slow cordiality Horne shakes Sim's, and we go off like the couples in Watteau[iv]—only not to talk of love but the safer subject of art.[142]

EC *Sunday, February 14.*

My Love is away with Amy Bell—I am away from my own identity. I want and want—my own Love, and nothing else. Last night I wrote the wee preface for *Sight and Song*. This morning after an hour of futile pen-scratching, I was carried swiftly from beginning to end of one of Geneviva's speeches for

---

would nod with the beat of his heart. This is now known as the "de Musset sign," an affliction caused by aortic valve regurgitation.

    i Thomas McLean's gallery in Haymarket showed the work of modern artists. McLean sold engravings based on the works he showed.

    ii Jean-François Millet (1814–75), an influencer of artistic realism in France.

    iii Selwyn Image (1849–1930), artist, poet, designer associated with the Arts and Crafts movement; Herbert Horne (1864–1919), English poet, architect, designer.

    iv Jean-Antoine Watteau (1684–1781), an influential painter of the Rococo school who popularized the small cabinet paintings known as "fêtes galantes," featuring lovers against landscapes.

Act I [of] *Carloman*. May the spirit illumine, raise and support us for the great drama![143]

EC *Saturday, February 27th.*

We start to town with our M.F. Valise full of evening clothes, which we deposit at the University Club—we prowl for gloves and return to a quiet lunch and a card from Little One, confessing how ill she has been. At Elkin's we buy the Reprint of *Modern Love*[i] and drive off to Pater's; as usual it is the house of Pater with the part of Pater left out—he is not there. [. . .]

Responding to music at a concert.

How strange the tone of these old instruments—what far-off, tinkling youthfulness! They cannot[144] express the subtlety nor volume of our modern emotion—the meaning, the experience, the acuteness in what we feel. They have a sunny, *gala* thinness, or a quaint sorrow that scarcely swells into passion. Men must have been half-crickets when this music satisfied them.[145]

EC This was the tale of the wedding (from Louie).[ii] [Havelock Ellis] rose, breakfasted, dressed himself in his velvet coat and was dressed by her in tie etc.

He sat by the fire and read *Nature*.

He remarked, "There are not many bridegrooms who would sit by the fire and read *Nature*."[iii] Louie was cold. He said, "sit by the fire child, and I will warm your hands." Then they went forward in the slush. The bride[iv] was waiting outside the registrar's, shook her umbrella (!!). The party was shut in a waiting room for one quarter of an hour. H. was not nervous and talked . . . there must have been something fearsomely unnatural in that easy talk. Then the civil marriage took place, the sun shining full on the couple through the Registrar's eastern window. H. looked handsome in the light—he was calm; his umbrella-shaking bride pale and disquieted! Bride, bridegroom and sister walked home arm in arm. Soon after the bride departed to

---

i *Modern Love* is a sonnet sequence published by Meredith initially in 1862, reprinted in 1892. The poems explore the failure of a marriage.

ii Louisa Eleanor "Louie" Ellis (1865-1928), a close friend of Michael Field's who worked as a dressmaker and collaborated with the poets on the creation of their garments. Ellis was a sister of Havelock Ellis, and through Ellis became a friend of and correspondent with Olive Schreiner.

iii Havelock Ellis (1859-1939), brother of Louie, a physician and author, and a pioneer in the scientific study of human sexuality. With John Addington Symonds, he wrote the first medical textbook on homosexuality in 1897. *Nature* (1869-present) is a weekly science journal.

iv Edith Lees (1861-1916), author and feminist activist. Lees was a lesbian, lived separately from her husband, Ellis, and had several extramarital relationships.

her rooms in town, travelling by herself in the Underground.[i] She gave an At Home that afternoon to which her husband came. They parted and only met again next day when they started for Paris. The bride was married in an ulster.[ii] This is a true account of the modern sacrament of matrimony. It is revolting. "Free love, free field"[iii] is sacreder.[146]

EC During the week we received an essay by B[erenson] on the subject of love in literature. It went to show that the matter of all literature that has the form of epic, drama or novel is the struggle of the individual against contending forces. In early days strength and cunning were the personal qualities needed for the struggle against death and doom. More and more tyrannous institutions, old and mighty became the foes of succeeding generations—first the struggle was between the individual and the Caste; next between the individual and the Family. The subject of struggle in both the last cases is frequently *love*, and on this subject nearly all novels turn. A marriage is the aim of English and American literature—the violation of one owing to social arrangements the aim of French. Northern lit, Russian and Norwegian, treat the problem of the individual's relation to Family with great freedom and novelty—giving more and more triumph to the individual—Tolstoy and Ibsen.[147]

EC On Saturday, March 12—while at tea a small book parcel is brought in to Sim, addressed Blackberry Lodge[iv]—feeling no good could come with that address she impatiently casts it down. I take it up, cut the string, open it and find it to be *Modern Love* and find in it an inscription to Sim herself from George Meredith.

"We dance a Dionysic dance, we sit with our chins in our hands and our vision away in the misty possible."

Then Sim writes: [. . .]

"Dear Mr. Meredith: *Modern Love* is known and honoured of us: and we love to remember with what fervour of admiration Mr. Browning spoke of it to us—For I imagine even the greatest of English novelists must still care most for his poems.

"While correcting your postal knowledge of us (we have lived just a twelve-month at Durdans, Reigate) may I ask whether it would be an intrusion on your leisure to call at Flint Cottage?

---

i The London Underground began running in 1863.
ii An overcoat with a cape, typically worn by men.
iii From Tennyson's anthem to chivalry, *Idylls of the King* (1859).
iv A former address for the Cooper family.

"We have often ourselves serious thoughts of dying,—one of us nearly did die last summer—[148] and we would fain not leave this earth without seeing what, I doubt not, the prophets and Kings of the next century will desire to see vainly. And we are not very far away. We can almost hear the bleating of the same lambs."[149]

EC We have been reading Huysman's *À Rebours*—it is the very word of decadence—the foam on the most recent decay, and yet there is something of meagre tragedy about it. One gets to know every dislike and like of the wretched des Esseintes—all his physical ills, his remedies, his food, till one feels to him as a nurse to her invalid. The chapter on Verlaine, Mallarmé, Baudelaire, Poe, the de Goncourt and Zola is a masterpiece of delicate, nervous criticism.[i][150]

EC *Wednesday, March 30.*

A dress-conclave at Louie Ellis's. Sim's wedding gown of soft anemone pink with French-brown edging is enough to cause a breach of promise of marriage. My robe of black and bright olive green veiled with black lace is severe and rather dark. Louie herself was worthy of Sargent's brush—a fine green tea-gown, boldly embroidered with damask-velvet thread and the highlights flashed across it with brilliant blood-red beads.[ii]

A trying half-hour with the Elk and the Roadman. Something has worried them—they have an anxious East-windy manner. *Sight and Song* is found to be too bulky to be held by the parchment (unmounted) cover of *Fêtes Galantes.*[iii] Suddenly our little book is disappointed of its clothes, and we do not know how to cover its nakedness. Olive cloth is suggested.[151]

KB *On Saturday, March 26th, Walt Whitman died.* [. . .]

Some of the holiest hours of our life have been spent with him. *Nevertheless he is gone*: he too is a phase, a period. The trials of life succeed one another too sharply; but this too must be faced. The things that thrilled us thrill us no more. It costs much to find Turner slipped away from one's mind as quietly as the dead slip from life. And then the poets . . . But the true courage is to face this. They will return into one's life no more forever. One comes

---

i Joris-Karl Huysmans (1848–1907), French novelist, art critic, and aesthete. His *À Rebours*, or *Against Nature* (1884), was a widely read decadent novel often credited as the "poisonous French novel" that corrupted Wilde's Dorian Gray. Des Esseintes is the novel's protagonist. In chapter 14, he reads Poe, Flaubert, Zola, Verlaine, and other authors associated with decadence.

ii John Singer Sargent (1856–1925), an American expatriate painter known especially for lush, gorgeous portraits.

iii A volume of poetry published in 1869 by Paul Verlaine engaging the eighteenth-century "fêtes galantes" tradition in painting as popularized by Watteau.

forth naked from the womb. Then one begins to accumulate; then one begins to drop by the way.[152]

EC A pretty girl comes in. The word *Miss Meredith* goes round. Louie brings her up to us. She says "We are expecting you to lunch." Meredith is better. We do not like the daughter. She is frank, cold, spoiled—shallow. Her complexion is very fair, her eyes steel blue, blond hair in masses, deep lips with very lovely curves. Dress—plain black, long fawn jacket, black lace turned over the neck, a black hat with pure blue ribbons. She is elegant, she bears herself haughtily—has no graciousness in the eyes. She is anything but a Nesta.[i] If his nature is like hers, I shall[153] hate him.[154]

KB *Easter Eve.*

We wake to whirling snowstorms. Today I resign my housekeeping: my loved ministry. No more shall I ponder pretty meals for Henry.

It is father's birthday. At 74 he is a perfect harmony in grey.

In the afternoon I simply give way as an ill-built house—I fall in.

With horror I recognise that outside of our art we are not living at all.

We do not walk with any of the great souls of the past; we live under the blessing neither of the living nor the dead. We are not thinking: we cannot act. And we care for fewer things day by day. We believe less, we hope less, and—God forgive us!—I fear we love less. We do not hunger less: we are hungry, and mowed up with husks.

We *must* study: the mind must labour with its hands daily, or perish.[155]

Michael Field travel to a Bradley family wedding in Birmingham.

EC *Easter Tuesday*

Off to the wedding![ii] [...]

Catching an express at Euston, we reach Birmingham one hour too soon—and pace the platform together, with that sense of hollowness of which the Present is convinced by the Past. [...] Fifteen cousins rise up to welcome us at Wilton House.[156] [...]

We storm the attic stairs, the attic—but we pause, so deathly is the sight that meets us—the dress laid out as if it were a corpse. Had I been the Bride I should have wept over and dreamt of that whiteness. Sim flies blanched with agony.

---

i Nesta is the vivacious, idealized daughter-figure in Meredith's 1891 novel *One of Our Conquerors.*

ii Probably the marriage of Mary Louisa Brooks, cousin to Michael Field, and Alfred Hall, celebrated at the Parish Church of Edgbaston, Birmingham, on April 20, 1892.

The Bridegroom, against all convention, spends the evening with his lady—she sinks in his arms; he carries her into supper. Heavens! Had I been the man I should have raged inwardly if so little had been left for the manhood in my love to overcome.

Wednesday—The Wedding Day.

Cold, raw: The morning a mere slough of waiting; boys at every turn, in unnatural lavender trousers, and at wrestle with half-fitted white gloves; the girls and mother harassed with details, the bride an East wind. [. . .]

At last the pleasure of dressing, the arrival of the flowers. Sim carries a great bunch of delicate roses and I advance bearing a lilac bush.

A sight of the bride, glancing at herself with cynical hatred from under the veil, which a young dressmaker's assistant arranges: a bride and not beautiful!

Her simple ivory dress becomes her form,[157] proportioned so slenderly. The bridesmaids wear white dresses trimmed with a buttercup-sprinkled white silk and rustic hats over which hang buttercups. They carry yellow posies.

We drive to church with Francis, who follows us up the nave—"to waft us on as a god." So curious to be with him on a marriage-day! The bride delays, the music irritates by repetition. At last she comes, scattering wild April smiles, finally giving her bridegroom a starry look, a real gift; I never saw her look so illuminated.

The seven brothers are pale opposite to me, the sisters make their posies quiver behind the Bride—she stands like a willing victim, but a victim to the first great Illusion! I feel as if I am assisting at some rite of an old world. The Illusion is strong as the Earth, but the worship paid to it must have new forms or new freedom if it is to be living as the power it celebrates. Then comes all the defamation of love by cake, champagne, stupid hopes, emptiness of the new condition—Ugh! But the cake is excellent—the honeymoon is indeed honey laid up by cunning cooks.

The bride bids a cool and gracious goodbye in her ruddy cloak and redblack hat. A storm of rice rattles over her. Shoes fly meteorically. There is no reason after this why we should be gathered[158] together. We go to our beds and last of all crown our fatigue with a family dinner which is sit-down. The evening is sad, gusty—an envious sense hangs about that the feast is gone elsewhere. The bride and bridegroom are not popular. The dark hours provoke thoughts[.][159]

EC *Saturday, April 23.*

A lovely morning. The leaves more like dewdrops than leaves in their lucid joyousness, the sky pale and happy. My love and I go to the station that I may see her off to Dover. We swear, with the bright world round us, that we will remain poets and lovers whatever may happen to hinder or deflect our lives.

Sim wrote in the train:

It was deep April and the morn
Shakespeare was born;
The world was on us, pressing sore,
My Love and I took hands and swore
Against the world to be
Poets and lovers evermore;
To laugh and dream on Lethe's shore,
To sing to Charon in his boat,
Heartening the timid souls afloat
Of Judgment never to take heed,
But to these fast-locked souls to speed
Who never from Apollo fled,
Who spent no hour among the dead.
Continually
With them I dwell,
Indifferent to heaven or hell.[i][160]

EC I continue to sleep with my Love, I continue darkling to be happy.

A description of a painting titled "Idyll" by Maurice Greiffenhagen.[ii]
   Monday, April 25.
   A young shepherd takes to his lips and his breast a yielding girl. She is huddled up to him—the blessedness of receiving, of being passive under love softly moulds the look of her face. Her [the rest of the page has been redacted][161] arms fall straight to the left, her bosom is pressed toward her throat by the lover's arms, her head nestles against his insatiable mouth. There is summer in her eyes and on her mouth while her cheek is kissed. The dark shepherd boy, in hat and violet-shadowed goat skin, takes a simple possession of her that is ardour at its purest heat. Her dress is gay blue, her hair burns a sorrel brown; poppies flap knee-deep round her—breezy flakes of scarlet against her skirt, dangling patches in the lighter, grey-green herbage. The slope rises by apple trunks to the sky, where a red sun sets submissively, while it turns the last poppy that climbs toward it into a tiny blaze of vermillion. There is an astonishing truthfulness in the picture—its subject is old as

i Michael Field published this poem in *Underneath the Bough* (1893).
ii Maurice Greiffenhagen (1862–1931), British painter and member of the Royal Academy. He painted *Idyll* in 1891.

the meadows, its treatment modern, modern—life in every sweep of the brush. It is instantaneously passionate. The figures are seen as if by someone standing upright as they. It is one of those works of art that "reveal what woman in herself must feel." The diverse sexual frankness of enjoyment in giving (or rather taking) and receiving is clear as in Michael's *Tiresias*[i]—also woman's more cloudless delight in her part than even man's in his. Rossetti's conventional poppies are lustreless and of the past beside this Impressionist dance of poppies.[162]

EC *Sunday, May 1.*

Smiling weather. In the afternoon my Love and I stroll round the garden-walks. Suddenly we speak of Meredith and clenching our fists toward Boxhill set to work to *will* with power that he be moved to ask us to lunch—we *will* and *will* with increasing emphasis of word and movement.[163]

EC *Dressed up and on the way to lunch with Meredith, his daughter, and the poet Richard Le Gallienne and his wife.*[ii]

Sim wears her Velasquez dress and black plumed hat—I my new dress of black cloth faced with olive silk that is darkened by black lace; black hat with olive bow, a lilac spray, and black and lilac baby-ribbons.[164]

EC *In Meredith's drawing-room.*

No special distinction in the few ornaments—rather a quiet and pleasant simplicity in the look of the little room than any individual note of taste.

Miss Meredith wore a dark serge, tailor cut, with gold edge and brass buttons, a white blouse and sky-blue bow. She is a nice maiden after all—a little spoiled and only distant through awe, which soon melts away.

Mrs. Le G. is a boneless heap of green Liberty stuff and smocking—over her heapy aestheticism she pokes her chin. Her hair is light and frizzed. Her features common—queer and yet commonly so; her eyes seem to curve like blue bays, monotonous and convex. Those Sphynxian eyes have betrayed Richard into his premature marriage. She is much below him—of the type of the artist's wife.[165]

EC *Strolling with Meredith.*

[We] reach the door of the Chalet. I enter—Sim enters. We act like two she-asses. I find nothing better to note than the basket of box-fuel and the

---

i Tiresias is the blind prophet of Greek mythology who transformed into a woman for seven years; also the central figure of poem 52 of Michael Field's *Long Ago*.

ii Richard Le Gallienne (1866–1947), British critic, essayist, and poet. Mildred Lee, his first wife, died in 1894.

cones that added make the fire sparkle. The room is wooden—on the floor some old and dusty Eastern mats—solid, old, inky desk covered with books and papers—*Revue des Deux Mondes*,[i] etc. Books on tables and chairs. Bookcase not that of a library but of a cultured reader. Fearing lest I should seem to be seeking a sight of M.F.—his volumes, I give small heed to the shelves. I see a large-paper edition of Carlyle.[ii] [166]

EC Again in our armchairs we talk as before only that I lend more undivided attention to the father, though the daughter is beside me.

He speaks of the hatred between men and women—he has known men who abhorred women and women who abhorred men. The depth of this sex enmity can be gauged by men's after-dinner talk. Separate education is answerable for much. He speaks bitterly of Fredric Harrison's sentimentality over woman's position.[iii] To root out from man the sense of contempt toward woman is the great point to gain, and this can only be done by giving her a knowledge of the world and an independent status. Therefore Meredith holds that the labour for the franchise is ill advised—it exasperates the deep opposition of men; whereas women's best course would be[167] quietly to enter the trades and professions, win their independence, and then enfranchisement would come as the ripe fruit of their still growth, for which their sex would be ready. Personally, he is fonder of women than men—he likes their rapid wit. To get men to understand him he has "to drag them by a halter up Boxhill."

He believes women have intelligence distinct from but equal to men's and that there is far deeper likeness in physical strength than appears owing to the false education and debilitating conditions that mould women. "I do not believe that nature would choose for breeding a strong and a weak—she wants a strong and a strong."[168]

EC *(In red ink) awaiting "Sight and Song."*

Teatime comes and with it comes the book—charming in its simple cover, the lettering perfect. Alas, the red-orange device inside, belonging to an earlier scheme, is out of place—a blot. There is terrible famine for our Mother-One in our hearts. Men are worse than dead when women's feelings are in question. Father is a sepulchre—spite of his kind attempt to be a sympathiser.

My Love and I clasp—knowing there would be little worth living for if either were alone in the world. But that will be provided for.

i The French literary periodical published since 1829.
ii Thomas Carlyle (1795–1881), influential and eternally contradictory Scottish essayist, philosopher, and historian.
iii Fredric Harrison (1831–1923), radical British jurist, author, and trade unionist.

We take our booklet out under the apple trees—the first book published at Durdans—we make the apple flowers rub cheeks with it. Then we read many of the Poems—it seems they[169] lack music, though the workmanship is good. It is a volume by itself; but will it interest apart from the pictures it translates? We are terrified. I cannot feel to dedicate this volume to the Mother-One—as I shall be able to dedicate *Stephania*—it is too much of another, too wholly due to our friendship with Bernard—the Mother shall never receive a second place—and the themes that are our sacrifice to her are ampler, more earnest. No—she may lay hands on this book; it does not lie in her breast.

O flowers of the apple, what is the doom of *Sight and Song*, how will it live—what is the perfect witness of all-judging Jove concerning its method, its achievement, its influence? and what will that Faun, that Bernard think of it! But the time begins in which we shall know, God willing.[170]

KB *Meets Mrs. Costelloe in town.*

She exacts we go to her brother's "apartement" in Paris—to live mostly at a *crèmerie*.[i] We will go, though we fear the *crèmerie*.[171]

EC As we are looking at this Costa,[ii] Oscar comes up; he shakes hands with Mrs. C[ostelloe] and therefore I put out my hand, which he takes (afar off) and never addresses a single word to me after. Sim bows, he returns the bow (afar off) and never addresses a word to her after. I have not often seen such rudeness—he is not of the men who can be rude offensively and yet escape. There is no charm in his elephantine body tightly stuffed into his clothes— with a gross, gorged effect—no charm in his great face and head of an un- select Bohemian cast—save the urbanity he can adopt or the intelligence without which[172] he can vitalise his ponderousness. When he shows himself as a snob he is disgustingly repulsive. We were not well dressed, as the day had begun with rain—we do not belong to the fashionable world—so Oscar rolls his shoulders toward us. When next I meet him in my choicest French hat I will turn my back on him, and most decisively. The artist strain in him is crossed by the vulgar-respectable. Gods and woman cannot endure such a cross.[173]

EC *On a walk with Mrs. Costelloe.*

In the gloaming she and I walked on Wray Common, and I told her I should never fight for any freedom to gain [that] which would perturb my

---

i A cheese shop.
ii Giovanni Costa (1826–1903), an Italian nationalist and painter.

art. I have only so much energy—if the god demands it, the cause of woman-hood must go hang. When I said I often felt I had no strength of Personal-ity—no defining will—she answered I had no conception of the force with which I impressed others—I had *virtue* in the Pateresque use of the term.[i] This is comforting to one who feels so pliant and generalised as I often do.[174]

EC (My Love has written of my Curls—"The Boy's hair curls more than ever. His head is simply in flames with curls, as if all his little farm-fancies had escaped from his skull and were turning somersaults for joy of their liberty—or is it 'hair the vine itself' as it says of Bacchus in *Sight and Song*.")[175]

EC A day of blight! In *The Speaker* an article by G. Moore on sex in art[ii] that makes one feel as if one were a negro—that would stamp M.F. as an artist with the stamp of inviolable inferiority—A clever article, frank, almost con-vincing in its downrightness for the moment—with a power of blackening the sky for us as the devil's wings do in *St. Antoine*.[iii] G.M. writes as that devil argued.[176] Then we take *Otto*[iv] to Elkin. The man seems in panic; he says nothing about the sale of the book, he "never smiles again." Does he fear, does he sicken over our morality? We make these sacrifices for art. G.M. says women will not make—or have we got our "dépit de juillet,"[v] our dog days' madness on us, and fancy all this?

Anyhow we are dark, we are irritated.

We hate London.[177]

Michael Field travel to Paris to stay with Mary Costelloe.

EC *Paris.*

Monday morning, June 20th. [...]

I have such a sharp impression of all this—Mary meeting us in a plum-coloured dress,[vi] a dubious look in the eyes set in so frank a face, the honey masses of her hair: then the sudden entrance into the little salon—the small torturous form of Bernard, his excited eyes, the shock of finding him differ-ent from my memory of him, the talk and drinking of tea, while he seems though uglier, to grow more triumphant in fascination than dreams had

i "Virtue," for Pater, represented the authenticity underpinning aesthetic expression and its reception.

ii *The Speaker* was a weekly periodical published in London from 1890–1907. Moore later reprinted "Sex in Art" in *Modern Painting* (1893).

iii Perhaps Flaubert's *Temptation of Saint Anthony* (1874).

iv Michael Field's 1892 play, *Stephania*, described the destruction of the Ottoman Empire.

v Literally, "spite of July."

vi Cooper noted that "B hates this dress and implores her to change it—of course in the end she does" (1892, 107r, EC).

made him. We go into our bedroom, which leads from the salon—it looks impossible at first sight—so small a bed, such dingy washstand, few chairs, and Mary's boxes. We have a sense we are beginning a life in which the impossible easily becomes possible. As I pass through the door, Bernard says, "How charming you are looking" and I feel an angry self-depreciation at the remark. [. . .]

[At dinner,] I am with Bernard—He again says I am looking very well; my hat throws delicate green on to my face. Again, I feel the same cynical wrath, especially as the tints of the hat are only demonstrating Bernard's method on my face. I am but a living example of what the New Salon can show in paint.[178]

EC *Tuesday, June 21st.*

We wake to a vine at our window (evoe, evoe!)[i] and Mary, in a tawny dressing-gown, with streaming hair above it and naked feet below, comes to prepare our cold bath. We open our bedroom door; Bernard twists round to us—he is there—and bids us good morning. Mary is in a white gown—she looks very positive, clear, and level. Seeing her and seeing him, I have a speechless weight on my whole nature—the beginning of "peine forte et dure."[ii] I scarcely say a word at breakfast, except with my eyes, that can always talk, when my voice is clownishly awkward.[179]

EC *Bernard's breakfast monologue.*

[God's] one command is: *Be contemporaneous!* The people who are so make tomorrow. To be contemporaneous is to digest today's meat. The great people of all ages are those who have been contemporaneous. [. . .]

He goes—we unpack. Mary shows me the studio under our vine-tree where a painter lives with his mistress—a *grisette.*[iii] We seem to live in the air of a French novel; there is a great strangeness in us—an awe that is not sacred. Then she speaks to us of life, of the dissolution of family bonds, of the divorce she hopes to get by residence in America. With her soft voice . . . Oh, it is like the delicious sweep of the scythe, mowing down what is ripe for destruction![180]

EC *Visiting galleries.*

Then Bernard announces that Michael has seen enough and must be left to digest—and our companions leave us. The Salon seems empty of all but

---

i "Evoe" is an archaic exclamation of Bacchic frenzy.

ii "Strong, hard pain." Also a concept from English law before 1772, describing the punishment for accused felons who stood silent, rather than submitting a plea.

iii A young, working-class woman who seems sexually available.

bewildering colours. [. . .] How curious our arrival at Rue de la Grande Chaumière—up the narrow stairs, a ring, and Bernard as doorkeeper! He has been reading to Mary—a rainy darkness hangs about the interior of the little Salon; but the kettle is boiling in the[181] spirit lamp, books are about—friendship that is a habit gives a piquant homeliness to the atmosphere. We are outside such friendship—dissatisfied, very weary, and with cold blood we withdraw into our bedroom, where I stay on our bed till it is time to go to Turval's for dinner. I am drear at heart, though my head is fervid with the sunshine of the New Salon.[182]

EC *Wednesday, June 22nd.*

These little breakfasts—how charming they are! Mary, stooping down to boil the eggs, as graceful as the *Tragic Mary* herself—blond hair and large white dress in a heap; then raised, as the egg is guided to its cup; Bernard, languid, nervous for a little while, the piteousness of insomnia in the blue eyes—then under the coffee taking strength and beginning to talk, his naïve, stinging talk, in which[183] culture, intolerance, liberation and the artistic virtue of his strange personality are united in a way that is somehow impersonal. My love, breaking roll and asking the provocative question at the right moment then, with a hunter's fire in her eyes following the answer. And I silent beyond measure, mixing my eyes alone with the converse, as in the happier days with "the Old"—putting the seal of a look on so much of Bernard's doctrine—while the crust and the strawberries stay a wearisome while on my plate.

They say they are going to the Louvre—we will go too. There is scarcely a welcome to us in the way they start off together. We are like two "souls forbid" on the top of the Odéon bus—our friends address us seldom. It is curious— why did they not say they were engaged if they are? [. . . Berenson and Costelloe meet up with an acquaintance and then] the three sit down in a way that excludes us. We look with constraint at the Botticellis then move, under the steering of intolerable pride, right away to the end of the Galerie des Sept-Metrès. We stand before the Mantegnas—but they are dead canvases to us.[i]

The three comrades form a snug little knot at the other end of the gallery before an early Sienese picture—Laughter and exposition flow forth from the knot—knowledge I am starving to hear. And we think of the day two years ago when Sim found me talking to the young[184] Russian, beautiful with the tints of Italy—an eagerness to charm in his eyes. Arthur was then accompanying us, fair as English youth could make him, jealous to the battle-point. The

i A gallery at the Louvre showing work by artists of the Italian Renaissance, including Mantegna and Botticelli.

dull rage in our hearts quickens and is heavy with tears. We wander into the Long Gallery—and every picture is but a manufacture; we reach the Salon Carré. It appeases us as if with the geometry of hell. I sit down, I think of the beloved Mother's joy in La Gioconda's hand—a gleam creeps to me from Correggio's trees in *Antiope*—the sultry quietness of the Giorgione is in tone with my mood.[i]

The trio comes; we exchange some words on the pictures that have found me true to them, and close to us Bernard begins to expound the little Simone Martini—he mentions another picture (I forget which) in connection and starts in search of it. We move with the other listeners: he turns sharp on us—he amazes me with the injunction "Don't follow me!" Our wrathful astonishment must have checked him, for he tarries to say to me "I hope you don't mind—but I can never explain pictures to several people *with any pleasure to myself.*" I return never a word but fix my eyes with a glittering contempt on him till he goes. Walking about becomes an exercise on burning shares. From that moment my life can be expressed in two words—infatuation and wounds.[185]

[...]

At lunch.

At the Restaurant table strife is soon ignited. Bernard sits opposite to us, moody, rather pale, with a vicious twist in his mobile eyebrows. Sim asks him to order for us; he curtly refuses, adding in a patronising tone that it would be very good for Miss Bradley's French for her to give her orders. Sim flashes lightning. "You don't suppose I am not capable of asking for all I want in French—'Garcon, deux chateaubriands—un bouteille St. Galuvier et une demi-boutelle St. Julienne.'"[ii] Even Mary joins in this insult, remarking it would be good for Miss Bradley to be independent. The shame I feel for him aches above all my anger. We address not a single word to anyone but Burke,[iii] who is puzzled by our courtesy. Bernard is silent. I lift my eyes and fix them full on his, an inflexible scorn in them, a very malice of irony. The beautiful eyes that front mine return a wild, irresponsible defiance, like that of a wood creature at bay. . . . I glance toward him sometime after—Joy! his hands are trembling. He has felt punishment in the excitable depths of his frame. Mary proposes the New Salon—we acquiesce; Bernard, half tamed and very miserable, anxiously presses the suggestion. Sim and I keep together.[186] We simply withdraw from the least nearness to him, at the steamboat station under the

---

i Another Louvre gallery dedicated to Italian Renaissance painting.

ii "Waiter, two chateaubriand steaks, one bottle of St. Galuvier, and a half-bottle of St. Julien."

iii James Burke, Anglo-American art collector and client of Berenson's.

plane trees, or on the boat itself. [. . .] There is a contemptuous, triumphant fever in my veins—a torment worse than powerlessness, almost. Mary, with a return of tact, manages to mix us together on landing: we pass under the Eiffel Tower—the old dispute as to its beauty rises among us, and somehow, without asking pardon, by means of the soft, dumb persistence of an animal, that little villain of a Bernard assuages Sim and walks with her. [. . .]

And fools that we are, we forgive . . . but between him and me the atmosphere is changed, the sultriness of thunder in our moods makes us henceforth for a day or two unbearable to each other—and *I* can say, makes me unbearable to myself.[187]

EC *In retreat together at the Luxembourg Gardens.*

There we face our situation.

When we joined Mary, at her proposal, in her brother's flat, we had no idea that her life and our lives would be spent entirely with Bernard—we had no idea that he and she were inseparable companions—we had no idea that we cared so much for him—that I should sicken of very passion for him. We did not know that he had lost the £400 a year, granted to him by an American millionaire for four years, and that therefore he was needy and beset with a grasping hunger for cash. We are in a tragic coil, as it is—We cannot go, without breaking all friendship with the only friends who attract us—Mary is perfectly sweet and full of confidence: also, an explanation would be required in England.

Probably knowing that as Michael and Field we are inseparable they have counted on long absences from our company and refreshing *encounters* at breakfast, afternoon tea and at night. Yet such a hope on their part is unfair; for we were induced to visit Paris on the condition that we should receive guidance to an understanding[188] of recent art, and Morellian[i] help in the Louvre. However, independent action is our only shield; we agree that we will walk together, plan our separate plans, have no expectancy in our manner—but this wisdom comes from the bitterness of our hearts, is sour and unripened. We feel there is much that we cannot grasp in the circumstances we encounter: the magnetic tremble Bernard and I awake each in each is an incalculable element: and we cannot trust the Sapphic frenzy that forces us, in spite of ourselves, to follow him.

But, while the bees are in the foxgloves and their boom in our ears, we hope with ourselves to be strong. Then we walk to Duval's and begin a dinner

---

i The Morellian method, developed by art historian Giovanni Morelli (1816–91), focused on artistic attribution based on the identification of miniscule details within painters' technique. Bradley and Cooper had hoped to receive help in utilizing this new method while in Paris.

of two for the first time. In the midst Mary and Bernard come—there is a dark callousness in his eyes, a want of repose in his movements. We rise long before they have finished and say in a composed way that we are going to have a stroll by the Seine. There is a sort of respectful encouragement in Mary's reception of our free will. I do not look at Bernard.

How my Love and I find once more the Paris of two years ago, as we wander, almost liberated from the present, by the river, look in at Varnier's, turn our faces up to the precious monsters of Notre Dame, and read again the words over the Doric little Morgue! The sky is great with rain—in the middle air a silence waits, on the ground we half surprise a shifting of the dust. As we reach[189] the Boulevard Sainte Michel the great drops fall, persistently fall, splash down and continue. We are drenched. At the top of the dark stairs Bernard lets us in—stupefied with the darkness, we enter the little Salon. The lamp is shaded. Mary sits full in its lowered light, dressed for the evening. Her "robe" is of white silk, striped with blue and trimmed with blue—a soft old china blue. Her chest is bare—the feathers of a white fan curl round her hand; her beauty is radiant. She has such a cool, yet smug effect, while the rain hisses through the pitch-black attics here beyond the open window. Burke emerges from the dim shadow of the sofa corner—and we appear before the trio like a couple of draggled Partlets.[i] The shock of admiration, combined with chagrin, is hard to bear. Mary excuses the toilet by a plea that it was so hot she could not resist the relief. We go into our room, furious, impotent—for my Love has only an ugly ancient satin, grey and pink—I thinking that in Bohemia one needed no evening attire, had put none in my box. A particoloured blouse of pink and rose, over a long black cloth skirt is all I can manage. The rain beats through us—we hear it with our ears, we feel it settle on our spirits.

I calmly go into the Salon—but how hot is my hidden suffering! I sit down, to hear B. say to Burke—"Does not Miss Cooper wear pretty colours—don't you like that fold at the waist?" Burke scarcely[190] notices a question that, if kindly meant, is abominably tasteless. I feel all the shame he should have felt and does not. My Love comes to sit by me. We will not desert each other. The Americaine arrives—in walking dress. She sits down opposite the radiant Mary, and soon eclipses her. Tying a handkerchief round her head, and not distorting, but changing, her features into those of a pious old lady she declaimed one of Lowell's poems[ii]—then with a smile, like the breaking of a firework, she makes the darkness of her eyes and

---

i Sleeveless, smock-like overgarments worn in the sixteenth century.
ii James Russell Lowell (1819–91), American poet.

complexion, the darkness of the half-lit room, coruscate. She takes a cigarette delicately, holds it with science, sets the smoke as a modern aureole
round her; chats, tells the inevitable funny stories with tripping humour or
with glancing appeals for companionship in laughter, drinks her Benedictine, and finally shoulders her violin, moves into the anteroom, and plays
from behind the curtain of night. Burke is silent, disquieted, in true English
fashion, at the pleasure she gives him. Bernard meets her as an equal, calls
her "Mandie," flashes his glance across hers, revenges himself for his defeat
of the morning by an assumption that we are not present. Mary, though
convicted of want of versatility, epigram, magic, sits queenly—bland, blue
and white—the *Grande dame*[.] [. . .] But Michael Field is as stupid, as
incapable, as Baudelaire's albatross.[i][191]

He is ignored, he is self-abashed, under a cloud. At last, the torture ends.
Bernard takes Mandie home to her mother.

The wee salon is in its small way Bacchanalian—cigarette dust on the
floor, St. Galuvier bottles empty, Benedictine glasses on the table, Mary's fan
on the couch. We hear from our room Bernard return, a parting, and the
slam of the door. We have fears of which we repent as they rise.

Thursday, June 23rd.

At breakfast we are all weary; we do not mix well in converse. There is a
sense of relief when "Mandie" appears to say goodbye on the verge of a flight
into Brittany. She sits by as we eat our breakfast—it is an insult to the animal
in men when one of their kind does not share the common meal. She and
Bernard do nothing but flirt—he opens his eyes and plunges them in hers as
if they were taking a morning bath—they grow fresher with the exercise,
more sweet and eager each moment; they wax in strength, they play with the
element they love. And she has tides of amber clearness in her eyes, shot
through with light, harmlessly provoking, agile in expression, receptive to the
utmost.

Then we needs must see the arch of "Mandie's" head—it is very lovely, and
we greet the loveliness.[192] She goes—we remain, and with him! No, he will
conduct her home. Mary tells us how she has just broken off an engagement
with an American millionaire—an egoist and a man of no culture.[193]

EC *Friday, June 24th.*

We go to the Luxembourg—as usual, Mary and Bernard together in front,
we following at a distance. How those two figures are stamped on my brain!—

i The French decadent poet Charles Baudelaire published the poem "L'Albatros" in his *Fleurs
du mal* in 1859: the poet-as-albatross is "Exiled on earth amid a jeering crowd, / Prisoned and
palsied by their giant wings."

hers so tall, with such independence in its sway, even independence of grace, for the forms and action have a certain angularity, yet every Frenchman who passes, arrested by the clink of her Châtelaine,[i] gazes with fascinated awe at the height, at the swing of this fair-haired woman: Bernard's figure only reaching to her shoulder, tragically dependent in every line—willful and adoring at the same moment—the rim of the sailor hat sharp above the thin neck, one little agitated hand [. . .] always resting across the back. He never walks with either of us—it would seem to be that he fears to provoke Mary, only that he avoids us when there is no question of Mary. He does not like our dress—can it be he is small enough to retreat at merely from folds and colours that try him? He takes us straight to the much-discussed Manet— *Olympe.*[ii]

"It is Cleopatra, who has just unrolled herself from mummy clothes, and the cat knows it." He pauses—"C'est la prostitution eternelle."[iii] Before this picture he and Mary leave us to go on to the Louvre: Bernard has been speaking of their companionship and ours—he leaves us with the profound remark: "It takes two to be impersonal; otherwise one is solitary."[194]

EC We go to lunch at Duval's by ourselves; then sit long in the Luxembourg Gardens, returning to tea. While we drink our tea, they persuade Sim to make public some parts of our Lange and Rosalie drama.[iv] Mary is the reader; the portions are Mrs. Evelyn's opening speeches. They seem as we listen the thinnest twaddle. I had resisted my Love to the point of irritable ill grace—but her eagerness to learn, to profit by counsel was too strong. Next the whole story is extracted from her and ruthlessly criticised. I sit in anguish—a self-conscious pain all over the skin, that seems to contain only the eclipse of the real self—despair. And—horror!—Bernard realises in a moment that he is Lange—that I am Rosalie. "You must make Lange a young man of wide culture—not like Symons or Horne[v]—in fact like me, as much like me as you can." After this the whole conversation is a very modern, very exhausting, and to me ex-[195]cruciating love-talk in disguise. He says Lange would *never* tell his love—I reply that Rosalie always felt antagonistic to

i A decorative chain worn by a woman to hold keys or other items. Also, a synecdoche for women's governance of the domestic sphere.

ii *Olympe*, featuring a nude woman making direct eye contact with the viewer, was first displayed by Édouard Manet in 1865.

iii "It is eternal prostitution."

iv Michael Field's unpublished, and sadly now lost, 1892 prose play *Old Wine in New Bottles*.

v Arthur Symons (1865–1945) and Herbert Horne (1864–1916) were English poets associated with the Rhymers' Club.

Lange—felt that he destroyed her most sacred ideals, though his modernity was hatefully interesting to her.

This goes on two hours till hunger ends the symposium, and we go forth to Duval's. There, I nearly faint with fatigue, shame, revolt: we order Chateaubriands—Bernard and Mary, soup, which quickly comes while we are kept waiting. Bernard, with one glance at my weary face, and a peculiar sympathy in his action, hands me his soup and gently insists on my having it. Mary looks at me, says nothing—but looks long.[196]

EC Finally, we sit in one of the anterooms—I go to sleep and am waked to return home in a cab. As we drive along, I notice Bernard, who sits on the little stool seat opposite us, looking at my hat inimically. When we are in the room at the Grande Chaumière—Mary and Sim preparing tea—he and I together, the little villain begins, "Miss Cooper, you will forgive me—I like everything about you, but your hat—these flowers in front are too dreadful. They try my nerves every time I look at them." He then takes the occasion for bullying our hats and "the vegetelles" we wear in them (all French flowers specially arranged by Mme. Véréna for Parisian taste!).[i] He wheedles me into a promise I will take out the offending bunch. [. . .]

When he is gone, I am absorbed in efforts to alter my hats. Mary[197] assists, and soon the table in our bedroom is a holocaust of grass-green leaves, red velvet, bright branches of spring flowers, a spray of dark cherries, green velvet, red ribbon. In wantonness of Bacchic homage to the hero Bacchus, at Mary's suggestion, we heap the Salon table with the garish spoil. [Berenson returns.] Mary is jealous as well as pitiful—the gay trophies of his teaching heaped on the table are unnoticed. When Mary, tired of the Turk, calls his attention to them, he seems to think we are all mad in a stupid way. Mary forces me to put on my altered hat—He remarks, "That green bow is good for you—you have something to thank me for." I get the creature off my head as quickly as I can, and in as underhand a manner as possible we catch up the bows and branches of the feminine sacrificial pyramid—disappearing with them. We walk savagely in the gardens—and at dinner he again remarks that my hat is improved—like a condescending prophet. What fools we were to humour him, and thus to derogate![198]

Sunday, June 26th.

We announce we have our own way of spending Sunday in Paris, which we tell to no one. After some time, B. answers he is sure we go to the Morgue. But we make no confession.

i "The vegetables."

Two years roll back—I feel I am again in Paris for the first time as my Love leaves me at the back of Notre Dame under the chestnuts and crosses the road. While she is away, I look up at the apse—I have a wish to see the people of the Morgue, but I no longer feel that strain at my heart that nearly killed me in this place two years ago, when I first prepared to look on death—death I had never seen, though my beloved Mother had passed through the change. It was something like the desolate terror I felt when I first looked at the sea into which I was to be dipped—I had come point blank into contact with a new element.

Now I am simply anxious to increase experience.

My love comes and with her I go to the mortal den in which death is confined. One's whole nature seeks to escape in what, if one were alone, would be a cry of surprise. Then all goes quiet in one, and the dead figures became as objective as waxwork. There are three men—one a dusky, tragic old man, with bent head, folded-in lips, and clenched hand; the second a most open-faced corpse, with a smooth French pleasantness on the wrinkled alabaster features; the third[199] a boy with fierce pitiful brows and a mouth that has become triangular. Their clothes lie over them—such utter "lendings." What strikes me more than anything else is the smallness of death, the way in which it makes limits that cannot be passed. I have before me the shapes of men some few feet long—but where is the magnetism that passing from these shapes could fill a room, fill other hearts, fill those flat clothes—where is the expressiveness that only used those features as the centre of its flight over the world? Yes, death is the smallest thing in the universe, with no beyond, no emanation. Thank goodness it breaks up! And in so far as we live shut up in bonds, without self-expression, mobility, freedom—we are but corpses and we are becoming every day more like these little models on their backs beyond the bars of the Morgue.

Yes, this is my Sunday lesson—that *life, life* is what the living must seek with heart and soul and strength and might. The only poor escape from the fixedness of a corpse is through the psychology that traces a past in the forms—a past is always piteous—it is sorrow *past* happiness that is over: present and future have alone to do with life—Heigh-ho, we must live, till this machine is cast from us. We go into Notre Dame—it is intolerable to be there—it is a grand Dead House with infinitely less to teach us than the mean one behind it.[200]

EC As Bernard and I go down the staircase and cross the courts of the Louvre, he reproaches me with my visit to the Morgue—It is not Greek, it is morbid and shocking. I defend myself—death is one of the facts of life, modernity reaches to all facts and includes them: classic antiquity ignored many; but the new art and literature is great enough to bear all truth. Then I tell him what vital lesson I had learnt at the Morgue. "I have never seen anyone dead"—his tone is exactly what I imagined the Faun's like. [...] There is a disgusted terror in Bernard's blue eyes—he adds "I was taken to see my grandmother lying dead when I was very little; but I don't remember it." No, there is not the least memory of death in this beautiful face beside me, quick with sensation, with thought, with fervent independence—racy with the present, simple as an animal's.[201] [...]

As we come home, we pause at one of the omnibus stands in the Champs-Élysées, under the trees: I remember that moment of gay foreign heat—the white look toward the river, the great omnibuses definite in the blaze. And as we walk together, my Love and I, by the Luxembourg gardens we wonder what will be the end of those two in front—always in front of us.

Sim and I go into the Gardens, more crowded than in the weekdays; we sit beneath a chestnut seeing and hearing the coolness of a spray in the grass. We meet Mary and Bernard outside Duval's. The crowd is dense inside—Sim nearly faints, is tetchy over her food, and makes us all cross and anxious. At night, in the little Salon, Bernard criticises several poems in *Sight and Song*. We challenge him to show[202] how impersonal he can be as a critic, face to face, and at last he begins—not without fear and some unwillingness.

We have confused the material of poetry, which is *feeling*, with colour and outline, the materials of painting. If we looked on a picture till we were on fire with it, the language we used would be poetic. [...] At afternoon tea B. has said that someday we shall give the very picture itself, drag the animal from its shell: then we shall write a *great* poem, as Rossetti did on the "Vierge Aux Rochers."[i][203]

EC Then we wander in the Louvre—desperate, ignorant wanderings. We had been decoyed to Paris by Mary's promises of Morellian teaching from Bernard, and we are left with no shepherd among the tangles of attribution, etc. Aesthetically we know the Louvre very well—historically, critically not at all. I am as deep in despair as *d'esclave*[ii] himself, numb beneath my ignorance. When we return in the afternoon Bernard is away; I retire to my bed, and from my resting place I hear Sim's frank voice questioning Mary as to the reason why Bernard makes no time to help us and offering *Money*! if he will give us instruction. Mary has not much to say for him but grasps at the idea of his earning some coins. Through the ceasing of a bounty from a private source he is poor, and is seized, like Midas, with[204] a desire to turn every-

i Rossetti's "Vierge Aux Rochers," or "Virgin of the Rocks," is an 1848 sonnet responding to Leonardo da Vinci's painting of the same name from 1503–6.
ii "The bondsman."

thing he has to do with to gold. Perhaps it is the Jew in him, at last roused to meanness. We have such a fear lest he should sink into dependence on others, that Sim gladly repeats her willingness to pay for lessons. We are not to speak about it to him—Mary must be left to settle the matter. We *all* go to Duval's, they in front, we behind. I know what they are talking about—I feel scalded with shame for him yet determined to act for his advantage. We sit down opposite them—there is a blue flame in his eyes, I just see, but do not meet. He begins at once about the lessons, refusing our proposal warmly. We answer that we cannot expect him to give valuable time and instruction it has taken years to acquire for nothing. We speak with such conviction, while Mary's sweet eyes watch us—that the pain dies from his voice, the angst from his glance, and an easy conquest is made. "But it seems so mean," is the last cry of the friend in him changing to the Master—but like the misery of Lamia's[i] transformation the distress is soon over with him—with *me*! Oh, how much there is to bear![205]

EC At Duval's we choose a table—they come in—the tall figure with the gracious face, the small one, with a look about the face of restive unworldliness. We watch them as they came up to us. I forget what we are talking about—he says—"Miss Cooper and I should marry—and be miserable ever after." I am powerless to shake off such remarks with irony or wit—I suffer and hate. But it is true—we give one another no pleasure; the fascination we have for each other makes us wretched.[206]

EC *Mary takes them to visit a nearby atelier.*
    We catch a glimpse of a half-draped girl. Upstairs the girls are chatting and putting up their easels. Laughter rings through the room—a buzz of happy occupation in the undertone. [. . .]
    But what is that crouching, yellow thing? The model, the first man we have seen in the state of nature at close quarters—in Lear's phrase he looks "unaccommodated"—dreadfully so.[ii] Though the day is hot—he looks cold—he has nothing but his black hair and white loin cloth. He poses—he is startlingly like a figure from the Morgue exposed—he seems to be made, not of flesh but of wax, beeswax—and black hair streaks his thighs and seat and bosom. I did not know that men were such savages, much to Mary's amusement. This man is no more to the roomful of young girls than if he had been

i Keats's narrative poem about the serpent-woman Lamia, published in 1820.
ii Looking at Poor Tom, King Lear states, "Thou art the thing itself; unaccommodated / man is no more but such a poor, bare, / forked animal as thou art" (3.4.113–15). Folger Shakespeare Library (n.d.), https://www.folger.edu/explore/shakespeares-works/king-lear/read/3/4/.

a block of naked wood. The thought of him makes the sunshine look bare when we go out. There we stroll through the gardens talking of art, women, the nude—to the gallery and again enjoy Manet and Zorn.[i]

We rest in the afternoon, for we are going to see *Salammbô* at the Opèra.[ii] At afternoon tea Mary suggests we should go in blouses because of the heat. Bernard turns to Sim—"You will not go in yours." "Why not?" "Well, you do not want to look a guy." "Then why should[207] I wear one?" asks Mary. "Yes," Sim says, "Why should Mary wear hers?" "O Mary can wear anything but you cannot." [. . .] "Why should you mind Miss Bradley's dressing as she likes?" "Oh, I am a man"—is the insulting rejoinder. I cannot remember what we say—I only recollect how Mary comes into our room and offers her feather fan; anything to break the brutality of the insult. I cannot think why we go—but we do.

Not a word is exchanged during the walk. On the omnibus I sit by Sim, and as we pass the Café opposite the Palais Royal, where we discussed modern Poetry with Symons,[iii] I mention the moment to Sim in a clear voice. The stroke tells—I hear Bernard's contemptuous, enraged voice deriding Symons to Mary. Nothing passes between us at the Opèra—He sits on the far side of Mary looking sullen, scared, and most unhappy. He fetches me some sandwiches—I thank him, with no glance. [. . .]

We drive home across the lighted river the darkness made great by the innumerable lights. It is very damp after sudden rain—no word is spoken. He is opposite. As we pass a gas-lamp near[208] Rue de la Grande Chaumière, I summon to my eyes all their power of magnetic anger and catlike brightness in the dark. I concentrate their gleam and contempt on his, till his lids drop. His eyes for an instant are terrified and ashamed. I ignore his hand in dismounting. We have to eat together. He remarks to Mary I look tired and am silent.

We say goodnight—almost as if it were a curse.

We hate him; hate him—I scarcely sleep.

Tuesday, July 5.

A lesson on the Paduan School[iv] at the Louvre—the best we have had. We are both distant—Bernard comes up to Sim and, in a voice, every tone of which is a wile, asks, "Is Michael enraged with the Doctrine?" (our name for

---

i Anders Zorn (1860–1920), Swedish painter.

ii An 1892 opera by Ernest Reyer, based on the novel of the same name by Flaubert (1862).

iii Arthur Symons (1865–1945), British poet, editor of *The Savoy*, and contributor to *The Yellow Book*, whose writings about symbolism were influential for British modernists.

iv The school of painting that developed in Padua in the fourteenth century, influencing the emergence of Renaissance art in Northern Italy.

him) I do not hear her reply. In the afternoon, while Mary and I are out of the room, he apologizes to Sim and is well scolded. Mary, who is becoming poorly and is in great pain, comes in with a letter and says that if he does not post it, which he does not seem inclined to do, she will herself. "O Mary. This is too bad—I am doing everything in my power to please you." Then in a reckless voice "It seems I can't please any of you. I shall go away." He does leave the room—We hear low tones and believe that he and Mary make up their differences with a caress.[209] [. . .]

Mary is lying down when he comes back to tea. "O Michael, you have forgiven me," he says in a worried tone, with a most serious appeal in his eyes as he turns to the window. His eyes win forgiveness, but he himself can scarcely be forgiven so easily, while woman is woman. He was guilty of the most intolerable offence—the humiliation of one woman by a compliment to another in the presence of both.[210]

KB We came home on Wednesday, July 13th. [. . .]

I leave P. to tell the Paris story: we are back in Durdans, with every feather plucked from our wings, convicted of folly in dress, of poverty and affectation in English, of false method in art (see *S[ight] and S[ong]*), of "taking things personally," of being Anglo-Saxon, of living away from Life. We have heard of a new god whose sole command is *Be contemporaneous*.[211]

KB *Contemplating the departure of Berenson.* They were gone and we were left to fumble about the earth as we might . . . they are not worldly; and we still are—but with a power of leavening—yes there is that in us—not the power of breaking down and building up *real* people have.

O Henry, Henry, my Boy, let us cleave to art—with a small *a*, and *grow* toward life, as toward the sun, not rend our path toward it. God bless Henry!

EC I am without my Love, in the twilight, when at the best one is sad to death. She is in Oxford—I am here a fragment. But I love my Art and will not dare to injure it—I love my own Love and could not do violence to her or myself—so let her not fear. Although "The Doctrine's" wonderful eyes—a Faun's crossed with the traditional Christ's—pursue me, that they have a charm that maddens, I will never go off to the hills like agave only to rend my own flesh and blood—my artistic personality. I die in the presence of the face I love—the man's.

There is no fellowship, no caress, no tight winding together of two natures, no tenderness when my Love is severed from me; and there seems to be no life in people—no life to be got anywhere—if one is *withdrawn from the Doctrine*.

to we were busy—P. talking, William Watson
& Hould Harris: they vanished. They were one
we were left to fumble about the earth as
night.. they are not worldly, & we still are —
with a power of leavening—yes there is that
too—not the power of breaking down & building
Real people have
O Henry, Henry, my Boy, let us cleave to art—
with a small a, & grow toward life, as toward
the Sun, not rend our path toward it.
God bless Henry.

I am writing my Love, in the twilight,
when at the best one is sad to death.
She is in Oxford—I am here a fragment.
But I love my Art & will not dare
to injure it—I love my own Love & could
not do violence to her or myself—so let
her not fear. Although those doctrine's wonderful
eyes—like a Faun's crossed with the
traditional Christ's—possess me, they
have a charm that maddens, I will never
go off to the hills like Agave only to
rend my own flesh + blood—my artistic
personality. I die in the presence of the
face I love—the man's.
There is no fellowship, no caress, no tight-
winding together of two natures, no tenderness
when my Love is severed from me;
And there seems to be no life in people—
no life to be got anywhere—if she is
withdrawn from the Doctrine
So I sit by my table doubly dead.

So I sit by my table doubly dead.
The remainder of this page has been redacted.[212]

KB *Friday even. August 19th, 1892.*

It is the eve of the Mother's death day. Among the flowers that garland her portrait are white roses and the sweet tuber-rose, and a vine pruning with its green cluster. We who are growing so close to the modern, are we growing further away from her? [. . .]

P. and I had a great talk last night.

We found there are moralities in "the Modern."

Courage is the first virtue—Courage to be oneself and win one's life.

And sincerity is like unto it—the putting away all padding from life.

Then there is the purity that abstains from pleasure to fit the body for more delicate sense: pleasure, and to give the mind freedom and leisure to function. From the first pleasure should be recognised as the end sought. We want to enjoy—to be happy: we want others to enjoy.

And the discipline is selection of pleasure. We cannot have high and low pleasures; we must choose. At every part of our lives, we are sacrificing one of ourselves. The question is which shall be free and enjoying.

And a great part of the discipline of pleasure is patience.[213]

Industry—especially in thought; but also unrelaxing effort for life.

And ennui made impossible by the multitude of thoughts and hopes. Ennui is the plague of life, punishing us when we refuse to be about our Father's business—which is why we must always remember that we should have life, and have it more abundantly.

It is *so* bright today—clear and joyous as she is. We are going to toddle towards the heath.[214]

KB *September 1st, 1892.*

The study is deserted; I am weary and sad; but a glorious telegram has been received from Grantown[i]; and I pray God take me straight to my Love. God love Hennie. Dear little Boy, it has been good for him to live and breathe alone—perfect Michael. But oh, it is most better when we are together. Oh, that we may be more and more together, closer, growing into one. How can I bear it that the curly head I love is lying on a pillow in Grantown tonight? But I shall smell Hennie in his little room at Edinburgh, and Heaven speeding me, on Saturday night I lay him on my breast. So be it![215]

i A town in southeastern Scotland.

KB *Thursday evening, October 6th, 1892.*

   Tennyson is dead. We saw it in the underground this morning—

Death of

Lord

Tennyson

Illustrated tragically

A penny

—but even the "posters" feel it was "beautiful" that the poet died so peacefully under the moonlight.—I am back in the days when "The Miller's Daughter" bounded my horizons—my way of looking at the Universe was unquestionably determined by Tennyson. Shelley was no part of my youth. I was saved by Shakespeare, and by Shakespeare alone.[216]

KB *October 12th, Lord Tennyson's Funeral.*[217] [. . .]

   It is lovely autumn when we come out. And so closes the Victorian epoch—An epoch already yesterday: it is for us, England's living and yet unspent poets, to make all things new. We are for the morning—the nineteenth century thinks it has no poets—nothing to lose, verily it has nothing: for we are not of it—we shake the dust of our feet from it and pass on into the 20th century.

   And who is there to go forward with Michael? The Laureateship will perhaps be given to William Watson, and then though the bald head of Swinburne sprout young unicorns, what hope or help for the future? The one poet who has attained is Robert Bridges, and his name is not even heard.[i][218]

KB Bernard writes that the reason there have been no women poets is because they have not dared to woo. England has a fair number of female poets, because a fair number of females in England are capable of wooing.

   Why are women silent? Is it true, what he answers: silent simply that they have not dared to woo. Let them sing themselves, their passion, nature's own unfathomable.[219]

EC *Saturday.*

   Mary is in Florence—They have met, they belong to each other—they begin the new year together and bless the old year by meeting. She has said "Oh, I do adore him"—but no woman can keep such words for herself, if they

---

   i Following a delay, Alfred Austin (1835–1913) was appointed poet laureate in 1896. Though William Watson (1858–1935) never received the honor, Robert Bridges (1844–1930) served in the role from 1913–30. Carol Ann Duffy was the first woman appointed poet laureate, in 2009.

are needed by another. She has been appointed for heaven and I for hell—that is all.[220]

Michael Field's summer narrative of Paris continued at the end of the book. Mary was ill; Berenson was to stay in her flat.

EC We hear Mary laughing, almost as the Darling used to laugh. Bernard has asked her to lend him one of her nightdresses—either he wears no such thing as a night shirt or is incapable of fetching one from his rooms. Mary has no clean one—so Sim is approached. She has one all lace and little tucks which is laid on his sofa bed. The whole affair is unutterably comic—only the young Dionysus can do such things with charm—But he can—the ridiculous becomes as winning as the appropriate. We bid him goodnight and are haunted in our beds with thought of the mystic bearded young face above the feminine trimming of the nightdress. We learn next morning he had been terribly hot and had been fretted in the strange attire. How I longed to see him asleep in his woman's robe![221]

Works and Days, 1893

EC *New Year's Day.*

A dark beginning. My cruel Love leaves me for early service, an unsatisfied heathen in our little bed. Then she starts for town to spend the night with Amy Bell. I am left to torpor, discouragement of mind and body. The rain raineth, and I pine, like wind round a corner.[222]

EC I have finished *Anna Karenina*.[i] It is Life—Life itself, as it appears to one who is in conscious sympathy with life—there is no difference between the observer and what is observed, except the *feeling* with which he observes, and that feeling makes his transcript Art. Levin's haymaking is elemental and yet so modern—the primal curse of man is made a blessing because it is shared with men—as Dolly's maternal cares are eased when shared with the peasant women. There is a greater miller in those scenes.

And Anna and Vronsky! I shudder thinking of their counterparts in actual life.

And I am finishing Gustave Flaubert's *Correspondance*.[ii] He is so like me; he excites by similarity—as two flints make a spark. He gives a sense of space to imagination—Language takes deep breaths of air.[223]

---

i Tolstoy's massive, multiplot realist novel (1878).

ii The French novelist (1821–80) whose correspondence was published in four volumes in 1893, anonymously (and mercilessly) edited by his niece Caroline Commanville.

EC *Attending the Athenaeum, 73, Tottenham Court Rd.*

We are desperately alone in this world that shuns us. What can it be! *Stephania* cannot be responsible for it all. We are boycotted in the papers by the men (Pater, Meredith, Hutton) to whom we have sent our book, and by even literary society. It is mysterious.[224]

EC *Saturday, January 28th.*

I want to write more about *Anna Karenina*. What I wrote the other day was so stupid. The book is comprehensive beyond every other I know. Passion, quieter love, birth, death, kinship, motherhood, the fields, the railway, the restaurant, the racecourse—every phase, every circumstance of life finds its place in the pages as in life itself. The unrest of passion and of doubt shakes like a pulse through the larger scheme. Passion finds its end in death, doubt in faith—they are too destructive to keep on—too finite when they are in earnest. But nature endures and the harvests—the relation by which life is begotten, the labour by which it is sustained: and this great persistence is felt all the more from contrast with the wrecking course of passion and doubt. These two contrasted aspects of strife and peace give the book its marvelous wholeness. Tolstoy has not yet become one-sided—there is a ripe balance in his outlook. The sex attraction that exists for itself is not confounded with that which draws two beings together to enrich the race; and faith is not yet synonymous with asceticism.[225] [. . .]

EC And the most wonderful thing is that Tolstoy follows life in each of his human beings and never makes a comment—he is as little talkative as existence, and as full of matter for converse.[226]

EC *Forced by illness to stay home from a performance of Ibsen's "Master-Builder."*[i]

I am close by the fire still when a box of flowers is brought to me. Do they come from the Riviera? No—from London, and this is the dear, briar-wood writing of my Love. I open on the vast, scooped petals of single snow-drops, and on immense violets—bunch after bunch, on comely lilies-of-the-valley, and a sprig or two of mignonette—all so generously grown, so prodigally given that I shall never forget them as a symbol of my own Love's love. I am proud of my flowers—women do not have such gifts—except from men—because they have not learnt through the centuries to give their love objectively in signs and lavish tokens. They give their hands, their lips, themselves, but nothing impersonal which they endow with ardency.

---

i Henrik Ibsen (1818–1906), Norwegian playwright who initiated modernism in theater. His *Master-Builder* was published in 1892 and premiered in 1893. Ibsen flushes psychosexual complexity from realistic representations of familiar phenomena.

But my flowers dilate my life as I breathe them, gaze at them, set them in the bowl.[227]

EC *Bradley and Amy return; Bradley argues about socialism with James Cooper.*

[A]s soon as we get home Sim rushes out to hear Amy speak about Christian Social Union to a few in a schoolroom.[i] By the fireside at home Hilda waves the shawl of comfort as the flag of independence[ii]—I see her movements through all I try to read, till the pages dance.

Sim and Amy return: conversation gets high on Socialism with father—A storm gathers, breaks—A crisis is on us. He says Sim[228] must leave. I join my hand to hers and we go out, not looking at him or speaking to him again. Hilda waves through our distraction. Then, note, the play of *The Master-Builder* is acted in real life, and Ibsen's power of giving blood to an Allegory tested, proved in terrible earnest.[iii]

It is my whole impulse to go with my Love—to sever all other ties violently and simply—her dismissal is nothing less than mine, if love is love: yet I find Little One sobbing by her bed, and then the casuistries of conscience begin. If I go from home entirely I leave her with Father, I close her chances of growth, I shut her up with interests of which she can never speak, I leave her to morbid depression of spirits—I should always believe that her vocation had "had to be stunted, and crushed and shattered—In order that mine might force its way to—to a sort of great victory." Yet I should not really have been responsible to the degree I should have imagined—such disaster would have been due chiefly, if not altogether, to her lack of *vitality*. [. . .]

Well, we sit and shiver and perplexity grows every moment more dazed. At last, we lie down for the night—but not to sleep. I go into a half trance of misery. My Love implores me to speak, but words have disappeared from my memory—I have no thoughts; my brain seems to hold its breath.[229]

The hours go on, with no change except that my lids grow harder, and the nervous thrills become less frequent down my spine. Then my Love breaks the silence by speaking of ordinary things, and words return to me, except when the crisis faces me—then they still elude my use. My Love misreads my

i The Christian Social Union, an offshoot of the Church of England, spread rapidly during the fin de siècle, exploring the role of Christianity in addressing social problems.

ii Hilda Wangel, a character in Ibsen's *The Lady from the Sea* (1888) and also in his *Master-Builder*. In the *Master-Builder*, Hilda waves her shawl after Solness has plunged to his death from the towering steeple he has built.

iii That is, an ordinary family dynamic reveals its explosive underbelly.

anguish—She does not realise that the troll in me, the artist, the lover in me, are on her side; the "helpers and servers"—volitions and desires—are all hers: only the sickly Conscience delays, fearing a raw place on my breast forever after—and that the helpers and servers should in the future keep flaying pieces of skin off other people in order to close my sore—in vain.

Finally, she sleeps. As the greyness of morning thins the dusk more and more, I grow in strength, I begin to reason—I determine, come what may, that I will force the whole situation with father, frankly, placably in the course of the morning. I will propose that Durdans be sold—that Sim has a flat in London, that I live chiefly with her, that every week I spend a little time at home (to free Amy) and that father comes to London or near it with Amy.

I will stand great and free for a little. I had told my Love when at last we spoke, that I felt she was forcing me up my tower, and that I should fall. Well, in spite of everything, I resolve to do the impossible. Then I sleep in the first daylight.[230]

I wake as one does after there has been a death in the house—a void and hungry consciousness of the unusual takes the place of the warm sense of familiar life that is one of the charms of waking. Sim stays upstairs—we carry on breakfast like actors. Father is silent, flushed, inscrutable—Amy and I talk trippingly. After breakfast I tell Sim and Amy of my plan. Amy says it is *impossible*—the very word that is my safeguard. I invoke the Mother-One and the Modern—enter the dining room, say in calm tones that I want to have a long talk and am met with the reply, "You want to tell me you are going to leave me forever." This plunges us in the midst of the subject. Father is very gentle, and acting under Mother's inspiration, gives me full opportunity for developing my plan. He is very pathetic, when he tells me of his affection for me—darkened, instructive, self-deceived, alas!—and when he says "I sit in this chair without an audience," Old Age itself takes voice.

Well, Durdans is to be sold—Sim is to go (she and father jar and excite each other), I am to go—and spending a little time each week at home—*but* father will not take Amy to town. All the rest is gained in the most loving, confidential way. There is no violence of speech or voice, nothing but wonderful cordiality. A power greater than we is holding us quiet—like the Zeitgeist. Even father is awed—almost[231] religious before it. I come out of the room exultantly free and great—There are hopes in the air—I wave in triumph. . . . My Love and I pace the garden—that is to be sold; look at the roses we planted and turn away.

A placid dinner: after dinner, I find out that my Love is dreading the idea of London as a home, now it is so friendless for us. This relaxes my will. Amy pours out her distress—so natural, so heartrending: dizziness strikes me. I sit all afternoon in the Botticelli Room.[i] [. . .] Sim comes to me. [. . .] an atmosphere of death falls on us—we consider, not the step, but the wisdom of the step. We remember that our visit to Rome is lost, if we set up in London—we remember that we must often part, leaving each other lovesick, that my life would be distracted, that our art would be hurt by noise and fret. . . . Finally, after tea, Tolstoy's Rule of Life[ii] rather than Ibsen's prevails—there is a new explanation. The morning's work is undone by the evening. We agree to go on the same—except that we have gained immense courage for the future— and down we tumble into the quarry—and Ibsen's *Master-Builder* has a Q.E.D. after it. The tragicomedy ends.[232]

KB *Saturday, June 24th.*

Father and Amy started for Scotland yesterday. Henry and I are living in the deepest conjugal bliss. We at once change our papers *Westminster* for *PMG.*[iii] [. . .] We both like our salmon cooked the same time. *We are so happy.* In the garden we set up one plant and put down another. It is the garden of Eden because we have our own way in it. This is delicious, but it can't last. That old serpent the Devil will be here next week.

In the evening Louie Ellis comes. We have a Sunday in the garden. She tells us of Olive Schreiner—Olive Schreiner home from the Cape after years of the brute, wild life of Africa.[iv] The ambassador pays his respects to her, Watts asks to paint her (he is refused); she goes the round of the great. Lovers from Africa come after her—to sink on their knees as soon as they land—one of them simply asks for the Beloved, demanding of Louie her friend. Meditating on all this I am filled with jealousy. This woman has been worshipped, she has known solitude—she has walked naked in the open air, she has handled politics, she has set up one, and put down another. I have lived at Durdans neither breathing nor being breathed upon.

KB *Wednesday, July 12th.*

Wet, wet, thunderstorms in the air.

The dear study is on the eve of spring cleaning. This morning the battle

i That is, the room Michael Field have recently redecorated with photographic prints of Renaissance paintings, à la Berenson.

ii In his youth, Tolstoy published precepts by which he intended to live his life, addressing topics such as waking, sleeping, eating, sex, the exercise of reason and imagination, and multitasking.

iii Michael Field exchanged the *Westminster Gazette* for the *Pall Mall Gazette*, opting for a rather more conservative choice.

iv Olive Schreiner (1855–1920), South African author, feminist, and antiwar campaigner.

of the Modern raged. The past was repulsed with great slaughter. Every Millet, every Turner has been banished from study and blue room. Italian art alone remains. This new god's[233] single command—*Be contemporaneous*—is harder to keep than all the ten old commandments.[i] Our eyes no longer desire the Turners, our heads testify against them, yet the pain of parting from them is keen.[234]

KB Mary says "You once said to me how you would love to be shut up with me on a desert island, where a ship never called. You kept on thinking so till about two months ago. I always knew you would get sick of arranging the seashells."

—"I should not have arranged the seashells, I should have arranged *you*."

Falling in love is the same to the Philistine as the artist. Like death it brings us all to the same level.

Strange how these two are falling away from each other! I knew kingdoms went to pieces, and that fashions changed—I had faith that great passions would endure. And to watch them perishing to see "the inferior work by a later hand"—the cynical self-consciousness undoes me.[235]

EC *August 4, Friday.*

By the evening delivery we learn that *A Question of Memory* is accepted for presentation in October. I get out of my depth in the future. My head struggles and nearly dreams itself into peril.

August 6. The proofs of *Underneath the Bough revised and decreased*[ii] lie on the breakfast table.

It is now August 11th—since the parting at Westminster what an intense smothered, smouldering life ours has been! That forestalled farewell, and Mary's omission of farewell, leaving our friendship like a letter without a signature, and the uncertainty how they two are affected by us two—the consciousness that between the morning and evening of the ninth day, something has slipped away[236] from England that leaves her a mere coast guard station, and a watering place for ships, the struggling with *A Question of Memory*—the fight with that mailed creature the Sun, the quiet stabs at the heart with morning, noon, and evening passings of the postman, the contrast between the spectral summer and the full-blooded autumn toward which we

i Michael Field redecorated their study according to Berenson's artistic precepts, exchanging more romantic images from the French painter Jean-François Millet (1814–75) and English painter J.M.W. Turner (1775–1851) for images from the Italian Renaissance.

ii In response to criticism, the second edition of *Underneath the Bough* (1893; 1898) was briefer than the original.

are pressing, reminiscences of enchanted and of shameful moments, mixed with an apprehensiveness that clogs our very breath—through this excitement and suffering, and recall we weave our slow Durdans days, talking a little sometimes of the potato crop and the deep knowing of the world to another man, and gauging the storage in our stomachs—of the pears that are a burden even to the parent stem![237]

KB *Discussing a newspaper clipping of a long interview with J. T. Grein, introducing "A Question of Memory" and announcing the date of the production.*[i]

August 23rd, 1893.

So at last it is all out. But what matter? The date is a consecration. Now at least we are to speak with living voices to men—to give them ourselves—ourselves and all we have of God.[238]

We have written to the Doctrine of the play. It is so wonderful! The kind of thing, if nature sympathised—one feels the bees would take home as news to the hive, the snail with his long horn eye would enquire into.

EC *August 29th.*

We start in pain of body for the Lakes. In the train we learn "O sorrow, / Why dost borrow"[ii]; our sandwiches are uncertain in taste, we have nothing but dry biscuits and cannot get food on the way. I feel reduced to an astral body.[239]

KB *August 29th.*

What a journey! We are rebellious against sandwiches and pass through the arid countries depressed and foreboding. [. . .] At dinner talk turns on Browning—"Have you keep an eye on Michael Field. When I die Michael Field can take my place."[240]

KB *III Verulam Buildings*

Gray's Inn[iii]

October 13th, 1893.

At last, we can write the blessed, the already highly-prized address—Verulam Buildings. We are quite, quite settled in this free, well-aired room. [. . .] I think our other journey in third-class discomfort, after the chill and blight of two and a half hours in the whitened sepulchre of Bacchus, as Henry des-

---

i J. T. Grein (1862–1935) established the Independent Theatre Society in London in 1891, hosting limited-run productions by private subscription, including work by Ibsen, Shaw, and other writers of literary rather than commercial significance.

ii From the "Song of the Indian Maid" in Keats's *Endymion* (1818).

iii Michael Field entered lodgings in London in order to be present for daily rehearsals.

ignates the stage on rehearsal afternoons, must have killed us. We both have chills and vague distempers; but the excellent housekeeper has cooked a leg of lamb for us with the delicacy that masculine wisdom has made imperative, and black coffee and cigarettes have made us ourselves—our Crag selves—not the nervous quarrelsome females we were fast feigning to be. Alack, Henry and I have quarreled like daws these last days—Henry is *so* unreasonable but behold him curled up at present in Fleming's[i] big armchair [. . .] and wholly happy.[241]

EC Gray's Inn on a wet morning—There is the sound of a wintry wind blowing along through the trees of the gardens, and with it a sound that blows along through one's ears, that comes whence, that goes whither?—like the wind, as great, as persistent—the traffic of London. The painted leaves of a plane tree beat the air that is misty with a confused look such as one sees on deaf old people. These leaves are green, but exhausted green; one or two detach themselves, blow along and fall uneasily on the grass. The trunk of the plane tree is profoundly dark tortoise-shelled[242] with gold patches—the darkness and gold both rich with the damp. A man and boy try to brush up the downfall of leaves—Gray's Inn round the leafy parallelogram stands solid and violet, the seats round the tree trunks shine with moisture, a cruel gleam that makes the body shiver. Now and then a brown pigeon, now and then a white one, reels amid the boughs.

This day, Cooper must stay away from rehearsal because she is ill.

It is difficult for me to stay away, I so love Rehearsal. It is wonderful to see one's words graving pictures, movements, persons—to watch a play being secretly fashioned down in the Earth.[243]

EC On Thursday I went to Dr. Russell Reynolds—ill, the colour of uncooked pastry, my[244] inside like an angry nest of wasps. I was sent home to opium pills and quiet.[245]

EC *October 26.* Tomorrow I shall be wishing my Love that deepest joy of being born again in the hearts of a multitude. She is gay and vital and does not mean to let anxiety spoil her Bacchic Feast Day. It is so wonderful for this wine of Life to be poured out to her on the very date in this vintage month when she was born. How I rejoice it; it is a splendid thing—a very gift of Fate.[246]

---

i Albert Fleming (1845–98), a barrister and resident of 3 Verulam Buildings, Gray's Inn, was a correspondent and editor of Ruskin, and author of *Revival of Handspinning and Weaving in Westmoreland* (1889).

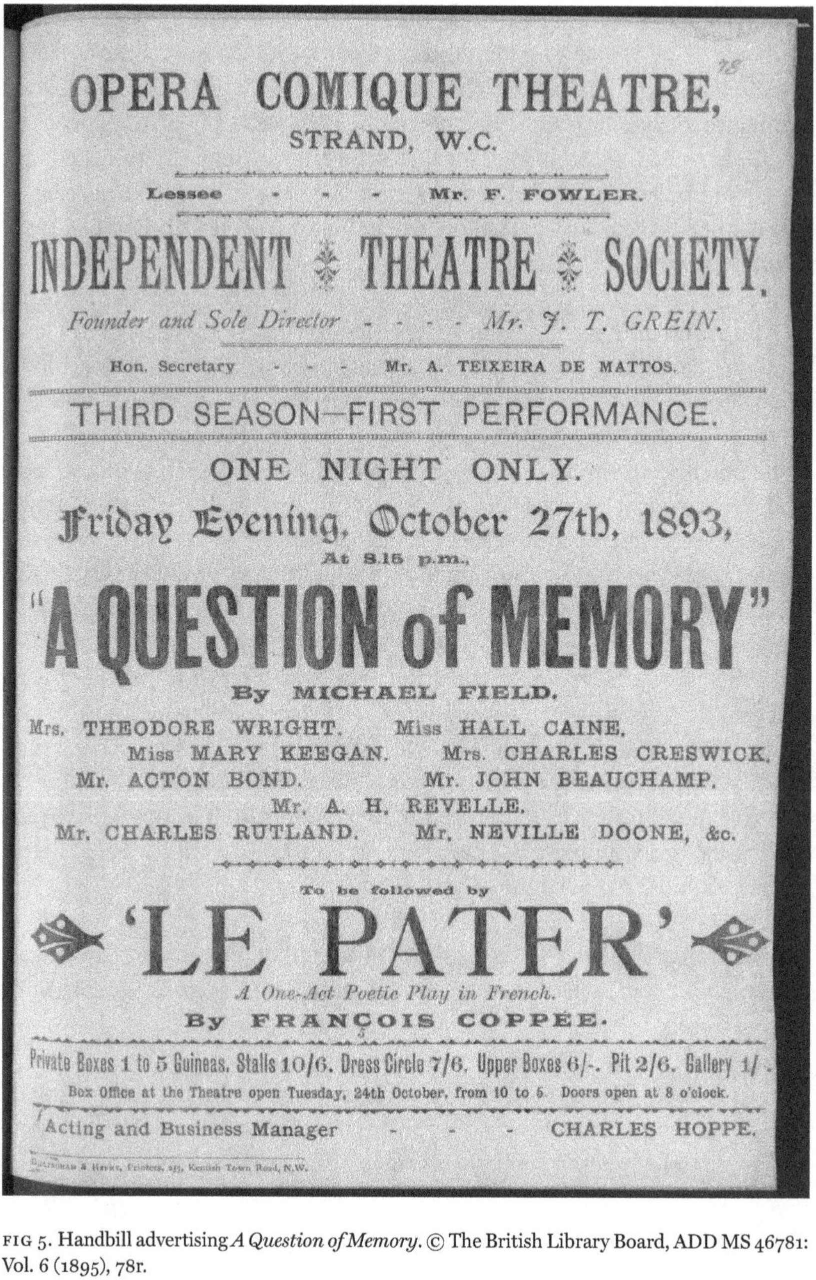

OPERA COMIQUE THEATRE,

STRAND, W.C.

Lessee - - - Mr. F. FOWLER.

INDEPENDENT ✦ THEATRE ✦ SOCIETY,

Founder and Sole Director - - - - *Mr. J. T. GREIN.*

Hon. Secretary - - - Mr. A. TEIXEIRA DE MATTOS.

THIRD SEASON—FIRST PERFORMANCE.

ONE NIGHT ONLY.

Friday Evening, October 27th, 1893,

At 8.15 p.m.,

"A QUESTION of MEMORY"

By MICHAEL FIELD.

Mrs. THEODORE WRIGHT. Miss HALL CAINE.
Miss MARY KEEGAN. Mrs. CHARLES CRESWICK.
Mr. ACTON BOND. Mr. JOHN BEAUCHAMP.
Mr. A. H. REVELLE.
Mr. CHARLES RUTLAND. Mr. NEVILLE DOONE, &c.

To be followed by

❖ 'LE PATER' ❖

A One-Act Poetic Play in French.

By FRANÇOIS COPPÉE.

Private Boxes 1 to 5 Guineas. Stalls 10/6. Dress Circle 7/6. Upper Boxes 6/-. Pit 2/6. Gallery 1/-.
Box Office at the Theatre open Tuesday, 24th October, from 10 to 5. Doors open at 8 o'clock.

Acting and Business Manager - - - CHARLES HOPPE.

Goodman & Hawke, Printers, 251, Kentish Town Road, N.W.

FIG 5. Handbill advertising *A Question of Memory*. © The British Library Board, ADD MS 46781: Vol. 6 (1895), 78r.

EC *On the morning after the play.*

   October 28.

It seems more natural to be dead than alive. We wake to the surprise of finding every morning paper against us; little Fleming falls before the crisis—he is too small a soul—but my love is strong, pours him out his tea, cracks jokes with him, and is able to convey our gratitude for this Gray's Inn Refuge. I am in helpless pain like a dumb animal at first. The *Times* and the *Telegraph* are worthy of respect in their blame; they have some good words for us and for our actors: the rest howl! [. . .]

Not a flower had anyone sent us yesterday, not a flower was given to us. No word, no letter, no visit, only the execrations of the Press! We say Goodbye to our found-[247]wanting host-guest and lunch together thankful to be by ourselves. There are caves in my brain through which cruel tides swing and rave—my stomach feels as it does when anyone you love is dead; my throat is dry and quakes from time to time.

I rise up from lunch and walk to the British Museum—the grim Egyptian deities and the Branchidae Priests support me more than the Elgin Marbles. I long to lie in one of those sarcophagi covered with hieroglyphics, and to know that the weight of ages would hold the lid down. I find in the Melopes and Frieze of the Parthenon a want of contagious life among the figures . . . gradually the stoniness of the sculpture strikes me with intolerable anguish, and I walk home, for the first time to cry a few moments. My love comforts me with tea, with a strong face and with tenderness. . . . Letters at last from Little One and Father, noble and confident—I leap up to Courage. I have reached the growing point in misery.

Then my love quails, she who has been so brave—The Evening Papers are worse than the morning—they are like a lot of unchained tigers. We are hated as Shelley was hated by our countrymen, blindly, ravenously.[248]

EC We mark with a hallmark the people who have the courage to stand by us. The abuse is hateful, but we cannot hate back; we simply grow bewildered like our Ferencz.

Not a soul has been near us—our rooms are full of the sound of a winter wind, on our desk are the Daily Journals. . . . but though everything is against us we are strong, thank heaven and our race! We have gained great experience, we have won the friendliness of our Caste, we have tried our forces for once, we have held an audience—*we regret nothing* (except Mrs. Creswick's acting!!). [. . .]

   EC *Recaps the night before.*

The first curtain fell with success. Young Michaelians came to our Box to

say the House was with us.249 [. . .] The Second Act was received excel-
lently—Miss Caine and Miss Keegan charming the people at once. Again the
Box filled. Poor Sidney came to congratulate us on success, for says he very
wisely, "Success is so much more encouraging than failure." [. . .]

Fewer people come to speak with Michael Field after the third act.

Grein, who had been estranged in manner, did not come and I felt suddenly as if I stood in a clearing where there was no humanity—where I was
a mortal alone. . . .250

Act IV was lost from the beginning. [. . .] [T]oward the end the Beattys
kissed, there was a laugh, and a shout of *no!* [. . .]—then we ran behind the
stage. The applause must have been good, for the actors seemed warm—I
cannot say I heard it and not once did I catch the word *Author,* although
Doone with rather Australian manners tried to force us toward the stage.251
[. . .]

EC With scarcely a word, I bore his remarks, and went to bed to sleep as
one does after a funeral. I woke feeling incomplete—I had lost my hope—any
anticipation; and there was no triumph in its place.

My Love wore her black and coral dress and a lovely green velveteen opera
cloak with silver clasp and black fur edgings. Two white flowers were bunched
under the collar. I wore a dress of shimmery beryl green—white lace, black
satin sash and breast bow, deep red leaves and a venetian red opera cloak,
with black fur edge.252

EC The next morning—well. I got up—sensation itself was sick—and the
thought of the newspapers made it heave. [. . .] They all said the same thing
without regret, without lenience, and without fairness. Such a tone of hate in
them! [. . .]

EC takes refuge alone in the British Museum.

I longed for the quietness of sculpture.253 [. . .] I longed to lie down into
one of the basalt chests and know that the great lid would cover me for ages.
The cat-headed Goddess became my one idea. . . . I fled home and sobbed.
Then the Evening Papers came—a storm of abuse before which even Sim
bowed. [. . .] The storm however remade me—I became as firm and as living
as before I had been overwhelmed. A manly letter from Dr. Todhunter,[i] a
word from Larkin and a brave packet from home: nothing else reached us—
no one came near us. . . .254

EC Actors look past you not into you—they give you the impression you are
an audience not a person. [. . .]

i John Todhunter (1839–1916), Irish poet, playwright, and doctor.

Tuesday

William Archer delivers himself in *The World* a merciless attack on our archaic style, with the admission that the shooting scene, if it had been as well written as it is finely conceived, would have been one of the most moving in English Drama.[i][255]

EC *Tells of rewriting that scene, and then writing a letter to Archer.*

"Eight years ago, you said in print that our use of the Elizabethan Method was enough to make a critic weep tears of blood. We do not ask so exhausting an interest in our mistakes—we want to realise where we go wrong and how we are to start afresh. 1590 is second nature to us—we sometimes fear it is first nature, for we are even accused of speaking Quaint Elizabethan English in ordinary life. It is very discouraging not to know when one is antiquated or when one is contemporary. We wish at last with all the strength in us to be contemporary; to write a direct prose with natural sequences. Of course, we allege as you anticipated that our style is a convention, but we feel its disadvantages more deeply than our audience." [. . .]

Sends Archer the rewritten scene.

"[*I*]*t shall*[256] *be well written* if we learn the grammar of our Art again. Your own words are the appeal we make to you, and we are certain you will aid us. The M.S. we send is the measure of what we have as yet learned; we want to know how far it is the measure of what we have still to learn. Mark the M.S. without reserve and kindly return it to Mich. Field, Durdans, Reigate." [. . .]

When I said to Addleshaw,[ii] "I would go through the whole experience again now that I know how it would end"—he replied "A man would not"— "But then you see, I am a woman and to bring out a play is experience of life—just what women feel so crushingly that they need. You men get it like breathing."[257]

EC *Attends a performance of "Measure for Measure."*

Oscar Wilde indicates us to Archer at the very moment Dr. Todhunter named him to me. The next moment my eyes met his—for what seemed like a great while, there was so much in the look, such waves of understanding, of fascinated magnetism passing from stall to dress-circle! It was a most Modern encounter—"frightfully thrilling." His eyes are like doors into a lethal chamber, but they certainly are capable of expressing Ibsenism in real life.[258]

i William Archer (1856–1924), Scottish writer and influential theater critic known for his early adoption of Ibsen and Shaw.

ii Percy Addleshaw (1866–1916), English lawyer and writer.

EC *Note in the corner of a clipping: "Women and Natural Selection, Interview with Dr. Alfred Russel Wallace."*

December 5. I read this before going to bed. I could not sleep. I thought I am not a dramatist unless I can evolve a plot—I am sure Pinero and Grundy[i] often think in plots. I said to my brain *evolve!* This is what it evolved.[259]

EC My Love and I quarrel—such a desolating thing—all my fault, I was in wrath against Sagittarius and reckless.[260]

EC *Archer writes to ask that they not send him the rest of the play to edit. He ends with a postscript:*

"When the play is published pray do not mention that any portion of it has been through my hands."[261]

EC *Last Night of Old Year.*

Mary Costelloe left us yesterday. The "Doctrine" is going to spend next winter in America without her, seeing his family and lecturing. She leaves him with firmness; she has seen with inexorable logic that he will make her pay for loving him just as the world does, and she pays equitably. It is fine to see a woman so logical in her affection . . . but her ecstasy of a year ago is gone on the same wings that have carried his youth away. When a young man lives in relation with a married woman, especially if the relation is ascetic as in this case, he becomes almost ridiculously old—with a sort of futile fatherliness about him, a trace of gout in his impulses. If she had never crossed his path—noble though she is!—then her atheism is absolutely a—quantity; not a liberating to universal life like his—with its deep race-Spinozism.[ii] All she says seems to ring hard against unexplained facts and formulated laws—all he says flows with the life of the world. Well—about this year.

The *Master-Builder* and the succeeding crisis gave me a far more solid influence over father, and much more inner and therefore outer freedom. In Italy I had a few days when there was spring rain on my love for Bernard, and I drank joy[262] as the little vines drink. [. . .] So much for my travels. The summer was draught, torture—ending in revolt against the "Doctrine" and a farewell Sordid—miserable. My one joy was the discovery of a power of using my new sensations in *Croquis*[iii]—the direct consequence[263] of Bernard's influence. [. . .]

i Arthur Wing Pinero (1855–1934) and Sydney Grundy (1848–1914), English playwrights.

ii The materialist philosophy of radical early modern thinker Baruch Spinoza (1632–77).

iii Brief prose poems that Michael Field, and especially Cooper, experimented with under the influence of Berenson.

Then came a plunge into *real* life at Grays Inn and the Opéra Comique. We have faced the technique of our art, we have faced (and for half an hour held) an audience; our aims have been consolidated by experience, our spirits tried by opposition. I am twice the woman I was this time last year—I am afraid just now nearly as bitter, for no friend stood by us, even to rebut false reports; and the one man who could have been of inestimable virtue to our art-life has withdrawn his aid. We asked him *to do the Impossible* and we all know how that ends.

I do not yet realise where *modernity* is taking me; I am moving with it as if down a stream, not using it enough for motive force like a waterfall turning a mill. But I do not get frightened—I maintain a resolute patience. I cannot define my position to Law and Anarchy—though I am certain that we are doing an unnatural and destructive thing[264] if we allow the claims of others to mar the freedom of self-realisation as the central need of our lives and the condition of happiness.

Underneath this certainty many dark troubles hide for me, and I hate to look forward to the hurrying years. But when I work at revising our play, imagine the plot of our new modern play, [. . .] and when I love my Love—the dark things seem to drown and I see how much self-realisation there really is in my life, though not in its daily conditions.

I greet "the unknown (1894) with a cheer!" May we finish *Carloman*, write a modern play of comedy with a serious interest, complete *Equal Love*, and tread on the stage with sure triumph. May we see Venice—may we even visit *The Crag*! May we gain a few friends, quarrel with none of our few old ones, and may I take the Doctrine as food, not poison, and withstand the Bacchial eyes!

May my Love and I have greater joy in our work, in each other (for we grow each year to find a faster bliss unite us) and in the life we conquer, the life we entertain!

Vale at que salve![i][265]

KB The little boil in my nostril is broken, and I walk unvexed through the palace of my brain.

We have not made a friend this year. [. . .] We are too quarrelsome, and this we must set ourselves to overcome in 94.[266]

---

i "Goodbye and farewell!"

CHAPTER 3

Domestic Negotiations

1894–99

TIME ACCELERATED for Michael Field during the second half of the 1890s, hurtling the women ever closer toward the twentieth century and promises of "modernity" that both teased and threatened. In their literary life, Michael Field remained productive even as audiences and critical regard dwindled. They faced dramatic transitions on the personal front, including the 1897 accidental death of paterfamilias James Cooper, father of Edith, brother-in-law of Katharine. Though James Cooper's death was traumatic, it liberated Michael Field into a new autonomy, including the chance to establish their own household for the first time. Michael Field seized the occasion to create an aesthetic marriage, complete with rings, a meticulously decorated home, a madcap male artist neighbor couple who knocked at all hours, and a fluffy, red, and occasionally violent dog cast in the role of adored child. Michael Field's embrace of the tropes of married domesticity signals the literary craft-edness of the poets' narrative—and an invitation to think about the darkness just on the other side of the light.

Works and Days during this five-year period conveys as much joy as frus-tration, as much contentment as anxiety. Take, for example, the distressing narrative of James Cooper's sudden disappearance—the speculation that he was murdered; the certainty that he was dead, even in the absence of his body; and the discovery, months later, of his corpse deep in the woods, on the rock where he fell to his death. Even as they wrote the narrative of this trauma, so intimate and yet so public, Michael Field found their way back to each other time and again. They wrote about exchanging marriage rings in the meadow where they imagined James Cooper might have died (he had not). At the same time, they wrote repeatedly about giggling with each other while tucked into bed at night, or rather, beds: at home, on the train crossing Europe to solve the mystery of Cooper's disappearance, in Switzerland, and in Oxford, on a bit of holiday.

James Cooper's death further opens domestic opportunities for Michael Field. Just over a year later, in early 1899, Michael Field reported their resolve to move from the patriarchal home, known as Durdans, and to create a married home of their own. In the 1899 volume of *Works and Days*, Michael Field shifted their aesthetic practice from the world of poetry to the creation of aesthetic domesticity via the "house beautiful." With the assistance of their friends "the Artists," Charles Ricketts and Charles Shannon,[i] they acquired the lease on a tall, skinny building in suburban Richmond. The house, "Paragon," had an unprepossessing facade on the Petersham Road. Its back, however, overlooking "England's River," the Thames, suggested to Michael Field the national and perhaps global significance of their aesthetic domestic perch. With further assistance from Ricketts especially, Michael Field decorated Paragon in the image of their art: a temple to Michael Field's marriage as an act of poetic expression. Domestic realignments of this period include the arrival in 1897 of Cooper's puppy, Musico, nicknamed Music, a basset hound, and in 1898, the star of the show, Bradley's puppy, Whym Chow. Michael Field hosted Amy Cooper's wedding at Paragon while also writing unkindly in *Works and Days* about how dull and conventional they found the couple. As they celebrated New Year's Eve 1899, Michael Field expressed contentment—but also loneliness—and their perennial sense of isolation.

Domestic privacy was both precious to Michael Field and oppressive; the symbol of the Thames remains just that, leaving the poets observing but not participating in the river's tidal flow. Michael Field were surely aware that there was danger in the worldly world outside; hence the ambivalence of their exclusion from it. The scandalous visibility of male homosexuality in this period, including the 1895 trials and imprisonment of Oscar Wilde, reshaped aesthetic flamboyance itself as a practice dangerous to its subjects. Wilde's experience was painful for Michael Field to observe. The sections of *Works and Days* written contemporaneously with Wilde's ordeal afford only quick glances at a worldly drama that struck very close to home for the women. Though female couples such as Michael Field were largely exempt from violent homophobia aimed at men such as Wilde, Bradley and Cooper were aware of the extreme vulnerability of those "like us." Michael Field's own ambivalence toward the performative homosexuality of the fin de siècle came out very clearly in their reaction to Aubrey Beardsley's publication of the first volume of *The Yellow Book* in 1894: "We have been almost blinded by the glare of hell." Michael Field wanted out; and they wanted in.

---

i Charles Ricketts (1866–1931) and his lover Charles Shannon (1863–37) were painters, sculptors, and designers who became close friends of Michael Field.

The final five years of the nineteenth century was full of signals that the eternal-seeming "Victorian" epoch was in decline, and that something new was set to arrive. Walter Pater, Robert Louis Stevenson, and Christina Rossetti died in 1894; William Morris and Sir John Everett Millais in 1896; Lewis Carroll, Eliza Lynn Linton, and Sir Edward Burne-Jones in 1898. The 1899 death of Frank Costelloe, husband of Mary Costelloe, liberated Mary to marry Bernard Berenson. The fact of the marriage in 1900 was exquisitely painful to Edith Cooper. The deaths of Ruskin, Nietzsche, and Wilde in 1900, and of Queen Victoria early in 1901, would only emphasize the growing divide between past and future.

Several technologies emerging in the 1890s heralded new ways of imagining the scope of literary and visual representational practices so important to Michael Field. Michael Field had long been accustomed to telegraph technology, which, among other things, delivered to them in Surrey near-contemporaneous news about the frightening disappearance of James Cooper in Switzerland. They were long accustomed, too, to the existence of photography as a formal medium for the capture of portraits and images. But Michael Field were shocked, in Switzerland, by the on-the-spot journalistic photography that "infamously" threatened to send images of James Cooper's corpse in situ worldwide on the pages of daily newspapers. The worldly world, most unaesthetic, felt increasingly immediate to Michael Field. Telephone and radio technology opened up new vistas for real-time communication. Automotive technology, combined with various fearsome prospects—"buses in the sky" and a tunnel under the English Channel—made the far-off newly proximate. Even in the world of representation itself, the emergence of early cinematic media—the screening in Leicester Square of films by the Lumière Brothers in 1896 and Edison's patent for the kinetoscope, issued in 1897—offered new technologies for storytelling that would eventually blur even further distinctions between high and low art forms. Contemplating the shift to 1900 on December 31, 1899, Edith Cooper worried about leaving their dead beloveds back in the nineteenth century. She also anticipated an exciting future for the twentieth-century Michael Field.

Works and Days, 1894

KB My Love—I leave her to write of it—begins the new year by a gay day in town with Mary and a Bohemian troop. I do not get to town till Saturday January 6th. [. . .] I get to town midday and enter deepening fog and "slush." On the threshold of an aerated I meet Mary, we lunch together at my club, thence to Burlington House, where we pick up the surly Burke, and proceed all three in a hansom to the borrowed studio, in Tite Street Chelsea, of little Rothenstein.[i] Two candles, a great luminous twilight, and the curly cub of an artist chattering incessantly as a bird sings. He is blessed in his poverty, lunching on an egg and some marmalade, and then taking a box for *The Second Mrs. Tanqueray*.[ii] He tells one incomparable story of Arthur Symonds.[iii] He and Symonds are together at the Empire. S. confides that he is just getting to know a certain distinguished artist—I think a dancer. Rothenstein knows her familiarly and after the performance the two young men mingle in conversation with the ballet girls. Rothenstein addresses Mad. X with careless Bohemian freedom. S. draws him back. "You must not speak to them in *that* way."

The man of *that* world laughs good-naturedly.

We hear Lane[iv] is thinking of bringing out a quarterly that is to be called *The Yellow Book*. The contributors are to be well paid. We feel our purses fill with guineas.

After ten we go to the house of the sacred ones—Ricketts and Shannon.[1] It is Whistler's old house and called The Vale.[v] As I am struggling to unmuffle from my furs and wraps, the door is opened, and an angel—just fresh from "preening," one would say, stands on the sill. He is wonderfully fresh and looks among us all like a living plant among artificial flowers. Once before I had seen the exquisite rose of youth piercing through London fog—but here was a bit of sunny grass peat with its own climate and delights, untouched by environment, moving along in an enchanted light—an untarnished creature amid smuts. Fairer apparition have I never seen. My heart beat approvingly as I ascended the stairs. Then we came to the plain sitting-room where Ricketts was sitting with his sentimental Christ's face, and waxen complexion.

We talk of the play, and our other works. *Tragic Mary* is rated our highest performance. "We must think immensely of our later work."

Sight and Song is alluded to lovingly, and Shannon says justice was not done to our play: "it *must* have acted if a fair chance had been given." One does not ask speech of Shannon; it is enough to see him moving about with

---

    i Sir William Rothenstein (1872–1945), English painter and artist.

    ii Pinero's scandalous play was first staged in 1893.

    iii Bradley is referring to English poet Arthur Symons, but she has misspelled the name as "Symonds," likely confusing it with that of poet and critic John Addington Symonds (1840–93).

    iv John Lane (1854–1925) founded the Bodley Head publishing house with Elkin Mathews in 1887.

    v James Abbott McNeill Whistler (1834–1903), American-born artist who sued Ruskin for libel in Ruskin's review of his *Nocturne in Black and Gold* in 1877. The jury awarded Whistler damages of just a farthing.

FIG 6. Charles Shannon, *left*, and Charles Ricketts, *right*. © National Portrait Gallery, London.

the tea tray, simple and serviceable, full of culture and refinement, and the gladness of a creature that has drawn days of free breath. That is freedom—to escape the mechanical in study and art, to impress one's own individuality on all things—not to wrinkle into anything.[2]

January 12th.

KB A really blithe, sweet birthday for my love. Amy gives her a fine Leonardo drawing—I a coffee-kanne and flowers. After breakfast we dance, brandishing boughs of white Persian lilac. My love and I walk, sunning ourselves like cats. In the afternoon we post off to the type writer *A Question of Memory*. The study looks particularly fascinating with flowers from the Riviera, and dried sea lavender; but my love, also in her black velvet, and great, drooping sleeves of moonstone lustre, is full of mystery and enchantment.[3]

EC *An answer to a letter from Berenson.*
   February 26th.
   "Please remind Field that he owes me an apology answer to a very affectionate epistle, and that in failure of such answer it is a temptation to believe that my expressions of friendship weren't *welcome*."

Dear Doctrine,

It is more paralysing to me to sit down before a sheet of letter paper than before a sheet of foolscap on which I must trace the scenario of a new drama or the beginning of a *Croquis*.[i] A letter isn't one of my forms of expression. I don't know where to begin or how to handle my own personality, or approach that of my correspondent. Nevertheless, I must make an effort to save you from the "temptation" of thinking your words of friendship were not welcome. I don't much believe in the reality of the temptation, because I fancy we both *know* we are friends, insofar as two people so much alike can be friends. Still, if you want my assurance—in answer to all you said about pictures and what our fellow enjoyment of them could do for you, I have only to confess that I don't write *Croquis* as I did in the summer after being with you. My sensations were at their highest power then; now they are lazy, and don't vibrate, and don't draw the right words to them magnetically. Like kindles fire in like, and though we're not quite two flints (I hope) we influence[4] each other on the same principle. [. . .]

If I don't like letter writing at most times, I like it less than ever when I'm in the midst of conflict, and all winter I've been in the state of Keats' *Lamia* when she was changing[5] from a serpent into a human being—a state of torrid transition. I don't know what I am or what I shall become.

The Modern [. . .] Yes, these two words have had significance for me of late. I wish I could get my change over, for it's not pleasant, or, more positively speaking, it's almost unendurable—a mortal strife. And you who can discover the "Genesis of the work of art"—is it true you think your interests so very remote from us artists? Have you no help? Even Plato saw what pitiable wretches we are, wandering between reality and illusion forever and finding no rest.

I analyse modern plays, watch life whenever I have chance, greet the spring as it creeps from the hedges and from the evening sky, eat my heart like a civilised cannibal, try to imagine that Discontent is a leader worthy of confidence, and work till my head reels and I cry aloud for amusement, which I find where I don't want it—in books.[6]

EC *March 5th, Little One's birthday.*

A blue sky, a day full of bracing light. On the breakfast-table this letter from Oscar—

---

i The brief prose poems Cooper experimented with around this time.

Dear Michael Field,

Write to Miss Elizabeth Marbury[i]
    c/o Lou's Exchange
    New York City
    U.S.A.

She manages all my plays. I have written to her.

I am a wretch not to have answered sooner—but I have no excuse; so you will forgive me—

Your third act was quite admirable—a really fine piece of work—with the touch of terror our stage lacks so much. I think the theatre should belong to the Furies—Caliban and Silenus, one educated and the other sober seem now to dominate in their fallen condition, our wretched English drama.

Oscar Wilde[7]

EC I think of the four natures intimately bound up with mine in continuance—My Love, My Mother, the Old and the Doctrine. My Love has[8] my rose-coloured Soul, the bloom, the expansion, the warmth of my being; my golden soul belongs to Mother—all the spiritual joy in me, all the poet in me "hidden in the light of thought." The Faun-poet, the lover of daffodils and the green world they live in—the tragedian, the wine-juice poet in me—these are my Love's.

To "the Old" I gave with my first kiss and the first plunge of my eyes into those silver lakes—his eyes, my white soul, the Dian of my Spirit—he has it with him, and no one will ever woo it away.

"Doctrine" has my blue soul—all that is witch-like, levin-like—and also the summer sky in me.

This I can say: that the four are all *living* equally—these recipients of my souls. Theosophists may explain or not how the two who are dead act with the two who are alive—but my own experience remains mine, if no one shares it in the universe.[9]

EC *Wednesday, April 17.*
    KB *The Yellow Book*[ii]
    EC We have been almost blinded by the glare of hell.

---

i Elizabeth Marbury (1856–1933), American theatrical and literary agent and producer.

ii Decadent periodical published from 1894–97 under the art direction of Aubrey Beardsley.

When we started to town, we were feeling depressed. It was one of those morose and leafy days which are the curse of summer in England—and it is almost summer after the heat of the last three weeks—days when the young green is viciously out of tone with the muddied stretch of rain-sky. We went to the Bodley Head to purchase our copy of *The Yellow Book*. As we came up to the shop we found the whole frontage a hot background of orange colour to sly, roistering heads, silhouetted against it and half hiding behind masks. The window seemed to be gibbering, our eyes to be filled with incurable jaundice. *La Réclame*, hideous befowled Duessa or any witch ever seen by the mind's eyes stood up before us as a shop where contemporary literature is sold. One felt as one does when now and then a wholly lost woman stands flaming on the pavement with the ghastly laugh of the ribald crowd in the air round her. One hates one's eyes for seeing![10]

But the infamous window mocked and moved and fizgiged, saffron and pitchy, till one's eyes were arrested like Virgil's before the wind of flame.

And the inside of the book! It is full of cleverness such as one expects to find in those who dwell below light and hope and love and aspiration. The best one can say, of any tale or of any illustration, is that it is clever—the worst one can say is that it is damnable.

But George Egerton[i] does not even deserve damnation, but something weightier—crushing out silence. *Education Sentimentale* by Beardsley[ii] and his bookplate are nightmares from some exotic house of ill fame. Faugh! One must go to one's Wordsworth and Shelley to be fumigated.

We think of changing our name to *Messalina Garden* to escape from the company of George Egerton![11]

EC Miss Robins[iii] came "upstage" to us fervently as actresses do. She is to write and arrange a meeting with us—will she? Actors and actresses are a *caste* apart however much society may relent toward them—one cannot take them seriously, except when one is removed from them by the footlights.[12]

EC Ricketts sits on the couch, sunk in his own shoulders, like some delicate flower in its leaves, laughing on a note that resolves affectation into sincerity. His mother was an Italian, which accounts for the activity of his hands, the ease of his lips in talking, the umber of his eyes, so much more expressive

i Pen name of Mary Chavelita Dunne Bright (1859–1945), late-nineteenth-century novelist and feminist.

ii *L'Education Sentimentale* was one of the prints Beardsley contributed to the first edition of *The Yellow Book*.

iii Elizabeth Robins (1862–1952), American actress, playwright, novelist, and women's rights activist.

than the ordinary English brown; also, perhaps, for the Christ-type of his head and features. His cheek is as finely hollowed as if it were the concave of a white shell—his little pointed beard is madder coloured and what hair he has looks like old thatch. His conversation is brilliant—but a coloured surface; not gemlike or metallic as Oscar's or Bernard Shaw's.[i] His remarks have sensuous content moulded by wit—they are not primally intellectual. He is one of those delightful people who seem complex but are simple at the end of a good talk. He is an ardent lover of Shannon, his elder by a year—loving him as My Love loves me—following him about with rippling banter and eyes that deprecate the Beloved's[13] willfulness.[14]

EC Ricketts told us in the garden he wants to get a carbuncle carved into a heart that he may give it to Shannon—"I want my ring," said the spoiled voice of the Beloved. These two men live and work together and find rest and joy in each other's love just as we do—two men whose life is complete harmony and two women—no wonder the male and female dual member is sympathetic.[15]

EC *Noting the twenty-fifth anniversary of her grandmother's death.*
I wonder if twenty-five years after our death anyone will pluck a flower for us!—a good mother has more chance of that kind of love than the greatest artist—blood prompts so much more tenderly than anything else.[16]

EC We leave them, and by four o'clock are climbing the stairs of Manchester Mansions to Miss Elizabeth Robins' aerie. A grave housekeeper lets us in, and we enter a small, poor, but refined room. The windows are shut and a stick of incense fumes in the room—till we fear that death is prepared for us and madly throw up the window. Over the clock hang portraits of Ibsen and William Archer. There is no sense of colour in the little room that is personal and shows artistic taste; but the green curtains and light walls and plain furniture are inoffensive.[17]

EC *July 11.*
I must go far back to June 26th, when we first saw Sarah Bernhardt[ii]—the air of London was dying of fever—we tried to get a bedroom opposite our club but revolted from the steep stairs and their smell—like that of entombed rashers of bacon. We fled even to the Temperance Hotel in Bedford Row—

i George Bernard Shaw (1856–1950), Irish dramatist, critic, and antiwar activist.
ii Sarah Bernhardt (1844–1923), a.k.a. *la Divine Sarah*, French actress.

though bent on the service of Bacchus, anything was better than steps and domestic fast. In the afternoon we went to the *Fair Women* [exhibition] at the Grafton. We enjoyed the dark sparks in the eyes of Lotto's Lucretia. How she irritates—one can't understand her. She has the eyes of several of the Bergamo[18] Madonnas—and lit dangerously.[19]

EC *La Tosca*—Weariness—long and deep.

Till Sarah comes in . . . A bunch of flowers and ribbons round a little witch's face that smiles till one laughs and flatters till one condones every-thing—even the unscrupulousness that stops the play for five minutes that it may gain a triumph of welcomes and acknowledgements purely personal. O Sarah! You are a temperament—you are hysteria and romance, you are a serpent of old Nile—but you are not a transcendent artist; and you are lyrical rather than dramatic—you show us yourself, as much as the old beauties showed their forms in the[20] Arena—so you show your own nature on the stage—your very self in your fascination, abandon, and . . . I can almost write disgrace—for the most adorable exposure has that element. "Je suis très bien avec la Madonne"[i]—delicious to hear the golden voice say it! Delicious to watch the smile come like incense from the mouth and spread through the being of a whole audience; delicious to watch the eyes loose their flight of arrows and become blanks of flittering alabaster for a moment, till the orbs return again to their archery.

This first Act made me Sarah's lover—I played the man to her every ca-ress—After that the charm went. Lots of things were effective, but never inevitable. The torture-scene left me unhorrified, with my "wittiers" per-fectly comfortable. I'll back the shooting scene in *A Question* against this scene any day for a thousand years to come. Even the scene with Scarpia is a romantic trick, not an imagined crisis—Sarah never reaches such qualities of a situation as sorrow or joy or guilt—she can only draw from it all its vio-lence or allurement.[21]

EC *Saturday, June 30.*

We cut dew-sprinkled roses as a gift for Amy Bell, and I start to town as I never do except when I am to meet my Dear—with a triumphant movement of my pulse like the swish of an arrow that must go to the bull's-eye, because it is sure of aim.

I see nothing in the [Charing Cross] pavement at first: then behind some masculine shoulders the milky plume, and the milk-white teeth of my Love—

---

i "I am very comfortable with the Madonna."

the black brim of her hat, the radiance from her face that is active as if it came from a planet—a world among all the fixed faces. We kiss and are complete.

In the afternoon my Love insists that I shall have her six-shilling ticket for *La Dame aux Camélias*, and gives herself to the Pit. It is hard to be severed so quickly but the interest of comparing Sarah with Duse makes the time short. In brief, Sarah's Margaret Gautier is Sarah; Duse creates a Margaret Gautier—a woman whose womanhood has Shakespearean humanity back of it—I say Shakespearean because it is at once as broad [22] and yet concentrated as Lear's or Desdemona's.[i]

When Sarah is on the stage we are always in the Salon of the Demimonde; when we watch Duse, already stricken with death, struck with Love, we are among forces that are destinies—the universe breaks into the trivial milieu, as it always does when our heart stands still.[23]

EC *Saturday Evening Tristan.*

We spin away in the breezy cab from Amy Bell's to Drury Lane[ii]—as we look round from our central stalls we feel as if we were not in London—there is an European character about the audience—not the distinctively English appearance of all the people who line a theatre even in town. The low dresses and jewels everywhere, the vast circle of the tiers, making the centre of the opera-house an airy cylinder to the foreignness of the effect. Then to hear the Band play an overture by Wagner[iii] gives one the freedom of Continents. Frau Klafsky,[iv] the Isolde, discovered in her red rheum-striped tent, is an Elgin Marble, suddenly waked to stupendous existence after years of Northern exile. She completely overwhelmed us and seemed to unhumanise the passion—her high soprano neutralized Max Alvary's diseased tenor—what has happened to his voice? He stands and moves impressively—and the cutting of his face is very Wagnerian in style—but his voice even outrages Wagner's most diabolical discords.[v] Frankly, the music almost hypnotized us, like a cataract—we could not[24] understand or analyse its volume—we could only experience its strength, velocity, and primaeval unscrupulousness—Michael actually slept a little while during the love scene.

---

i The play adapted from the 1863 novel of the same name by Alexandre Dumas fils, sometimes known in English as *Camille*, and later adapted by Verdi as *La Traviata*. Here KB insists that EC take her costly ticket for this production, featuring Sarah Bernhardt, while KB herself will sit in the cheap seats. Margaret Gautier is the play's tragic protagonist.

ii London theater constructed in 1663.

iii Richard Wagner (1813–83), German composer, most notably of operas.

iv Katharina Klafsky (1855–96), Hungarian operatic soprano.

v Max Alvary (1856–98), German tenor known for Wagnerian roles.

We toiled upstairs for strong coffee before Act III and came down feeling that the coffee had made the necessary passes to wake us up from the mesmeric state we had been in. How we enjoyed ourselves![25]

[. . .] We rose and left the Opera house when Tristan died. Isolde, coming like a giantess, with her unsympathetic voice, frightened us and we fled, feeling we could not bear incomprehensible music, after our hearts had heard so well.

We drove in the coolness of midnight back to Porchester Terrace knowing very deeply we had been[26] near a work of art too great for us to measure in a single night with the compasses of the brain, but sufficiently akin to our imaginations for us to divine the greatness we could not measure. It grew greater to us the further we were from the Opera House, greater as we lay in our bed—greater, greater every hour we have given to thinking of it since.[27]

EC *Monday, July 15.*

Mary comes down unexpectedly—and finds me with half my hair in pins and Michael, with her front open—both toiling to get a new front made out of some Correggio sulphur silk.[i] These little accidents—due to life's tactlessness—are of no consequence, except artistically, and because they are all told to Doctrine by Mary's gossip of a tongue.

She sat down and finished the front as capably as she would swim or paint one's throat. She is a woman capable before ordinary life, self-assertive, with frank, genial eyes that enjoy like a child's; she has no more pity than a child—she experiences rapidly and shallowly, yet taking great interest in the experience, her temper is even, but her tongue unkind, and her face kind—an unmodelled face, that only marks with wrinkles if it takes any marks and is pleasant from the black-chalked brows, the calm freshness of the smile from the eyes and the growth low down on the brow of auburn hair. She loves and talks about it to the man she loves and others, as if she were in Eden.[28]

EC *Thursday, July 17.*

A few days ago, Michael, in full disgust at the *Yellow Book*, wrote as follows to the editor Harland—*à propos* of our little prose poem "Rhythm" he had accepted for the second volume.

Dear Sir,

I must request you to return my typed copy of "Rhythm." I dislike the *Yellow Book* both in its first and second number, and greatly regret that in a

---

i   A hand-woven Dupioni silk with a shimmering texture and visible slubs. Here perhaps in a color that reminds Bradley of the saturated coloration of Correggio's paintings.

sudden rashness of sympathy[29] I proposed to contribute to it—It has been all my fault, and I should not ask you to return an accepted paper if your delay in printing had not convinced me that you feel M.F. is not an ingredient in the Yellow-broth . . . as for metaphor's sake I must name it. Trusting you will see that I do not write in a spirit of contention, I am

Sincerely yours etc.

In response we have the following on an open p[ost]card—

"The Editor of the Yellow Book can in no case return rejected MSS. unless stamped address envelopes for that purpose are provided by the sender."

We reply to the Cad—

Durdans Reigate—July 17

Dear Sir,

I extremely regret the unbusinesslike omission of stamps. I punish myself for the informality of enclosing a half-penny stamp for the card on which you explained my mistake. And I enclose fully addressed, stamped envelope as the return fare of the MS I have asked you not to insert. Sincerely yours, etc.[30]

EC *In Ilkley, the spa town in West Yorkshire.*
Tuesday, August 17.

The wind rides everywhere in wild disorder and deafens us with showers against the window. I make our bedroom in to a chez-nous—that's always the first thing I set about in strange surroundings. Then I stretch myself on the bed, calm in spite of the tyrannizing wind, for my need of rest comes from profounder caves than those from which hurricanes issue, it comes from the secret places in which my life is continuously fashioned, it is a need of my being.[31]

EC *Monday, September 10.*

Disturbing letter from Mary, that dresses all my wounds and makes me as sick as a dog. Bernard is on the Atlantic—she has parted from him, happier than ever, because they have surmounted "a crisis" with Obrist.[i] Yet she goes to Obrist to look after him as a friend as soon as Bernard has left her. I am sorry for Bernard when I think of him going back to his mean Jewish home, above which he has risen so immeasurably. As for the rest, if he drowned in the Atlantic the Earth would be a happier place for me! He seems to lie me on the planet as though it were the wheel.[32]

i Hermann Obrist (1863–1927), German English sculptor and designer.

KB *It is November 11th.*

Twenty-six years ago Alfred Gérente died: I have been looking at the old journals. Goodness, what a sentimental girl I was. It is marvelous God suffers such creatures to continue. How diffuse, and boring, and ridiculous youth is! And yet the passion of those days, in the midst of all this folly, was perfectly genuine.

Why then do I feel that past self break into dust as I read?

Quai d'Anjou

Her fellow watcher was called away, and she was asked would she remain with the corpse. She nodded to show she would not be afraid and forced her eyes steadily on the bed. All she saw was a dark head, laid deep in the hollow of the large, French pillow, the line of the sheets and ordinary coverlets below the head, and, where the heave of the chest showed, a large crucifix. The very thick lashes lay in settled fringes on the cheek—that was the only sign of death. The girl sat quite still, as she had been left by her fellow watcher. She would have liked to remain so, by herself, all night without stirring. Thirty years after, when she was an old woman, she desired the same thing.[33]

EC *Last night of the old year.*

[. . .] We have worked with joy and lived at peace.

I still don't *love* enough; there is no fire in my heart for anyone—the red sacramental glow for my own Love excepted, and the demon fires over the Doctrine's fathomless pool in me.[34]

Works and Days, Jan.–Oct. 1895

KB *January 6th.*

The day ended with a matinee of Oscar Wilde's new play *An Ideal Husband.*[i] The best saying in it is "I always have my memory under very good control."

Brilliant comments on life by puppets, yet Oscar in this play has got down a little deeper into human nature. He exposes the folly of the[35] woman who worships her husband, but he does not make her loveable. She repels, and one's heroine must never repel. A heroine may be a great monster, like Becky Sharp,[ii] but she must attract. One feels of Lady—that she is poorly furnished

---

i Wilde published the play in 1894; it premiered at the Haymarket Theatre on January 3, 1895.

ii Rebecca "Becky" "Lady Crawley" Sharp, protagonist of William Makepeace Thackeray's 1848 novel *Vanity Fair.*

beside Mrs. Cheveley. Even women with principles may have some charms. Lady—might have been foolishly, grotesquely adoring, and yet have won our hearts; as it is we pity her husband for having married such a fool.[36]

EC *Having met a combative Berenson at an exhibition.*
He says dreadful, pitiful things in his incessant undertone—words of re-proach against M[ary]—of distaste—of separation . . . then of adoration—veering words, wrung from the strength and weakness of his manhood. And *I* have to listen! Well, it seems to me as if an iceberg had sailed into the midst of my life—as if every breath of air in me were cold—Anything might happen to me, I should not feel it—and all the time I am so laughably at home in the situation, able to note what he says and does, and to speak with befitting gravity but no deep concern.[37]

EC B. said "M[ary] has read too many wicked French novels" and "She may be thinking of me in much the same way in which she thinks of her husband"—Retribution![38]

EC *Following a visit from Logan Pearsall Smith*, who sat talking of Pater and Impressions, and finally his desire "to win us to prose." How weakening that cry is to us—it seems like a Time-quake under us!
Yet after all every age needs its own *résumé*—and needs the help of the Daughters of Memory[i]—needs the compactness and universality the poet alone can give; the greater the age and[39] the richer its prose the more it re-quires its tables of memory from the past. [. . .]
We have worked well—but after work nothing remains to be done, but to rest one's tired head and look into bitter hollows that one has dug or that have been dug round one.
On the night of January 29th, I had this dream. Michael and I were in an Italian Duomo visiting a Tomb on which was the effigy of a beautiful Youth, painted to look like life. The board-floor was shaky round the tomb but treading lightly we came close: then the effigy turned over from supine to prone, and we saw the inch-long lashes of oaten-gold lift and pale mocking eyes opened on us, while a fine, smiling tremour quickened the mouth, and I cried out "*I have seen the Renaissance!*"
The effigy[40] then came down and Michael would kiss its hands and cheeks while I shivered lest she should catch the plague. Then the figure returned to its tomb and sitting with drawn-up legs watched us go toward the door—I

---

i Mnemosyne, the goddess of memory, and her daughters, the nine Muses.

heard a strange noise like a pebble being rolled about "It's his tongue moving," I thought with indescribable fright—and sure enough these slow, stony words came from the beautiful mouth "I—can—lend—you—a—pair—of—scissors." We fled at the highest pitch of terror.

And in the morning came the cruel letter from Florence, and the severing letter was written to Bernard. Oh, if it could sever—we might grow strong, but . . . we feel that all the while fate is watching us with a subtle Renaissance smile. Every pastime is as cold and heavy as the moment before a snow-storm—we are cleft and yet clinging at the same time—we are fools.[41]

EC The days went on—at last on Sunday morning Michael's voice called me through the ceiling, she being down early for breakfast, "A letter!" I ran to assure myself of such news. Yes, he had written,—a charming, sensible note that would not let us relax our hold on his friendship. He wrote, "Now Michael, you will not for so slight an offence, if indeed offence there was, cast me off. And for offences much, a thousand more, greater, you would be silly to cast me off. I consider you, and value you as my friend, and I am not a person to let go. Besides, *there* I should remain, part of your mental furniture, only I should become a thing to stumble against, instead of a friendly thing to[42] sit on. People don't separate easily when they have got so much from each other as I have from you and you from me."

I half read the letter, and then before I knew what was come to me, I was sobbing slowly as if I should almost die of it, and yet my brain had grasped that joy was the fact beneath this despair. I have never cried for joy before—all morning I cried from time to time. Joy generally comes as a summer day after a day of tempest—not with the long reluctance of the spring after winter.[43]

EC *During a visit by Michael Field to Italy.*

We started, after a long morning with Berenson's photographs, to call on Vernon Lee,[i] accompanied by Miss Cruttwell.[ii] Such a walk!—a gray sky making the wheat of the *poderi* glow green into one's very brain. . . . We passed the stream where Boccaccio and his ladies sat in the coolness and told their tales: finally we arrived at Il Palmerino.

We saw a gaunt Sibyl, in a tailor-made black dress, vine-dresser's hat and apron, sowing seeds. It advanced—it was Vernon. She looks fifty; she is thirty-nine. She is very ugly—her mouth an earthquake of teeth in a fissure; the face very long.[44] The eyes with a look of greed for discussion, the eyes of

i Pseudonym of Violet Paget (1856–1935), English essayist, novelist, and aesthete.
ii Maude Alice Wilson Cruttwell (1859–1939), English artist and art historian, and follower of Berenson.

an intellectual Vampire. Yet there is much suffering in the expression, a sadness that one pities. The features are restless and have a sort of ghastly good breed.

The bosom-friend of Vernon, Anstruther-Thomson,[i] is a splendid example of the thoroughbred Englishwoman to whom horses and dogs are as familiar as books to us—a noble, handsome, easy woman, she too is strapping tall. The tiny house has no charm; it is crowded, awkwardly disposed, and like its mistress has no central unity of purpose.

Vernon was very stupid in what she said about Art—about Huysmans—and the metallic conversation went on while the poet sat in dual quietness. Then came the return: a huge shepherd-dog accompanied Vernon—these Italian watchdogs are the terror of the *poderi*; we say they are the form in which devils now appear. We were nearly at the top of a hill, when the dog of Vernon's great enemy sprang from a wall. Terrific noise! The dogs close under the vines: the three immense tailor-made women rush in with sticks: Vernon's ghoulish appetency for the strife, the dominant long back of Anstruther, like the leaning tower of Pisa, over the combatants and our nice Miss Cruttwell's violent promptness of visage remain with me and will forever. Diabolic[45] howls, slashes, black arms grasping tails, calls for *Acqua!*—a peasant woman with a vine hook—a coil of brute fury in the wheat . . . and we fly down the hill, down, down; shamelessly, quakingly we seek holes in the hedge. At last, on a little knoll the creators of William Rufus and Canute exchange a dialogue.

Michael (distracted): Henry, what are you afraid of?
Henry (in a calm silver voice): Oh I'm afraid of being killed.
Michael: Don't stir! I forbid you.

And there we stuck, till a voice as cool as a man's called out, "Do come on; we shall be so late for dinner." "No" says Michael, "I'll not pass those dogs till they are chained." "But they are," contemptuously adds the voice. Michael and I shake with inextinguishable laughter when we think of the fierce, tail-gripping women, all teeth and courage and pugnacity—and of the timid poets, the worshippers of Vikings, trembling lest an infuriated cur should fill his mouth with their cheeks.

I sow the flamelets of pomegranate leaves on their wild bush, ruby flamelets, and gathered the mealy white heath.[46]

---

i Clementina "Kit" Anstruther-Thomson (1857–1921), Scottish writer and art theorist; partner of and collaborator with Vernon Lee from 1888 to about 1898.

EC Lovie and I waste the night in pain and reproach. We are still tired, excited, not ourselves. I contend I shall be better when the forcible demands of this religious season are slackened. I conceive of religion as I conceive of Art—one must be a saint just as one is a poet if one is a religious at all— As yet I cannot see that the two callings in their perfection are in the least compatible. I choose to be the artist [. . .] at times of spiritual festivity or meditation.[47]

EC On Sunday night after talk about Carducci's *Satan*[i] and about Oscar, I dream that we stop at a restaurant halfway up a mountain and a woman far down the table begs to speak with us when the table d'hôte is over, for she has heard things against us. "Oh," says a woman on Michael's left "what an interesting talk that will be. I suspect it will be about your works." Michael[48] replies "I have no fear at all about my works—I know quite well they all come from Satan." At her right hand, I whisper, "For goodness' sake, don't say these things—remember the Oscar scandal."—How characteristic both remarks![49]

EC *Berenson ignoring Michael Field as they prepare to depart his villa.*
    Such absolute lack of response nearly kills us—we wonder if we have voices at all, or whether we are only mad and dream we can be heard. At Asolo,[ii] perhaps this ghastliness will be dispersed—there, we can talk to those who still believe in us and are affectionate to the thoughts of our hearts.
    My own Love is so unnatural with this void treatment she said she would like to kill herself—she! and then she cried, and always her eyes are *ternes*.[50]

EC In all this it is marvelous to find how Bernard and I have been thinking on the same lines, only I have had most interest in the creation of the work of Art and he in its effect on the lover of Art. My definition of beauty was— *that in the (objective) world that attracts emotion.*
    And my definition of the work of Art was—*the reissue of an emotion of beauty into the objective world as an object.*
    Really, we are made fearfully alike, that we should have been thinking the same thoughts[51] like this all winter without a word on the subject having passed between us.[52]

---

i Giosuè Carducci (1835–1907), Italian poet and 1906 Nobel Prize winner for his contributions to poetry. His *Hymn to Satan* was published in 1865.
ii The hilltop town in Northern Italy, onetime home of Robert Browning.

EC Bernard wants the few, the cultured, in his world, and strives to bring a few more into that company that his world may be more to his mind. He is not a poet, or he would not be contented with so few. . . . We want our work to give cosmic emotion to a very world of listener—poor poets with their maimed selves!

It is so strange a thing in psychology if two likes meet, one must neutralize the other—B. simply effaces me from existence; I cannot be myself; the words come from me like Dryads cursed out of their trees, when they come at all. I sit in silence, registering my agreement with all he says by changes of expression in eyes or smile—and I feel like a phantom and so blessedly clumsy I could rate myself!53 [. . .]

Miss Cruttwell objects to the word "sexual" in Bernard's definition of Beauty as "the sexually desirable." Then a great discussion takes place—or rather an immense duologue—between the unwomanly woman, who puts intellect above emotion and suffers shame from sex, and the little God who founds the whole world he experiences on sexual passion.54 [. . .]

"And intellect—what, pray, is that?"

"Intellect is merely a misappropriation of the funds saved in the sexual bank." Then he goes on to show that intellect is the product of natural selection; the power developed by the strongest in their struggle for life—the instrument of their sexual aggressiveness—sexual power stored, and finally devitalised by being used no longer for its direct purpose.

(I had discovered this for myself—"Intellect, I wrote, can never create; Emotion [in its three forms *instinctive*—sex love: *conscious*, volitional excitement—and *instinctive-conscious*—Art-production] is the only creative force in the Universe.")

The one primal fact of psychology is Sex . . . self-preservation is secondary and dependent on one's need of expansion and self-expression. We eat for the sake of the creative instinct in us. "It is impossible I should withdraw 'sexual' as the core of my definition of beauty."55

EC It is wonderful how [Berenson] enjoys Sex ideally (he has told Mary that he is himself absolutely virgin) and how one can enjoy it56 with him in the same way and by the same spirit.

EC reports on Michael's view, shared by Berenson.

The best children are those conceived in hot passion . . . illegitimate often and often becoming artists and men of genius. This idea of seeking the healthy mate is not a civilised One. Man has developed his power of sex from a periodic restriction to an always present influence; and this passionless, intellectual search for the healthy mate would be restrictive to sex-power and depress its efficacy.

Imagine the lovers in Browning visualising a healthy child as the end for which they live! If we bother Nature at her work of natural selection we injure her work that in her[57] infinite benignity she does for us—leaving us free to love.[58]

EC On Friday night a question arose as to whether jealousy could be the subject of a great work of art. B. denied it was sufficiently primary and elemental, and contended that Othello's love and the corruption of his noble nature and not jealousy is the real subject. But B. did not say what he should have said—that Jealousy is not a life-giving emotion—only a defect of sexual life—and therefore not a genuine poetic subject.[59]

EC *Tuesday, May 8th.*

Browning's birthday . . . and we spend it at Fiesole,[i] not at Asolo. Well, he was the only other man to whom my eyes gave a whole passion. I made him lord of heaven and earth when he was alive, and I love him in no other way there and here.[60]

KB At lunch talk of man's presumption in thinking all beauty is made for him to look at. Whereas man is no more than a single Stilton cheese in a row of Stilton cheeses.[61]

EC Custom "cruel as frost and deep almost as life"[ii] has shut the lips of most women—but Sappho has sung her sensations, and Christina Rossetti her suffering, and quiet Miss Elliot, in *The Flowers of the Forest*, has sung in the boldest voice though few have ears to hear—woman's eternal sex-need of man. Emily Brontë has shown the sheer elemental force of passion in a woman can equal a man's.[iii] Why what would those ballads be if one took from them the story of woman's unsurpassed love?[62]

i The town near Florence where Berenson eventually established Villa I Tatti as home to his coterie and collections; in other words, Michael Field spent Browning's birthday in a space associated with Berenson, not Browning.

ii See Wordsworth's "Ode: Intimations of Immortality from Recollections of Early Childhood" (1804): "Full soon thy Soul shall have her earthly freight / And custom lie upon thee with a weight / Heavy as frost, and deep almost as life."

iii Christina Rossetti (1830–94), English poet. Jean or Jane Elliot (1727–95) reworked the Scottish folk song "The Flowers of the Forest" in 1758. Emily Brontë (1818–48), English novelist and poet.

EC Intellect is not only the stale deposit of Sex; I mean—the impotent result of Sex, but it may also be called one of the most important officers in Death's police force.

For the true function of Death is to regulate Life from the outside—Death is the great Regulator. It prevents life from growing rank, enfeebled; it presses it back within forms that tighten themselves and become efficient. Intellect, being totally unproductive and therefore not a life-force, is a regulative one, and by Science and by morals it guards Emotion and Sense against themselves. All Society is bound by the cold claims of death, at present is held in form by them—they are the "necessary restraints" we hear so much of. But the aim of Culture and Religion is to minimise more and more the regulation of life by death . . . to make life self-regulating and true to itself.[63]

Works and Days, Oct.–Dec. 1895

EC Mary writes that he and she have made a fresh start—all differences at an end; and that they sit together and think domestic thoughts of the future . . . Whew! "The Doctrine is ever celibate" he said in Paris. If he became *domestic*, I do think this flaming habit of loving him would be broken forever . . . what no crime of his could do—his domesticity would do, I shudderingly believe. Imagine Bacchus with the poker of the hearth in his hand instead of the thyrsus. Curse the thought—curse it bitterly![64]

EC *Celebrating Michael's birthday.* Then in family style we play *Jacobi*[i] as long as it can command our interest, and then Mick and I read old Year Books: we listen to a story that is told, and listen smiling at the story's truth.[65]

EC I feel we are moving further and further away from him; and now when my restless mental sight looks and looks, as it does eternally, I find it fixed on the image of Pylades—my beloved Pantomime, in *The World at Auction*—not as it has been for years on Bernard's eyes and lips—the Dancer slips in front of the Beloved. I know I am created to respond to Bernard's fascination as a sensitive-plate to light—only now there is no light, and I am mercifully blank. *Wednesday, November 20.*

Yesterday the repulse of our friendship—today the outrage of the world. I open the *Daily Chronicle* at breakfast and find an article "The New Woman—and the Old" (obviously by R. Le G.) ^No—he did not write it^ that states of *Attila* that it is "an excursus against chastity, obviously written by the most

---

i A parlor game related to bridge.

harmless and well-behaved of ladies"—etc., etc., through a column of willful misunderstanding, insult, and ignorance. Of course, Father has to see it. . . . We fly to town as soon as possible—try to get places for *Trilby*[i] in vain[.] . . . We go down to our desks—but under the Reading-room air I decompose, and my courage becomes as deaf-mould, and Lucian's sallies of the *joie de vivre* sting me stupidly and make me feel apprehensive, and the silence creeps up my back and explodes in my head.[66]

After an unsatisfying lunch at their club, they return to Reigate to find Father reading "Attila." He hands them a brief review in the "Scotsman"; it demon-strates understanding of the effort and offers praise.[67]

EC I carry it to Michael—"This has saved me. It has established my sanity. I know I am not mad now." Then we each confess that all day we have been in a horror of[68] dread that we really were going insane, dwelling on danger-ous subjects and writing what we did not mean from lack of balance. It is awful to dread that one is nebulous—awful to realise that anyone putting a straitjacket on one would not seem out of place. No voice had reached us—except the desperate voice of Elkin, the insulting voice of Fleming, the muf-fled voices of Mary and Bernard, the outraging voice of R. le G. ^*The Chron-icle*^ not a word of greeting, of intelligence . . . it seemed as if we must be mad to think we should have such a word. [. . .]

So three Scottish voices speak into the silence, rend the solitude—that is enough: my gratitude rises like a wave twenty feet high . . . it might submerge these good Scots if it broke over them. I don't expect one word of comprehen-sion from London.[69]

KB Deliberately I said to Henry the other day—"Henry let us go together into a dreamland, and there be shut up."

There is a world of noble spirits and enchanted nature, a world where we may listen all day long, or speaking feel the quiet in the air that comes when there are many listeners. And in this world of dreamland who is there one may not meet. Surely if there be any world the dead haunt for holiday—for doubtless the dead have their great and practical affairs, faring on, fighting upward—it is this.[70]

EC Curious how close the resemblance between Imperial Rome and London of Today—not in customs, but in tendencies due to laxity—wealth—degen-eration! It is a mirror—a review of our times.[71]

---

i The 1895 play by Paul M. Potter, adapted from George du Maurier's 1894 novel.

EC Now we are reading *An Amazing Marriage.*[i] *Jude the Obscure* (Obscene) I could not read. Offal was thrown in my face—thrown powerfully so that it could not help but hit. I turned away forever from the thrower.

Hardy[ii] appears to me to be in Hell, not on Earth. He has no pulse for life—he blasphemes what he has never experienced. I felt this when I met him; he seems less than an echinus, alive in the limitless sea—he was echinite—the mere petrifaction.[iii]

Sex with him is the fidget of necessary antagonism in a world that had better have been sterile. The "still, sad music of humanity" played under the law roof of his pessimism becomes disgraceful noise.

All the functions and deeds that should be unconscious are self-exploring and abominable.

He is the scribe of the Tragedy of Science—neither an Artist of Apollo nor of Dionysus.[72]

KB *November 29th, Friday.*

This month has been a month of red-hot iron. This morning—Meredith's letter, in answer to my pleading he should break silence—He has little to praise the characters or line of *Attila.* . . . "Perhaps," he says, "You meant the reflecting of their light on the sex mania current. That would be satire: quite enough to kill your poetry. Will you come and hear more." *We hope to go on Monday.*[73]

EC I simply do not write of what has happened—It is an abyss into which it is futile to throw such stony pellets as words . . .

I feel as if with one hand I was lifting a free-throated trumpet to my breath, and with the other graving my funeral inscription across the block on my knees.

My womanhood is dying—the poet in me waxes to archangelic—I mean the poet who is the figure of my hopes.

Outer life is a rose from which the amber, keen centre has been nipped— the zest of the intricacy is gone.[74]

EC *Departing Meredith's home.*

One goes away chill—one's being unexercised—the conversation one has heard is like marvellous conjuring; one's mind is in a dazzle—but one's

---

i George Meredith's final novel, published in 1895.

ii Thomas Hardy (1840–1928), English novelist and poet known for his provocative themes and sharp social critique. *Jude the Obscure* was his final novel, published in 1895.

iii An "echinus" is a sea urchin; an "echinite" its fossilized form.

nature has not received virtue nor been eased of the pressing of its own virtue.

In Browning an overplus of Intellect was vitalised by the heart.

In Meredith the living Heart rarely kindles the overplus of Intellect.

He sits by one a Stranger—almost belonging to another planet, where the laws of life are reversed—and the head generates.[75]

His great women, so completely of this Earth, come from creative depths where *The Mothers* hide in caves—inaccessible to Welsh wrongheadedness, and Celtic antipathies, modern self-consciousness and sententious sterility.

Michael speaks to him of our delight in his *ladies*, "women untainted by religion and untainted by lust." His face gives thanks for the appreciation.[76]

EC Town is harass and a visit to Amy Bell in the city—my brain fights against the noise till it is bruised. . . . I return sick and vibrating with headache.

A notice in *The Times*: "The writer who calls herself Michael Field has already established a claim that what she writes should be read"—then follows the story sympathetically told . . . and that is all.[77]

EC *The last night of the old year.* [. . .]

Well, to the year! We have done *Honoria*—or *Attila*, rather; we have done *Carloman* (laus deo!)—we are well on in doing[78] *The World at Auction*—the two last, I believe, will be masterpieces.

The Croquis are not going to be published—Bernard nearly slew any care I had for them—not as *For That Moment Only* . . . perchance in magazines from time to time. We have been to Florence and proved that I can never be Bernard's friend . . . but only become more and more the victim of his fascination, his cruelty and meanness. I have touched moments with him that made the universe gold—I have gone through woe that put me to death for weeks. Let me set it down: *I love him* inexorably, by fate—as I give him up *by choice*. In him all that fascinates me in myself parts me in another, who has the sort of beauty my face seeks after. It is a kind of self-joy, a kind of recognition of the dearness of one's identity—that is such a terrible attraction in Bernard: that, and his likeness to Dionysus—the vine in his features. His dishonesty about Nietzsche has been the moral shock of this year[i]—the trial and condemnation of Oscar has been the horror—a spectre thing through all the seasons.[79]

---

i Cooper refers to her discovery that Berenson had presented Nietzsche's thoughts as his own.

Works and Days, 1896

EC On Saturday we hear that Paul Verlaine[i] is dead—poor Silenus of the Damned turning sometimes into St. Francis of Hell. I shall[80] never forget how his eyes licked us like an adder's twofold tongue as he read us his fervent pieties in Bonnard's Inn. Grasses, raindrops, little sounds, infinitely delicate tendernesses of Earth were revealed to him in the midst of lust; abasement and adoration and the child's love in the midst of superstition. They say his last hour was terrible—after all it was the flesh that adored and loved and bowed before god-nature spirit that is *life* and peace.[81]

EC *February 9, 1896.*
    A day in town—first at Henson's, looking at stones . . . How I worship the soft, mobile rays of a star-ruby . . . a thing marked by nature as a talisman. Also, an Alexandrite, worth £120, green, to the eyes, but under lamplight glowing red as if it were [a] grave that gave up the secret of an old murder that had steeped in. Next, to our silversmith's in Vigo St. where we see some more of the old Berlin ironwork.[ii] I like wearing it, because it is the best of its kind, the last marvel iron can attain to. Gems must be perfect to give me joy and I shall never have a perfect gem . . . so let me have perfect iron . . . This is a great principle of taste.[82]

EC *February 10.*
    Every day we are feeling more and more how savourless the days are without Bernard. . . . We *make ourselves live*—we don't live, except in our work. We are *in relation* with absolutely no one. We even have to set to our pleasures as with a windlass. Breath itself appears the result of mechanization— not the gift of God. Yet we do not regret, and we feel we are worth much more than two years ago . . . So we bear the hateful pain of growth and nearly die of it.
    His face is struck on my eyes continually—often when the bird twangs of the garden strike my ear . . . and I meet him in many galleries after many years, and confess that he is love to me, and yet, though I imagine every impediment gone, we can never be one another's.[83]

---

    i Paul Verlaine (1844–96), French poet, major figure in the symbolist and decadent movements in literature.
    ii A style of cast-iron jewelry popular in Germany in the early nineteenth century. Vigo Street in central London held many literary associations for Michael Field; it was the site of the business of publishers John Lane and Elkin Mathews, later the Bodley Head, which later launched Penguin Books.

EC We live without the Word—speech that gives life to time—we only talk nonsense to one old man of seventy-seven—a kind father, but always unendowed with personal and interesting conversation.

We live as we do not want to live in every way, not able to shape our meals to our desires, nor our household existence to the bent of our temperaments. We live without pleasures that come unsought—*but*

We live with solitude like that out of which the Earth was created—

We live creating and rejoicing more and more in the creations of great men—we have books, and in the summer, roses, some great memories that are actualities . . . Mother, Robert Browning—Paris, Italy—and Life is making us Worshippers. Not time yet for the eternal repose of Morpheus!!—and a Future may draw our eyes to itself someday.[84]

EC *Monday 24th.*

A choice lunch with the Artists at Chelsea. The beautiful even numbers—two poets and two artists—give something Pythagorean to our intercourse.[85] [. . .] Ricketts breaks in white foam of conversation, incessant subversive of every word that resists—brilliant, yet somehow slipping off memory.

We are assailed to grant the new publishers a reprint of *Fair Rosamund*, scattered over with roses. We must stand to our old works if we are to stand: we have many "very bitter enemies" and to face them with our whole career is the strongest policy. We ask—why have we so many enemies? We make out that the nom de plume was a cause of enmity, the way it was kept, the way it became known, the way it was unacknowledged and acknowledged. "One lady in literature is unmanageable enough—but two!!"[86]

EC We much enjoy the artists—their simple ways, their love of art in all the arts, single-eyed and flaming. We do not quite understand them; one knew nothing of them. They are the friends of Oscar, of Whistler, of Rothenstein[i]— and they seem fated to befriend our work, and to be associated with us. We are lightly apprehensive; but we cannot reject the only offer of kind feeling we have met with for years.[87]

EC *Good Friday, April 3rd.*

In bed Love and I talk of the five past years. . . . We have been suffering wearily of late from the dullness of life without Bernard and Mary . . . we have lost our palates for living and the misunderstanding with the Artists has weighed on us, because, from them we drew a little gust—

i Sir William Rothenstein (1872–1945), English painter and art writer.

About a week ago Bernard returned my volumes of Hegel's *Aesthetics* without even an inscription of thanks—I knew what it meant—I had not written about *Florentine Painters*,[i] and this return of my Hegel was to mark finality—It was a blow given to one who is unconscious—I did not feel it—it was nothing . . . pain had gone too far before it fell. But Michael somehow took it differently . . . the old days roused in her held awake and made *now* ghastly.[88]

EC My love starts for town . . . I go to this our book for companionship . . . the breath of the day, what makes it a day, goes with her.

A red silk bodice sewn with garnet and aquamarine beads comes for me from town in the grim mist of the morning.[89]

EC *Visit from Cousin Francis.*

[O]ver coffee, F[rancis], M[ichael], and I chatted of everything literary and classic. . . . He told us of the delicious saying of Henry James,[ii] describing Meredith and Hardy by the choice of words in the titles of their last books, turned vice versa—"Meredith the Obscure, and the Amazing Hardy."[90]

EC *Friday, April 10.*

Great things done in town—we have revolted from our dreary lamp and live determined to have incandescent light . . . so, to Hart and Peard's to get a suspended lamp.[iii] At last we attain a lovely design, which we arrange to be carried out in blue native iron. Then we buy sunshades of tropical iridescence—like plumage of strange birds half cloud and half the spectrum—then a fair thing of a toque for Michael, and a flax-blue sailor hat with black velvet and quills for me.[91]

KB *Loss of Despatch Bag.*[iv]

All the birds of heaven left their roosts because of this loss. Our souls are dyed black and blue and our hair is blanched with the agony! Let me tell the tale.

---

i Hegel's *Lectures on Aesthetics* were originally published in 1835. Cooper speculates that Berenson was miffed by her failure to write to him about his *Florentine Painters of the Renaissance*, published in 1896.

ii Henry James (1843–1916), British American novelist and essayist.

iii Hart, Son, Peard and Co. was a firm of architectural metalworkers in Central London until 1913. By "suspended lamp," Cooper probably means an electrolier, a multibulb electric light suspended from the ceiling. This style of lamp was associated with the Arts and Crafts movement.

iv Akin to a messenger bag.

We leave Lostwithiel[i] in a cruel wind—A lady suffers from train sickness. We have between gusts of wind and . . . other gusts!!! Henry appears sullen and apart. Our fellow-passenger falls into deeper and ever deeper humiliation; and the blasts from the north become more keen.

Taunton: *ausgang*.[ii] The despatch bag is laid on the refreshment-room bed. [. . .] I begin humming devilishly over a bath bun when lo—our packages are counted—the despatch bag is gone.

Telegrams at High Bridge we await reply. Henry is scared livid—beaten, guilty, hell-doomed face is what I cannot bear: so, the Heavenly Ones remove that burden quite away from my soul.—I have that dazed Bag to comfort; not a stone of my own spirit is stirred. I pace up and down the High Bridge platform in the blast—finally "the beautiful feet" of the Station-Master publish peace. *It is found.*

I patter and cackle my approach, announcing safety with a smile through the window, and bidding Henry be thankful for the big tears the crystal sluices well undammed—I begin to move our things and bodies to the Glastonbury platform.[92]

EC *June 1st.*

Amy and father start for Italy . . . A noble adventure for an old man in his seventy-ninth year. He wants to see the "land of lands" before he leaves the land of the living—most touching romance of a truly romantic nature.

As Michael says with father in Italy and the incandescent light in the study we[93] are not backward in *modernism*![94]

EC I am reading mad Nietzsche[iii] in translation. How he whisks up the obvious into suggestiveness, colouring it with rainbow-hues or sulphur according as he is poet or atheist! He stimulates as no logician or exact thinker could— his logic is of passion—his thought a grasp after neglected truth in a sort of dance of personal idiosyncrasy—astonishing.[95]

EC My Love and I are further on in our love, getting nearer to the flame-wax core where the Divine ripens is the fragrance and future—every year we are deeper in love, more tenderly attuned. Fate has given me much of the Trilogy to do apart—but I look on to *Anthony Derivian*[iv] for a fated union of all we each are as poets—we can quarrel with hate in this her one harshness.

i A small town in Cornwall.

ii "Exit."

iii Friedrich Nietzsche (1844–1900), German philosopher, critic, poet, and novelist.

iv Michael Field planned a play titled *Anthony Derivian, or, The Abbott of Glastonbury* in 1896. The whereabouts of the manuscript, if one existed, are unknown.

We have had no publishing—no violation of life itself to bear—what mercy!

Of course, in such a household as ours, we have had fret and anxiety on us enough[96]—to spare—but we are above our cares even as St. Michael above the scales of the Dragon.

We have had strength accorded to us in greater measure—more cheerfulness, fuller life in the midst of discord or weariness.

We have not gained a friend—it is hard to keep up sympathy with the named people we come in contact with. 'Tis pity![97]

Works and Days, 1897

EC *Leaves and flowers.*

Gathered at the Knoll where [Father] was so happy and where he sang the day before he died—Wednesday, June 23rd.

Three smaller flowers.

Gathered by Smutt when we exchanged our rings.[98]

EC *1897. New Year's Day.*

All night the drain men were emptying the cesspool next door to the clang of the old bells—we by our bedroom fire heard both the wholesome sounds in a dream. At the very turn of old year into new we embraced with the simple wish "A happy new year"—I like all these forms in their purity.

The morning is hot and wet, but we don't care—Best to begin obscured, drear even, than too bright.

We meet dividends, bills—an Apollyan fight with addition and subtraction and past extravagance.

At Redhill we have a gay tea with Delia and Lygel, who have been won by blue china and blue Xmas cards. We tell them to make good resolutions on the last night of the old year to the voice of the bells, but to break all the next day if they would prosper.

However, we go back to face my condemned allowance, and Michael proposes extreme pain as a heaven-sent punishment—that the £5 to be paid down for *Rosamund*, and dedicated already to buying her my marriage ring, should be devoted to the settlement of my financial woe!—and yet there is a cleanness in paying every bill, and we grieve in a kind of bliss.[99]

KB *Liphook.*

I begin my first entry into our Year Book in the tiny morning room of Hartford Cottage, Hants. We have fled from Reigate, as from a land of abortions, drains and damp. And it is good in this still country, though we wake the mournful hedgerow, and long sheep rack, and the tree that has no sense of style, but grows dowdily for the cow. We are content. [. . .]

I feel as a bulb below in the manure, bulb-stuff, no feel or push of the flower in me as yet; but distinct consciousness. I am bulb-stuff, *not manure*.[100]

KB What games we have by our bedroom fire at night! We lie in our bed, read proofs and poems, and stick roses in our ears.[101]

EC *March 23rd.*

With Meinhold's *Sidonia*[i] to return as ostensible reason and the fate of *Rosamund* as real reason, we call at the *Dial*.[ii]

Holmes, the clerk, receives us and puts into our hand a copy. . . . It is partly green as the summer peascod, with the creamy rose trellis, the roses crowned with briar-thorns and under them fat doves transfixed with arrows as thoroughly as St. Sebastian. The half binding is of mist-like blue, flecked with leaves and shapes in brownish purple—the most restless effect ever produced by a volume. The green is sharp, the design complex—the whole binding seems the result of the first spasm of spring, that is to release Oscar, on the imagination of Ricketts.

But the doves!—sentimental, revolting—for what is sentimentality but the impureness of purity and therefore the unlimited loathsome—we suffer inexpressibly. The relation of cover and book does not exist; there is nothing of our beloved Rosamund in His Valentine symbol, so obvious, so unlovely. The Clerk demonstrates the tragedy involved in the plumpness of these birds, that he may be quite full of the corn thrown to their kind before the[102] Houses of Parliament—it is the fair large roundness like that of the Judge in *As You Like It* that makes the pity of these smitten bodies. Fancy shooting a lean dove! [. . .]

I have to drink an immediate soda and brandy at the Club to lift me from the languor of collapse.

Two arts cannot marry on equal terms—one art must live in polygamy with the others, if there is to be any combination. Wagner discovered that the musician amorously used poetry, drama, painting, as lord of a harem. We are suffering from the equality of marriage between our drama and Ricketts' designing. Fools![103]

---

i Johannes Wilhelm Meinhold (1797–1851), Pomeranian priest and novelist; his Gothic novel *Sidonia the Sorceress* was published in 1849.

ii An art magazine founded by Charles Ricketts and published between 1889 and 1897.

EC Michael's words (nearly two months after).

We are in God's providence, close under his shadowing Hand. We cannot see His Face . . . the sweet, old father is gone, whither we know not, save that underneath that shadowing hand we know that all is well. A rose morning in June—a telegram came to me, brought in, through Amy's tenderness to her sister by a Quaker friend, a neighbor—"Am afraid Father has met with 'an accident.'" I went up the stairs—I heard the voice of my darling—"Master!" in cooing, gayest call, and I had to break the news. We were both at our work—at the words "Tombs, tombs, tombs" when the shadow fell. Then for more than a week we lived in the muffled rose-dark of Durdans, breaking now[104] and then from the hot blackness of the little shrouded house to the garden, where was Eden in white and red.

We were only spoken to these days by telegrams and the one true Quaker friend. First, we heard of a reward offered, then of Italian navvies[i] . . . at the thought of murder, well, there were a few moments then when I felt as if the walls of reason would give way before the pressure of my passion—but all that while I could not move.

Mechanically I sent word we were ready to start . . . but I knew well I should break down on the way. Last of all came a word from my little precious Amy, saying the Valais Government,[ii] whom may Heaven requite, were trying to force her to say she had given up the possibility of crime.

At that word, and also because I found Zermatt was going to be abandoned as if there were nothing further to do, I arose, and Henry and I in a dream travelled on past the rushing Rhône and past the wild singing Viège, down in the eddies of which we believe that sweet, gray white head was hidden—we went and met and our beloved little Amy stole back at her prayers into the little English house while Henry and I went on the *Craies*,[iii] following every conceivable Route, questioning the railway authorities, questioning the mule man—only at the end to feel this death is in God's keeping.

Our Sophocles taught us patience. Thank God for literature, the literature of the dark days with its long reaches far into the world to come.[105]

KB Henry writes to Amy—

—I am sure of the end. Darling, in the white dawn when I asked our blessed Mother to help us as she has through so many tragedies, my soul saw her clearly and the wings of her spirit were no more folded over us to cover us

i That is, laborers.
ii The government of Valais, one of the cantons of Switzerland.
iii The "Chalks": the White Cliffs of Dover, en route to Europe from England.

from cares, but pointed erect, so that my sight went up to them, as if they were sunbeams. I felt somehow that she had a new treasure with her, all the humble love, the years of devotion of her bridegroom, living at her side. [...]

For us the tragic loss of so sweet an old father is awful beyond words, almost beyond feeling as yet, except in tears that rain on.

It is so impossible to realise here in the home round which he has turned his whole life in love for us, thought for our future, toil for our pleasure, that he will never see the plant we have set in the beds for his eyes, the melons reared for him, the noble roses he gave us. With all his faults of mood, his tenderness, affection, simplicity, sweet paternity, chivalry, poetic temperament and beautifully gained ripeness, his trust in God and his loved ones, made him indeed dear and irreplaceably precious.

EC It is much to us to think of the dark years spared him—of his glorious translation into the Kingdom of truth and light.[106]

EC *Monday.*

At last I feel I must write of him—my sweet old father, so much myself. He may have been murdered (might they be flogged and hanged who would dare do such an infamy!) or he may have fallen over a rock, straying from the path, or he may have gone of his own will, in mystery and peace to his Beloved, called to her from among the snowy mountains she adored in her maiden days: he is gone, leaving us the little home he put his heart into for us, the fiery roses, his gift, his plastic wood-carving, and the memory of his own personality—a great one, of gripping virtue, lonely, proud, violent, affectionate, tender, jealous, quaint, simple as a child's, hearty and yet dark as night when the evil spirit from God came upon him, with something of an early blush in his few moods of joy—despondent, complaining, piteous, excitable, reverent, loyal—his impress is on everything by the hearth and in the home, on everything he touched, on the hearts of the few he loved.

With such a nature, it was impossible for others to weave him into life— the attempt was doomed to failure. One could but twist one's own threads with his and remain unwoven into general existence. Round Michael whom he loved with passion,[107] round me whom he loved with devotion, round Mother whom he loved with veneration, he simply created a wilderness. There must be *his* love and a desert.

He nearly killed me with nervous fear and anxiety, I dreaded the least conflict between him and Michael as the end of my home life with him, I dreaded some violent scene, I had a sense of doom growing with the years; no man could be received by us with comfort or dignity, every friendship was blighted as it rose to growing vigorous by his hatred—yet I loved him and love him—we love him, Michael and I, we twain—with an overwhelming force. He created a desert round us and built an altar in our hearts. [. . .] Sometimes the pain and fear he brought me almost made me long, out of a life-impulse, for his death—but now fear is cast out; my love for him is perfect. He was to me as Oedipus to Antigone—only Sophocles can express our bond and my mourning.[i]108

KB *Saturday.*

Henry makes his will: we pack—finally we take a carriage to the bank and deposit the strong-box and our dear Manuscripts with the Bank Manager. We turn to our Rose-Garden, and kiss and breathe, and ask for the unopened lilies: then we start.[109]

EC In sad twilight, the train, and the *wagon-lit*[ii]—

The little padded den makes us laugh—living, humourous laughter. We ask for our bed to be made up and one bed springs aloft while the other remains. We stifle outside at the very look . . . we enter and the door shuts. Ha! Beds in all the space, rugs to our knees—the window, it has a modern scientific spring . . . cannot be opened by the[110] human being! The door! It has a modern scientific spring—cannot be opened! The mere human being must come to an end and beats in death-struggles against the door. At last rescue arrives; the bed above is wound down to the bed below, the ^mere human being is^ hand trained to the springs, and we sleep . . . we can get no coffee . . . and this is civilisation, the roof and crown of it![111]

EC We walk up to Mont Rose—the Zermatters look to me most repulsive—the spawn of vile conditions of life: they might all be assassins.[112]

Speculating about where he might have fallen.

No, the Bridge is impossible. . . . Yet we go back to the hotel to hear from the agent of the Secret Police that if Mr. Cooper could come back, he would say, "That was where I perished."

After such an assertion from the spectre called up by the Swiss authorities, we hear the voice of our own father say, "Rather than believe this, believe I was murdered." [. . .]

I say goodnight to the Matterhorn and its one star. We sleep at least in the same land where *he* sleeps forever—that is much to us—and we are there to serve him, to do the work of sons in his honour.[113]

---

i Sophocles was the Greek tragedian whose Theban plays featured Oedipus and Antigone, father and daughter. Antigone was born from Oedipus's unwittingly incestuous union with his mother Jocasta. Oedipus died in exile.

ii That is, sleeping car.

EC We have had a terrible night: we are too much out of joint to be able to climb up to the Schwartz-See. Michael sobs and cannot eat and wildly straightens our room—there is the estrangement of grief between us, for grief can be a very Até[i] [. . .] [W]e go up to the knoll where *he* was happy the morning of that last Wednesday and sang to himself—there we read of Ædipus and his mysterious call in the foreign land to his death. The death of our beloved was Sophoclean. We wander where he picked his spray of Alpine Rose, we lie on the damp, sweet-smelling hay.[114] [. . .]

    EC We confess on our return how we have been hoping for a dream to clear the mystery—we do not want to know *his* grave, it might take away the blessing from this land—we should like that sacred as the grave of Ædipus—but if we might know the spot he last trod before carried off into the secret shades we should be at rest. [. . .]

    Here we find precipices sheer over the gnarling stream, a bridge that is treachery itself. Deep spiritual conviction deeper than the witness of a dream, comes to us both—*this is the spot*. We shudder as we see—we feel for a moment the hideousness of[115] that dread form . . . who has its lair in these Gates of many guests—that Hound-aspect of Death, the untameable horror at its portals. . . . the rocks are so fierce, the stream so steep in its velocity. But all change, if sudden, must be a wrench—and our beloved could but have known a second's cruelty.[116]

    Later, Michael Field will learn that this was not the location of James Cooper's death.

EC *Wednesday.*

    Brave, assured sunlight. While I write to the Consul, Michael goes out and sees a ring of warm, broad gold in the depths of which a sapphire grows blue of darkness like a mountain lake. The ring is almost a wedding ring, yet something beyond. Here is the *cadeau*, the chain of love that will bind us together in spite of fire and scissors. I go to see it, and then my Love insists I shall try some rings. They say nothing on my finger till at last a brilliant guarded by two pearls takes possession. He costs £10 . . . it is paid, and the glorious chain of love and beauty is mine to bind me to my Love. But we do not give the rings to each other—that must be done by the Matterhorn Bridge. We are quite gay and eat little Madeleine-cakes.[117]

    [. . .] When at last we are near Matterhorn Bridge, we dismiss Franz, and go to our mead by the torrent where we read the Burial Service for him, but not to that spot. We sit down, our feet buried in sweet willow herb and there plight the troth of our fresh life together—a life that springs from the deep

---

i Até was the Greek goddess personifying folly and its consequence, suffering.

tragedy we have shared from its brim to its hollow—we who love him, whom
he loved with such peculiar passion—loving me that I loved Michael as he
would have loved her. [. . .] Then I pluck[118] the willow herb in its branch, we
wash our rings in the Zmutt and suddenly Michael, filling her hand, drinks
to him. That I cannot do—I feel it is the lover's right. We walk home in unity
of spirit.[119]

EC *Friday.*

Brightly burnished last day! The turmoil of having to leave Zermatt has
surged through the night and sleep has made us laugh like demons with
hysteria. In the dark, Michael gets out of bed and strikes a Lucifer on its
box[i]—there is a flare . . . Michael holds the fiery box out, sawing the air with
it, but so vague in mind that a long pause ensues before she said magisteri-
ally—a slow and heavy emphasis on the word!—*Water!*[120]

EC *Back in Durdans a month later, August 23rd.*

A "dust to dust" day—all the world falling, it seems, to pieces from very
grayness and futility . . . yet my basset hound comes to me in a big box, and
we run him about the garden till we could weep with exhaustion. But what
curtain-ears he has—folded and tan: His body is white with a great black
spot on each flank—a white river runs between his eyes to the end of his nose.
He is a most dignified, sentimental beast: we quote at him

> Sir Launcelot mused a little space,
> He said "she has a lovely face"
> God in his mercy grant her grace
>   The Lady of Shalott[ii]

Basset is a still dog and though only five months old has scarcely a trace of
puppyhood. Yet we have not had a tranquil meal since he came, and the night
is a space of dread to our forethought.[121]

KB *October 26.*

A body, supposed to be Mr. Cooper—discovered in a pathless wood three
hours from Zermatt.[122]

Two clippings from the Daily Mail:

"The body was found by two wood-cutters at a spot about an hour's walk
to the east of Zermatt.—his right arm under his face. His clothes were still in

---

i That is, a match or "friction light."

ii From "The Lady of Shalott," published by Alfred, Lord Tennyson first in 1832. Cooper
quotes from the revised version Tennyson published in 1842.

Zermatt.

Oct 26th.

Directly after lunch - the telegram

A body, supposed to be Mr. Cooper dis-
-covered in a pathless wood three
hours from Zermatt...

Press agency.

2nd Telegram.

Message says body man believed from
description Mr. Cooper found in pathless,
mountain forest three hours from
Zermatt outside track of tourists

to go

Where the years are long, the long long years.

a good state of preservation, his jewels being all intact. His hat was discovered a few paces from him and his stick fixed in the rock."[123]

KB *Large mourning card, KB hand.*

To the beloved, abiding memory of James Robert Cooper,
of Durdans, Reigate, Surrey;
(aged 79)
who was lost on Midsummer Day, 1897,
and found in the Wittiwald on October 25th of the same
year, beneath the shadow of a rock, as if sleeping.
"The Lord Himself is thy Keeper."[124]

EC The coffin has not been closed till, at our arrival, the Vice-consul can identify clothes etc., by our description—the loved features are gone—so the Mother's letters, her portrait, the Dresden portrait of Michael and me, Amy's little hooded portrait—when she was his "little Pickie"; an Iona ring from Michael, and the birthday flowers, with a few roses from his garden are put in by M. Seiler.

There Hennie and Michael identify the objects found, the carbuncle, studs, watch cord, case, etc., then we go the graveyard to choose the spot in twilight. We select a place under a yew-tree on the side of the brave mountain. [...]

A Hamlet gravedigger[i] hobbles forward on the darkened stage of this mountain cemetery.... it is weird—the white sun is still on the very hilltops above the slope on which *our beloved* was lost. After dinner, I go to the Mortuary Chapel where he lies under the figures of Madonna, a military and a bishop saint—I go there to bless all he has been to me, to be near him[125] at last, the Old Pop he longed for, in a foreign land.

October 30th, The Day of his burial.

[...] We pace with that dazed shuddering sense of necessity that takes one through a funeral. The summons is brought, and we descend into the cold street where the poor coffin (the best that could be got) stands covered over with its hardy mountain garlands. As we walk through the village the cross of Alpine-rose leaves is carried before us. The people are respectful but unsympathetic.[126]

EC *At the burial:*

The people stand and gaze ... foreign, foreign!! The ropes that cling to the coffin as one's heartstrings to the dead are not horrible to me, but instru-

---

i That is, the clowns who open act 5 of *Hamlet*, debating Ophelia's fate and discovering Yorick's skull.

ments of blessing that give the secret earth what belongs to its secrecy. There is for me happiness in the top of the soil on the lid.[127]

EC I am sent upstairs—and Michael comes to me in a harrowing passion of hysteria. Photographs of the rock, and one of the dear body, have brutally been put into her hand without a word of warning. . . . Yet in her agony her one thought is to get possession of the infamous cliché[i] (not taken for judicial purposes, but as a bit of private speculation by a poor wretch of a Zermatt demon?) and dash it to pieces.

Her torrent-will overbears all opposition and the thing is brought and executed as if it were one of the Lord's Chief Enemies. The fragments are thrown into the Visp.[ii] The photograph of the rock we are overpersuaded for the sake of Zermatt not to prohibit in the journals, caught as we are in the hour of mortal weakness when the grave is being closed in our own lives as well as in the churchyard. [. . .]

Visiting the place where he fell.

By a fallen fir we stop—beneath the rock, a woodland-rock sixty feet high (they say), with woodland mould, Alpine rhododendrons and fir-refuse at its base. I shall never cease to see or cease to endure what was shown and done—the blackness where he had lain and given his flesh to the wood, the guides poking their Alpine stocks and axes into the sacred mount, giving back the breath of corruption. [. . .] Without warning, they had just flung a stock of wood from the top of the rock on to the spot where he lay—it will tear through me till I die—brutality loosed on me and almost an avalanche to my mind.[128]

EC Why, oh, why did he go so far to the East, Zermatt before him—just on to the tract where search was given up as utterly needless? The mystery is as deep as ever—it will be hard to keep the mind from hunting, hunting . . . but the mystery has no future in it, no anxiety, and in the name of life, we must strive to cease asking, when it may not be given us, seeking, where we may not find.[129]

EC How close he is to me now the wide dread of months is gone, now we know something of his death. With all the sorrow he has made us bear through his faults, they were perversions of love, and the pity of them alone remains, while the greatness of his love, all the more magnificent because husbanded, is the wonder and delight of our mourning.

---

i A photographic negative.
ii The Vispa is a river in the Visp area of Valais.

Like me he was terribly true to three or four beloved ones—he gave them simple love, bare, absolute, tender, necessitous—by others in the world he was scarcely known, but always liked, because of his balancing voice and good, bright eyes.[130]

EC *Thursday.*

That demon photographer at Zermatt demands the cliché and proofs. I write to the Vice-Consul that the cliché is smashed and scattered. I beg him to threaten the rogue with the judge's instruction. When shall I have to cease to fight for that dear father![131]

EC *Edward Whymper[i] pays a visit to Durdans.*

Like all people of fine strain who live much by themselves his talk is often on the things he likes to eat and drink, and he has many "fads." His sugar must be sifted that he may have only a suspicion of the fattening sweet in his tea. He rolls on the couch, bows over Musico and kisses my little hound. When the hour comes for dressing he asks if we have a strong desire to see a black coat—"I don't think it a pretty thing to see[132] but if you wish it can be put on." We pray him to do as he likes, and he wears his gray suit at dinner.

He likes his dinner! I have paid eight shillings for his golden grapes—the only other fruit, tangerine oranges! In the midst of dining, he breaks out "Now don't you give me tea tomorrow morning." We are instructed in the kind of toast to offer. "And an egg," Michael suggests, "*two* eggs." Michael and he have their weed together and a suggestion is made that he should get us, the infirm, to the top of Mt. Blanc[ii] for a Contract—"dead or living." "And the dogs?"—"That, madam, would add considerably to the contract."

When Michael leaves the room, Whym asks if she has been married—At the negative answer he appears astonished and remarks "I don't know why I should think so, but she has the manner of a married lady." Michael and I make our bed shake with laughter at her stories of the young Mr. Bradley who died in the Canary Islands—"You must have noticed I could never bear the mention of a Canary" sobs wicked Michael and I attend to these disclosures of a hidden past!

The hero of the Matterhorn is not punctual at breakfast—the coffee grows cold, and the toast grows cold and the eggs grow cold. All morning he is studying our Swiss bills, disentangling them as if they had been sent to

i Edward Whymper (1840–1911), English mountaineer and artist, among the first to ascend the Matterhorn in 1865.

ii The highest peak in Europe, situated along the borders of France, Italy, and Switzerland.

him. We take him up Reigate hill; our discourse is simple and most friendly. When he goes after lunch we miss—the only guest who has given us the feeling of _____ [133]

KB *Monday: Boxing Day.*

A new trouble—yesterday suddenly while we were all seated at lunch Eva, our housemaid, went entirely out of her mind. She began to talk utter nonsense. I answered her calmly, but as soon as she had left the room, we agreed her wits were gone. It was an awful moment—of Zermatt acuteness—to hear a sober, loving, faithful human creature, contradicting herself—the fearful way of madness. It makes one feel how all sin is negation, some *no*-ness of one's most inward, real self. And madness is of course sin without responsibility—Durdans seems to be gradually turning.[134]

EC *New Year's Eve accounting for 1897.*

We have learned some of the lessons of Love . . . how we loved with every vital and enduring fibre in us that Beloved Lost One, who had brought into our lives so much of their pain, their harass, their loneliness. But we loved him—we had written of him, our dramas were of him; I myself am of him, and Michael loves me and makes me as herself for that simplest season that is yet profound as life and fate. And all the trouble of a jealous, passionate temperament being removed, we can know how piercingly sweet his nature was in its faith and tenderness, in its *virtue*, in its appeal and its answers. He gave us love—lover's love . . . and when to the full it could not be returned he rejoiced to see how we loved each other, and in our love he wondrously gained some sort of fruition.[135]

It is beautiful to think he ever approved our love and has sealed it by his death. The bond between us is a new thing in strength, in reach, in profundity, in vigilance—that bond of the rings by the Smutt, that bond of diamond and sapphire. And Michael is singing of him with an open wound of passion and sorrow. . . . [I]t is our new marriage hymn.

We have learnt much about Death—the mother passed it so radiantly, we were blinded to Death, we neither felt nor understood it. Before the blow fell on us in June, we had foreknown all of death we put into *Anna Ruina*—it seemed as if we shadowed our own experiences. But now every day we are learning more and further on of the bitter-magnificent spells of death.

We have learnt more about man—the faithless lying, the mean greed and meaner cowardice of the self-seeking and of the priests of such—we have learnt how faithful a few souls, who are not brilliant or amusing, can be; how mighty is the fellow feeling that can bind a noble stranger to one's service.

We have learnt life deeper, deeper, where it wells up below the black rocks with all the possibilities of its currents and surface hidden in Earth's own night.[136] [...]

I have had the great new joy of possessing my basset hound, of laying my hand on his modelled shoulders and lovely head, and of drinking the mild glamour of his raised eyes. He has filled voidness for me with his sports, his unconscious lustihood. Bless my Beloved for him.

The bells are ringing—and what of New Year?

We begin as in a desert on a cleared space looking in each other's faces ... the old home-life gone, Amy absorbed in a new love ... there is almost something of terror in all this—but I am convinced that the dead in unison with the Spirit are working intensely and mean well. I think joy may have come to us this time next year on one of its springtides.[137] [...]

EC We shall have rising life as we watch our dogs, our garden, and our little home growing more beautiful. I think we shall have more friends and be less hard on them, if they only will *give*.

And shall I see my little Dionysus of my youth—shall I see those eyes and lips again? I totteringly think I shall have to meet them and hear them. How when I think of Life in the image that expresses it to me, Bacchus—I must think of the mortal I love—now almost as impersonally as if he were a legend of imperishable charm or a faunish sculpture. And in so many ways he resembled father, and so has his own new link with my being.[138]

Works and Days, 1898

KB *January 11th, the Vigil of Henry's birthday.*

I am tossed and restless. Not a new planet—a tantalizing comet that disorders the heavens—has swum into my ken[i]—It is there—and who looks at Venus, when a long light with a tail is in the sky. When the novel is only interesting because it is novel, it becomes a bore.

This new male guest with his veiled Catholic face, and his ritual, is distressing to me. Oh for the spirits of gemlike quality, that are!

One such walked beside me thirty-six years ago in the Abbey Fields at Kenilworth and told me of the little Babe born to him.[139]

KB *Whym Chow.*

Friday evening, January 28th, Whym Chow arrived—a dusky, sable—a wolf with civilization's softness, an oriental with musky passion-white rolling

---

i From Keats, "On First Looking into Chapman's Homer" (1816) eyeballs, and the power of inward frenzy—velvet mariners and the savages of eastern armies behind.

I suppose our new love of animals is a desire to get into another kingdom—we reach after the kingdom of the dead—we can penetrate into the kingdom of animals. [. . .]

Saturday morning.

Alas! Heavy news by post: the children have still to pay to the thievish government one hundred sixty pounds! The Chow turns on us the white of his eyeballs and shrieks. . . . I am ill [. . .]. Henry, great Boy, rises to meet all these oppositions. My blest, my only Love for ever, and O my poet. The revises of the *World at Auction* have come. Heaven keep us sound!

February 1st. The great birthday. We rise from wrecked couches. We have no flowers ready . . . We have the chow. I rush to him at 6:30. His fury of greeting floods my heart with joy. Is one little passionate heart so thrilled at my waking? Heaven bless the chow.[140] [. . .]

KB We read in last year's White Book of the pathetic health drinking in soda water.

O great deep heart of Love! He is with her now—and from wine to winecup of soul healths are drunk—and blessing invoked on us the poor benighted ones of the thrice famous little homestead. [. . .]

Thursday, February 3rd.

My precious ones have given me my little Emperor, Whym Chow of the fiery heart. The first day I took him out, he escaped; at every attempt at recapture, the seven devils the sweet angel is possessed of howled and moaned in their torment. Man and boy and mistress sought by suasion . . . but the sack alone—a strong sack—sewn up hastily by St. Peter from his relic sheet for the purpose[141] restored him to our arms. He entered, and my heart resumed its place among the lungs, and chemicals, and the flooded arteries!

Poor Man!

When we first lifted him up, he turned on us the whites of his eyes, oriental white—with the sprung lustre of a sword from its scabbard, and yelled. He has two notes—like his mistress!—the first passionate personal protest and revolt, the second a long moan, full of impersonal tears that such wrong should be done in the world, and such cruel hearts allowed by Providence to beat.

As for his religion, it is *me*. I can be a good god to anyone who loves me—so responsive, so utter. [. . .] [W]rite on gold with a silver pen. Send me a child's *History of China*, for all I can do is to utter the name of Confucius!!! And I am nothing, except historical.

His mistress writes, "feed him yourself, and there will soon be to him no other person in the world."

But it's not the feeding.

That is what wins me. He greets me when I go to him in a morning, as mortals greet the sun—brushing away the milk, and scattering spray to the winds.

He is infinitely beautiful, with every beauty, except the beauty of holiness.—It is almost painful to see how his little brows are chafed by temper—sheer shock at the atrocity of men and things—the Swiss—one has only to mention them—and he [142] rolls his eyes to the sword glare.

I will never make him a Christian dog. I will civilise the seven devils.

—Oh, I love him!

Hennie loves him.

He is Michael's own little brimstone soul.

Hennie loves him!

Amen.[143]

EC *Palm Sunday.*

I am alone in the study with the golden Chow at soft oriental stretch on the couch opposite—his chafed, devoted eyes on me—what unEnglish supple dignity he has!—he gives no hospitality to his pride—it is a mere housemate. I adore Whym Chow—I admire and love my noble Basset hound Musico (both registered in the *Kennel Gazette*), but Musico is sensitive without fellow feeling, cumbersome, pining (he has the sport dog's little unhappy whistle) and, in spite of his superb plasticity, he is inexpressive to emotion. Whym Chow is yellow fire throughout[;] there is some white clay in Musico's soul—and his ears will split.

Robinson of Redhill has done some wonderful heads of Whym—one great vignette hangs opposite our bed. We have [144] the furry Sweet in seven different pictures. At the same time my Love has given me pictures of herself—one with Whym is perfect in solemn protectiveness to the little creature and beyond him to all her Beloved Few . . . to Henry, and to the thought of the dead, left to the living in trust. It stands under Whymper's great photograph of the way up the Vale to Zermatt—It has the same gravity of tone and a light on the brow like the snow celestialness that shines over the unseen Weisshorn.[i] This corner where Zermatt Valley and the pictures of the Chow hang round that grave face with its lofty tenderness, a little remote, shows up our lives as they now are—At every moment our dogs claiming the care of our hands, the watchfulness and admiration of our eyes, the service of our feet—and always behind us thought of that Valley of the Shadow of Death, those clinging for-

i Major peak of the Swiss Alps.

ests, and that magnificence of air above them, in the space between the mountains and round their forms. Two other pictures of my Love in her black satin evening dress have quality. One is a noble head out of characteristic pose—but Byronic in effect; the other a three-quarter face of sweet composure and full of sorrow's charm that Keats knew about.[145]

EC I have scarcely written for a quarter any word of our life—but there have been moments I would not lose the clear impress of.

In January, while we were suffering the distress of being without servants and feeling ill—the negatives of the photograph the wretched man [the demon photographer] Fumex took in the Wittiwald come from the consulate, at last wrested from the Knave.

One I saw—the dear form bowed in a nest of Alpine rhododendron—deep among leaflets, and forest tranquility, with boughs of fir traversing the thicket. "He is made one with nature"—and one's eyes see how sacred and wholesome (Göethe's *heilsom*)[i] it is to be wound in her arms and sleep out the mortal passing away under her light. It is the very calm of pity that comes whenever I see the exquisite detail of the nesting shrubs and the sleep which is the same as the "sleep that is among the lovely hills"—yet is *his* sleep to us.

We have a most beautiful, enlarged photograph of his likeness before he was married . . . We scarcely now regret that we have no record of the gray, floating sweep of hair—for this early picture has the eternal, permanent Virtue of our Beloved—the beauty of his passion, courtesy, the guarding up of his heart in his eyes, at once fresh and[146] melancholy, kind and recluse—the humility of his goodness, the spiritedness of his faults.

Ah! What was the end of his days!! The obvious belief is that he strayed—for the valuables were found. . . . Strayed *from paths*, against his unfailing cautious habit, strayed wildly, persistently, unnaturally.[147]

EC We have had to face, Michael and I, the anguish of spring cleaning that means the removal of all belonging to the Dead that must grow dead and useless, all that has not the life-evoking power of the true relic. The dear One hoarded, thinking the trifle put by would "come in"—we have had bitter toil among superfluities of vain accumulation, half dust and moth already . . . but out of this flat horror, this weary staleness of suffering, we have gained one precious result—a cabinet in our bedroom of veritable relics—things that speak of the power and love of the Beloved . . . tools he used for his carving,

---

i Johann Wolfgang von Goethe (1749–1832), German poet, playwright, novelist, scientist, and critic. By "heilsom," Cooper probably means to suggest the healing qualities of the image.

the words he wrote on our letters received the morning of our play, a portrait of him in his youth with a collar to his cheekbones and his eyes with their fine, solitary cloudlessness the same then as when we lost him. This is the compensation worth weeks of fatigue and nausea.

We have at last a pale old cook, who[148] is the very Genius of the Range—standing by it to measure with Minos' scales, to stir as Medea stirred her cauldron;[i] she is old and calm enough to produce flavour, she is patient enough to create proportion; the fire burns temperately in her presence—the pie before it enters the oven is as restorative to see as to eat when it comes out. There is peace in the kitchen—out of it none! [. . .]

What with [servant] Kate Crisp, the dogs, the East Wind, money affairs, ill-health (I have even had that Methusalal[ii] disease asthma) and the new invasion of responsibilities and impertinent claims we have no time for our life's work, and the great Irish Drama stands aside while things of no consequence triumph. But this shall not be when Easter is over; the house clean, Musico taken walks by the Vet's Groom, and Kate either coerced into order or _____.[149]

EC Oscar's *Ballad of Reading Gaol* is not literature.[iii] To experience experience won't make art—it must be imagined as well as suffered. I see this so clearly when I look from the beautiful photograph of our little Chow in front of our bed to the photographs of Mantegna and Timoteo della Vito[iv] on the same wall. Robinson has presented all he could see of the body and soul of our Chow in the best light, at a vital moment—but the subject of a work of art must be transmuted from the centre—and it is only the superficies that the photograph from life can reach.

So with Oscar; the real part of his work is mostly arranged experience, not imaginatively translated experience; and much of his work is special pleading—rhetoric the cold-hearted with hot voice; and some is deliberate appeal to the weaknesses of the English public, and therefore is an attempt to commit hypocrisy. The book contains an immortal outrageous paradox—a very

---

i Minos, the mythic king of Crete and one of the judges of the underworld, and Medea, the sorceress of Greek myth who cooked up recipes for rejuvenation in her brass cauldron.

ii Methuselah, the biblical patriarch said to have lived for 969 years.

iii Wilde wrote the poem after his release from Reading Gaol in 1897, and published it in 1898 under the pseudonym C.3.3., denoting the cell block, landing, and cell Wilde inhabited during his imprisonment. The poem offers a meditation on the execution of a prisoner convicted of murdering his wife.

iv Andrea Mantegna (1431–1523) and Timoteo Viti (1469–1523), both Italian Renaissance painters. Cooper is referring to the popular late-Victorian decorating practice using photographic reproductions.

Colossus of the kind. "We needs must kill the thing we love." Oscar was sent into the world to generate this stimulating monster.[150]

EC *Holy Thursday.*

The toil to keep our home going on wears us out. As Michael says, "I am just turning to thought of the Passion, and I am assailed by the prices of egg whisk and jelly bag." Even at night, while we are striving to read the first act of *Anna Ruina*, jam is delivered, and the boy says that when the ten train is in he will bring a milk cheese. Painters in the garden—Carpenter in the house . . . I am dragged along from one duty to another in a state of victim-fatigue.[151] [. . .]

How lonesome we are—deep lonesome. We cannot get anyone to come to us, when we want a little human-help at these seasons, such as Easter . . . we live entirely with our dogs and flowers and (lately) with our worries. Day after day we speak to no one, and if anyone comes to lunch or dine, it is some parasitical woman, who would draw our powers of life out of us, not renew them with rich leaf mould—suggestive, exhilarating converse.[152]

EC Alas, the day hardened in light and breath. We went into the garden and I began gleaning rose-sprays oblivious to the need my Love had for me. I thought her satisfied with Whym Chow. But a great desert of loneliness stretched over her on a sudden, and she went in to weep.

Tonight we have read from the old Year Books and looked at our pictures of Whym and his mistress, also at Ricketts' woodcuts.

Music is still pining, and has a thin light in his eyes, a thin expression on his nose. We have had a boy—the vet's groom—to exercise him, and I believe Music feels as a pain the stranger's hand on his leash. He is affectionate to the death, as only the sullen can be. Well, we shall not forget Musico refused his breakfast on Good Friday—I wish he had not.[153]

EC *April 20th.* Dr. Ryan[i] comes to see Amy . . . why?

There seems to be no admiration, hope, or aim in his visit—nothing alive. He is weak bodied and holds his top hat on his head just like Sam Weller,[ii] only that there is no hammer or glad human nature under the brim-blue Catholic eyes, with a veil of discipline over them, and that queer patience in them, as of the mule, that convent education always leaves behind it. A good, minute soul—slower than the tortoise—interested to the bitter end in every

---

i John Ryan (1855–1933) married Amy Cooper in 1899.
ii A comical bootblack from Charles Dickens's *The Pickwick Papers* (1836).

detail of its own experience. A bore, a "funny man" and a "devot" in one—also a worshipper of his Mother![154]

EC *Ricketts and Shannon visit Durdans.*

The Basset-hound is admired as gloriously sensual; grave, dignified, admirable as that most admirable of animals—the pig. His feet are dwelt on, and the dawn of a three-fold lustre in his eyes at the sight of food. Whym Chow is equally—almost equally—appreciated, his free foxlike attitudes, the gold of him: also his sensual delightfulness. His flesh when stewed has a flavour of plum, so Ricketts has heard. He is re-named Nuzzle and Musico is re-named Collops. Rye [in light pencil, Ryan] is too much like a dog to accept in the least, and he feels the cold atmosphere, poor Mamie [light pencil, Amy]! [light pencil, EC; Ryan was then Amy's accepted lover.][155]

KB *May 4th.*

My Mother's Wedding Day. The house is now without sound, both Babes gone to the Westminster show of pet dogs. I might be alone, the last of my race, left with three guardian dogs to lick my feet.

It is more than sixty years since that wedding day, yet I wreathe the portrait of my own sweet Mother and desire nothing better than to curl up in some remote corner of heaven and be caressed by her . . . I give maternal love, because I am so utterly a child. If one has fulfilled one half of a relation, one[156] knows what is requisite for the other half.[157]

KB *Lincoln, May 29th.*

Yes, we have kissed Music's star and torn ourselves from the jasper-glittering gold of our adored Whym Chow. We leave Little One with Dora Pease,[i] who wore a flaunting old Japanese costume among our black Paris fashions last night and gave us the heartless gossip of the Pearsall-Smith, Sellar, Phillimore, B. Shaw sets.[ii]

I said a true thing of B. Shaw—that he takes himself with *serious* humour and becomes a sight for gods and men—only those who take themselves with light humor may maintain their dignity. Dora looked like a Jap doll dressed in England for a suburban shop—Whym Chow bit at her with Oriental fury of outraged good taste.[158]

i Sister of Edward Pease (1857–1955), cofounder of the socialist Fabian Society.

ii Robert Sellar (1841–1919), Scottish Canadian radical journalist and editor; John Swinnerton Phillimore (1873–1926), British poet and scholar; George Bernard Shaw (1856–1950), Irish playwright, author, Fabian; awarded the Nobel Prize in Literature in 1925.

EC *June 2nd, Thursday.*

We are in great grief on account of our golden gleam, our life's joy—Whym Chow. He has been ill, under doctor and vet for mischief in the blood and an abscess. When I read Amy's reassuring, devoted letter, I turn white with utter fear and Michael ages in sorrow at the news. What he is to us—his passionate love, his chowing—the bond! I dare not cry—my stone would melt into a fountain; it would be a case of Niobe.[i] By a solemn act of faith we commend him (as far as Earthly protection is concerned) to our Little One—and, for the rest, Michael has a private time with Heaven, and gives us of the strength of it. If we should have to hear that our little Whym is taken from us—well, we must be ready to bear that. But we hope very much and believe that the Wee will be allowed to stay with us. Michael is cold as I, least her stony heart should crack, if once she let the flood of tears rush in. She won't—her heart belongs to us.[159]

EC *July 13th.*

Dr. Garnett[ii] comes over to lunch with us. He likens Whym Chow to a bear—a most respectable beast. He tells us a story of Swinburne's[iii] fame. Swinburne had fallen in a fit one day at the British Museum. A few days after, Dr. G. at an Eating-House heard a waiter telling a petted but illiterate charge that if he looked in a certain direction he would see Mr. Swinburne. "And who is Mr. Swinburne?" "—the man that fell down at the British Museum, and 'urt is 'ed." O Apollo![160]

EC *Friday, September 23rd.*

We visit the Artists at 8, Spring Terrace, Richmond.[iv] They have never been so frank, simple, and friendly.

The little house is delicious. There is behind a small lawn with that kind of thrift about its poetry that is so touching in sweet town gardens: it has a vista of little apple-trees in avenue, the Oxford Bust under a canopy of ivy and Verrocchio's Cupid and Dolphin by a tumbled wall of grapevine with grapes, green and hard as jade.[v]

---

i Niobe, the Greek goddess of snow and winter. After her children were killed by Artemis and Apollo, Niobe became the emblem of maternal grief.

ii Richard Garnett (1835–1906), author and philologist; Keeper of Printed Books at the British Museum Library.

iii Algernon Charles Swinburne (1837–1909), English poet, novelist, and essayist associated with decadence.

iv Residence of Ricketts and Shannon from 1898–1902.

v That is, sculptors in the classical and Renaissance styles.

The large room is gray and white filled with Sheraton furniture, old Shef-field plate and Greek pottery.[i] On the table a few violets, the wriggling steps supported delicately in a glass with columnar neck and a single dandelion dock learning from a bit of old china. Lunch in the willow-green parlour (fowl, chocolate and custard pudding and banana-fritters—a food for gods at a picnic in a pine-forest). Above my[161] head the original drawing of Rossetti's *Mary Magdalen*,[ii] discovered by the artists in a print shop. The discovery has made Rothenstein say "then there is a god."

Their Table—ah they beat us. They have forks with pistol handles (both green ones and silver);[iii] they pour their claret from a Sheffield jug—they have a *saucier* that stands an idol in the assembly. We admire an old Sicilian wine cup full of mignonette—the fellow is instantly offered to us. We bring back a lithograph of Shannon's and the portrait of the twain.[162]

EC Ricketts expounds his genesis—born of a French Mother, who was bred Italian and had Spanish blood by her father—coming into life at Geneva and educated in France, he has nothing of his Anglo-Saxon father except Rick-etts—his name. "I am a mixture of races"—"You are a claret cup." Michael gives bow and smile. It is her speech of the evening.[163] [. . .]

After dinner our friends come upstairs to give us some advice in re-generating our bedrooms. Ricketts, at the sight of our Morris bed, cries out with fervor "You must have dreams in that bed"—Unfortunately he turns to the Zermatt-cross—"What is this cross, with its shocking point?" Oh, I think of the hands that had welcomed theirs and go cold. They know nothing of our agony.

They have to fly for a train—but remember their genius.

Tuesday, October 4th.

Julia Domna finished and written out.

That abyss of motherhood closes, and I am glad to look down it no more. Would I could have reached the poetry I heard as I conceived the prose sce-nario . . . heard it as if across space, from the ball of another planet! But it was not to be.[164]

i Sheraton furniture: a late-eighteenth-century English furniture style; Sheffield plate: met-alware made of copper fused with silver; Greek pottery: samples of pottery from ancient Greece appealing to aesthetes and analogous to Michael Field's use of Sapphic fragments in *Long Ago*.

ii A preparatory drawing for the painting *Mary Magdalene at the Door of Simon the Pharisee* (1877) by Dante Gabriel Rossetti (1828–82), a founder of the Pre-Raphaelite Brotherhood.

iii Pistol-handled forks, with a curved grip that was easier to hold, gradually gave way to straight-handled forks over the course of the nineteenth century, as metalworking techniques of the Industrial Revolution made lower-cost, durable implements more widely available. In other words, just as with their Sheraton furniture and Greek pottery, Ricketts and Shannon's flatware samples were beautiful items from the past.

EC *In Oxford.*

We attend our first University Function—the installation of the new Vice-Chancellor[i] . . . The atmosphere is close as if aware a small solemnity is about to begin. A row of women—rather slices of womanhood—propped against the wall: beneath, their intellectual lord and masters in the guise of dons, beings who have no valour, no copious expression of force, no straightness or novelty, because they have knowledge—[165]only seek Intellect, the destroyer.

These men and women, unnatural and out of place side by side, have nothing to do with society—which is the word of action and of woman as married powers—the will to Live and the Eternal womanly making unison. It is one measure of the difference between men's lives and women's that men are used to having Latin—I enjoy the sound as if from some old cavern's mouth.

These clerks do not manage ceremony well—there is no eurythmic sense in a protestant ceremony, and Englishmen are so angular and bashful. The red that the doctors wear is glorious to behold.

I should not like to live among these quaint, desiccated, urbane Oxonians and these women on their knees to sex as Deathliness.[166]

EC Holmes is a good, good-tempered creature with a native gift of fun, and a mind and wit that are portions of stars that have broken off from Ricketts' sun.[ii]

He gives us the sense of that banter in the midst of which Pater lived at Oxford and tells us how at a service in the Chapel of Brasenose Pater thought he would slip out after the Bishop of Oxford who was going to the vestry to prepare for celebration. Suddenly the Bishop turned and bowed to the altar—the bow was returned by Pater.[167]

EC Lying on our bed, our dream bed, yesterday afternoon Michael and I came to the belief that we must part with Durdans for life's sake. We could only *just* keep it up, having no margin for pleasure; and then the air is injurious to us, and the foot of a friend never passes its door. To stay would mean we sold ourselves to the Past, to Association, to the Comfortable and the Sad—with ill health ever gaining on us.

i Sir William Reynell Ansell was installed as vice-chancellor of the University of Oxford in 1898. In the UK, the vice-chancellor is the top academic and administrative leader of a university.

ii Charles Holmes (1868–1936), painter, art historian, Slade Professor of Fine Art at Oxford, and later director of the National Gallery.

We think of Haslemere[i] as a new neighbourhood; for after all we are in our tastes country ladies, loving a garden and dogs more than any other things. Oxford would be soothing, but oppressive, and we should soon hate the dons and their women. So, we dream ourselves into a fervor over a Haslemere Cottage—the tension of undecided fate relaxes on my temples. But oh, the soil, the Durdans garden! I fear the way in which[168] its "body and beauty will unprovide my mind."[ii] I am weak the moment I think of the three hundred grape hyacinths preparing their dusk charm among the rose roots; of the fritillaries growing strong on their own little territory; of the sanguines, and furnace gold of the lilies, the garden of autumn crocuses under the autumn-bearing roses.

To tear myself from my own soil is like tearing myself from my body—are they not the same thing? I feel all that happens to the Earth of my garden as if it happened to my flesh. And the wrench is more acute just after November, that month of the perfect garden, adorned as a bride for her bridegroom, descending out of the heavens. I have lived day after day for the sake of lilies more perfect than any that will ever be born, of roses from fairyland, of grape hyacinths, dog-tooth violets, alstroemeria in breadths of colour such as spirits alone may see. Yet these dreams are at my heart of hearts quickening it. And the garden is dear for what it was to us in our great sorrow: for the sake also of that brave, pinched form that still hurries with round shoulders and military step, about it whenever we think of the old days.[169]

Then beyond this trouble of giving up Durdans, and the trouble that comes to me from the Catholic marriage, is the trouble of straitened means. I love generous ways of life; the possibility of being lavish with the gladness of a fountain. I keenly love the nobility of a free hand—I enjoy the considerations shown to liberal outlay. All my coins henceforth will be set up like palings round my desires. All this makes me very wicked, absent-minded, and deadly sorrowful: but through it all I grasp at one jewel hope, the wedded life with my Love in our own home. So much to go through before we reach it: but if we do . . .

Light of my life, I shall forget all this time, or bless it as one blesses one's nurse when one is well.

The rest of the page has been redacted.[170]

EC *Christmas.*

Michael has said what Christmas is and always has been—a passing of phantoms.

---

i The village in Surrey where Michael Field visited the family of Mary Costelloe Berenson.

ii See *Othello* 4.1.226–27. Folger Shakespeare Library (n.d.), https://www.folger.edu/explore /shakespeares-works/othello/read/4/1/#line-4.1.226.

But at breakfast came Dr. Ro's merry engagement ring—the merriest-looking I have ever seen; and Amy no longer belongs to herself or us. This event in the midst of a mirage of memories makes the day still more curious and curdling underneath our affected blitheness—for we do try to flash back the glee of the sapphire, rubies and diamonds in spite of our deep private sorrow.[171]

EC Michael sent the Artists each a sonnet—to Ricketts "Fifty Quatrains" (the Kings), to Shannon "A Train of Queens."

This morning we receive a letter from [the Artists]—

Dear Poet,

We never having had any poems dedicated to us before do not know quite what words to use—in fact what words are beautiful enough to thank you for your gift of verse! Needless to add a certain coldness has come over us towards our respective poems. All the butterflies are nested in delicate places chosen to suit their complexions—the postscript is entirely enigmatical. Are all the dogs going to be drowned? Singly or together? Who is going to do it? If you are really going could the curtain bed be removed?

There is a house at Petersham[i] old-fashioned with garden, near here, close to the river and near the most beautiful park in the world. You must really explore more fully. Believe us.

Yours very sincerely

The Artists.[172]

Now this is not only a very nice letter—it is a sign that "casts its bright beams of light" upon us. On Christmas Day I went round beloved Durdans Garden and felt detached from it—the anguish allayed and vague as it becomes before final party. Since, I have been aimless and dead as to hope. . . . With this letter hope and life leap at each other's necks and swing in dance.

Petersham, an old house, the river, the Park, and above all the Artists evidently want us near: our change of abode would not be friendless.

And there is no doubt that Michael and I ought to be severed from the past somewhat; its tyranny is aging us—I have long felt to be eighty, and the walls of Durdans to be pre-sepulchral in their sacred imprisonment.

KB *Extract from letter to Artists.*

"Your letter with its news of the old house at Petersham enchants us, and Henry's face grows springtide with its joy. We will come, and our dogs will come, the curtained bed and the kennels, two final carts bearing our roses, vines, and lilies!!"[173]

i A village within Richmond upon Thames, near the home of Ricketts and Shannon.

EC Now I can talk of Petersham—Give me a name on to which to cast my threads and I weave—the void before me turns me into a congestion of meaningless skeins.

Amy has received a card from his mother, who now knows of the engagement, inscribed "with a mother's love"—she is gone out for the day and night.

Michael and I are together and alone with the wind and our future.[174]

Saturday, December 31, 1898

KB And this I say if both of us being alive and well, we write our next year's New Year's Eve from *Durdans*, we shall deserve the curse of heaven.

Columbus did not discover America by carefully wrapping himself in a great cloak.

Our harbour must be the opened.

We must fling the bulbs by handfuls to Destiny.

Durdans is now a coffin that should be closed.[175]

EC We have been detaching from Durdans—our adored little home, with its garden and the twining about it of *his* memory who gave it to us. I trust this year looks on the deathbed of our home—for I feel we need a new life, a resurrection; and a great chance has been offered to us at last—the chance of founding a home, where my Love and I can live a married life and make our own associations and weave our modes of enjoyment, and be[176] our best each to each in newness as of green spring.

The Courage we shall need will be gigantic—it will grow in might if we seek sincere quality in it.

We have made no new friends—but the Artists are more and more our male doubles in what they enjoy, live for and assimilate. [. . .]

"No new friends," so I say—why, we have learnt the whole previous nature, we have adored the love and faith and passion of our Whym Chow. We bless him, our dark-red beam of a happiness from the depths of the heavenly clouds—ripe, ripe, dark rapture. God bless our Chow.

And the other dear dogs are far dearer than last year—they have come out of their hearts, as if out at doors, to draw us in.

Old Sarah, the cook of many years, feeds us with delicious meats and old memories—Ellen, the housemaid long waited for, has almost a sister's eyes and keeps our home and loves our dogs with fidelity.[177]

EC I have just put out the lights, and bade farewell to the parlour where he used to sit, where the soft gray hair attracted with such comeliness in sunshine or lamplight. The bells are ringing out the Old Year—Chow is at my feet, my own Love in little nightgown and socks reading the Zermatt sonnets. I have kissed the carbuncle ring on her finger—my loyalty to the deathless Old that can never be left for the New.

I feel we shall *found* during this year—it will be a colonists' year—which means hard conditions, suffering, endeavors to be overcome by patience, hope, house-founding. We shall have to toil for our joy, my life's Joy and I—but heart to heart we shall have strength, and heart to heart we shall be blessed. We shall receive a home as a crown to our day—a home for our marriage.[178]

Works and Days, 1899

EC *1899. New Year's Day.* [. . .]

I am very sleepy and we agree to treat this day as the borderland of New Year. We cannot be strenuous till tomorrow—we are calm. There is much that is convalescent in us after the most harrowing last day of the old year we have ever spent. [. . .]

We have had much talk. Now we have determined to give up Durdans as a *sacrifice to Life* and to seek with courageous will for a new home among the strangers[.] [I]t may be that Durdans will be given back to us—a new home we have won that we shall as truly found as if the soil round it were not dear to our[179] hands and feet and eyes.

But it is only by striving to leave it we can be blessed if eventually we stay under its roof. We must *prove* destiny, and then hold fast that which is good.

If fate—I mean, the Wisdom that has proved itself unassailable—gives us back Durdans, we shall alter it fearlessly, selling all those things that are not become virtually associated with us as poets; we shall lead a new life with our God and our dreams.

Human fellowship we shall seek after in seeking for a new home, and more engaging country—we may find there is little hope of either, since we hate town life and are too apprehensive and sad for deep country life. Sometimes I fear we have been too long in the desert for us to care for any daily converse with mortals—we only can find friendship if we turn to God and our Dreams—If this prove so, we may be restored to Durdans, where we could dream and worship in quiet without the fret of the unassimilated round us.[180]

KB *First day of the New Year.*

Petersham! A refreshing letter from the artists—with this memorable sentence—"We think you should in this vortex of excitement talk of flight, but move with caution." The old house at Petersham we fear is palatial. "I feel," Ricketts says, "You should nestle in a tiny house in England, and live on nothing in France or Florence during winter." Yes, later on, but while we have our kennel and Chow, and the harbouring of all these bulbs and roses, we need space. [. . .]

EC Ricketts with his own hand has written the long letter. Shannon afraid exhaustion should set in forbids more—"Shannon says I must not say any-more—in fact this is his hand-writing. There is one house[181] with a long strip of wilderness overlooking the green which ought to be seen. We will go first and frighten away the rats and drains." [. . .]

Accounts, dividends, bills all morning. I join Michael and Whym Chow in the garden. Michael is very hopeful on Petersham; I am very much tired and sore in the brain and as I look at every clod with bulb under it, of the roses sappy and pierced by buds, at the well-compassed work of the garden, so satisfying at this season—I sulk.[182]

KB On Wednesday, I have a great attack of hysterics—I have not even Dur-dans to cling to. I have put away my dead in Durdans. It is unsanctified, and unclean, and cannot be renewed or blessed to us any more until we have proved our willingness to give it up.

And whither shall I take my beloved, where fare with him in this mortal world. We are unsummoned by love, or welcome—save in our nook of Petersham.

But patience! We look for the sign and will go up the hill with sacrificial knives well sharpened—On the same sad Wednesday I go with my love into town and bring her her betrothal-ring—an old-fashioned, hand-fast ring.[183]

KB *Tuesday, January 9th, 1899.*
I wake to feel the firm earth gone from me. In all our sorrows we have been sustained by the firm thought of home. Now we have no home, no one *who is ours* to return to. We must found a home.[184]

EC We plant too much faith in restlessness. We seek with a fever in the seek-ing, and no solid goal. Where shall we be next Birthday, I and my Love and our Dogs? Life's solution of this mystery will be peace: the mystery is distrac-tion and the desert. I long for Time to say to us "peace, be still." Lovie brings me "from Durdans" one mezereum-flower. I spend the evening in bed and in pain and in sleep.[185]

KB *Describing a visit to Richmond and lunch with Ricketts and Shannon.*
Rejoicing in Hope [. . .]

At lunch I see the Old Sheffield jug—Fatty. "One ought to have very beautiful furniture and objects that are dear, calling a chair 'Jennie'" for example. [. . .] After lunch—coffee and sloe gin—of the hedgerows, of the flowers in the hedgerows.

I grow enthusiastic and the artists describe how, with waving of hands. I shall tell my fellow there are ten bedrooms and two bridges. In a cab, we reach 1, Paragon—the straight, old, red-brick house, with its pretty white paint and old pillared doorway. [Down at the bottom of the garden by the river,] I look[186] houseward.

High up in the sky, I see a bay window.—"What is that"—"Oh, that is your bedroom." *That*—with England's own river in smooth, country-stream flowing by!

There is no garden, but a roof balcony that we must make a tile of Paradise, planting it with rose trees in pots! and carnations in boxes, and mignonette, and trellis perfumes, till the odour strikes the stars.

I return, the news as a gift in my hand. [. . .]

EC *Shannon's Letter.*

Dear Poet

First Floor Enter from street on drawing-room floor; double room with balcony at back overlooking garden and river. You can descend to the garden from this floor. *Two windows to each portion of the room.*[187]

Front door Entrance to house had eighteenth-century pillared door.

Second Floor On floor above two good bedrooms; one facing river having a large bow window—The other room a magnificent eighteenth-century fireplace of marble and carved wood.

Third Floor Above this, two more bedrooms.

Staircase Staircase, pretty, carved balustrades—paneled probably underneath the wallpaper.

Ground Floor Dining room charming, odd shaped, overlooking river "with little cabin" projecting over garden attached herewith christened "sulking room." Large pantry, very old-fashioned leading into paneled room given over to servant.

Basement Dear little kitchen and old-fashioned scullery.

Garden Room for three rose bushes which dog can destroy in fourteen minutes—seven minutes if helped by another. Little wooden summerhouse overlooking towpath. Three roses still in bloom today. Wall taller than a man matted[188] with minute Ivy (not observed by the Poet).

The garden is at such an incline that the Basset sitting at the top of the garden would at once stride into the river if it was not for the door. Unprecedented opportunity for pushing relatives through doorway at high tide.

You are on the Petersham Road, in a nest of beautiful old houses, minutes' walk from the precipitous town garden full of rooks and sparrows who feed from your hands—they spit out currents—so ask for seed-cake—five minutes' to ten minutes' walk from station. Petersham Park in sight, Hampton Court near—Kew a good walk—charming walks by the river.[i]

The house must not next week be judged by its furniture only by its possibilities. Neither must Richmond be judged by its winter aspect.[189]

EC *Exploring Richmond. Lunch at the Star and Garter.*

The air of the Terrace is almost Parisian—it makes one feel happily elated. We descend the town-gardens. *No Dogs!* I point and leave the moral to strike.[190]

EC We leave the Petersham Rd. for the towing path and go along, beyond the place for embarkation, to a gate, a wall, a small arbour, above which is the humble red old house, a strip among others. Then we go back to its street entrance.

Alas, the walls are yellow brick with only red bricks round the windows, and the garden is asphalt and a few ferns under ivy-mold soil. The lovely white door is an unsupported piece of loveliness.

It opens—a delicious little hall and staircase—a sunny room, and through long windows the sweet Thames flowing softly. This room would be the study. The dark cool room behind the Sheraton Drawing room. The bedrooms are large and low and beautiful to dwell in—even the attics are not common attics—though we shall be sorry if we have to banish guests there. The parlour and sulking room are *home*, with all the attractiveness of the word. The kitchen is bright—but pantries and scullery dark and, we fear, smelling ill—expert necessary.

The garden bed would hold one hundred fifty roses and many bulbs—the rim of soil under[191] the ivy-hung wall would hold lilies and herbs, pansies, daylilies and auriculas. An arbour watches the river-door on one side, an acacia tree on the other. Without the danger of Musico's presence we could make this miniature garden a symbol of Eden.

i Petersham Park is a public park in Richmond upon Thames. Hampton Court, the palace of Henry VIII, is also nearby. The Royal Botanic Gardens in Kew, founded in 1759, combines vast gardens with facilities for scientific research into plants and fungi.

Advantages

Lovely little rooms and passages
Nearness to the Artists.
Nearness to the Gardens, Terrace, Park, Petersham, and the Thames.
Outlook on to white river air, and its tidal currant.
A gravel subsoil.
Something brisk and joyous about the genius of the place.

Disadvantages

Nearness of place of Embarkation, with loafers and holiday makers.
Extreme ugliness and humbleness of approach.
The dirt, viciousness, and degradation of lower Richmond on the way to
    the station.
(The drainage, with light thrown on it, will not always be deterrent, I
    believe. And the fact of being at the edge of the river will not, I fancy,
    prove unhealthy—the subsoil being gravel and the current of breeze
    frequent.)
No place of freedom for the dogs.
A basement.
A woman next door who plays and sometimes sings.[192]

EC We reach the Artists in time for three-quarters of an hour's talk. Ricketts receives us depressingly—he is so afraid we may come and be ill—he is
contrary as a savage. "Really, Ricketts," says the confident Shannon "you are
talking like a doctor."
We promise quiet thought and a lawyer if we entertain the beloved little
hovel. Our butterflies are poised on old glasses. The "gee-gee" carpet[i] has a
ground colour of dead roses. "You must lie down on it" commands Ricketts.
I fall like Whym Chow in a heap—then become conscious of my huge winter
coat and see myself a black Russian Bear before the eyes that love bony grace
and veils. I rise sensitive. The Artists always seem to regard me as a new ex-
hibit in a deep-sea water tank—I feel I ought to blink and expand my lips
with spectral novelty in every movement.
We are introduced to "Fatty," "Swallow" and "Bulfinch"—the three new
Sheffield jugs—also to the "Jack-in-the-Box," named Dr. Ibsen (and a perfect
portrait) and to the Christmas God "just like God the Father seen by Blake."
(He had the grey Capuchin and the wild, windy eyes.) Ricketts forgets to
hand us our bag when we enter our cab—we discover our loss too late.[193]

i A hand-knotted rug from India.

EC *January 20th.*

Yesterday I was holding the whole *Times* in front of the fire in Michael's bedroom: there was a bright stab at it inside, the whole mass was flame between my hands. The moment was perilous for a smokescreen blocks the opening of the chimney—there is scarcely a hearthstone and a mere brass rim of fender. With shovel and tongs and most deliberate movements at last I got the flashing heap on the top of the fire and breathed again. I even trembled for half an hour after. How near one is to death among common movement. Time, there is no need *we* should recognize this[.] Death should be out of sight behind a blood-red curtain, that life may dance and be healthy: but only a gray veil is between us, and we always see the menace that should be thickly hidden—therefore we halt or trip in our measure and are languid.[194]

EC This must end—we should mop and mow at each other if we stayed wholly with death and the dead. The Thames-side house at Richmond would limit us fearfully—and our animals more. We have been turning with zest toward the old house at Petersham to which our dreams went at the beginning of this year. The lease will be out in seven years and £200 premium is asked—so the [...] Artists will not lead us into temptation and keep us from sight of it. We feel that to fling a £100 each to seven fat years would not be crazy almsgiving.

So we write for a permit to Shannon; and also we write to our lawyer Daniell for him to gain all particulars of 1, Paragon. Certainly Richmond-Petersham is the one goal this planet sets before us—and the life of our wills flows toward the Thames. Dr. Hewetson says the Thames Valley is healthy and the river mists would not be worse for me than the climate of Reigate.[195]

EC We love the lowly, bright Paragon—we shall soon make our tiny front gay—a very smart little front, with paint and latticing. And the river arbour can be made a kennel for Musico. The Parlour! It is perfect! The "hovel" is sweet smelling, sun-full (except, alas, at the back)—a strong, comely,[196] loveable strip of a home. After lunch at The Star and Garter, Michael and I "foot it" in the Park—Michael Bacchic in a blessing content and in magnificent wind . . . it seems as if there were some life for us yet.

And while in *Mon Abri*[i] a great barge passes like a ghostly whale that has taken to one of the rivers of Paradise, being dead. The fleet stealth of the apparition is delicious—it glides hugely. And there we lean on Richmond Bridge where the people will gather to see the Chow and Basset take their

---

i "My Shelter." For Michael Field, an early and short-lived nickname for their new home.

waterside airing. The tide swings down and overflows the path of the sunset across it.

And then we buy flowers—and the man looks as if he were entertaining angels that would stay or at least return—four bunches of freesias, four of anemones, and a love-knot of Neapolitan violets—We have to travel part of the way home third class—to know the separate existence of each penny in our purses.[197]

KB *Mon Abri, Thursday, February 9th, 1899.*
—I sign my will, Dr. Hewetson being witness. I toil extremely with doves, and dogs, and house [. . .], and orders for the garden that is to me as a churchyard, round a disused church. The flower-man comes, bearing gayest daffodils and tulips of a rare rose satin over daintiest underlinen. I rush to the shops for stamps and change.

As I reach the door of Durdans, I am met by my Fellow. She embraces me with the greeting—"You are the Mistress of 1, Paragon, Richmond." We kiss over a bunch of white, fragrant stalks I carry in my hand—then lunch, and the letters of reference that the trustees may be satisfied, and Chow and I tell [Amy]— bearing to her at last a joyous telegram, and more walks in the moist garden where the Snowdrops are bursting, and the hairdresser to cut and wave;— never have I done, or been subject to, in one day, so many divergent things.

Henry dresses exquisitely in garnet-necklace and bloom bodice.

We send to the Artists "an annunciation by the flower of allspice" (two blossoms—sole on our plant)—Michael Field, At Home, March 25th and all days following—1, Paragon, Richmond.[198]

EC It was exhilarating to gather my Love out of the very wet rain and tell the news through a kiss that 1, Paragon is ours. I feel *renewing* as a process that is as yet a wild confusion in me—but the certain movements of the confusion tell me that it will become a dance. "Sweet Thames flow softly till I end my song." Indeed the song in my heart is an Epithalamion[i]—a marriage song of absolutely joined lives: a dream that Eros returns to us after the years of a lifetime as a gift.[199]

EC At night Michael and I in the hollow silence of Durdans arrange and furnish our Abri Rooms, creating them ours, till sleep is banished for half the night. [. . .] When we are growing older, we must not touch our love with the

i A form of poetry celebrating a marriage, made canonical by Edmund Spenser's "Epithalamion" (1595).

lyrical—we can but magnify it by the touch of the tragic. All other appeal is sentimental.[200]

Sunday, February 12th.
Shannon writes—

We are glad to hear that you are glad. We are also glad for a gray blue Persian Kitten who is like a lamb, a bear, an elephant, a pig, a moth, a caterpillar, a mouse, your gloves and Ricketts' pocket handkerchief. When you come to Richmond it shall scratch the Chow. C.H.S.[201]

EC We receive a most genuine Ricketts letter[202]—no dictation to Shannon—Ricketts himself pressing his pen with the instantaneousness of his own nature.
He says—

In colouring a house, see that the temper of each room is kept. When a room hides from the sun provide it with colours and hanging that love the shade: the green of green shadows in the heart of a wood, blue of that blue haunting a grot, the colours found under the sea; place also mirrors in it that listen to you, that look like pools. In these cool rooms various objects may be hung or placed—shadow is kind to ugly but useful books.

In rooms that love the sun use colours that love the sun also: white, ivory, gold, yellow, fawn, some shades of rose even. In these rooms the objects should be well-chosen; the sun is angry with ugly thick shapes but loves the corners of delicate frames and dainty furniture. Here the mirrors should be allowed to *talk*: provide them with subjects of conversation, carnations, roses, anemones, woodbine, rings on hands, fruit in a basket or on a silver dish. Chinese embroideries.

In all these rooms strive to keep the furniture close to the walls as in Persia. The air and light will love you for this—a rare carpet may then broad in an open space, lady friends will not overset snowdrops in slender glasses or bump against things and male friends or relations will not leave hot briars or smouldering[203] cigarettes upon satinwood—or even galoches. We beg you to kiss the Chow behind the left ear for our dear little Cat. I think a mess of basset paws [. . .] might induce him to leave Durdans—if not there is still the river gate. We shall expect to see your roses in an ebony car drawn by zebras; you of course will arrive in a chariot of ivory drawn by pards.[i] Please consider us in the matter of meals or other small matters of assistance. Your slaves on the date of your arrival.[204]

---

i That is, leopards.

EC Then Shannon writes a correcting card "I have repented—warm colours should pervade the house, warm blues, warm greens, warm whites, warm everything." Also, I have a letter from Amy accepting with a thrill of joy my offer that the marriage should take place from Paragon, Richmond, with father Thames to give the bride away.[205]

EC We talk about Paragon and its furnishing—the Artists will mix our paints. They want us to have the walls of our parlour covered with the gold of the Dial-Screen at Warwick Street—then[206] to treat it in a Dutch manner and devote it to tulips.

Ricketts is enchantingly poetic on the behaviour of flowers under sunlight in different stories of a house. In the sunroom above our parlour, that should be devoted to bowls of flowers, anemones would become like butterflies and flit to the corners of the room from which the cook with a duster would have to brush them.

Flowers simply take wing when they are high up in the sunlight—while below, in our Dutch room, the anemones would never leave their bowl, but glow quietly in their place. The sunroom must be ivory or have walls of Indian matting. A hall should be ancestral . . . no effort to make it speak of oneself should be taken—it should be yielded to the passage of the generations to the transitoriness of comings and goings—this is to keep me from an expensive paper.

The lower rooms should not have such light tones and light furniture as the higher rooms as the sun stoops to them and does not play through them fancifully. My Queen Anne bedroom must have a neutral wall and every gaiety crowd into Michael's river-bedroom.[207]

EC We tell Ricketts of our sale of books to realise the price of Michael's wedding present to Amy, "An old silver Dutch tea-pot with one dove on the top"— "to exclude the other pigeon" smiles Ricketts finely and with joy.

The Artists will hire the dentist's boat (You must have one tooth a year drawn to win the privilege of hiring it) and lie alongside to watch Amy and her bridegroom disappear behind an island.

Ricketts gives a quaintly true description of Paragon—"a doll's house in front and the poop of a vessel behind"—he thinks the combination perfectly delightful.

What makes Ricketts so essentially an artist in conversation and in composition is the quality of strangeness by which Life becomes art. He has many weaknesses, many whims (that with him are not affectations, but tendrils out of the very stock of his nature)—but because he can make all that he touches unfamiliar he belongs to that Kingdom that must differ from the world if it is to exist. Personality is the [208] power of a will to impress the world; genius the power of a will to translate it into another world.

After long talk on the Paragon, we turn to the Italian journey. May they come back alive! Shannon thinks of drinking soda water! Ricketts has a foreign body; but Shannon's digestion is English. On the other hand, Ricketts shrivels up at the thought of custom houses and Italian spoken by gestures. We fire them with the desire to become slave-owners and have a gondolier at their call for a whole week. [. . .]

Ricketts offers us any of their lithographs or woodcuts to put anywhere at the side of a mantel shelf, behind an umbrella stand.

Now I must relate a strange thing—[209]the spell of the "gee-gee" carpet over me. It simply makes me awkward and enormous. Three times I kicked it in to rucks in the floor, with helpless imbecility of movement; and the strangest thing of all is that I felt where my soles touched it to grow elephantine—my knees were to me as bolsters, my dress was Esquimaux in bulk—my boots—well if I had vast turtles as feet, their shells could not have been heavier than my slave-leather. And Michael knew all this by merely looking at me, saw I was amplitudinous. Curse the gee-gees!

Shannon takes us to the station—he has a delicious gift of leaving you without parting, without disturbing the counting of life by a jar as almost everyone does. We part like ships even at a railway-station![210]

EC The wretches of artists contemplate starting for Italy about April 20th, which will hurry our work. They smoke at the Paragon and turn over Morris papers,[i] with puffs of *Whew! . . . My goodness . . . Crikey!* But their creativeness seems paralised and we only settle the guestroom with Morris "Blackthorn" and blue ceiling; Michael's River Bedroom in the "Larkspur and Rose"; grot with Old Woodbine paper; Sun Room with ivory paint; Dutch Room with gold Japanese paper . . . in the Sulking-room we want Morris' "Acanthus": it is described by the artists as "liver and bacon."[211]

EC *Wednesday, March 20th.*

To Guilford to get table, chairs, sideboard—necessary things—*Result*—we sit in Williamson's shop and Michael buys for me my wedding present for Richmond . . . a small tea casket (call it not caddy) of ivory and tortoise-shell—the loveliest object I have ever loved; "nothing too much" dreamt into shape.

---

i Wallpaper designs by the Arts and Crafts movement designer, author, and socialist William Morris (1834–96).

And we buy old cut-glass liqueur glasses and old silver egg spoons, and three of the most perfect coffee tables with seed legs! There is in our behaviour a riot of luxurious contrariety.

Walking around Durdans garden.

There is a sense of the dead about the fragrance and entreaty of the air. I feel to lean on the father's arm and with him overlook the teeming bit of Earth that was his that will, we trust, continue to be ours!

And it is a terrible joy to feel my own Love's arm where his used to support me.[212]

EC *Thursday, March 30th.*

We also visit Miss Combes and buy from her her grandmother's small oval mirror and some old blue China. She likes to know where they will be. "The things are my own—I have no one to leave them to"—what a comment on the severance from one's race that is the abnormality of the single life or the forlorn life—*The things are my own.*

She has got some perfectly ridiculous animals—a crowned lion and zebra, and some yellow turrets for tapers (perfectly absurd!) that I shall be charmed into buying for the paneled room.[213] [. . .]

There is a little picture of the Chow fast asleep along the Ilkley on which Mother[214] died, with the Cross they put above father's Zermatt grave, and Whymper photograph of the Zermatt Valley, over his head. No one can understand how sacred to us this scrap of our heart's doom is—how dear the creature that soothes it . . . our little Chow of the night-time.[215]

EC This last week I have chanced to take up and read, while drinking coffee in Amy's little room, some of the *Sonnets from the Portuguese*—they have the hideousness of newborn animals. It is the recent and callow love that is so painful to me in them . . . Love should not come as a *new experience* to any woman—she should belong to Aphrodite the first time she looks at her face in the mirror—she should feel behind her the inheritance of Eve, Cleopatra, Queen Mary, Juliet. Womanhood should be the Evocation of Love—and the ancient sovereignties of the god be hers by right.[216]

EC *Ricketts irritates by talking about the Vale Keats instead of home decorating.*

At last, we start to look at Spanish Rugs, with many conjurations that we will leave Ricketts to settle everything, breathe "it is too long" if we very much want a carpet, and with such fuss of caution and self-importance as man so amusingly makes when he goes to a shop in woman's company. There are no gee-gee rugs to be had.[217] [. . .]

EC He refuses to enter Liberty's[i] to see a piece of old Venetian brocade specially chosen out and we retire to St James' Tea Rooms with nothing accomplished and an atmosphere of ineffectiveness round us.

As we drink tea Ricketts tells us how he and Shannon are making their wills.[218] [. . .] They dare not go to Italy until they have given their Hokusai Col to the British Museum, their bits of Antiquity to Oxford; and left all their work in the hands of Sturge Moore.[ii] So they have got Whitaker's Almanack[iii] and are their own lawyers.

Without the lawful intervention of Sturge Moore, Ricketts' sister, who has married a German doctor, would claim his unpublished cartoons or Shannon's family in the depths of Lincolnshire would wish[219] "to have all dear Charlie's drawings." "If we make our wills we think the little railway accident will not occur."[220]

EC *Wednesday.*

Michael and I put on our scallop-shells and away to Toplady's.[iv] The things are well-chosen with the restfulness of love. Ivory-coloured Wedgewoods, Sheffield egg cups, Dutch sconces greet us, and inside an American accent, a pleasant face that reminds in black and white of Mary Costelloe's pastel effects, and a most serviceable pleasure-seeking kindness.[221]

I buy a Demon's toasting fork, two lovely sconces, and Michael a cut-glass, silver-mounted mustard pot, "a real Toplady article," for Amy. We really enjoy ourselves—these Americans set life capering—strange that all *"the set"* should now be "fizzing" over furniture and we be contemporaneous!

After lunch at Club, we buy at Morris' the Brussels carpet for Michael's River Room. Ridiculous Miss Toplady! I am glad I have enjoyed her wares.[222]

EC *Saturday.*

Again to Miss Toplady's.

We find French stuffs of exceeding value—a Triton-woven stuff such as

i A shop founded in 1875 by Arthur Lasenby Liberty, known for its decorative goods, including imported textiles, furniture, wallpapers, and clothing.

ii Thomas Sturge Moore (1870–1944), British poet and artist, and later also Michael Field's literary executor; Katsushika Hokusai (1760–1849), Japanese painter and printmaker. Ricketts and Shannon ultimately distributed works in their collection to the British Museum, the Ashmolean Museum in Oxford, and the Fitzwilliam Museum in Cambridge.

iii Annual book of articles, facts, figures, and tables published from 1868–1997.

iv Miss Toplady was a London curiosity shop established by Mary Berenson and her brother, Logan Pearsall-Smith, as a means of exporting Italian art and antiquities. Between 1898 and 1905, the shop influenced ideas of connoisseurship in London, and also played an instrumental role in Bernard Berenson's curation of the collection of Isabella Stewart Gardner in Boston.

waves are made of for the River Room and blues that never will forget the sea. I buy an iron knocker from Siena, a Wedgewood sugar basin and coffee pot.

A gentleman doubted the existence of Toplady—he was invited to meet her at afternoon tea—great tension due to hope. A telegram. "Ill—unable to come. Many regrets. Sell suite for £70—Toplady." Surely the telegram proved the real existence.[223]

EC We go forth, we two, to found a home. I and my Love, we have chosen each other with all our strength, inspiration, and yearning—may our home be a rest, a place that fosters, and makes warmth; may it be pleasant by its riverside and shelter joyousness![224]

KB *May 15th. Last Night at Durdans.*

Between noon and one o'clock I looked out and a van was being thrust through the lime-tree leafiness—There was a second one behind—two coffins to receive all that remains of the home *he* made for our shelter; two brutal coffins.[225] [. . .]

Well, Father remains and Durdans remains—they are both of my life stream, of myself.

The rooms are walls with papers on them I know and floors of straw and lumber—so Durdans ends, to remain forever alive as on Jubilee Day with its banners and roses, or on Midsummer Day 1897 with its gray irises and the sprinkle of wild sweetbriar starlets beyond.

I must sleep . . .[226]

EC *Whitsunday, May 21st, Paragon.*

Our beautiful meadows are misty, the buttercups hide behind the river-mist; the full Thames has many boats along its mid current.

The Chow is at my feet in the River Room; Michael is at Petersham Church.

I am thankful for my towering little home; and almost welcome the many trials it entails as a pledge it is not too perfect.

The servants have behaved as only servants can, and brilliantly supported the arguments for slavery—no one has done the work promised; we live among workpeople, unfinished rooms, ladders, complaints, and gabble. But the tides swing up and down our river, and the light is full of the water, and the greenness of the meadows rejoices calmly in its own plenitude. Also our rooms grow toward sweetness. The carpet is down in the River Room, the solemn Queen Anne Room has its pictures, the Durdans study begins to reincarnate itself in the Grot.[227]

EC I came home to find a strange letter that had not come through the post laid on the study table for me—£100 from my dear Love, tenderly given at sacrifice to herself, that the weight of my heavy expenses might be lightened.[i]

I had wings—clean, weeping joy. Our little home would not have a comer's weight of debt on it—Beloved!

After gardening, we lie down in the study—Music and Whym sharing the Morris Couch with me. We have not changed for the evening; we have worked ourselves into callousness—the cotton blouse is thus as the satin bodice. We yawn and sleep—the dogs yawn and sleep; the room is a cave of sleep.[228]

EC *On the anniversary of James Cooper's disappearance.*
Midsummer Day, June 24.

This is such a strange anniversary—spent in the home Michael and I so longed for, our first married home. Everything is so much sharper than last year at Durdans. For days we have felt the shadow of our majestic and terrible sorrow coming down on us from the mountains. Yesterday E.B., who has been to Zermatt and undertook our care of the grave, writes of it as only a relative would—with passion, without efficiency. I long to tend it with my own hands and to make that bit of foreign land a portion of my country. To think he died and is buried *a stranger*, he who always hugged home and was never for trusting himself to the unfamiliar.

More and more, as I go with him through his Midsummer Death Day, I am sure he strayed and did the almost impossible by descending to the rock, over which he fell, in spite of his years and the extreme difficulty to one totally unused[229] to mountain-climbing.

He slid down and it was fatal. There was a shock—the hands laid against brow and heart . . . then unconsciousness in all probability, and it may be long unconsciousness . . . for I sometimes think that when I had that revelation of joy and felicity on the Saturday morning at dawn, it was the moment of his actual release. Perhaps the souls of *both* Father and Mother have touched mine as they parted from earth—Heaven knows how close and vital my being is to their life of life![230] [. . .]

How little anyone knows about us! They think we have lost an old man, who hindered the expansion of our lives, who often rendered us rebellious, who was good and limited. They little know we have lost our profoundest lover, our Curse laid on us by the Mighty Love, the fashioner of my genius, of

---

i Cooper's personal resources were merged with those of her sister, Amy, by preference in their father's will. Bradley, a generation ahead and partaking of the same family resources, was more affluent than Cooper.

Michael's inspiration, the form that rules our lives, the pulse of our Fate—the tenderness that is an abiding grace to those who have once known it. His power is inconceivably terrible.[231]

It has nothing to do with our end—it is in force whether he lives or dies. Yes, here it is, as it was, as it will be. He encompasses those he loves with his unsurpassable love, his utter influence—his darkness.[232]

EC *Wednesday, June 28th.*

Sarah and Ellen leave us—unregretted of is sad; but they have been so self-ish and disobliging, so iron in their tyranny over mistresses of broken nerve that their departure is deliverance. As soon as the door shuts Whym and Music constitute themselves[233] our police. It is most attaching of the dogs.

We climb up and down the stairs of Paradise till our limbs are on the rack.

Then our new maids arrive—silver and brass of fine quality, so they appear. Lightning sweeps the river—meadows, rain crushes our roses. It is strange, and we ascend gladly to our beds.[234]

EC In a grovy field, beyond, the artists want to build a house—a builder's house of two stories in which they are to live till they get a very old house in which death will come on them while they are still furnishing rooms. There must be so many rooms they will never know in which they[235] will die.[236]

EC We see our new home in perspective as we walk—it is good to see it—its simplicity, its harmony, its river-lit charm. And we are grateful for these gifts in spite of our clear sight of its disadvantages—its steepness, its unpopularity with servants, its age and infirmity. We find its little garden is like a rich bit of carpet in our hearts. This home of ourselves—not of our past—is close and extraordinarily precious to us.

We see our new lives in perspective—[237] [. . .]

EC *Wednesday 23rd.*

Artists came to dine. Ricketts enjoys the reeking old baize on our satin-wood table that smells "like stupid Pater."[238]

EC *Sunday, September 10th.*

"Blessed are the dead which die in the Lord"

—because of lice.

To strive with this small infantry—

—to put on for helmet the hope of cleaning, clearing them out is enough.

Whym Chow [. . .] is all over minute sores; the fleas had found a nest for themselves where they might lay their young on Music's back yesterday; and were bringing forth thousands and ten thousands in our streets. And this, though our hands smell of lye without ceasing.[239]

KB *1st October, 1899.*

It is Sunday—the first Sunday of our married life. The river is deep and flowing; there is a river too in our hearts flowing deep.

She is above me, or below me, in the house, she only—gladness in her steps.

We are intensely desolate, yet so snug and warm, a squirrel in its winter nest.

The wind and rain have been wild and sweeping—the west edged with gold. The dead are gone, the little bride is gone; but the dead remain.

The dead have bidden farewell, the bride has bidden farewell; but the dead return.

In the autumn, in the spring they come to us, but the little bride will come no more forever.

For death binds; it is Life that severs.

We have her old terrier abandoned in the house. She is gone, the little bride is gone forevermore.[240]

EC *The story of Amy's wedding.*

On the 24th Francis arrived, and Dan came in red with river-bank fishing.[i] On the day itself I was toiling like the Marchioness[ii]—in pantry and paneled Room. I only saw the bride drink tea in her violet Fisher coat[iii] and[241] skirt and hat with gold and white jasmine in white chiffon—an end of chiffon curling itself round her neck, like a half-veil.

I scarcely go into my old brocade blouse and violet skirt before news came "it is all over—Miss Amy is Mrs. Ryan." No waiter had arrived; Lizzie, our third maid, had bleeding at the nose—Sarah was in bed, Crofts was pale as eggshell china.

I slashed at the Fowls and only left them when the arrival of the bridegroom's parents and the rest of the party was announced. They came in by our little river gate round which Michael had lavishly gathered palms, bamboos, late roses, clear-blue plumbago and white bavardias.

Michael and I so entirely lived where these people were and so entirely

---

i Cousins from the Bradley side of the family. Francis Bradley had proposed to Katharine Bradley in their shared youth.

ii *Little Nell and the Marchioness* was a play based on Dickens's *Old Curiosity Shop*, written by John Brougham and staged in New York in 1867. The Marchioness of the story was a poor servant girl rewarded with marriage to Dick Swiveler after nursing him back to health.

iii A full-length fur coat.

left the sacred kingdoms where they were not, that the entertainment was a success, and all shoals were avoided.

A maternal butler gave us of dishes he bore close to his breast [. . .] . Michael's glorious fruit—grapes and quinces, pears and lustre plums—lay among garlands of stephanotis, firm as marble, sheeny like satin, dropping odours—divinely mystical.[242]

Our rooms endured the company very well—they ceased to be intimate and schooled themselves to be receptive with dignity—and the light from the Thames silvered them.

Our quiet little bride and her bridegroom left us by the river-gate, passing by the palms, bamboos, late roses, clear-blue plumbagos and white bavardias, while rice beat them and old shoes were flung after them.

Outside the door was the river, the beautiful old bridge, the tide of wave and light and wind—an angler who looks once and angles thereafter. The pair walked away along the towing path and waved from under Richmond Bridge.

So it ended. We bade farewell to the strangers—and returned to the strange house full of broken mats, piled fruits, champagne glasses, and the sweetness of tuberose and of stephanotis clutching one's sense intolerably.

The weariness—

The blankness—

The relief.

The horror as if the precipice of fatigue and folly over which one has been hanging.

The sense that the Dead were removed, as much as the Dogs we had sent to stables.[243]

KB *Sunday, October 8th.*

A most happy day, though outside it begins in winter mist and winter. [. . .] [W]e watch the sun drop red behind the elm-branches, and are much with our dogs [. . .] moved by the extreme devotion that constrains them to forsake the warm study carpet and lie down on the Italian matting in the Sun Room at our feet.

Henry dresses our altar there with sloe gin in the old Murano bottle:[i] we sing

"Lilies and light and liquor: liquor, lilies and light"
'Tis thus the sweet hours flicker
'Tis thus we claim delight.[244]

i Sloe gin is a sweet liquor made from sloe berries. Michael Field keep their sloe gin in a bottle made of Venetian Murano glass.

KB *December 7th.*

I toddle forth with my two dogs Music and Whym on the towing path, in the grey mist. I am not anxious now, and I fall to meditation. Suddenly, almost close to our door—a heap of gross human refuse.—I turn away in disgust and anger, and a little further on, along the same path, I find a dropt rose, fair, still delicately fair, and without soil.

And I linger: but modernism lingers to emphasise its disgust and passes by the scarcely perceptible fairness.

One common towing path for us all—but we may each determine what shall arrest us.[245]

EC *Christmas.*

So strange a day—unguided by tradition, none of the old things in the old places, Amy gone, Dick gone: Memories without their local habitation. A holly twine along the dresser in the hall; a mistletoe bough in the study; fir behind the tombstone cross from Zermatt and mistletoe in front of all—these are our decorations.

The Sun Room is lovely with small orange-trees and boughs, with specimen blooms of rose Chrysanthemums, stars or Medusas and with the breathing balm of freesias.

Michael and I give each other no presents—our gifts (mirror and shelves) had not arrived—Michael writes a Miltonic sonnet to our Queen while the Christmas letters remain unopened. The day is a day of grace and light in the air—damp underfoot.

We take the dogs across the river and give thanks for our climbing little home. As Michael has said all goes well at first during the afternoon—then our little Chow, who has been poorly since yesterday, makes us very anxious. Turkey appeals in vain to Michael . . . the Chow does not eat.[246]

EC *The last morning of the Old Year.*

Amy has been with us and gone—she came the day after Christmas, and we lived the old life together seamlessly for four days. Now she is gone, and Michael and I watch each other in a little round mirror of Ricketts' design that hangs on our gold wall and reflects our life in its circle—this new life of our deepest desire realised for us. Michael looks most dear in that mirror with the glints of joy about her lips and eyes in the Dresden portrait and a face made plastic by Experience—How strange it is that Experience to be noted vigorously on our faces is experience of suffering—so few people have any eyes for the artist-work of joy. . . . It is not popular or [understood].[247]

[. . .] After lunch we lie on our condemned Chesterfield couch[i] and look round our white sunroom aglow with spring warmth. The river is a stream greater and greater by virtue of its own expansion toward its banks and the meadows. We lie "warm in the wraps of love" and realize in a calm like that of old age that we cannot ever have such an afternoon again—cannot wait the birth of a new century together and in our golden room by the waterside sunset we read the passage in *Stephania* about the millennium.[248]

EC I find Michael has lighted her altar candles and set our fourteen volumes on the altar, rededicating them to the new century in which they trust to live, praising the God of life for the joy we have had in their creation: our passion this year is gratitude—which is the looking round on all that has influenced us and beholding it is very good.

Michael has tried to go to church—but has returned from the husks.

It is terribly moving to leave our great and beloved dead in their century— it seems as if time laid over them another coffin lid. I feel a mourning and lamentation that can take no voice. But how I bless the era that has given me the love of Father, Mother and a noble poet. How I shall always bless the last year of that era, for without any impiety, my love and I have been able to dwell in our own home by the great river of England and to dwell there in unity, in devoted happiness.[249]

The year has been just what was foretold to me—a year of the rebuilding of life—full of the dusty trials of the mason, made small by the details that build up a whole. We have scarcely worked at all. Michael has done some dozen good sonnets—[. . .]

This is all: yet much has been accomplished. We have founded our beautiful little home after the wrench from Durdans. We have made each room beautiful at great cost and by great economy, and as we were able. We have established a great friendship on gold foundations. Amy has been married from our home and gone to make a new home. She is happy in the state of marriage—her husband has a fixed appointment.

Finally our domestic arrangements are not defaming and impossible as they have been for many months, and as harass withdraws, our[250] minds lie open and fallow to the spring. Surely looking round we have reason to behold this year has been very good.[251] [. . .] Motorcars clatter by—the amusement 1899 ends with. Ah me![252]

---

i A large couch, typically upholstered in leather, with rolled arms. This one is condemned because its replacement has already been ordered.

EC I do not hear the Bells—Over the river the hovering of time comes to me alone. I feel our new century will open to us much joy and trial that needs joy and faith to bring it to good. We shall begin a great new drama of the Renaissance, but while we write it we shall have to strive for its trust in life it embodies.—Like our century we shall face the difficulties of an empire building when circumstances are stubborn.

I believe both England and Michael Field will win. We have to conquer the pressure of detail on our lives, of constrictions on our power of travelling—we have to be plastic as we have never been.

We have to conquer the pain of Bernard's probable marriage with Mary, to hold ourselves strong against their old fatal influence.

This year built our circumstances—the century will find us building ourselves. I do not feel 1900 will be a peaceful year—but the strain to us and England will be athletic not weakening.

My love lights the altar-flames—O to worship more constantly to obtain the triune blessing of creativeness.[253]

We cannot love each other more—but we can strengthen each other more and cheer each other more.

God grant us some time in this new hundred years to grow and multiply our works—so much time has been taken from us by sorrow.

It will soon be midnight when 1900 draws breath—1900—the Father and Mother were not to see, that we see. And the road of our desires is in front of us as far as we may look!

O Century, with the End we may never reach—we shall be strange to these one hundred years off as the heroes of the French Wars to us of the cycles and nerves!

Dear God, to think the very century in which I was born is almost asleep forever. I bless it as it falls asleep.[254]

Little Chow stretches himself—

The river is silent—

The air is very silent.

Strength and joy be with us and with the year that is born, strength and joy to England.

For us, my own and I, all that our "life in one" can be under the eyes of God in our home by the Thames.

All hail 1900. Welcome through the silence.[255]

CHAPTER 4

Crash

1900–1907

THE FIRST FEW YEARS of the twentieth century found Michael Field in a period of relative quietude, marked around the edges by gloom and apprehension. The arrival of the new century brought a more direct reckoning with "modernity" than ever before. In 1901, Bradley and Cooper were proud to complete their own decadal census form, recalling the circumstances of ten years earlier, when they were daughter figures in a father figure's home. Now firmly established as householders themselves, Michael Field enjoyed curating occasional social events involving familiar friends Charles Ricketts and Charles Shannon, their future literary executor Thomas Sturge Moore, and on several memorable occasions, William Butler Yeats.

At the center of their home and their hearts? Whym Chow, Michael Field's unruly and occasionally aggressive canine lord and master, in whom they reposed the most intimate elements of their private relationship. Just as "Michael Field" provided the organizing principle for Bradley and Cooper's identity as a writer, Whym Chow, another masculine figure—son? husband? deity?—provided the women with an organizing principle for their intimate lives. The intimate and the professional converged in 1902, during Michael Field's summer holiday in Rottingdean when, during a visit with the family of Rudyard Kipling, Whym Chow brutally killed the Kipling pet rabbit. Michael Field basked proudly in glow of the Chow's violent masculinity.

By this time in their career as a writer, Michael Field's published work met with almost no positive commentary, minimal critical attention of any sort, and negligible sales. The play *Anna Ruina*, for example, sold just nineteen copies from its publication run of nineteen hundred. In *Works and Days*, Bradley and Cooper stewed over the impression that the world had left them behind. Yeats's solicitation of Michael Field's play *Deirdre* for the Abbey Theatre in Dublin spiked hopes that were dashed by his rejection of the play after he had read it (and further still by the production of his own play by that name for the Abbey Theatre in 1907). This was a personal crisis as well as a professional one: in 1900, Bernard Berenson finally married Mary Costelloe, foreclosing the narrow channel of hope nurtured in Edith Cooper's heart for the past decade. In 1903, Tommy Sturge Moore announced his intention to marry, precipitating another crisis in Michael Field's social circle: "no man who is married can be a friend." News of the engagement of Bradley's cousin Francis, who had proposed to her in her girlhood, left the poets shaken.

A rapid series of closely felt deaths further left Michael Field with the sense that they were out of step with time. John Ruskin, so formative to Bradley's early development as a thinker, died fewer than three weeks into the new century. Friedrich Nietzsche, so formative to the artistic and philosophical development of Bradley and Cooper, died in August 1900. "Oscar"—Wilde, of course—followed too quickly, on November 30, 1900, in Paris, a broken relic of aesthetic splendor after serving his two-year sentence for "gross indecency" in Reading Gaol; Cooper struggled with De Profundis, Wilde's harrowing jailhouse letter to his lover, published posthumously in 1905. Weeks after Wilde died, on January 21, 1901, the "Victorian" period finally concluded with the end of Queen Victoria's life at age eighty-one, after nearly sixty-four years on the throne.

The concept of modernity, a source of inspiration and desire for Michael Field through the 1890s and their acquaintance with Bernard Berenson, became a source of apprehension early in the new century. Michael Field's later-in-life social conservatism found them on the wrong side of history as fervent supporters (Bradley especially so) of the British side in the Second Boer War in South Africa. Victoria's death offered Bradley the opportunity to write scathingly about the myths of "progress" that had proliferated during Victoria's reign: "Growth of suburbs, growth of education among the poor, an unmitigated evil—extension of franchise, and growth of free trade, unmitigated disasters.—the growth of trades unions, the damnation of the future. [. . .] The growth of sentimentality—toward crime; and of science craft (the priestcraft of the Victorian age) insidious, berotting influences." If such prospects of social mobility were not bad enough, modernity as represented in modes of transport was odoriferous and intrusive to Michael Field; the possibility of a tunnel under the English Channel and of an omnibus in the sky were the logical extensions of the buses rattling on the Petersham Road by day and night. Further reinforcing the impression of encroaching violence, the suffrage movement, so compelling years before to both Bradley and Cooper, was radicalized to the point of prison hunger strikes in the first decade of the twentieth century.

The most frightening violence of all, however, took place far too close to home to contemplate. In January 1906, over the course of a day featuring multiple botched attempts, Bradley euthanized Michael Field's beloved Whym Chow. The dog's precipitous decline, likely from meningitis, left Michael Field stunned, shattered, and at a loss for how to go forward. They gave serious thought to decamping from Paragon, home no more in Whym Chow's absence. They saw the dog's shining coat everywhere they looked, reflected in the satinwood, mirrors, and other gleaming surfaces of their aesthetic home. The painter and designer Lucien Pissarro kindly produced cards announcing Whym Chow's death at no cost to Michael Field. Cooper poured her grief into the sequence of elegiac poems published after her death as the collection *Whym Chow, Flame of Love*.

Early in 1907, Cooper informed Bradley of her conversion to Catholicism. Though Bradley followed suit, the moment that Henry and then Michael converted, each independent of the other, marked an "end" for Michael Field. This was not the end of their lives, though those ends came soon enough, in 1913 and 1914, respectively, just as modernity hit hard in the form of the Great War. Nor was it the end of "Michael Field" as an author; he published up through the end of Bradley's death and even beyond. What ended here was the mutual intimacy imbedded within Michael Field and between Michael and Field: the inspiration that made one of two. As we read through the years before Whym Chow's death, the end is in sight, visible in Cooper's frustration, loneliness, boredom, and conviction that the world is moving forward while she is standing still. Catholicism offers her a shell, preserving the authorial function of Michael Field while realigning the women's private and intimate relationship.

Works and Days, 1900

EC *January 10th, Settee Day!*
  Michael writes early on January 9th:

Artists,
   Will you come tomorrow Wednesday evening—before nine—not to bid farewell to the Chesterfield, but to hail the new settee?
   The Magnificent has been done—the Boers of barbarous scruple repulsed on every side.[i]

i Michael Field were passionate in their support of the British army in its war with the Boers in South Africa (1899–1902). The war erupted over Boer resistance to the expansion of the British

How dare Cowper sing the sofa . . . so cool and presumptuous.[i] Even the Artist traced *our* sofa with a trembling hand.

I write as madly, as foolishly, as St. Paul this morning. I am still drunk with the hot milk of last night—the hot milk we drank to Sir George and those Devons. *Michael.*

It came, Michael writes to Amy, from Guildford, the deep orange thing, burnt deep with the sun like the coloured races.

And the old Chesterfield was carted away. [. . .]

The Artists came. They bring a little cushion covered about with China-men, or, as they put it, with poets looking up at "poetesses" to console Michael for the loss of the comfortable Chesterfield. The old Poet has[1] to be duly propped up with ever more cushions from "the Grot," till at last the head is supported and the brain acknowledges haven.[2]

EC *January 12th.*

I am glad we shall be together, we who keep the first birthday in our new own home. The Dead like the hearth uninvaded when they would press close.

It is a joyous day, that gives on the sense of sound as a gold trumpet tube, when it glows becomes reverberant to the Spirit. I am keeping indoors with the lovely rooms we are filling with such love and thankfulness and springing life, with humour and even laughter.

For the first time since 1897 we found ourselves dancing a turn—in "the grot."

My Love has given me *L'Oiseau bleu*—the brooch designed by Rick-etts[ii] . . . Byzantine, wonderful—also three great[3] pearls in a ring—three bubbles of milk from Hera's[iii] breast. The Artists said they were tranquil—Shannon saw them in a portrait. Also, two Sheffield salt cellars—the glasses springing like flowers from the plated ground—the tendrils to hold them by rather heavy, as the Artists truly remark—but the glasses so captivating.[4]

EC. The Artists were summoned to tea on Wednesday to give their opinion as to an old mirror and an old Italian bowl from Toplady's. It happened they

---

Empire into the Transvaal. The British fought a brutal and destructive war against the outnum-bered Boers, until the Boers surrendered in 1902.

i William Cowper (1731–1900), poet and writer of hymns.

ii "The Blue Bird." Ricketts designed the enameled brooch, decorated with garnet, and had it fabricated at the London workshop of Carlo and Arthur Giuliano. The brooch is now in the collection of the Fitzwilliam Museum at the University of Cambridge, and Ricketts's sketches for the design are in the British Museum.

iii Hera is the goddess of marital harmony and the protectress of women in childbirth. She is also one of the twelve Olympians.

FIG 8. *The Blue Bird Brooch* (*L'Oiseau bleu*), designed by Charles de Sousy Ricketts and made by Carlo and Arthur Giuliano. The gold brooch depicts the shape of a bird on berried foliage. The bird's body is enameled opaque turquoise with enameled translucent green wings set with a garnet cabochon. The berries are made of seven coral cabochons and the bird's eye is a garnet cabochon. Height 4.7 cm, width 4.8 cm; 1899/1901. Photograph © The Fitzwilliam Museum, Cambridge.

were [5] late—we had finished tea and by chance were making Basset drum out "God Save the Queen" with his drumstick paws.

They, as symbolists, thought the sounds meant no welcome—the entertainment at end and looked like flight. [. . .]

We are determined to have a real judgment by both Artists separately. We toss a penny—Shannon is doomed to pronounce first—so Ricketts is left alone in the Gold Room.

Shannon likes the bowl and would certainly have the mirror—it is charming, and would look well in the Gold Room. Ricketts is summoned—he has been having a secret cup of tea and secretly feeding the Basset with a lump of sugar—He likes the bowl—it is unexpected and "chummy," what Rossetti would have bought—the mirror (taking [6] my side) he hates, as a bit of romantic furniture, as bric-a-brac.

Instantly Shannon fades from his judgment, excuses himself with a kind of hot haste of shame.

Curious! There are some people born whose opinion is all judging and makes a culprit of anyone else's. We used to go over like that with *Doctrine* . . . we do still with the Fairyman and no one else melts our thoughts of men and things.

It was tragicomic to see the process in poor Shannon. These radiant pronouncers make one see with their light—that is the point; and in their light who can stand?[7]

KB *Sunday, January 21st, Death of Ruskin.*

It is very much to me, the news of his death—touching me not with grief at all—with music—with music one has not heard for years—and an indescribable sense of precious relics that one has not seen—for a moment exposed—of the past that is with one forever, and has been neglected—of the past that is only attaching—when it is fugitive, and lest, and reappears.

How I loved him!

—For years, best of all creatures on the earth.

Good is it that he is away from the misery of this sinful world . . . but as I sit and watch the dick-birds hopping[8] about, and the sky, already a little restless with the spring—I don't like to think his eyes will enjoy these things no more.

For the earth was his and the fulness thereof.[i] And he has left us for creed so much—labour, and peace, in worship—the joy of the servant of God—that recognizes the smallest little chickweed His, and loves His work all the six days through.

—And this joy is simply unknown to the moderns, who love their cribbed, idol orchids, the work of men's devil hands; love the potted, tainted flower, in its mimicry, its self-absorption, its grotesqueness, and care nothing for the creatures that bear us the honey, the light, the dew.[9]

EC On Saturday afternoon, while Francis is away at a Matinée, Michael goes to Spring Terrace to borrow *The Importance of Being Earnest*.[ii] The Artists propose an advertisement in the *Daily Mail* for a new companion for Michael, who will like all winds, and will not eat soup, or chicken or cod with shrimp sauce.[10]

i Psalm 24:1.
ii Oscar Wilde's 1895 play was a hit at London's Empire Theatre, until it abruptly closed during the scandal of Wilde's "gross indecency" charges.

EC *Tuesday, April 9th.*

Nutt[i] sends statement of *Anna Ruina*—a good name Ruina—Queen of Ruin. Only nineteen copies have been sold! We have to pay £15, as by agreement, and the excellent David is then still a loser.

No wonder I regard publication as merely fire insurance. We have no readers; before our work a beautiful desert swims golden . . . who shall say what is on the other side—but I am soothed by the solitude—Michael is wearied by it, alas!

After we had abstracted the £15 from our income, we went out, Michael and I—together at last, after weeks of separation. I bathed in the west wind; I saw almond trees throwing a rose veil over the bareness of all their trees; I felt that companionship two lovers can only feel when the world has living walls round them, of air and trees and sky, instead of canvas and brick.[11]

EC The Fairyman brought marrons glacés.[ii] Michael was digging round the Solomon's seals in the garden: Ricketts stepped on the balcony and breathed *Michael* to make her turn to the sweets.

She turned—one warm glad rose round her snowy teeth—and was soon wooed up. She reports there though his voice had a fairylike discretion of secrecy, his appearance on the turret of ivy stems was ineffective. He looks very happy—I thought with creation—but no! With foolish plays and the buying of satinwood. The Artists' rooms are full—so they are going to buy more. Alas, the hateful[12] amberwood will take them from Richmond to some Palace in town—a studio that is to be built by a millionaire within Holland Park. We both feel as if we could weep—the river darkens, the future grows small. But not a stone is yet in place on the purchased site—only the hateful amberwood glows in chambering masses at Spring Terrace and takes much of the sunshine from the prospect of our lives.[13] [. . .]

KB Henry said to me yesterday—"Your face is elemental—is of the elements, mine is of the spheres." How true this is! He hears the music of the spheres—far off on the rim of all the agitation the happy buzz of the infinite and ordered swirl—I feel only the havoc of wind and fire.[14]

KB *Thursday, May 15th.*

Our last day in the [New] Forest.[iii]

I am full of dreams. Henry and I give up Paragon, and come here, leaning up against Nature, taking the comfort of her loveliness. Here we close in for

i Alfred Nutt (1856–1910) was a publisher and a scholar of Celtic folklore.
ii Candied chestnuts.
iii Michael Field visited the New Forest in Hampshire annually for many years.

our sunset, and here we die. We may travel and spend weeks in London, but *our final home is here.*

Henry dreams this little parlour full of his choicest satinwood and the Sheffield plate—but rare bits of Roman and Venetian glass on the cupboard and shelves. Whym Chow will be happy here—and there must be a Great Dane in the yard. Music, bless the dear hound—Yes, Music must be here too. "For of such is the kingdom of heaven."[15]

EC *Weekend at the Montague Arms, Beaulieu.*

Michael is sitting for a moment in the porch, Whym at her feet, and I am in our beautiful bedroom at the top of the house. Suddenly a great dog (a bobtail) attacks Whym and hangs on. [Michael] seizes Whym in her arms— the worst thing she could have done, as Jack clings on his loins with a tenacity she fears means the death grip. Then she gives a shriek—like that I heard in the distance when grandmother lay dead before Michael, like that I heard from the high bedroom of Hotel Mt. Rose at Zermatt when the terrible photograph had been exposed to her. *Michael can shriek*—a wild cry that loses all earthly body, Banshee-like, a wonder to me and to the frightened world . . . and I have been three times doomed to hear it afar.[16]

Whym Chow was uninjured.

EC *Describing her illness.*

My River Room was too hot for me at noon and I was drawn on an Ilkley into the Queen Anne Room. That Ilkley, my rack, my bed of Hell! And the first time I went so into that other bedroom, it was strewn with lint, cotton-wool, bottles, "foods"—and I realised I was very ill with a big illness.

The omnibus outside came up to my brains, rolled over them, and left them prone. Brilliant flowers from my brother John kept drawing my eyes to them, as they boasted of their pomp and splendour—poppies, gladioluses, carnations, roses of Spanish blood. Whenever my Love had to leave me one of the devoted maids was with me, and I liked the kind hand of Lillias pushing back my seaweed hair. She told me tales of all the people she had served and I was at the theatre—so hot I was and ready to magnify everything.[17]

I got a baby's bottle that I might drink water at night when I wanted—it became a magical pilgrim's bottle—slyly emptied at once, till wind took the place of water. I wore a brown Jaeger shawl[i]—I was the cocoa-queen delayed on my passage to visit Queen Victoria and finding my quarantine dull-dull. "Nothing happens." I wailed . . . and shortly after I nearly died in a heart at-

---

i From its founding in 1883 until the late 1920s, the Jaeger company produced animal-fiber clothing and textiles that they claimed provided health benefits.

tack that left me gray as bones for hours on hours. I have written of the gray country I nearly colonised. There was a magnet's power in its absolute solemnity I shall always feel till it draws me to itself.[18]

EC *Monday, July 23rd.*

Mary Costelloe comes to dine—brixsome, ruddy as David the King.[i] She is triumphant all along the line of her fate.

In the midst of dinner, I feel some announcement is on its way: I drink some brandy, confiding my heart to its care. Mary speaks of the villa she has been preparing, of Bernard's lack of interest in it. "The house will be ready by November, so we shall be *married*, I suppose, on the last day of October."

Married—to occupy a house!

Married—only (she says) for the sake of her mother and children.

Well! Bernard has had all the pleasures of change and of art this year, and has confessed (oh, strange artlessness for her to confess his avowal!) he has not once been happy. He now has miserable health. I would not be Bernard—

I can see him as I met him before he had been spellbound, at the Hotel de l'Opéra, in Mrs. Chandler Moulton's Paris Rooms. "Stay," she said, "to see a beautiful boy" . . . and he came in lustrous as a pomegranate flower, packed with ideas as a pomegranate fruit with its seeds, a dazzling energy. His very glance stung refreshingly, like spring water. Then—and now, infirm, he approaches a perfunctory marriage.[19]

KB *Monday, August 27th, 1900.*

Nietzsche died on Saturday Aug. 24th. This news reaches us penned up in our cottage most miserable and dejected, unable to drive, not strong enough to walk, trembling at every change of weather, without books, or secondary occupation.

And from all our friends comes story of sickness, or of home-return with chilled hearts.

[. . .]

A mouse is nibbling, nibbling at the cupboard, happy in his effort to win what his nature requires. [. . .]

EC Nietzsche—the great Thyrsus-bearer![ii] What he has been to our lives—but he used the Thyrsus too much to spear and cruelly transfix the world, not enough to deliver it and to set it dancing. One must not toss the

i   1 Samuel 16:12 describes David, king of the Israelites, as "ruddy."
ii   In *The Birth of Tragedy* (1872), Nietzsche characterized great drama as the juxtaposition of Apollonian and Dionysian forces or, roughly, order and disorder. The Thyrsus is the staff of Dionysus, associated with fertility and hedonism.

Thyrsus with bitterness in the action, in the aim; or solitude is made round the dancer, and he is a maniac if[20] he is not in company with others. A lonely Bacchant is a madman. . . . I must write of Nietzsche at another time—the North Wind binds my brain.[21]

KB The artists and we are like mushrooms lifting the pavement of the world in silence, Henry grimly observes at breakfast time.

Wednesday, October 10th.

Greatness, Henry observes at breakfast, is a way of using luck to advantage. Henry is greatly strenuous, fighting the winds, and giving me force. I shall never forget how I returned from town the other day to find he had put my brains into perfect order.[22]

EC [Ricketts] is come to talk about *Mrs. Daventry*.[i] The plot is Oscar's, not the dialogue, which is crude, direct as Oscar could not be.

His characters always spoke literature. In ordinary life Oscar had a marvelous power of giving the character and conversation of men who shoot and bathe all day or of society women talking about art, or remarks made by his children.

He once acted a drunken host taking his guests round his picture-gallery and dabbing the pictures with his napkin. He came to a portrait of Peg Woffington by Hogarth[ii] "now that I call sensual" he said with an emphatic dab. So with all the others—in the drunkard's opinion they were either sensual or not sensual—*Voilà tout!*[iii]

It was splendidly acted and would have made the fortune of a scene. But in his plays Oscar chose to sentimentalise his wit. There is nothing brutal in his work—it is intensely urbane. [. . .][23] At each quotation of a crudity (enjoyed and half commended by the perverse Fairyman) the comment follows "Oscar could not have done this"—"Oscar could not have done that—He was too old-fashioned and proper."

"I think Michael will prefer to be old-fashioned and proper with Oscar."

The Fairyman flies off at Michael's unrivalled saying as on wings of joy![24]

EC Ricketts thinks an artist's *entourage* should contradict his faith.

When we were "going in for every folly" and visiting theatres every Saturday, we bought old oak and Jacobean furniture.

---

i *Mr. and Mrs. Daventry*, a play by Frank Harris (1855–1931), Irish-born American editor and writer, from an idea by Oscar Wilde.

ii *Portrait of Peg Woffington* by William Hogarth (1697–1764), portraying Margaret "Peg" Woffington (1714–60), Irish actress.

iii "That's all!"

Now we are serious about our work, we surround ourselves with satin-wood.

So with the Artists—they hold that Art should be strenuous, profound—and they buy smiling Tanagras and Japanese drawings with their fragile decorative grace and leggy satinwood. It is well to have a smile round you, when you are grave.[25]

EC *News of Wilde's death*. The shock[26] withers Michael as with the wind of the ages. What tragedy!

The foolish punishment for an odious offense, that should never have been made public or lighted up by law, has killed Oscar's mother, his wife, indirectly his brother, and now himself; while leaving his children orphans branded outrageously.

Now I can think of nothing but the quality there was in him—the pleasur-ableness. This is so rare a gift of personality in these days and is almost the only that matters in the social life of man as the art of living. In work and in life there was, spite of all his degeneracies, a breeziness of high places—yes, even a breath of thyme. I have met most of the "moderns"—none of them blew a breeze or had any fragrance like Oscar at his best.

His intelligence was a warm climate, because the emotions set for the shores of his mind. His terrible wit wore white gloves, it was civil, it was *mondain*.[i]

His face was like a rich yet ungainly fruit, and his glance[27] was the light-speck on it—a benign, dazzling focus for his ripeness, his rounded tempera-ment. He made folly itself a very big thing.

December 7th.

Michael goes to Spring Terrace and the artists are not down. An hour or two later Ricketts opens the door to her. She is come to speak of Oscar.

"But I would rather not hear. I have stopped Holmes and Rothenstein who wanted to give details." *Michael*: "What I must know is whether anyone who loved him was with him when he died." Ricketts answers "*Yes*: Bobby Ross and Young Turner.[ii] Poor old Bobby Ross [was] quite devoted to him. We must speak of other things." And he begins to quote Spilling's letter about gemstones and my pendant. But as he speaks of the jewels inevitably he returns to the great theme. He learnt Michael gathers at *Patience* on Wednesday.[iii]

---

i "Worldly."

ii Robert Ross (1869–1918), journalist, critic, and Wilde's literary executor; Reginald Turner (1869–1938), journalist and novelist.

iii *Patience* was an operetta by Gilbert and Sullivan that premiered in 1881. A satire of aes-theticism, its central character, Bunthorne, is often regarded as a surrogate for Wilde.

"I am Wilde"—the thrill through the audience. Then someone remarked "How sad it is about Oscar." Ricketts has been upset and got over it; Shannon seems as if he would be[28] very much upset. Michael asks the Fairyman to come on Saturday evening or Sunday, if in the mood. She will not again *introduce* conversation on Oscar.[29]

EC So we approach Oscar's Death. Shannon was told very carefully just before a meal. He said "Oh!—when did he die, where and from what?" Then "I can't believe it is true" and turned in silence to his meat. Since[30] he has never mentioned the subject—except to declare on two different days "I can't believe Oscar is dead."

Bobby Ross is a "fidus achates"[i]—clever in a way, subservient, stolid. Turner has charm. Michael at last asks when and how Ricketts met Oscar.

He sent drawings to Oscar, then editing *The Woman's World*.[ii] They interested the editor, and Ricketts had work on the paper. We enjoy a rare story of the imprinted stocking too good for transcription. Then, when the first number of *The Dial* came out, it was sent to Oscar, who next day drove down the Vale, Chelsea. The next week he came by again, the next twice, and ended by coming to jaw three times a week. He told Rothenstein that the Vale was the only house in London where he would not be bored.

They once talked about worshippers with Oscar. Ricketts contended what he always holds that: . . . "but it is a very unkind criticism of you"—gods should never come down from their shrines.

Michael demands an explanation—he murmurs with a voice not ignorant of panic, prefaces to our plays, a shocking sonnet to America in a journal; but it is[31] much too serious to speak of.

Michael, as ever innocent before accusation, declares that if she had been dubbed coiner or forger she would not be more astonished. We are such hermits and our work so removed from the world.

He iterates like a scared bird against a wall and prefaces, the Prefaces, the appeal—it is so damaging. "But I will not say any more."

Then he continues—Oscar had to confess he was a late divinity who needed worshippers and liked them to throng his courts. But Ricketts he said was an early, man-eating deity who no sooner saw a worshipper than he caught him and tore him to pieces.

With reference to Mrs. Oscar, Ricketts dwells on the great opportunity she lost. She was urged to act with spirit, with breadth—she failed—and ever

i "Faithful friend."
ii Wilde was editor of the *Woman's World* magazine from 1887–89.

after she was nothing; her husband was an unpleasant subject, and she a ghost it was not pleasant to see.

Had she given him limitless devotion she would have had all the sympathy and admiration of all. She once called at the Vale with a Charity Album—Ricketts did a landscape, Shannon some charming Cupids. She was much pleased, and they [were] most anxious to [do] anything[32] they could for Oscar's wife.

Suddenly the conversation turns on the Whistler trial and Shannon's attitude. "We few Artists in the world must always back each other"—that is the Artists' precept. Shannon was called against Whistler. Pennell[i] must be murdered, because, like MacColl,[ii] he is a journalist in Art and discusses in public its secrets with which the public have nothing to do. Shannon knew Pennell to be right—that the lithograph must be cut on the stone, but at the last moment was clearheaded enough, without giving away his conviction, to protect Whistler. He was cross-examined for three-quarters of an hour.

An angry artist after the trial was heard to remark against Shannon that he did not believe in gloves (Shannon had gray ones) and Vandyke attitudes, but in work, showing how Shannon had thrown sand in the eyes of his own side, for Whistler's sake.

Michael remembers the brief visit to the Vale Press at the *Dial*, when Shannon and Holmes come in from the trial full of man's joy in the discomfiture[33] of his fellows. [. . .]

The Fairyman eats and continues—Oscar had wit and humour. Other men have wit or humour. He had the flash that comes from sharp encounter, and the summer lightings that play round a subject. Beside this, he had a strong sense of the comic.

He concludes with a story Oscar told of a female relative who lived in the old ancestral barn-like mansion of a village in Ireland. Near it Peek and Frean[iii] built a country house and carriages drove up to it for dinner-parties and social occasions—peers and notabilities of the neighbourhood.

The old lady of eighty wondered, grew indignant, then determined that the old hall should be thrown open to company after many years of solitude. Flowers were ordered from London, carpets laid, many candles[34] set alight.

The old lady descended on the eventful day in satin and all her old jewels; she visited the candelabra; she visited the supper table. The time went on, the candles sank. No one came. She watched the clock.

i Joseph Pennell (1857–1926), American artist and art critic.

ii Dugald Sutherland MacColl (1859–1948), Scottish art critic, artist, lecturer, and writer.

iii Perhaps Hannah Peek and George Hender Frean, founders of the biscuit company Peek Freans.

Time went on.

The candles sank lower and lower—

At last they went out.

No one came.

The old lady had thrown open her house and had sent out no invitations; if the hall was open to guests of course they would come. She went upstairs to a bed from which she never rose.[35]

EC *Last day of the Old Year.*

Only two of those who have died this year have been Michael's dead— Nietzsche and Oscar; both have been tortured by tragedy, both careers were storm struck and destroyed. But both men had fearless intelligences plastic and warm—both had the divine daemon at heart, though shame and sin and folly were close against the shrine.

We mourn them—they played such marvelous feats with life—they leapt about it, they threw strange colours on it, they made it novel, they made it expressive.[36]

EC [T]he perfection of the life Michael and I enjoy with each other in our work and in our home has overcome the pain of Bernard's marriage with Mary on the 29th.

She has toiled for her crown—I never raised a finger; she deserves the rite, and I am unforgotten still. He is unforgettable, as the few I have loved are— they stand in emphatic life, the dead and the living equally assertive in their beauty and desirableness as the planets in the night.

So Bernard is a star—Amy Bell calls him "a Jewish picture-dealer, not the man for Edith." And I have vision of his eyes on mine and our natures tangible to each other in that absolute alliance.

My own beloved Love is knit to me with stronger grip and sweeter, for Death has ratified our bond, leaving it secure for life to enhance; and when this happens the bond is at once more solemn and more gay. We are joy to each other in a profound[37] interchange, and more simple and tender in our wayfaring side by side.[38]

EC We know this new century will be ours before it ends, though no one will write a word about us now, not one of the old friends whose desertion of us has been bitterness of Sodom.

In this century of women agitators and women's cause—no word of our work, of our being alive!

But at last no ripple of happiness is thwarted by the world's rejection of us—though the complete sentence of silence under which we write is, it almost seems, a plot of the Fiend's. We say *get thee behind us!*[39]

EC The Century's first birthday comes on apace. The bells are rocking. . . . Bless my love and her love and lover![40]

Works and Days, 1901

EC *Review of dinner with Artists at New Year's.*

Of course Ricketts protested that he was of the nineteenth century and always would be—the wonderful century of Keats, of French literature, of Beethoven and Wagner. He had nothing to do with[41] the twentieth century. He is an undiscovered master of the nineteenth. In vain we protest that we trust to unite two centuries in our work and Shannon asserts that he belongs to the new century and savours the opportunities it gives him: the Fairyman declares he remains with Beethoven. [. . .]

After glasses have touched, Shannon's plate begins to dance. I watch him at his ratiocination—so stolidly reasonable. He thinks there must be a joint in the table that has sprung, so he moves the plate; and when it still feebly lifts places his thumb on the edge. Really, I am pumping air into a little bladder under it that is reached by a long tube under the tablecloth. The trick has driven a doctor away from a dinner party, convinced of evil spirits—but Shannon after an instant's as-[42]tonishment considered and acted. Ricketts confessed he would have thought it was the champagne, and striking a finger point against his cheek imitated the complacency with which Yeats would have received the attention Spirits showed him.[43i]

KB *It is Tuesday morning, January 22nd.*

Our beloved Queen is dying.

Yesterday John and Amy were with us. The presence of John was intolerable. He was full of getting the rhythm of the Latin prayer for the Queen to go right with Rex instead of Regina—this, though he could see how our hearts were wrung.

Our Beloved, our Sovereign Lady. God knows I would die now this moment if so she might be spared in full brain-power and strength of soul, till

---

i Yeats was a famous believer in spirits, and like Michael Field had convictions about the near-presence of the dead.

she could pray that good prayer—"Lord, now lettest thou thy servant depart *in peace.*"[i]

How pathetic that our people, as soon as they knew their Queen was gravely ill, took everywhere to singing the National Anthem. How moving too that she is said to have asked the Princess Beatrice if her people still loved her . . . that last doubt of the aged and dying whether they are still loveable. Loveable! the young are loveable because the spring is with them; the old are loveable because God in his beauty is with them.[44] Wise old Barlow[ii] has found out what the trouble is—obstruction in the circulation of the brain; and now my one prayer is that our beloved sovereign may die—that science may not for a while keep her from receiving the state of the blessedness of death.

For us—the rest of the lives can be but sequels—the big volume is closed.[45]

KB The great illusion of the Victorian Age is the illusion of progress.

Because at the beginning of her reign our streets were paved with cobbles —therefore.

Growth of suburbs, growth of education among the poor, an unmitigated evil—extension of franchise, and growth of free trade, unmitigated disasters.

—the growth of trades unions, the damnation of the future.

The growth of sentimentality—toward crime; and of science craft (the priestcraft of the Victorian age) insidious, berotting influences.

The synthesis of the reign—Imperialism.

The great virtue to be cultivated "hardiness" and the love of beauty.[46]

EC On Monday the Old Century will be really buried with Victoria: all is new as if Revelation were accomplished as far as England is concerned.

This has made the last fortnight so strange. We face unsanctified time— without parents, Queen, landmarks or traditions. The licence of the unauthorized terrifies us singularly.[47]

KB *Census Sunday.*

1901

Yes, it is Census Sunday—Henry the head of a house—and of a house in Richmond—the miracle. Ten years ago—the beloved Father; now the grave at Zermatt.

---

i Queen Victoria died on January 22, 1901.

ii Sir Thomas Barlow (1845–1945), British royal physician and baronet who tended Queen Victoria at her death.

It is appalling to think of what has happened in the decade—Henry's Dresden illness, his enchanted convalescence—visits to Italy—the play, the great disillusion, the battered years of cynicism—the tragedy—the years of dumbness and frustration, the re-[48]setting of life and happiness—the New Friendship—the new life together, the steering our little ship ourselves, instead of being irresponsible passengers—the great turning to lyric form.[49]

EC I have just signed the Census Paper, as Father signed it ten years ago. I can see his silver hair outspread over the blue document—I can hear our laughter and discussion, and the sudden anguish of silence when he wrote himself down as a widower.

And now, like Shannon, I write myself as head of a house, and like him entertain as guest or lodger the choicest of my sex—the beloved one, single and f.—even as I am.

We, dramatic writers, living on our own means, with our two servants, both single—what a quaint household!

We ourselves both from Warwickshire, they both from London.

And as I write the Thames runs by cloudy and energetic with the south[50] wind—the river that binds our days together with its influence of light and tide. [. . .]

If, ten years ago, I could have seen my lovely old rooms, my glowing bits of satinwood, my darting and lustrous river, my long-bodied hound, and could have known I had all these things, with the complete fellowship, day and night of my Beloved, a joy almost too terrible in bliss would have been over me—and now it is within, it is of my heart, it is my very life. My gratitude is commensurate with my joy.

And next Census—will it find us by our River? I believe it will find us together and that is enough to satisfy all hope.[51]

EC *Saturday, June 29th.*

I am inspired to go to Sloane Street and buy blouses of lawn, simple as angels' vests in their perfection. The delightful woman at the shop says she will deliver them herself at Richmond that we may have them tomorrow. She establishes her dominion over us by the great sentence "I see the urgency of the situation." Did she really foresee Bernard?

We have a merry lunch with Dr. Caroline Sturge (Dot!)[i]—a meeting of old Cliftonians—the ancient days served piquantly with the most modern sauce.

---

i Caroline Sturge (1861–1922), Quaker physician and midwife.

They were for relatives and Sturge Moore and we fired them with the lust to know their poet of *l'oeuvre du siècle.*[i] [52] [. . .]

Sunday, June 30th.

It is a day following a night of thunder-rain. The garden has a look of elasticity like that [which] comes to people after food; it is full of leaves and soft, half-spilled roses that are outwardly bright beyond all custom of brightness, but sunk at their hearts in damp.

The heat and damp together make one languid and apprehensive and there are clouds before the sun and birds singing easefully.

I stack my white drawing-room at each end with lilies. I set the great roses the rest in piles against each other round my bowls. On the Sun Room table thunder[53]bolt irises, on the mantelshelf Malmaison carnations.

Slowly for an hour or so I bring the flowers into the places they befit. Then with a little increase of hurry I dress in my simple white blouse of finest lawn, with Ricketts' ornaments.

Then there is a long pause. I pace among the vases. On the balcony the long-flowered lilies are streaming into bloom, out of rain-clogged pots. At last, a cab drives up—a discussion of fare at the gate. Michael says "Yes—and he is as handsome as ever." My heart plunges inward down an ocean. I begin to tremble and am saved. I rise and calmly greet Mary and her husband. Chow barks—bless him!—and Michael sweeps us back into the Sun Room, saying "Let us all go and be happy together."

Bernard and I out by the wall with only the little Japanese plant *Kōrin*[ii] between us. He has lost the colour of his youth from eyes and skin, but he is luminous with sweet silver in his face, and a burnish as of fine silversmith's work on his beard—his eyebrows and lashes resemble the swell and wave-dips of a silver stream. The beauty of profound ideality and of discipline sanctifies and gives repose to what of the old, rich loveliness still remains. The patience of the expression[54] is the direct gift of Dream—it is Oriental and religious.

We speak simply, with a depth of gentleness in our voices, of my white rooms—Bernard says they are the most beautiful he has ever seen in England; they are full of light from the water, that is the nearest possible substituted for Italian radiance; and the sense of space in them is delicious. They do not make you feel as if they bowed your shoulders down, like most English rooms, and there is nothing trivial about them—all you put your hand on is beautiful.

i "The work of the century."

ii Furuya Kōrin (1875–1912), Kyoto-based artist and designer associated with the Japanese Arts and Crafts movement.

He glances darkly several times, at the Artists' wreaths of pictures round the rooms—the spacing of them is at least perfect . . . and he keeps a dark, controlled silence.

He looks at my jewels *L'Oiseau bleu* and Music, admiring the first somewhat as true to good traditions of design, and giving the faintest praise to the "dog thing and its barbarians." How Ricketts would have struck his heart!

We speak of my health, of his health, of how the breeze from the river at Westminster has exhilarated him—of St. Moritz, its air that sparkles and makes one sparkle—of Pontresina and its Germans. Again a cloud drags itself over the lustre of his face and the [55] old bitterness is too copious on the tongue. He hates the Germans and where they are he must not be.

We go down to luncheon. Before he sits at the table, he insists on entering Michael's little writing room. "Oh Michael!—A real St. Jerome's study, and in such order!" He looks round jealously—at the portraits of the Artists and returns to the table saying that Michael's sanctuary is full of "unmentionable gods." Pan, she confesses, has taken the place of Bacchus in her worship—cruel Michael! The old divinity, hearing this, darkens through all the silver lights and shadows of his face. Then patience comes over the divine's dissatisfaction, and he looks sweet enough to overthrow all other gods by their own consent.

There is speech of an American lady who had shot herself and died in agony under her husband's eyes for the sake of a cold lover—"A Woman with every consolation that education, interest in higher things of mine and art etc. give—I have no patience with her. And she imagined she did this for love; that never should do anything but make us a little uncomfortable." For a moment I feel the air a little awry. As in [56] old times—but I am unnerved by the attack and my calm makes it so absurd it is not repeated once after.

Mary and Michael both condone the suicide. Bernard is shocked at their attitude—He is a thorough sceptic and feels it may be wrong to take one's life—no one knows, and, except where honour is blasted, he thinks it is nobler to give the nobler chance sway over one's actions.

We talk of Perugia and the asparagus we ate in rivalry, of Fermo—of incomes. When I tell him I put my money in a number of little bags, his Jewish nature breaks out into pitying amusement. "O Field, what a dear thing you are!"—and his voice has the reverence of tenderness in its deprecations. He knows our income to the last pound. He thinks there is a leakage in our expenditure for us to be so straitened. Our grim maid Lillias looks at him and grows affection as to Whym Chow. His eyes bind her with their philtres—I am amused to see her subjugated, like Kate Dufter at Durdans. When women are near him, they are always to be blessed! [57]

We return, after Michael has taken Mary and Bernard down our quaint little garden and he has been fretted and puzzled by the god, the Artists' Bacchus, set by the arbour among vine leaves; we all return to our seats in the Sun Room, to take our coffee and cigarettes. The sky is more threatening, and the great sheaves of lilies only look the whiter and more dominant. Bernard says, "You must come to see me—You know I have a home now, but it will never seem quite like home till you have been there."

Michael begins to question as of old—and Bernard to talk of the folly of the intellectual standards of the Victorian age and of our youth. Science can never be anything but method. Intellect can only register life whether of the senses, the emotions, and the will. There is talk of poetry. "O Michael, poetry is about the dumbest things I know—It has to use words, but it only begins beyond them, in what they suggest." Pindar is Bernard's present greatest poet. He brings his subjects so well above the horizon, he is so noble, so stirring to the soul.

Less by exposition than by instinct,[58] we find Bernard is on the path of what Ricketts calls the "New Moralism"—claiming me and Moore with himself as disciples, also, I fancy Santayana. I think Gray's[i] translation in his *Spiritual Poems*, beginning "Beautiful Soul" expresses exquisitely the mood that to us is blessed. "Choosest the path where many a lily blows"—well, I certainly have chosen that path for my love in my white, lily-thronged room.

It begins to rain and to become cold. Michael proposes we ascend to see the view of the bridge and my Adams mantelshelf;[ii] I am glad, for I have been sitting a short while opposite to Bernard and side by side with Mary. His eyes on me for the first time have been an anguish and my heart has flapped.

Standing in the bay window upstairs I meet his eyes on me and he says to Mary, "Field has become very beautiful—like an Italian picture." Mary responds, "Like the head of the Poldi Pezzoli."[iii] He continues, "Yes, Field, you are very beautiful." And I reply quite simply, "Then it is due to the white river and my white walls." They go up to look at the guestroom and I descend to light a fire in the Sun Room.[59]

I am bending over the new flame when he comes down alone. I rise and our hands join. He shakes mine Hamlet-wise, up and down, and says, "Dear Field, it is delicious to see you again and just the same"—"And to see you again, the same Bernard." I sit down by the wall, and he draws up his chair.

i John Gray (1866–1934), poet and Dominican priest.

ii A mantelpiece in the neoclassical style of Robert Adam (1728–92), featuring ornaments such as urns, swags, and fluting.

iii Gian Giacomo Poldi Pezzoli (1822–79), Milanese collector of Renaissance art, and founder of the private museum Museo Poldi Pezzoli.

"And did you think I should not be the same Bernard?" A shrug. "Who could tell—friends do change sometimes."—"Ah, there may come a cleft all through life, but this is very rare. It is beautiful to find you so at peace."

"Yes, I have reached a great peace. For about a year I have felt it." "I do not always feel it like you; but for months together I do. I too began to feel it about a year ago. I knew all those six years you and I were travelling the same road. I knew I should find you where I was."

He tells me how the hatred that is felt for him (on account of his success and his tongue—"If I am silent they hate me and if I say anything they hate me the same") mars this sense of peace. "It is the most dreadful thing to be hated."—Michael and Mary come down and we go into the Gold Room for tea, while Mary convicts[60] him of flirting with Italian ladies, much to his anger—of holding the hand of one lady "Because I am very fond of her."

I don't care—none of the thrusts come near me. Bernard and I are one and the same to each other, and I don't want to be anything more or other. The Italian ladies may hold his hand and welcome—just as Mary has her wife's demands on him.

We part in the hall touching each other by our eyes rather than our hands. It is deeply, peaceably goodbye.

Then he joins hands with Michael—who remarks "the eyes are a little duskier but they are the same eyes."—"Oh, they are the same eyes?"—looking back.

"Only a little duskier." Michael rejoins as the door closes.[61]

Works and Days, 1902

EC Who can rejoice with Time and his scythe-cut years—where is the immortal gladdening that must come down on a feast-day!

The ritual of New Year's Day is the reception of dividends, the burning of rubbish, a raw state of mind, a body lax with vigil—a sense of fetters clanking round a womb with child—the iron of temporal circumstance noisy even above the foetus of a year.

I hate the day—it is abominable.[62]

KB *January 12th. Henry's birthday.* [. . .]

Our happiness is very deep. My love is as a crown to the life dearest to me, and we are blest in our home and work.

It must be our business to show forth God's strength to this generation— His strength. His power: their slow decline to hell who are "passion's slaves."

Facing the judgment of Henry's parents and of my own, I still feel our sin is extravagance: we must spend less on objects, to keep quiet pastures for the mind.

Whym, with lovely, puckered wrinkles, is asleep before me, quite well.

Henry is growing a lovely little aureole round his well-shaped head.[63]

EC [W]hile the damp gray of twilight has grown close to the full, scarcely-rippled river, Michael and I have talked of the past decade—of tragic happenings and an illness.

My love for Bernard.

The play and its failure.

The break with Mary—the six years of apartness—the blight of cynicism.

The tragedy in Scotland with Father and Michael and its lay of shadows.

The Tragedy of Zermatt.

Amy's Catholic marriage.[64]

The parting from Durdans.

Rheumatic fever a second time and here at Paragon a year and a half of care and re-rooting, nearly as bad as tragedy.

The only year that was comparatively free from the torment of pain and anxiety was 1896—and then in that brief renewal, how we wrote and worked, with strength and freshness!

We both feel this is an opening decade that will eventually greatly change our lives.

We must have more carefulness over the expenditure of money, more carefulness for thoughtful and gracious living, more carefulness of the life of the spirit in the daily hours. More love for each other we could not have, but we must see that the Graces always stand by it.

I do not feel forty—I feel less aged by far than at thirty. Youth comes to me through joy as I have never had it by right of time.[65]

KB *The last day of February.*

I went yesterday to the burial service of our dear old friend, Miss Vickers.

I shall miss her, as one misses a very quaint and beloved piece of old China. In the first year of Paragon she was our one household, and intimate friend. She furnished us with our servants and our doctor; when we needed furs, or silks, or fragments of English lace—she had treasuries.

She made us the little gray frocks in which we went to Mother's funeral. She made us the long black coats in which, in the great year 1890, we swayed through the boulevards of Paris. She made Amy's wedding dress. Last of all she was concerned with a dainty little Gainsborough bodice made to please Painter—she traveled with us through a long and significant piece of road. She had wisdom, not insight; but sound proverb wisdom.[66]

EC *The Artists return full of the aquarium.*

They have seen a brown bear with a head like Chow, they longed to hug—an octopus dilating with gastric strife, anemones biting bits off crabs and lolling their tentacles from columns of jade or jasper.

The plaice and soles gave such joy to Fay; he takes the part of a sole and swims, erecting his fingers into the dignified and intellectual tortoise-head, and giving the white velvet fins, the elegant movement through the tank, the obliteration when the sail is at end and the creature drops softly on the sea mud.[67] Then he rolls with quaint one-sidedness as a seahorse.[68]

EC For a few minutes Fay bleeds over Oscar and his fate—the awful blot on civilisation of the way in which the trial was conducted, so as to do all the harm it could to the public and the offender. The judge's speech was so outrageous it was practically suppressed by all the papers—every diner at the Savoy and every undergraduate of Oxford would have been struck in public.

Walter Crane from the Balcony next door peers down on us.[i] He will report Michael Field two old women of about the same age. Each numbering eighty years, curiously wrapped about in furs and seeking to control the antics of spirited dogs.[69]

EC *Thursday, June 5th.*

We wait—

Yeats[ii] and Tommy come.

The first motion of Yeats is to seize a book for bread and support in his shyness. It is Ricketts' *Hero and Leander*, and there is not another book in sight.[iii]

We leave him to recover, then Michael shows him the river and the pendant. The miniature he finds most lovely but does not know which of us it is.

His shyness makes Tommy more familiar. The stranger manifests that we are somewhat intimate after a year's friendship. It is an easeful truth.

i Though the socialist artist Walter Crane (1845–1915) was loosely affiliated with Michael Field, he did not live next door to them; the poets had clearly devised a nickname for a nosy new neighbor.

ii The Irish poet and playwright William Butler Yeats (1865–1939) received the Nobel Prize for Literature in 1923.

iii Ricketts and Shannon illustrated the book *Hero and Leander* by Christopher Marlowe and George Chapman, and published it with Ballantyne Press in 1894.

At dinner Yeats is fearfully shy at first, doctrinaire and "cansy," but he gradually becomes warm and vivid in his monologuing. He is dark with[70] a Dantesque face—only not cut in Italian marble!

His hair dribbles in a Postlethwaite manner on to his brow.[i] I wanted to give the order to Lillias to bring grape scissors and cut the locks.

His eyes are abstract and fervid. When he speaks of spiritual things, and shakes back his forelock, there is a smile like an atmosphere on his eyes and brow.

The mouth is for speech—the hands flap like flower-heads that grow on each side a step and are shaken by the wind. At first the gesture spells one; then it irritates, because it is a gesture and is not varied.

Yeats is not of us—as Tommy and the Artists and Bernard are—he is a preacher. He preaches some excellent things and some foolish things. He knows our plays well and seems to care for them with insight. I was not prepared for this.[71] [. . .] His wit is rhetorical—not the instructive mischief and drollery, the moment's wild happiness in some contrast, that is so engaging in Tommy. He is an evangelist—quite sincere in his exposition and persuasion.

We have some more amusing glimpses at George Moore—calling in a policeman to know if the law requires him to eat his landlady's omelette, or gazing at the Amateur Dublin Actors of the Clerk fraternity and pronouncing "Well, you are a seedy lot."

Yeats reads a little prayer to the psaltery—a most charming poem—all the Archangels appear in it, with shoes of the seven metals.

Also he intoned as if to the psaltery Keats' Bacchic Ode.[72]

EC Yeats says that in his first review of us, written when a college youth, he remarked we did not dream or saunter enough.

Poor George Moore, who wails over the way in which characters become faint under Yeats' handling, would find in this lack our safeguard.[73]

EC *Tuesday, June 11th.*

Michael is just dressed to start after ticket for Yeats' lecture, and I to accompany her as far as the post office, when Shannon and Tommy appear on their "bikes."[ii] Shannon looks as if he had been "stripped, stopped and new papered"—as fresh[74] as a newly decorated house.

I never saw such a change. He likes the Palace immensely and already has

i Jellaby Postlethwaite was a cartoon figure created by George du Maurier for *Punch* in 1880, satirizing the effeminate mannerisms of aesthetes, and particularly Wilde.

ii Bicycles were a technology of the early-nineteenth century. The development in the fin de all but finished ten pictures that had been waiting for light. The clarity and elasticity of his mind are marvelous.

Tommy seems a cobweb corner by him and by his well-knit form. Tommy looks forlorn of all grace. They are both boastful of man's superiority in doing everything—like braggart soldiers, woman does not respect them the more for speaking on that theme swellingly.[75]

EC We travel with two women—hermits in a pair, Nietzsche would call them—"fellows" we call them. The lover is an intense featured[76] woman whose love of ideals would devour the very flesh off her. The beloved a silly little thing of about two and twenty with whitish blue eyes, and frolicsome smile. They look at each other from the center of their eyes—and I know they are lovers.[77]

EC *Thursday, September 10th.*

Michael has been getting a divine dress made by Louie Ellis of gray satin and old silver—a thing one admires like a work of nature—a silvery sea or the dew-drenched cloud of a mountain.[78]

EC *At last September 18th.* The Artists arrive in full evening dress, as ordered. I receive them.[79]

"And your fellow?" says Ricketts and begins to look round the curtains and furniture, as if she inhabited a nutshell.

Then she appears in gray satin; "It *is* the Eighteenth Century," so he praises. We have large-flowered lilies in chorus, and pots of spraying white specimen lilies, and Malmaison roses, already wooly and two centuries old.

Also I have preserved some sprays of his maidenhair and show them in the silver-gilt cup.

Menu

Orleans Soup
Cod à la Crème
Partridges
Tomato and chutney salad
Stone cream and green-gage jelly
Coffee amaretto
Apples, malta oranges and muscat grapes
Red Hymettus, Spanish Chablis—Cyprus

---

siècle era of safety and comfort features, as well as pneumatic tires, led to a significant increase in their popularity.

Michael, descending to dine, says she is going to forsake the eighteenth century just as she is clothed in it, and try to become of the Renaissance.

Shannon declares he has a sympathy with the eighteenth century. "My dear boy, you know nothing about it. Michael and I[80] understand its reasonableness."[81]

EC On the following Sunday, Havelock Ellis comes to see us. Louie has told him I am become beautiful, and he wishes to see me! I don't know if he sees, but he does not look.

He is just the same, only the Samsonic hair is grizzled, and the impressive face more set and benevolent. He is of his past self—as Thelwell is—only the Warm Widower is less depressing company than the Hushed Husband.

He seems to have his being in the fear of the wife of his bosom. He bored me to the point of sleep—he was a large poppyhead poultice.

Only once did life flash out between us. I said I had the eye of a sailor for a dog in the distance and he brightened and confessed he turned in another direction with his dogs if he saw another dog[82] afar off.[83]

EC I dreamt myself last night in the company of Havelock Ellis.

He remarked "We have at last reached a stage when we are able to tell a lie."

Immediately there was a burst of religious music from the next room, and we became quiet, thinking of the days gone by before we were artists in falsehood.

He also asked me for cigarettes to "warm the man"—and I could only find some, steeped in water—so I put them for the fire to smoke and to dry.

When at last I presented them half dried I was rewarded by the assurance, "Now the man is warmed."[84]

Michael Field paid a visit to Rudyard Kipling and his family.

KB It is Saturday, October 11th.

I walk round the great weedy garden of nasturtiums, the rabbit in his hole, and leave Chow in the garden.

I come in: I look forth—Chow and the rabbit are one—Chow pecks, the rabbit rolls, and Chow pecks again. I run forth, I shriek[85] and chase. He locks and closes again, and again—

Finally, Edith[i] extracts and exalts the rabbit apparently lifeless—I return to Henry.

---

i Probably Edith Ramsey Chichele Plowden (1854–1911), artist and woodcarver; friend of Kipling.

Slowly my boiled blood cools; we set the rabbit up under shelter of shavings, we leave him munching a cabbage leaf, and I find Henry, quietly stretched on his couch at the Alfonso murder scene, adding certain little cries and flutterings and follies of collapse.

But the Chow! The incident has made a man of him. I shall never forget the air with which he dashed in, and drank water, like a young hero who flings aside his casque and refreshes himself.[86]

KB Rudyard Kipling's rabbit died on Monday—slain by Michael Field's Chow.[i]

He was but a white lump by our flaming little Minister Whym—but I am sorry death came so leisurely.

The morning of Monday Whym startled a wild bunny that flew among some boys at punishment drill. They boasted the red dog had given them a better time than the virtuous had spent.[87]

KB It was strange when Tommy and Yeats were here. They are real poets, moving about, gurgling their lyrics, flapping their wings. And beholding them, I said, "then I surely am not one of these."

Yeats has nice black hair—the bloom of the dark grape on it—and he has gentleness. He hates inversions, judging a poem as it would or would not have been a fine thing said in speech. He cadences one or two of his little lyrics—one he always repeats to a positive lilt.[88]

EC *New Year's Eve.*

Whym lies pointing his golden nose on his blanket, so sleepy to the bells and my pen and my fond love of him—lying with shut, slant eyes.

Bless him! I profoundly feel his dear companionship in the New Year!

God keep him—and my dear Musico, whose eye has been bumped today! Poor man, he rolls it underneath his brow.

Never have my beloved and I been closer in our love, because so intimate in our creative union—the power is so between us, so divinely of one by the other, that it is impossible to think what our work would be[89] if we were dissevered [. . .].

It is a joy that is not fulfilled but is rising.

Our love is "soft, creative, fostering, free"[ii]—it has never been lonelier. It has never been more prevailing.

Michael is asleep on the bed—completely worn out with the week's work

---

i Rudyard Kipling (1865–1936), Anglo-Indian novelist, poet, and journalist, was awarded the Nobel Prize for Literature in 1907. His Nobel citation noted his "virility of ideas"; hence, perhaps, Michael Field's glee over their dog's slaying of Kipling's pet.

ii A quotation from Michael Field's play *The Tragic Mary* (1890).

on *Tristan*. My love and her chow are both asleep. They will have to wake for the newborn year to bless them.

I have never less wished a year to go than this strange, unhappy dominant year.

I have never welcomed more rapidly or with more ardour the incoming of a new year—so convinced I am of the goodness and revelation of its quality and its purpose. [. . .][90]

They are firing cannon. I don't remember this virile welcome to another year. There is another salvo—and in the quiet darkness Orion is a creature of light—made all of light, above the swing of the bells to and fro.[91]

Works and Days, 1903

EC At tea, very late, Fay quietly arrives. He always comes when Michael says *come*. This time he has hurried from a man who seemed as if he would buy a picture.

Fay is charming—a serenity in every sense, his voice content, his eyes divining, a touch of the listener in the way he speaks, as if he heard before he made discourse. Yet he is full of fun and tells how Yeats with a volatile sweep of his hand sent his wine glass into Tommy's soup, while Tommy had an expression of pain that his soup should have been chosen to be flavoured with wine.

Yeats bored with his poetry and dogmatism, praising the thirteenth and early fourteenth centuries against the Renaissance. At last Tommy grew surly and remarked they cared in their literature only for fighting and adultery— "the whole duty of man" was the reply of the prophetic one.

Then Michael and Fay resume the talk of Wednesday evening on manners. What does he mean by saying manners should cease between intimate friends? He does not like bad manners or etiquette, but intimates that friendly converse is an escape, is freedom—it is like having no clothes on.

"Ah but we don't see our friends so." What can he say?[92]

[. . .] "I believe you would like women to have no morality at all—none toward god, or nature or man."

"Absolutely none."

He then describes woman—the real unmixed woman—she is a wild,[93] destructive creature—so desirous of wandering that as Renan[i] says in the Earliest ages she had to be stoned to be made to keep to the hearth at all.

---

i Ernest Renan (1823-92), French philosopher, biblical scholar, and progressive political writer.

Only Motherhood enables her, keeps her from wandering, unites her with what is permanent and yet even in France where her maternal instinct is predominant, it is dangerous to the development of the nation. Women do harm continually, but with surprising innocence—it is wonderful.

Etiquette has been made by man as a check to this freedom of the woman.

"You think men are made to save women from themselves."

"Certainly."

The woman who restrains does infinite harm—she is the worst of dangers. She is full of weak idealism—idealism that is a convention. Men have a sense of realism; few have this conventional idealism. It is as much a pose, as that women do not, may not care for adventure, while men have love of adventure bred into them whether they will or no.

Fay declares he cannot love—the microbe has not yet called to itself other microbes and become a disease of any kind.[94]

So much Fay!

One must never stop Man when he confesses himself out of his sex—but one wanted to tell him women play with men of genius—are amused, as they ever crave to be amused, by them, but do not love them—the soldier, the man who acts, who pulls them "through the door has them forevermore."

I forgot to say Fay only asked Yeats in the first instance to dine because he said an excellent thing—that the Irish love what they see to be right and the English hate it.[95]

KB We have heard that Maud Gonne—the woman to whom Yeats, the poet, has been engaged fourteen years, has married a colonel, and entered the Catholic Church.[i]

Well may Tommy say women should have no control whatever over their lives.

Again, by how slender threads our own happiness hangs.[96]

EC A few days after [Tommy] writes of Maud Gonne and how she is gone from poor Yeats to a Colonel. She and Yeats had practically been engaged fourteen years—and she *changes* her religion and her love without a word to him.

"*It is dreadful*—women should not be allowed to settle their lives"—declares the misogynist Tommy.

I am sorry—this seems one of the hardest things a poet can have to bear.[97]

i Maud Gonne (1866–1953) was an Anglo-Irish actress and republican revolutionary. Though Yeats proposed to Gonne several times, she married the Irish republican John MacBride in 1903. MacBride died by execution for treason in the Easter Rising in 1916; Yeats named MacBride in his poem about the Rising, "Easter 1916," outraging Gonne.

EC Fay has heard more of Oscar's death "less hateful than I had feared; a week's unconsciousness and then extinction."

Fay also heard directly the story against Rothenstein, who said once—"It is extraordinary how sensual English women are! My dear fellow, one talks of French women!—but!—yesterday I passed a row of English schoolgirls, and will[98] you believe it, as I passed every one of them smiled!"[99]

EC In midafternoon Tommy has the audacity, after being warned from Paragon, to bring his sister—a raw, but sagacious, young carrot. She is more disastrous than a wife—the tie is looser and less a necessity—therefore more resented when inflicted on the patience of others.

I am sorry for her—He should not put a woman in that position—or learn anything of Woman from her.[100]

Friday, May Day.

The Shagreen box[i] comes. I have said to Grace[ii] we will have it as the great peace object—peace at any price!! It makes in the Sun Room a solid block of green.[101]

EC The old Shagreen Box is considered dear (at £6)—although it is exceedingly fashionable.

Ours is very much damaged. He (Fay) opens it—it is very nice inside, he acknowledges, as he looks at its crimson bed. "You should put in it a packet of love letters, a lock of golden hair, black at the roots, a faded rose, and the bill of a bracelet."[102]

EC *Saturday, May 9th.*

Last night Grace dined with us and told us that the old Venetian glass was now to be seen at Toplady's.

So this morning, off we go, right into a yellow fog and St. James hanging over us like the cliffs of hell. What weather! She leaves gluttonous and sleepy with overeating of rain—heat in the rooms, cold of death if the windows are opened, thunder, fog, torrents, showers, gray skies or glittering irony in the light. *Ma foi!!!*[iii]

The glass in fog—gloaming not attractive—but I find a red stone in old

---

i Shagreen is a form of textured leather, probably in this case derived from stingrays; a Shagreen box would have provided luxurious, decorative storage for ordinary household items. Bradley refers to this box explicitly in her will.

ii Mary Grace Thomas Worthington (1866–1937), cousin of Mary Berenson; shopkeeper for Miss Toplady.

iii Literally, "my faith"; colloquially, "indeed" or "well."

silver that will do for my *goutte de sang*[i] to be worn on a red velvet round my executed throat (Fay's comment at Rottingdean). Also we bear away a pharmacy vase of Murano glass in which roses and irises can really drink crystal and be glad.

For nearly[103] an hour we pace the underground station, trains driving through our brains and advertisements raping our eyes.—Horrible!

But in the train a workman with a girl animal and a baby is forced for lack of room to travel with us. Perhaps the girl is his wife—perhaps not—Anyhow he is the father of that babe. In masterly silence he hands it [a] bun, and when it gets restive, with a gesture commands it shall be given him. He sets it by the window in his strong arm, while he reads the paper. The babe responds to the calm strength and hands back.

Then the intelligent eyes of the father leave the page for the babe's face with a smile in them of a tenderness passing anything women can show. Or is a smile that would exercise attraction on God.[104]

EC *Saturday 23rd.*

Michael went to hear Weingartner[ii] conduct Beethoven. Behind her like hoary Babes sat Arthur Symons and Havelock Ellis.[105]

KB *1st Sunday after Trinity, June 14th.*

Last night I received this note from Yeats.

Dear Michael Field: I have been asked by the committee of the Irish National Theatre Society to ask you to let us see your *Deirdre*. I forget whether you have quite finished it, but perhaps you would let us see what you have done. I am confident we could give a good performance of the play, should it prove as I am sure it will, adapted to our methods.

I hope you will consent to let us read it at any rate. You had better write to me c/o Lady Gregory[iii] Co. Galway. I shall be there sooner or later. I am at present with Hyde.

Wm. Yeats.[106]

EC It is strange to be writing in *Works and Days* again—for two months I have hardly written a word of the wonderful days—

"*Gold*" *Tristan* being ended.

"*Flame*" *Tristan* being conceived and achieved.

---

i "Drop of blood."

ii Felix Weingartner (1863–1942), Austrian conductor and composer.

iii Lady Isabella Augusta Gregory, née Persse (1852–1932), was an Anglo-Irish playwright and poet, a force behind the Irish Literary Revival, and cofounder of the Abbey Theatre.

"Deirdre" being wrought out and ended.

Beside this the grappling with our wills and that time and fate after us. And much entertaining—a little going to town. Round us was the wildest weather and then came the wind-flowing glorious summer.

I must try to set down a few hours I remember sharply from the glowing drift.

In May, Edward Whymper visited us. He is sixty-three now but the face looks like rock covered with thyme—hard with will and clearly sweet with good-temper and humaneness. I received him in the evening with both hands—he was mild at once, wanted to drive us round the Park, and brought out three of his magnificent mountain photographs, with a glance at the artists' small bits of[107] black and white in the Sun Room—"Are these in your style at all?" Our dinner of made-dishes is quite wrong, but we invite the pipe. He visits a friend up the hill and returns to the pipe, to accepted Whiskey (the best possible) and to talk wild and merry talk about federating the Indians of the Rockies after being accepted as Chief on the strength of his blankets and marrying seven squaws to be called Monday, Tuesday, Wednesday, Thursday, Friday, Saturday, and Sunday. Sunday obviously the fine lady. Saturday the marketing matron, Friday inclined to look after the household morals, Wednesday the cook. Four tents are gone—the distribution is clear— ending with "Sunday and myself."[108]

EC *Sunday.*

Tommy comes to talk over our wills and what we are to do with this book.

We do not want it to do harm—we do not want its vitality, its real confession injured. We have to leave the problem—but I think Tommy will "execute" us in respect to all other M.S.S.—even if *Works and Days* is not left to him.

He is too unfortunately close to Fay; we fear influence.[109]

EC *Tuesday.*

It has been torrential downpour—dark and damp are the hours.

By the morning post a letter from Tommy—it ends—"Hoping that you will not be very horrified at the facts revealed"—the Will? What are the facts horrible enough to affect it?

Michael turns to the beginning: he confides a great secret; he is going to be married to his cousin Marie Appia.[i] Alas, our bequests can never tread the

---

i Marie Henriette Sturge (née Appia, 1872–1956), was Thomas Sturge Moore's cousin and eventually his wife; she worked as a translator.

Appian way! It is a shock . . . and for Ricketts: it breaks up the little celibate company—we lose a friend for no man who is married can be a friend; the old wine is not for new bottles.[i]

We have received Tommy as such for the last time. We understand why he was not "life enhancing." Surely it was only honourable to tell us he had already consulted another about our Executorship—can there be friendship on any ground flushed by Hymen's[ii] torches?

For him marriage was predestined. He was very marriagable. Mercifully she is a Frenchwoman—[110] he will be a prisoner in the first division, grace to this. But he ceases from among our few friends—that is the trouble; and we have so few!

Dark and damp are the hours. Janet[iii] comes for the night, looking quite Early Victorian in her black fringed gown, white square collar and bunch of coral for a brooch. I find an opened letter on the writing table left by Michael—it is from Yeats—in young lady or Lady Gregory typing and rejecting *Deirdre*:

My dear Michael Field,

I have read *Deirdre*, and I am afraid it would need a far bigger stage than we are likely to command for a long time to come. The company has just given up the idea of acting a plan of Suderman's[iv] for the same reason. I am inclined therefore with your consent not to offer them the play.

To speak quite frankly I do not like it as well as your other work, and I should not like it to be the first of yours to be offered to them. Did you ever try your hand at a one-act play? They are far easier to construct than a long play.

I have myself as you know been writing one-act plays in prose lately. I have done this chiefly as a discipline, because logic (and stage success is entirely a matter of logic) works itself out most[111] obviously and simply in a short action with no change of scene. If anything goes wrong one discovers it at once and either puts it right or starts on a new theme and no bones

i A cautionary parable of Jesus in Matthew 9:14–17; Mark 2:21–22; and Luke 5:33–39. Cooper began a prose play titled *Old Wine in New Bottles* in 1892; location of the manuscript is unknown.

ii In Greek mythology, Hymen was the son of Apollo by Urania, one of the muses; he is the god of conjugal happiness.

iii Likely Janet McHale Image (1871–1951), a former music hall dancer; married designer Selwyn Image in 1901.

iv Hermann Sudermann (1857–1928), German playwright and novelist.

are broken. But I suppose every playwriter finds out the methods that suit him best.

Yours sincerely

WB Yeats.

Michael, under guard of Fay, writes back:

I quite agree *Deirdre* would be much too elaborate for your stage. I shall be glad therefore if you will kindly return it to me as once registered. I shall be leaving home shortly to enjoy the second spell of sunshine promised to us.[112]

Yeats's one-act play "Deirdre" opened at the Abbey Theatre on April 1, 1907.

KB Tommy is engaged. He tells us this in a letter, and a strong tree from our slender group of celibates is lopped off.

Already he has taken counsel of "Marie" concerning a matter we entrusted to him in confidence.

I go to the Palace. They are hiding their displeasure. Fay regards marriage as a kind of death. The good circumstance is that the bride is French. I speak of life as a kaleidoscope, and of the new and varied shapes it may be shaken into. The simile does not sparkle.[113]

EC Michael had told Logan we did not want to meet Santayana in a crowd.[i] Mary turns it round that we do and insists on our driving up to tea to meet Santayana.

How vain! An old botanist who collects books of poems when they fall to the bookstalls and to pence begins to read endless twaddle with lunatic transitions.

What patience Americans have in amusing themselves! Bernard laughs, the sound coming out of him as a woodpecker's laugh—a simple,[114] natural sound. And Santayana laughs too, but his laugh is like that on ripe cherries—a vegetable glory. We scarcely exchange a syllable with Santayana.

Young women come in—one with the little parrot-perk of aesthetics, her little hard clever face saying "Pretty Poll" in its every turn. She could not creep into interstices—she has no creeping loveliness of recognition or sympathy. And the old botanist blabs of his dry herbs or more lovingly of the grot at Kew, while Santayana sits with eyes to which "all the world's a

---

i The Spanish American philosopher, poet, and novelist George Santayana (1863–1952) was an influential figure in twentieth-century discourses of aesthetics, naturalism, and materialism.

stage"—strong Latin eyes and round features that look with the comfort of a purple plum.[115]

I read at the window with Chow. Michael in her 1750 gown and Gainsborough hat stands with her book under the yew.

Mary and Santayana enter very hot from the inauspicious walk. "It seems to me you have not caught the mood of the day. It is not a day to clamber up a hill, but a day to watch the bees going in and out of flowers" reproaches Michael.

But we are soon at the point of friendship with Santayana. He is eagerly self-indulgent before Life, like an ardent theatregoer—his courtesy is to other spectators. He does not know indignation or[116] remorse—they cannot be generated from a spectacle.

He visits his sister in Spain every year; he has a passion for distinction, for everything that is mathematically conceived—perfected by forms—and abstract in matter. But he has written poetry and we understand each other by that freemasonry.

I note the large lustrous contours of his face—the blandness of his speech behind teeth—glitter, the black of his eyes "of blackest black our eyes can know" with their rampant vision, the curb in his carriage as if a brilliant-eyed thrust alert with morning.

There is a look of comfort about all his lines *et dans le velour de sa voix*[i] and his eyes move over one seizing one's significance with the haste of enjoyment that is for a moment only on a shifting stage. He is very young in mood—even in physical make, though his forehead is bald—young in the curbed neck in his grasp of vision, in his lushness of physique and rounded laugh. He likes Earl Russell[ii] because he is like a boy—because he is despotic, knowing his own mind, and because[117] he remains unchanged—if such a thing were possible to say—he is a sun to many comets.

In the Common Room at Oxford lately he heard one of the ablest remarks I have heard this year. The Question was put—"What is orthodoxy?" The reply was "Orthodoxy is Reticence."

Michael had two of her games to amuse us. The first: tomorrow is St. Bartholomew's Day.[iii] What class of people or what people would we wish to massacre?

i "And in the velvet of his voice."

ii John Francis Stanley Russell, 2nd Earl Russell (1865–1931), known as Frank, was a barrister and politician. After he was tried and convicted for bigamy before the House of Lords, Russell worked to amend laws governing marriage and divorce. He was the older brother of philosopher Bertrand Russell and, as an early adopter of the motor car, was assigned the number plate A1 in 1903.

iii A Catholic mob, fearing a Huguenot uprising, initiated a two-month siege on Protestants on St. Bartholomew's Day in 1572, killing as many as 25,000 people.

She would massacre all clever people.

I would too—and that young woman who sat by me (I think to myself). Santayana condemns Kipling to suffer—but afterwards reprieves him.

Mary would immolate all who are oppressive to their families (except men of genius). Mary is not able to reach unconditioned hate of class.

Santayana cannot hate—he is too intellectual. As he quietly makes a point his eyes, that forcibly hide much reserve, shyness, terror of the wild creature at intrusion on its secrets, have a gleam, a flash of securing radiance pulsed from their depths. I describe my hatred—it is a bruise[118] made by the stroke of an intolerable temperament—a great bruise that never ceases to be black.

Michael in the night watches confesses to remorse—thinking of the bad things she has done; Santayana is afraid he is very young—he thinks of plans. Mary has daydreams and leaves money to needing friends. "Five hundred pounds for me" laughs Santayana purringly.

Much of the talk is of St. Francis[i] whose Bacchic joy in all creatures Mary identifies with Walt Whitman's. "Help me!" Michael cries.[119]

EC Roger Fry, his wife and Mr. Dickinson of *John Chinaman's Letters* and the Platonic Dialogue come to tea.[ii]

There is charm about Roger Fry—the "bouquet" of a special kind of red wine. He has humour—so, too, in crochety, family friend, coffeehouse way has Dickinson; and gaily goes the time over the toast and strawberry jam.

We enjoy our allusive literary English humour fantastic, full of tolerance and banter. We are so glad no American, Jew, or Alien is among us.[120]

EC [Fry's] wife is very tall, with the attitudes and style of 1884–86.

Ill-health has made tragic the moulding and tint of her face. Her eyelids have the purple veiling woods have when they are severe with winter. She is sweet through her tragic austerity.

The blue and white stripes of her dress wind round her as if tying her long limbs.

Such a pleasant afternoon.

---

i St. Francis of Assisi (1181–1226), patron saint of animals.

ii The painter Roger Fry (1866–1934) was a member of the Bloomsbury Group, founder of the Omega Workshop, and the critic who coined the term "postimpressionism" to describe the counter to the impressionists' naturalistic representational style. He was the lover of Vanessa Bell. His wife, Helen Coombe (1864–1937), developed serious mental illness in 1910 and lived the remainder of her life in a mental hospital. Goldsworthy Lowes "Goldie" Dickinson (1862–1932) helped to found the study of international relations. His *Letters from John Chinaman* was published in 1901.

Dickinson believes that fundamentally he can only understand and there-fore like Englishmen.

How is it I can never talk to Bernard as I did to these men? He has never found the key to my voice. The milkman's roses are breathing out their night sweetness and they will be sweet when the door is opened tomorrow.[121]

EC *We are drinking tea, and (Herbert) Horne is giving some idea of the Art-ists years ago.*[i]

Shannon is to Bernard and Horne's minds, the woman in the marriage of fellowship—he is more receptive than Fay, more obstinate, less intellectual—in old days, more gay in pose.

What has altered him?

Ricketts and the Muses.

Ricketts leaves a personal[122] and most peculiar mark on the people he has influenced—

Holmes, Moore, Shannon.

"Yes, he is a profound influence."

"The great god Pan." It is hurled out, all the smart and malice of two years growing lovely with passion in Bernard's eyes, that are for that moment only as in his youth. The covert smile from under which he hurls evokes the coun-ter smile in his auditors of implicated intelligence. Michael, recognizing the thrust, recognizes it is best to stand when one is struck.

"Certainly," continues the avenger, "it is Mr. Ricketts and Mrs. Shannon. I noticed this at I Tatti.[ii] In all fellowship, as in marriage, you can trace who acts and who is acted on. Yet, as in marriage, the wife reacts on the husband, Shannon's views very much influence Ricketts."

Shannon is the arch attributer.

He used to be called the Irish Apollo.

Ricketts is wholly a foreigner—his impression on one is that of a Frenchman.

Bernard is candid. He says with his ripe malevolence "I am saying all the nastiest things I can—not the[123] cruelest." "Oh, say the cruelest too" says intrepid Michael. I leave a few of "the nastiest things" in privacy, but the cruelest we do not hear.*

[*] God and Magog—the scarlet woman are a few of the gentlest ex-pressions.[124]

i Herbert Horne (1864–1916), English poet and designer.

ii I Tatti was the villa in Fiesole, Italy, where Bernard and Mary Berenson lived and enter-tained throughout their married life. After Berenson's death in 1959, the villa, its gardens, art collection, and library passed to the ownership of Harvard University, his alma mater, comprising the Harvard University Center for Italian Renaissance Studies.

EC This afternoon we have been to High Buildings to see the Frys. It is a house to love, with its benignity, its low hedges, its loved formalism, its bee-haunted flowers.

We have tea in the white chamber with its French mirrors, gold-striped settee, Leeds vases of Paragonic severity.[i]

Mrs. Fry has a sky-blue skirt and sash, a white blouse and coral chain. She is tall and pondering as a stork. Yet she nestles in altitude and appeal—her willowy movement envelopes one. She has no more a complexion than the stones of Amiens that have known the disasters of the wind of centuries; yet her eyes [illeg.] and lips where they meet and nostrils have[125] "quiet coves" where one can enjoy "mists in idleness."[ii][126]

EC Bernard loves to talk to us, and talks to us[127] as to no others because we are such exquisite listeners—we allow him to be creative in converse.

He loves, like an *improvisatore*, to weave a fantasia of speech on a theme—to produce a living web of speech by which he creates his thoughts and as he realises them rejoices. [. . .]

I quote the example of Lady Gregory's treatment of Irish legend, as contrasted with the old texts. This leads to a talk about Irish literature—the dream-expressiveness that is its single virtue—and about Yeats. Bernard once met him, when he[128] was hardly noticed by Yeats—a personage even then.

Yeats talked intensely and volubly—yet he struck Bernard as being serious and therefore sincere in the midst of what looked like pose. Bernard feels him more "considerable" than any of the younger men, because he has a universe and because he has reached vaguely the symbolic nature of Art.

"Tommy" Bernard finds only an experimenter in technique, a *poseur* in ungrammatical willfulness who one day might be pitched into greatness on a happy discovery. He has no Universe, and therefore he is cold.

I emphasise his freshness of sensation that is restively seeking to mould language to its turbulence of impressibility.

The remainder of the page has been redacted.[129]

EC Roger Fry, his sister (very Fry of very Fry),[iii] and his Willow-wood wife came to tea.

---

i "Leedsware" pottery, often cream-colored and featuring openwork weaving, was first produced by Hartley Greens & Co., founded in 1756. The company closed in 1881 but was restarted in 1888.

ii From John Keats, "The Human Seasons" (1819).

iii Joan Fry (1862–1955), Quaker campaigner for peace and reform; she helped her brother raise his children when Helen Coombe was hospitalized.

Miss Fry brings me a generous handful of peach Rudbeckias. She wears roses round her hat—pink, definitely unreal as the roses of a Dresden shepherdess. She is a delightful creature—unexpected in her quiet judgments, in her quiet fun, that has a strange ideality about it—and begins where no one else is gay. All of her is womanly.[130]

EC *Tuesday, September 29th.*

A dreadful Michaelmas—Alas!

My finances are in darkness. Michael and his angels are fighting the Dragon of Deficit.

My head loses its balance worse than my banking account; it loosely whirls round the fixed idea of getting straight. I am intolerable.

Michael and his Angels save me, and before we go to bed this most miserable day is illumined by Gospel and Collect for the Feast and love-poems of "The Old."[131]

Thursday the Artists come to dine—

Yesterday Fay wrote: "The Artists have not forgotten—could they forget? We expect Berenson's left ear toasted on a silver charger with red pepper strewn thereon as a savoury." So we give them sweetbreads as Berenson's ears—while the poor little Doctrine is on the sea, feeling very bad: he sailed yesterday for America.

We are looking well. Michael in her gray satin eighteenth-century dress— I in striped white and black, the "Music" pendant at my waist, the "Bluebird" brooch hung as a pendant on the neck. This arrangement is instantaneously acclaimed naughty.

Michael wears no Ricketts jewels—but lays the Pegasus Pendant on the Sun Room table—this is instantaneously condemned. Taking up "The Pegasus" in the course of the evening, Fay remarks, "This ought to belong to the Palace."

We have the first Neapolitan violets in the silver bowl—smilax and purple vine round the Leeds bowl and a pair of satinwood-yellow chrysanthemums in the glasses on the mantel shelf.

The dinner was *economical*, but turned out capital—better than many[132] at double its cost—

Parmentier soup
Stewed halibut
Fried sweetbreads in cucumber sauce
Leg of lamb
Stone cream and banana jelly.

Not once did Fay offer one of his cigarettes to Michael.[133]

EC The golden thing is—an old Dutch piece of Satinwood, a harbour and a hold for *Works and Days*—and my birthday present. It is soft as a woman's hand to touch—soft with its blond age. It is a little heavy in build—but the wood is fine, of the darker umber sunset kind.

It is one of the personalities of the house.[134]

EC After tea [Fay] speaks of Queen Elizabeth and how she interested Oscar—she and her race. Oscar was present at a country house when letters of hers to Leicester were discovered. Oscar had also been present when Edward II's tomb had been opened and saw the body preserved—when someone touched a jewel, and the corpse was gone with that touch. At the end a ring was missed from the King's hand. All the distinguished company was searched—it was found at last on the respectable person of an old gentleman belonging to the Museum, who had been lured into this strange sin from the paths of an innocent life.[135]

Oscar loved the Tudor Catalogue. John Gray had a love for the race and also Swinburne.

Then Fay gives us Oscar's scenario for *Anne of Cleaves*. She is the lovely woman represented by Holbein in the Louvre. On the voyage to England, she falls in love with a young English nobleman—the ship keeps nearing the King's country—what is to be done? Will they make an old governess play the part of Anne of Cleaves? No—she will disguise herself till she is detestable to the King.

Henry in disillusion flees the hideous bride and divorces her. Afterwards one day the king hears the lute from an old London garden: he gets on a courtier's shoulders and looks over the garden wall. He is enchanted by the lovely lute player. Then he learns it is Anne of Cleaves, his *divorcée* now married to her English nobleman.

A very charming little play! Oscar was delighted with Mary Howard, and much interested in the babe found walled up in the chapel at Holyrood and wrapped in [a] cloth of gold. It was thought to be the *real*[136] James 1st—the first Scottish King of England being a changeling.

Fay says he cannot express what Oscar was to him and Shannon for a whole year. His brilliance was inexhaustible, and beyond the immediate enjoyment they received an atmosphere—a wonderful, false atmosphere was produced for their work in which it throve for years. They breathed an ideality—a warmth toward things the mind that they must have to live bounteously—that life, especially in England, crushingly denies them as artists.

Then Fay says how Oscar loved to talk of Ellen Terry when a little model she married Watts, and fell under the iron rule of Lady Holland (Watts being that lady's illegitimate step-son).[i] The poor little thing lived in a nursery up-stairs and was gradually eliminated. The crisis came when Watts had a din-ner of Bishops, connected with the decoration of St. Paul's.[137]

EC Michael has brought from Miss Toplady's a Venetian pharmacy pot in old Murano (or a fruit jar) to see if it is a bait to the Artists—it is: bite bite. They each proclaim it desirable. Then one sees what Fay means by making money *imaginative*, when he makes a glass pot full of imaginative cre-ativeness. He sinks a Eucharis lily with a gold ring in the midst of the water, puts on the lid, and watches the flower as a seaweed lift itself with that support of growth, which is the strange and beautiful power of the watery elements.

Crystals come to nest round the edges of the form of the flower and the form itself is an insubstantial[138] pageant belonging henceforth to art's little magician![139]

KB *St. Stephen's Day.*

It begins—the fight to erect ourselves above ourselves. Fog and a corpse wind underneath. Henry is strife with his ills. . . .

EC Oh, but we had a good Christmas Eve. Michael became a Child "as if a rose should shut and be a bud again"[ii]—she had a Christmas tree! I decked it with red and white candles and seashells and black and white paper but-terflies round a black wool devil, with such a horror of a tail. His poodle, grown white for Christmas, looks out with white sheep's malice round a bough—a pearly Japanese fish sails the air, and a woolly clown asks all eyes to mount.

Mistletoe sprays up as a French fountain from the white Leeds bowl wreathed with intricacy of coralline holly berries—ivy leaves round the mir-ror—the red and black of holly wreath demon and butterflies trickle down the wall in the great Mandarin's necklace. We startle the little tree with glow-worm lighting; and then in a[140] frenzy I begin all round the holly bush, with my best kicks and springs—washing my face as if gathering ocean to my brow— . . . but my heart! I had forgotten; and its breathless heave refuses childhood to me.

Christmas Day itself is flat—very cold and lifeless is the earth.[141]

i Terry was married to the painter George Frederic Watts (1817–1905) when he was forty-five and she was sixteen. The marriage lasted less than one year. Lady Augusta Holland (1812–89) was a frequent subject of Watts's portraiture.

ii From John Keats, "The Eve of St. Agnes" (1820).

Works and Days, 1904

KB *New Year's Day*: More and more I feel this, we are weavers of the stuff of time.[142]

EC *On her birthday.*

My gift from Michael is *Placidia*[i]—the satinwood chest that enwombs *Works and Days*.[143]

EC Then talk goes to the meeting with Bernard and the friendship with Oscar.

Fay says they and Oscar never talked anything but inspired "rot." As women, we probably have no idea how playful men are among themselves. Fay said scarcely anything—nothing serious—Oscar tried all his newest paradoxes on them, elaborated exciting, fantastic projects.

Before dinner I had shown Fay our two letters from Oscar and delighted him specially with Oscar's desire to see our characters in golden masques (we are to show these letters to Bobby [Ross]—as two bricks in "the legend").[144]

KB *Wednesday, February 10th.*

Shannon calls it "Solomon," and the tinkling within "The Song of Solomon."[ii]

It is the most perfectly successful achieving, of all the jewels. Its doors are to be smeared with ambergris, so that it may appeal to all the five senses. In its soft cloud a star beams. But it is not as a ring it excels.

Blessedly, an old, cleaned, favourite blouse, low, square, with velvet stomacher, turned up[145] and I put the ring on "breastie" by a gold chain, the full Pegasus ornament below on black velvet.

Henry and Painter fell to adoration—I could have laughed at them. But we were all very happy, and there is no conversation to report in the Year Book.

My beloved wore a new blouse, and the Chinese necklace, and looked the sweetest. Her grief had been I shall have nothing to wear. But that gracious old blouse had all the effect of a "Sling."[146]

---

i Placidia is the mother of the protagonist Honoria in Michael Field's 1896 play, *Attila, My Attila!*

ii Ricketts created a gold ring set for Bradley with a cabochon star sapphire dome above a mosque-structure containing a loose emerald. The "Sabbatai" ring is now part of the collection of the Fitzwilliam Museum, Cambridge.

KB Frances Power Cobbe died on Tuesday April 5th.[i] A very brave, a very gallant woman. But for the sake of the most[147] precious things of the spirit, for the sake of the savour of the vines, and the fragrant substances of earth.

One must make protest against her. First of all, born as every woman is to be man's helpmate, she hated man (as man), and boasted that she had not been desired of him, or desiring.

She did not produce flower or fruit after her kind.

May she energise in Mars somewhere!—perhaps—there among the canals she will do less harm![148]

KB *May Day.*

Marie is like a sod of green turf. When Tommy pecks, he will find the daisy, the grass, the wholesome worm . . .[149]

EC Marie is dusk, responsive to the country air as blueberry.

She has ableness of character—the true Protestant strain, and ability—her English is wonderful in attack—and a bright-eyed independence of phrasing makes one laugh as at the motions of a healthy living creature in the meadows.

Now and then she has the gesture—a trick of the brows that reminds me of Michael's old friend of Paris days—Miss Gérente—who strange today—Marie describes as almost a "great grandmother" to her!

So it comes about that we learn from Tommy's bride how the good little soul, the sister of Michael's supreme love, Alfred Gérente, came quietly to her end in the Deaconesses Home, with *pasteurs* to pray with her, and, by favour, her beloved objects round her—all her mementos. How strange is life—how strange!

Tommy read the gazette—but badly, monotonously.[150]

EC A silly letter from Tommy, suggesting that through a woman he could get an opportunity of reading a play[151] of ours to a junior partner—he also a budding poet. If [the junior partner] is interested he will ensure the play having a good hearing with his senior. Michael replies—

Merciful heavens, how can we thank you for this opportunity of being read by a "budding poet"! Out of the mouths of these babes and sucklings would you perfect our praise? Not for one instant would I abide being sniffed at by these doubtful Thomases, not one of them capable of considering the

---

i Frances Power Cobbe (1822–1904), a prolific author and prominent feminist and anti-vivisectionist.

matter in hand. Surely you forget who have welcomed, us who have given us their homage. Browning told us to wait fifty years, and apparently we must wait. I asked you to help me, and you have diligently tried—but on impossible methods—as if you should propose the pawnbroker to me if I were in sore straits for money. Like the Duke in "My Last Duchess" I choose never to stoop. But I choose to publish *Tristan*, and I will.[i]

Sincerely yours,

Michael.[152]

EC The men we know all believe that a woman's one need is to love a man—that is enough, for it is her ideal.

They think so . . .

But woman's own ideal is to be loved—she wants herself infinitely surpassed, her power of loving left behind by that in man. This is why she is religious and Christian—this is why the man who loves is her adoration and her dream.[153]

KB *Saturday, September 10th.*

The lease has been finally approved, and in faith and calm we wait its signing. It said in Isaiah—If ye believe not, surely we shall not be established.

We believe; and we are being established.

We begin our seven years—afresh—and the new lease of life is not to imitate the old lease. It is to be a New Paragon, new in its ideals; i.e., its central idea is perfection; not whereas we have sought perfection in the grace of life, now[154] we seek it within ourselves—and in external things as the expression of ourselves. We recultivate our personality, left fallow for seven years. Truly as regards our spirits and our minds, these have been lean years. Slowly we have come up from death and torpor, injured to the very bone, we have crawled about and got things done for us, till, as regards direct contact with life, we are as clumsily ignorant as the fishes in the sunless cave of light.

EC But friends! We need human voices as well as the sucking hum of the oars. We have got into solitude—and it is a hard thing to get out. Michael said of this last spring "we were nearing suicide"—the terrible menace was in the condition of our days.

---

i Browning's 1842 poem, a dramatic monologue in which the speaker says, in reference to his (now-deceased) wife's supposed flirtations elsewhere, "Who'd stoop to blame / This sort of trifling?" Michael Field did indeed publish *Tristan de Léonis*, in a volume with two other plays, in 1911, as "the author of *Borgia*."

We had lost touch with life, as if we were sphinxes, or Chimeras[i]—we neither bought from our fellows, talked to them, mixed with them. I have a quite infinite flush of sanity from the daily shopping with Michael. To hear her drive a little bargain is like a wholesome buzzing of a bee to my ears.[155]

EC There was a great Painter named Ricketts
Who showed us that Art has no thickets:
> He cut his way through
> With his own Ricketts Blue,
This marvellous painter named Ricketts.

There was a rare critic named Bernard
Authentic, "and but by a turn" marred—
> He never could rest
> In Art's pretty nest
Till he'd scattered the nestlings, rare Bernard.

There was a fine woman named Mary,
Who never of pleasure was chary—
> She drank all her fill,
> Yet never did ill
This Child of Renaissance, blessed Mary.[156]

There was a fair painter named Shannon,
As bright as the parquet he ran on,
> An apple-bloom face
> Yet in "Toilet" his grace
Put to shame all the fairness of Shannon.

There was an Archangel named Michael
Who used his fair spear as a pike well
> For encounter and prick;
> Though he hurt to the quick,
All hailed him Angelic, dear Michael.

There was a young painter named Ricketts
As subtle as snake of the thickets
> As cruel as bland
> Yet a power in the land
Like Eve's pretty Lizard, this Ricketts.[157]

---

i Both hybrid figures from Greek mythology associated with femininity. The Sphinx had the head of a woman, the rear of a lion, and the wings of a bird; she would kill those who could not answer her riddles. The Chimera was a fire-breathing figure comprising a lion, a serpent, and a goat.

Works and Days, 1905

KB *On Edith Cooper's birthday.*

January 12th.

It is a net of pearls I give her, and the shy elf meets me at the door as I return from the dusk, with the quaint, drooped hangings of pearls in lines parallel with either cheek. It takes splendour to secure, and save from wasting on the air, the five substances and perfumes of which her face is composed.[i]

Moving about in that brilliance she is as a star. She enchants me, and I beseech her not to remove her headdress. Yet, if she kept it on, I should not sleep for gazing on her.

Her head is designed for ornament. It does not summon the crown, or garland, but the headdress.

I wish to retain no other memory of this birthday—save the pearls as they appear, and reappear in her hair, and as candles to her cheek.[158]

EC *Following the death of KB's doves from leprosy.*

I have suffered with the doves—never shall I forget seeing the poor little lepers—once such soft consorts—laying their doomed heads in their wretchedness close together and waiting—love there in the almost blind horror. Their cage was a *memento mori* such as could turn worldlings into saints . . . all the round bounce of the happy creatures gone, every trace of beauty removed by infamy and corruption—no voices crooning,[159] no wantonness, simple and courteous—nothing but vulture heads gathering into ridges of horn and a rubbish-heap of feathers. Yet the specialist looked with kind eyes on them and hoped to fill these little scenes with tender life again and piercing sounds! Alas! So they suffered on till death. And we disinfected the room, and we burnt the cages, and there is noiseless air no longer giving home to our ear.[160]

EC I cannot write of it—words are not elastic enough—there would be meaningless explosion if they were used. One crunches on the rock bed of humanity as if for a spring—and the wild silence can have no victim.[161]

EC *February 23.*

Fay sails. What a misuse of the imagination it is to picture the absent and their doings! It is setting a great positive to negative work—because

i A snood made of pearls strung on delicate thread or wires; in Buddhism, associated with "Indra's net," signifying the interconnectedness of all worldly phenomena.

Imagination affirms all it sees, and Reality denies and deceives imagination—turns it into "fond imaginings," makes it the dupe of facts that are playing it false.[162]

EC *Responding to the posthumous publication of Wilde's "De Profundis."*

I cannot yet write about Oscar—[. . .] it is Tragedy in phrase and pose— yet it is often genius with the sword of Light and the song of Beauty. The praise of Christ is the inside of a little golden book of Devotion would I read among the April fields at Eastertide.

The book wants analysis—as one would give to *Hamlet*. . . . [T]o discover its character taxes one, and I am[163] too full of *Borgia* and *Tristan* to have spare strength of brain to test the quality of these things lifted up from the *De Profundis* of aestheticism—not of the Psalmist nor of the Funeral Service. I must wait—reread.[i][164]

EC We have again talked through the telephone—oh, we need nothing but the voice to be to each other.[ii] All my love is in her generous laugh, with its little pricklets of amusement. Nothing delights us so much as chatting to each other. And Michael says she understands why the Dead talk such nonsense—What logic would any lovers utter?[165]

EC Fay agrees wholly with Michael on the Oscar book: "though I think you overrate it, you are right—he felt nothing but the effectiveness of things; underneath his skin was a constitution of porphyry or adamant or some substance out of which the Romans made busts of Emperors like Nero and Caligula."[iii][166]

KB ". . . But what will become of us—unpublishable, unactable, irritating?"[167]

EC After dinner we hear much of the later Oscar and of the success of *De Profundis*. "Death can make even genius respectable." So Fay says—of course; death is the one leveler, the common doom—all men feel the kindness of equality before that one and only Democrat of the Universe.

There is no question that *De Profundis* has only the depth of a personal

---

i Wilde's *De Profundis* is a letter from Wilde to his lover, Lord Alfred Douglas, written during his imprisonment and published in 1905.

ii Early telephone technology was introduced in England in the late 1870s, with exchanges proliferating around the turn of the century. Coin-operated call boxes were introduced in 1906, just months after Cooper was writing here.

iii Porphyry is a form of igneous rock, typically reddish and coarse-grained; adamantine describes a substance that is hard and unbreakable, like a diamond.

and momentary expression. We follow the narrative of the decline and fall after that prison life. It is inexpressibly woeful—it is not tragic.[168]

EC One must never meet the past face to face in its nakedness—one must leave the black velvet mask on that face, or all is marred.[169]

EC *Friday.*

I have a night that ends in early dawn and the slow teardrops, one or two, when earth is as a solitary star in voidness and one lies in the star alone.

Amy is removed from England in a few hours more.

Fay has been unkind.

Tommy unvital.

Even Mary goes to join Bernard in a day or two.

We have no friends, no neighbours—we have before us the stealing on of years, the conflict to live, mid age and old age—no readers, no friendly encouragement—unnatural conditions that dehumanise and unnerve, for to work at tragedy and poetry in silent rooms, debarred from much reading by delicate sight and from conversation by the absence of our kind is unnerving and uncivil—alas![170]

KB *September 30th.*

I will resume this neglected journal.

Yesterday—the Palace—farthing buns that Michael eats in cluster, as bunches of grapes. A dull caller—he descends the abyss of the lift, and Fay comes back, cross-legged dancing on the air. Swart goblin! It is in these moments of demoniac joy one feels him, what he is. "Let us live," I say—"Take me to the study"—and we pass to "Venus smacking Cupid." The little creature is crouched weeping at her knee—a body quite limpid in its clay—lovely: Venus is not Venus, and not smacking. But the Cupid is so living, so tremendous sweet, nothing else matters.

We have long and intimate talk.

EC I too will resume this neglected journal (Oct. 5th). Why so neglected? Well, September has been a mountain of Purgatory: the weather has hugged me indoors to suffocation-point; cold fogs, cold rains, or the warm slackening damps of the grave. We have been afflicted with inhuman melancholia, that[171] does not bear to be remembered. Our isolation in Paragon under these circumstances has been a curse. Day after day we have spoken to no one, save our ever-soothing dogs. And the sense of great powers of converse lying by in ever-corroding inertness, in seclusion that is not even safe from time, has been despair to us—despair on the dangerous road the end of which Wordsworth foretold gout and solitude—who can fight such an alliance?[172]

EC *October 11.*

Francis is engaged. We have wished it, for as the lonely airs blow over life from the common future of mortality to have some time warm and nestled in homeliness is desirable for those who are aging. Marriage is the natural shelter "to drive the winds away."

The unmarried are shelterless and deserted. Francis is wise and we approve his choice. But this event of good to him is only another dropped leaf from our nearly bare tree of friendship. To Michael the dropped leaf carries down memories of a June greenness long ago and a little shrine of Aphrodite Alcaeus decked[i]—and to me the dropped leaf means almost the last listener gone.[173] Francis loved to hear, to question—all the imprisoned fountains of speech in me flowed when we were together. And, of course, for this the frankness of a common condition of singleness was essential. Marriage is the tomb of all other real relations.

This bareness coming round us is alarming. We fear we shall breathe in no man's land—a little desert in the midst of others' fields of wheat and sheepwalks. A ghostly breathing place where only ghosts should be, not creatures of vivid converse.[174]

KB In age what furious jealousies gnaw the heart! We are starving—and lips that are laughing beside us close on the golden apple.[175] Francis is engaged—Tommy's son is born—one event makes a void where there has been greenness and the other no way brings to us mirth or rejoicing.

In age one ceases to have impact with life, unless one is a grandparent. Then life visits one tidally, the waves still break at one's feet, and the little flowers of the hedgerow greet you as you pass. [. . .]

A change is coming to our lives, some wide, undreamed independence, something to be shared together of my Fellow and myself.

Tommy's son—I return to him—I am churning some small verses to his babyhood.[176]

KB *Friday, Nov. 17th* is the name of this great day of joy and reconciliation.

Henry starts forth in a still frost [. . .]. I profess indoors, and then follow after, and scan the loved wild figure silhouetted against the snow-verge.

i Alcaeus: a warrior poet from the Isle of Lesbos and, like Sappho, a worshipper of Aphrodite. Given that her cousin Francis had proposed to Bradley long ago, this might suggest a road not taken for Sappho and Alcaeus to join as one in worship of Aphrodite.

How I love her, and desire her, and curse the pain I gave her—dull in a cloud of sleep to the moonlight vision of last night. She read to me the Diane and Henri love-scene.[i] [. . .] Through the filings of moonlight some things I missed, and some I doubted, and I was blunt to all the fineness of conception.

Besides—Tommy had written to me—blatant and coarse in his paternity—and I was hurt that he could do this thing, so infamous in a poet. I was stunned and helpless.

In the night there were alternate hours of waking and asleep, and unheard tears were shed. Henry spoke to me in harsh, strange tones. I did not heed; I was hard as to the reproaches of the delirium. Then—the dawns—and after the dawns she read to me—till the air was full of moon raindrops; and we became[177] again one soul.[178]

KB *Paragon (we return November 21st, Tuesday).*

Joy—and like an allegro movement is our return. We come back to north air—light full of crystals, chrysanthemums—cooing doves—exquisite parlours.

My most Loved is[179] as a Star in the midst of all this Beauty. Like Cleopatra, she knows what she wants. She comes home to lay hold of it. Vigilant, alert, and gloriously accomplishing. [. . .]

Today, the second day, all the old temptations set in. A west, wet gale—flaccid bodies—But we have learnt the great lesson of living to today—of making each day a revealed beautiful thing to give to God.[180] Henry strives victoriously.

I do not know at all what Heaven would have with me—certainly *myself*.

It is, I think, a law in the art of life that we must always conceal the state in which we temporally are. Youth—the least ashamed state—is most over-come of shame at itself. The youth is ever apeing the man. Age too must never allow itself. It was Regan who said, "Being old, seem so."[ii]

All precious things remain or recur. Those stones are called precious stones that forever emit light and colour.

The real saint lies uncorruptible in his mould.[181]

---

i From *The Tragedy of Pardon and Diane*, eventually published in 1911 by Michael Field as "the author of *Borgia*."

ii A paraphrase of Regan's speech to King Lear (2.4.233): "I pray you, father, being weak, seem so." Folger Shakespeare Library (n.d.), https://www.folger.edu/explore/shakespeares -works/king-lear/read.

KB I come up and hear I may listen to the great trial scene.

She stands before me curled up in a corner of the settee—the manuscript on a small table before her—and stands—her arms stretched wide, her hands clenching as she reads—and reads. It is a new thing, strong and blowing as from a trumpet. It is conceived of her own soul, and issues at a blast. The flowers of her similes are fresh as those that flash from the trumpets of Amadís of Gaul.[i]

There is in it no complexity, or "fine feeling"—or muddle motive. It is clear chiseled as the rocks.

I feel as a mother at her daughter's bridals. Without me this day had not been born, and yet it is her day.[182]

KB The New Song

Yea, we had been one soul, and we divide.
She stands before me, and with hands clasped tight
Reads forth . . . As from a trumpet's night
Blows the new song, and flowers are on its tide.
She stands alone, elected, glorified,
As we had never been one soul. O Height
I worship from my space of lower light,
O mountain crest that I am meek beside!
What of this glory that is kindled mine?
My Dear, the wonder—for I am not stirred
As by another's rich, announcing word
Rife from the tomb, sounding now far away;
But veritably, of my blood, I lay
Such claim, I grip thy clenched hands,
   I am thine.
St. Catharine's Day, Saturday Nov. 25th.[183]

EC Nerves jarring sometimes on the beauty of Michael's love to me and mine to the beloved Michael. Ah, impiety! Hope and confidence almost unattainable, except by overtaking them in a dream of fame after death.

Solitude of friendlessness quite terrible—days and weeks with no converse, save with the dumb expressiveness of our dogs—and the daily chatting with our two maids. . . . Tommy lost by marriage,[184] becoming nothing but a Nurs-

---

i Amadís of Gaul was an early-sixteenth-century chivalric romance written in prose, and eventually satirized by Cervantes in *Don Quixote* (1605). This is not an especially generous characterization by Bradley of Cooper's work.

ing Father in a household that is all nursery—as a lair is all for the cubs ... Fay more abstract ... no one else. Any women who do chance to come, dismal failures, unable to think or feel about the creativeness of beauty, or to take life with humour, which is the gentlest form of detachment by which it is recreated into an art of life. Where we breathe and have our being women are absolutely inferior creatures to men, as animals to human creatures.

The solitude is the chief of the dark spirits: we must not depend on our Kind. Sometimes the solitude is so strange we feel that some slander must have infected our presence, unknown to us—sometimes we are sure of this. We might have been in prison.[185]

EC How one's ears beat, as one listens to the air on which 1905 dies and 1906 is born! The ears tingle with the stillness.

I do not ask personal questions of the tingling spaces—but I feel my Love and I and Chow shall be together to garner what this year 1906 has brought in its course of marvel and of immediacy of life.[186]

EC The Dead be with us! Ah, they know the secrets of all springtimes—may they be with the flush of life due to us from tonight!

God bless us all—my own love, Henry and the Chow. The bells are almost unheard—they are but a whirr in the shell of the dusky night.

1906—welcome.

The Cannon of the Royal Borough have just severed one year from another. I can hear now the surge of the bells to and fro. The night is very cold and deliciously still—the new born.[187]

Works and Days, 1906

EC *With Mary Berenson on Cooper's birthday.*

Husbands and wives should never read each other's letters—she reads B.B.'s—and tells him what to say to Ladies ... but there are many people who will not allow two pair of eyes to rest on what was meant for one pair of eyes. ... In a flash my eyes convey to hers the reason of my profound silence toward "Doctrine."[188] [...]

January 13th.

Such a river to walk by ... the most beautiful fabric in the world! ... Is it sun I am feeling as if I were being turned into gold? And are my eyes really seeing red when I close them? No wonder Whym Chow, fighting eczema, grins and is aglow. Spring! Oh, and Spring tides![189]

EC *Sunday 14th.*

And they think basset a dearer dog than Chow—in celestial wonder at them in his chair.

He has been bad with eczema—felled sometimes and needed the muzzle for treatment and has climbed the chair at sheer command with dragging paw. (Written after his death.)[190]

EC *Friday 19th.*

We had been growing anxious over Chow's stiffness in standing or climbing—and the golden front paws lay out rather long. In the evening panic came on us and [we fetched] the Vet. Only his assistant could come. He said the dog was suffering from local paralysis from constipation—a common disorder, needing the pill that should be sent. Chow lay at our feet near Michael's green couch—he looked at her with all the sight of his little soul. She hated me, when I said, "How Chow is looking at you!"

Saturday 20th.

The Vet says Chow will probably be well by Monday. . . . "He will not—he is seriously ill," Michael comments. I try to assure myself she is over-anxious.[191]

EC *Having convinced KB to leave for an evening with the Artists.*

I have to press her to go because the vet has not been. But she so needs change and I do not feel in any dread. As she leaves Chow makes an effort with straight forepaws to hold up to the window for his fond goodbye. I help him and get him on the end of the couch—but the straight forepaws straddle over it. I say *yes* to zealous eyes, but as we go out of the Sun Room instead of turning down stairs he walks into the wall—It freezes me.[192]

KB There paces my Chow in mental peril—wandering witlessly—and above me lies Henry of the broken heart.

Friday.

Yesterday—a specialist Sewell—"I am sorry, it is a bad case—I cannot say he will recover." Yet if Chow were his dog, he would "give him a month"—there is chance, though it is vague chance, for life.

EC *Sunday*—how terrible Sundays are!

Milestones of doom to us as a family. Today I have had the worst loss of my life—yes, worse than that of beloved Mother or the tragic father—my Whym Chow, my little Chow—Chow, my Flame of Love is dead and has died—O cruel God!—by our will!

Wednesday after Michael started for the Palace, I took my Delight[193]

[for] a walk on the towing path. He had been suffering from eczema of his tail and from a strange stiffness of limb the vet called rheumatism: but Michael had breathed the word Paralysis and we had a vague anxiety, indeed she had felt slightly ominous for some months as the Beloved was showing what we thought to be signs of age, little touches of disobedience and difficulty, a little less alacrity to follow up stairs.

As I led him along the towing path, I noticed his frenzied pace, right on in one line of speed, with scarcely any snuffling. L—, at the River-Gate, called me in to see the Vet, who had promised Chow would be well on Monday. The dear little head was pointed to the wall at the back of a chair in the Gold Room. "But this is very serious"—and a candle was held to the leonine eyes that hardly blenched. Polar cold struck through me. "You anticipate meningitis?"—"Not that yet, at least, completely."

Chow is ordered to a darkened room and quiet. How terrible to sit mid most of his ravings and wait to tell Michael the dread diagnosis. Swiftly the fell disease grew, as[194] if grown conscious with being named—By late evening the beautiful little Whymmie was pacing for hours, though he would lie down at his Minnie's word and got some sleep, while she lay on the green couch in grot. I upstairs was distracted between terror and wild hope.

Next day specialist—Sewell—called in—sickening suspense till he comes, and grips the situation with eyes, lips and nostrils like grappling irons. Chow's beauty admired—his strength and condition as well as his glorious coat. "He has a great deal of strength—the case is a very bad one but there is a vague hope. If he were my dog, I should give him three weeks or a month."

We determine to do this; and we set about arranging to nurse, removing all the broad ruby head might knock against in its soft and cautious butts. Mostly Whym visited the corners of the room with "distrait" nose; standing humbly on his proud feet, or else he whirled round like a stately werewolf with such terrible rhythm as drew the imagination into its circles.[195]

[. . .] Yet in the afternoon we take him round by Messina's to the towing path, he romping among the ivies like a creature of another earth. The river damps invade me and at the same time a discouragement spreads out into Despair, at the thought of our Resolve.

And I go back to find the ceaseless diagonal lines and the circles. Impossible to hope!

Saturday.

In the night of Sunday, Chow has one hour's sleep and Michael lies by him on his sheepskin rug in ecstasy. Soon the regular pad of the wolves over the dust-sheeted matting—the food and water held to the nose for recognition by the touch, unaided by the now sightless and contracted eyes.

The pacing becomes of mechanic stubbornness—a thing of danger to the brain of the watchers. I see it in dream: it scares me; I wake with nerve ends like scalding water and with a great passion at the heart that little Chow should be set free from all his misery. My poor love comes to me dazed with sleep—Whymmie has dropped.[196]

KB *Monday.*

I go down to order Chow's coffin and grave—I see him—not curled up dead and dripping in his basket as I saw him yesterday—though then he was quite sweet—the face still scowling a little at death—He lies rigid, and very beautiful—quite glad now to be still—holding as in a casket his royal love for me—not the flowing gold now—but there, there the treasury for me of the dead heart—the glorious little frame is a tomb to his passion.

Hamlet—over Yorick's skull is not like that—"there hung these lips that I have kissed so oft." But every throb of that heart—and all these dances of joy round me—are hardened and softened—therewithin—under that tawny fur.

Such a moving little chap he looks! I am so proud of his love.

What he would have been to me in age!

My Dear, My Dear!

Oh, it is the great strain and stretching out of this love to me that has brought him to his death.[197]

EC O beating of the manifest wings of Pain! Under the pulsing cold that is within me I tell her I am sure that this unbearable torture must end for our Adored—inexorably during the night I have seen *it has been coming on for long*; there is only the chance of one to a hundred he could ever get over a disease that every day strengthens.

We send for Dr. Williamson—the morphine given while the loved Chow has to be held by his own is thrown up; and from this bungle at five in the morning till the vet comes at eleven my Love is left with her little doomed joy. But there is something to do!

Out of blindness and perpetual motion of the lovely feet and perpetual bumping of the brow (save when it stayed against Michael's knee, arrested by the soft patting, and then with gentle insistence pressed on to reach the opposite wall) out of all this, Whym Chow snuffed the morning air with his free joyance. I saw him in the midst of the ivy leaves in the front Garden a happy Bacchic cub, the ivy doubly alive against his flaming fur. Earth, air— how he snuffed, and my agony knew he was going to leave them. How I loved him, how I printed him on my[198] mind—Little Chow, God bless thee; Little Chow, God bless thee!—the crease of ruby down his brow, the soft almost blue-shaded ears, the roughness round the neck, the tender swirl of silk where cheek and ruff were at one ... and the affaire's legs—so lean and sturdy—such energy and singleness! Oh my Whym Chow, my little Chow. Chow!

Michael, who needs must kill the thing she loves, determines he shall have full joy of the Earth. The little frenzied one is led round by the towing path . . . I see him enter the river door for the last time. I wanted him to trot on lead from rose-bush to rose-bush.

Then the vet.—

Chow is left in the garden, pacing and breathing. I hear the vet and Michael go down. I bow in prayer—

I lie, where he used to sleep, in an agony of submission. My love returns white—she has had to hold her adored while the sleeping-draught was given—she, his adoring mistress. She comes to me while the sleeping draught is stealing Chow from life . . . she is called down . . . A moment or two after I see a [199] basket carried down the garden to the river door—my sweetest, my most beloved is in it, sleeping the death sleep.

How can I see it pass: am I paralysed?

And I hear the brave Michael has started to meet her beloved and to see him after the final injection has been done. She insists on the bullet . . . So as a gentleman her Chow should have died—but no one may fire in Richmond. The fair little body has to be taken to Twickenham.[i]

When she enters our desolated Paragon, home no more forever—she says, "My little dog is at rest—at rest, you hear it—he is at rest." It is like having the sound of icebergs that gnaw and laugh and then break up. It is hideously and greatly tragic. Our grief is blind, is potent . . . we scarcely touch food, but bring back to order the rooms, now grown so hateful that we realise we must go.

"Yes," I say to Michael, "we must let Paragon and get a little flat in town." All the night more unnaturalness of our life there appears more naked when Tommy comes to supper. I do not see him—but Michael has courage to give him supper in the gold room, where with [200] all atrocious circumstances she parted from her joy. [. . .]

That first night without him in the little tower we kept for our Magic Joy—the floors like unconsciousness; the passages tunnels—the glowing sat-inwood furniture, Chow [201] matched, like objects out of Mars, found with last things in the deathly moon.

And the sense we shall not have love's breath in the solitudes of night anymore, the change of posture that banishes fear.

---

i The suburban town of Twickenham is just across the river from 1, Paragon.

The waking in the Queen Anne room with paralysis of all that encourages one to rise for another day—even tears now too arctic to flow.

And the floors with no living movement about them not a gleam of life among them—the floors—

Old Music called up . . . the old dog pining a little, and he moves about the floors.[202]

EC Oh, the bitter tears for that silent hall the symbol of a silent world where for us there is no welcome.

Whym Chow, Whym Chow—Oh my little love!

Rain on the shores of a dead sea God has smitten—my tears and Michael's.[203]

EC I write to Marie Sturge Moore:

My dear Marie

You have understood.

That we should have lost Chow is, as you say, "awful news." Poor Michael after four days of nightmare nursing and six hours of bungled efforts to put our most loved to rest, has broken down completely and is suffering dreadfully in nerves and head. I am only less smitten.

Marie, those who really knew us understood that in this bare world we went to him as our brazier of love, the flames and the incense, the motion and thrill we found perfect alone in the passion Chow had for Michael—a love that has consumed his life in eight years, when he should have lived eight years more.

The boy who for seven years has served us writes "he was your only and dearest friend you had at Paragon," and our landlord here said simply when we spoke of our grief, "Why, of course, he was your all."

Chow was too noble to be demonstrative, so only those who lived along with us or who were very penetrative realise that this loss is heavier than any we have had, in a certain way. That we are human beings and he an animal makes no difference: there is[204] one coinage for love throughout the Universe and he gave us divine measure.

Michael is now like a queen without a crown, a goddess without her attribute: we live shorn days, and desolate is all before us.

One thing alone is certain—we must leave Paragon *at once* if Michael is to be revived. We have put it already into agents' hands—it is memorial to the eye, and a grave-vault to the heart. We must make all things new.

Here Chow is missed by the good people, and we look on haunts about which his little live body seemed to flame. I am trusting the mighty air may enter and revive Michael, but when it has no intimate comfort in its cruel actuality . . . well, even air that is of the moved pinions of a god is but a weak aid . . .

Thank you for your true sympathy.

Field.[205]

EC The pacings of our little Whym are on me . . .

I am restless from the centre of the mind [. . .] [G]ood Mrs. Riches wipes the floor, and moves the dear father's carved chest into the middle of the room that it may hold the little coffin of the Creature of Love who seemed to embody his own love for[206] Michael, so of one kind of heart to her were Chow and he—the little creature born for Michael on the day she knelt by his coffin in the dark Church at Zermatt.

Michael has always felt in Chow the presence of that devoted consuming love in its nobleness that went into the unseen eight years ago.

Tuesday, January 30th[207]

Tender preparation from my Love—tenderest and unforgettable.

I am in the paneled room—there is the full furred head I adore—He lies toward the chimney piece, the legs straight out as in the happy days when he was sleeping, the face with the plainness of his repose, even a bright glint of the eye as when I entered—and the flank is long, is sunk among the ivy leaves and the flaxen tail quite down and hidden over the eyes the bullet-mark—the loved ears as pliable, as dearly soft as ever—the fur with all its gentle silk, its harsh threads, its fleece of the distaff, its ripples and its shag . . . all its gold, umber roam and palest amber—yet no warmth at the base of the fur, no spring of light, the dayspring, on the surface of colour.

And as one looked out the familiar[208] attitude one trembled with terror at it because it would never change . . . the impatient, vivid Chow would never change . . . what rigour! Sculpture and yet not apart from actuality—Terror! yet the dear man looked beautiful—flowering sapphire—like wine-drenched sprays against his muddy brow; under his dark little chin a nest of wine-coloured Christmas roses, a few of our snowdrops among them; the Bacchic ivy in strands around him.

I gave him the best lock of my hair from its roots, and one of my precious blue shells, and his Mistress dropped between his paws her fire opal (he the fire, she the opal—both born in October).

And we gave him her sonnet to him and words from her to him and the inscription

Whym Chow
Flame of Love
Born October 29th 1897
At Rest January 28th 1906.[209]

EC *Whym Chow was buried in Paragon garden.*
I see [the coffin] lowered and the four men with uncovered heads; but old Forbes, who has led our Whym for months, stands covered and unmoved before Death.
His fate is sealed.[210]

EC *In response to an insensitive letter of condolence from Ricketts.*
Well may he be jealous—Michael and I love Chow as we have loved no human being—for central to us is his Love—our Flame of Love.[211]

EC *Transcribing a letter from KB to Ricketts.*

Try to learn a little of what we suffer. I could have been happy in age with Whymmie—alone quite alone. Whymmie is my eternal attribute.
I am St. Katharine now without her wheel—her power, my grace are gone.[i]
I must see Paragon no more. My little Gold Room is where I parted with Chuckles—the Grot is where he paced and paced in frenzy; my comfort, that he snuffed the fresh morning air there from open windows, that my voice almost to the last was recognised.
And all this Henry feels, only sharper, because Henry loved me in Chow. I am glad that perhaps you are not going away.

Michael.[212]

EC *Friday 16th.*
Lucien Pissarro[ii] has acted with such perfection. We sent our little card for Whym Chow and asked if he would print it in his most beautiful type—we would give Chow the best. He sent two slips on vellum and his own paper, refusing all payment with sympathetic courtesy.

---

i St. Catherine of Alexandria, the Christian martyr who was ordered to die by torture on a spiked wheel; the wheel broke under her touch, and she was then beheaded.
ii The French artist and printmaker (1863–1944), son of impressionist painter Camille Pissarro. The younger Pissarro, a friend of Sturge Moore's, showed Michael Field several kindnesses later in their lives.

We sent him not as in return but as a mark of friendly esteem a Zaerns-dorf *Tragic Mary*. A dozen exquisite cards are sent printed—simple thanks for the *Tragic* are returned, with a hope that in the spring we may visit *The Brook* and the episode end on its human dignity. A quiet thing begun and ended of its own virtue.[213]

EC Last night a most barbaric letter from Mary—evidently, she had miscon-ceived and thought we did not wish reference to Chow's death . . . but the cool business she made of suggesting to us[214] places abroad (the only sympathy of a modern is to suggest to you a place to go in sorrow)—her boiling desire to tell of B.B.'s attitude at the feet of Contessa Carlotti when she knows the jar of such vulgarity.

—Well, Michael suffers another cleft—a new fissure in grief, that makes yesterday wide apart from today. No wonder Michael cries for Whymmie, even blind and frenzied, by these human creatures!

But, well, well, we mortals gave him back to sight and the sweet ways of his genius—for among dogs his mind had genius. He could feel and provoke the most wonderful emotion.[215]

KB I have often reproached Henry for never having written to me a love lyric—now the Chow songs well up to me—the love poetry of those two watching faces at the window.

And I have no longer Hennie alone, which was death to me—Hennie with Little One—wayfaring with me—wayfarers, wayfarers—yea, even the dear Father through his forest—the little one in his love pacing—frenzied—at his mystic task—wayfarers, wayfarers we journey—*our goal within us*. The king-dom entered, the sacrifice lifted up.[216]

EC Michael has often said I loved Chow too well. I hear her voice, "You must not love him like that. You must remember Chow has to die." And she has warned me I should bring tragedy on myself and on Chow if I so adored him. There was wrong in it—to grip what must pass as if it were irremovable: but along with this, growing as the wheat with the tares and not to be plucked up till the Last Day, was a force that held his little spirit forever. The Mother holding me with spiritual bond, yet judges.

On the dear Father's bond of eternal love there are the shadows of the Past: my bond with Chow is one of pure love, free of judgment, free of clouds—Love in its very fountain beat of eternal freshness. And that love is for the love he gave my Beloved. No wonder there is a mystery—one that, like Eros' bond with Psyche, must be secret and undamped through life.[217]

KB A letter from Mary—She is near me in Chow's worship—"she understands too well how I loved him."

—Poor Mary and if either she or Doctrine lost each other they would go to Japan, and seek new acquaintance.[218]

KB *Ash Wednesday—*

We wake and comminate one another. Henry finds I live too much in flux—not rising to Being—I dare say he will put it better—I cannot understand.

My great sin is *Mortality*—especially as it exists in memory—the mental moments must not photograph—I must break the negatives—too much ever I grieved over the vile exposure of the loved Father's body photograph—these things are of the transitory—Memory—Mother of the Muses—is incorruptible.[219]

EC *Sunday, March 4.*

Our last Sunday at Rottingdean. We have passed through our mortal anguish of loss to the realisation of that word of St Paul—"as having nothing, and possessing all things."

All our little Whym Chow is ours—Michael and I are closer in spirit; for we love in unity with the little Spirit of Flame our interchange. Thirty poems have welled out to my Little Love and made me forget memory, which one must put under one's feet as everlasting Life puts Death underfoot.[220] [. . .]

Pissarro has done the beautiful little card that is our pledge to Whym.

And from Robinson of Redhill the little head of Chow, taken from Florence's (Amy Bell's maid) photograph of Michael holding Chow in her arms at West Lulworth, has been returned a masterpiece of sensitive beauty. Here we have the little soul . . . and why?

Whym was in his mistress's arms bearing for her love what is intolerable to a Chow—symbol of all he had to give us of freedom to share the whole of her life. And Florence was in a highly wrought condition of second sight when she snapshotted this moment[i]—hence its almost unendurable sensitiveness of expression—almost barely radiant from so new a little soul.[221]

EC And now tomorrow we have to go back to Paragon, home no more—to go with no golden burthen in our arms, no more bearing with us our one perfect

---

i Possibly suggesting clairvoyance or mysticism, or perhaps heightened imagination. The "snapshot" was introduced in 1900 along with the Brownie box camera, by Eastman Kodak.

love—save as our deathless joy and light, but denied us in his sweet, sweet earthly life.

We have to go back—face memory, and constant suggestion of mortality, and be true to the holy mystery we have [222] had strength to enter among these infinite curves of Dawn and under the tonic airs.

I have been able to resolve to have my dead, not in memory, but in being. Others are faithful to their dead by remembrance—I by essence.

I am sure a very sensitive film would be able to show the form of Chow by us—actually here. He is of every hour, of every moment rather—with us of the grasp I had of him and by virtue of the soul he won through his mistress. I have written him thirty poems.

O Chow, my little Chow-chow—my Whym! And where we go there you are also.

God support us through tomorrow!

Close, close to us, little Chow! [223]

EC *Paragon*—a faded fairyland. The golden Prince whose home it was—gone!

We realise it was *his* house, we are but relics. He filled it—now it is silent as if Fay's terrible silence had laid her ice curse over it. Every lovely room is meaningless, as a grate empty in the summer—and any green boughs of cheer we may try to put over the vacancy only makes it ridiculous.

I shall never forget the return—that plunge in a past as into a tomb. [. . .] The sunroom with its vain anemones from Brighton, the weeping maids, the meal served beside a vacant chair [. . .] [a]nd everywhere a hollow that produced a resonance through the brain.

And so we shall go on . . .

I am writing this, Monday, March 12th, when two ladies come to look over the house. Though there has been scowl of rainy snow, the light comes to make Paragon attractive. They are charmed and at the way it is kept. After lunch in a glittering flood of [224] light the river begins a great flood under a stray wind . . . glitter of the two floods the gold and the silver a flight of colours from the large-flowered anemones and the pale double tulips about the surface of the twofold floods.

The satinwood is radiant fire as Chow's coat—the Sun Room one flickers and splash of brilliance.

O my last little home—the first I ever had with Michael! The young leaves of the roses seem to be tossed from the garden into the room as from Bacchus's crown . . . at this moment Herbert with offer from the people to take the house at £70—I paying them the extra £5 . . . for I had actually got wrong in my own rental and thought I paid £75, not the £70 I do! "Can a mother's tender care . . . etc. yea, she may forgetful be!"[i][225]

EC Our first applicants for Paragon are unreliable. I reject slashingly the importunity of an interested Agent. . . .

Continually our "lyric" bedrooms woo us to stay; or the Music of the sun-room, dynamic as a choral ode, assaults us, from the midst of glowing satin-wood and glowing anemones. Always, I worship the beauty I put behind me. Only death is here. We cannot reach our Flame of Love; we cannot reach nature, or a happy garden; no friend crosses the[226] doorstep, and the relaxing air is doubly pernicious now we have no form of gaiety, no shape of hope, to raise us up from depression. We live here under the suggestion of death. [. . .]

I feel that no one can even be expected to understand our earthly loss—No one knows how lonely we are, without human successors, and in the world rejected from among our contemporaries as if accursed. We had but one devoted lover, spirit to spirit, our Whym Chow; between us and him there was "the first secret of the world" as Oscar says of love.[ii][227]

EC *Transcribing a letter written by Bradley.*

The reason we are breaking away from Paragon is that here the life is memorial—and I must pass my days weeping for the patter of the little feet and the warm breath on my hand. This is mortal.

We must dwell—not without him—elsewhere. Every day we must offer to God, who surely created Chows that day He made the stars, a little nosegay of fresh love and praise. I am beginning to be able to praise God for His golden gift—and for our being all together still.[228]

EC These walls sometimes shriek like mandrakes when we threaten to remove their shelves and appurtenances. But whether we let or not we *vacate* in May. We go forth simply for our souls' health. Were we to live only a memorial life and Michael stomping on archangelic foot, vows he will not lead a memorial life.[229]

---

i See William Cowper's hymn, "Hark, my soul; it is the Lord" (1768).

ii From *De Profundis*, referring to Jesus: "He saw that love was the first secret of the world for which the wise men had been looking, and that it was only through love that one could approach either the heart of the leper or the feet of God."

EC *In Oxford.*

Then at Abrams, where we bought our first things after Zermatt, Michael buys me an old, very fine satinwood tray. How in a dark furniture shop a bit of satinwood glows and heartens like Chow! All satinwood now is to me as a tablet of gold to his fur.

Here those years ago the artists were buying their first satinwood table when they came on Michael. I buy Michael a silverware Bowl, a lovely little Sheffield cruet and two excelling iron trays.

There is relief in this buying—it seems a pledge to some kind of life. I know we felt like that at Oxford eight years ago (just when Chow was being fashioned for us)—we felt like that though our Dead lay forth unburied.[230]

KB *Wednesday, May 23rd.*

Flame of Love!

I say to myself. If we walk in the light, as he is in the light, we have fellowship one with another.

Yes: when we walk in the light where little Chuckles is, it is marvelous how our fellowship with one another springs up.

I believe we are being kept at Paragon that we may overcome the terror of the little grave and wholly dissociate this from the spirit of Flame that is our sure possession of God.

And in this let us rest and be happy.

In this I am divinely happy.[231]

KB Modernism is an amazing thing.

I have received from a relative a proposal to return a memorial card—my mother's—a memorial card sent to my mother's niece—

Part of my reply

In the old times—we lived on the sanctity, on the Victories of the dead—the little Trafalgars[i] they had won for us, the fresh ground they had conquered for the spirit, the tiny colonies they have founded were our pride and our possession![232]

EC I have said the truth to Mrs. Turnbull writing "To you with your loss, so profoundly deep (her only brother) I yet can say that our loss of our Golden Flame of Love, our adoring Whym, must always leave a wound full of living blood that may well at any time."[233]

---

i In 1805, under the command of Admiral Lord Nelson, the British navy defeated the French and Spanish navies off the coast of Spain.

EC And my love for Whym Chow is the very core and living of my whole heart.

Even Michael in herself alone is not quite at that origin of all that is profoundest in my love—her dog just reaches it first and waits for her impatiently to come into her mightier possession than his. [. . .] And now it is all passed, behind—and I have him in eternal mode, my own forever . . . but yet it was sweet again to see in another how his eyes shaded protestingly at the unbesought hand (and on the head) to see this and all the sweetnesses we had when we were rich, who are now so poor.

No longer sharing this life with him, our Beautiful, our Little Love.[234]

EC *In Dublin.*

To sleep in a room among the photographs Michael bought years ago— among old things from Durdans, with Chow's sweet little Durdans face to greet us—and to be in Ireland!—well, after such fatigue one ought to have slept; but hellish toothache drives me to midnight unpacking while Michael sleeps.[235]

EC I am held by sickness as under *jujitsu*[i] . . . yet these tables penetrate me with their wild-honey shine and their stately maze of inlay.[236]

> **KB** But, if our love is dying, let it die
>   As the rose shedding secretly,
> Or, as a noble music's pause:
> Let it move rhythmic as the laws
> Of the sea's ebb, or the sun's ritual.
>   When sovereignly he dies;—
> Then let a mourner rise, and three times call
> Upon our love, and the long echoes fall.[ii]
> After midnight Saturday, September 15, 1906.[237]

EC *October 29th, My New Birthday.*

Then I receive my most exquisite presents: *De Profundis* in the white cover with Fay's three globes of heart-moving symbolism in gold; an oyster shell holding in its iris concave a lovely, gold-shadowed precious pearl; a handful of chalcedony (one of the foundation[238] stones of the New City) that has closed securely round a little fount of living water "whose fountain who

---

i Japanese martial art.
ii Later published in the volume *Wild Honey from Various Thyme* (1908).

can tell?"—lovely symbol of our life held in the mystery of the Blessed Trinity, safe from change or waste.[239]

EC *Sunday, November 4th.*

We have suffered less from the traffic of Hell this autumn has brought to our quiet Petersham Road—the motor buses that rush past every three minutes to turn at the Petersham Inn.

What an age this is! The crash of speed the only delight of the inhabitants thereof. People will tolerate anything—mournfully the houses quake—the air fills with sickening oil, the brain registers avalanches of steel. . . . This is a great trial brought on us—that may drive us from our reinstated Paragon.[240]

KB *The New Year Book is purchased.*

One thing—it cannot contain—I thanked God as I touched it—not the parting with Chow.

To part with one another will not have that bitterness or strangeness—we three are forever one: when it came—in the frenzy, and terror, and without promise in the dying eyes. [. . .] I knew nothing of God's Mercy. Nor of his wondrous little gift back to us of the Golden Life. Our sacrifice has been accepted and we are at peace.

God keep us in our little home—and yet we are ready to go forth.[241]

EC And—Oh, Truth—*Vera veritas!*[i]

My Love and I and Chow are together and garner what this year 1906 has brought of marvel and of immediacy of life.

Though our Whym was taken at once from our mortal sight and touch and the dear's habit of being in the flesh—let me say rather in his golden fleece—at our side, we are closer to him now, more instant to the marvelous love of his heart and soul than when he lay on our couch.

And ever is he living by our hearts and thoughts and conception are with us both and with each, prayed for, dwelt on, adored forever and in the might of the Divine Majesty—*Sancta Trinitas.*[ii]

There has been an element of surprise that satisfies in the course of our destiny—we are both lost in the marvel.[242]

EC *Last Day of the Old Year 1906.*

There is thaw and a languid world—a light touching the river and the sky that is not of this year. And the birds sang this morning of another year.

i "The real truth."
ii "Holy Trinity."

Profoundly sad the goings of the past time have been to me as they concern England. She is under a treacherous government, one that loves all her foes and will possibly hand over her crown of glory—her circle of sea—to promoters of a Channel Tunnel. Then England will be discrowned forever!

The whole of life and government now is for the brute mass—as if Athens had laid out of her art her life for the satisfaction of her Slaves.

To give these brute masses satisfaction food must be adulterated, all objects vulgarised, books entirely written for them, manners lost, the capital of the land squandered, the seacoast betrayed, motor buses raging, smelling—and the only dream to be allowed other motor buses in the sky!

Speed is the one God and Motors are his angels.[243]

KB O Little Whymmie, so much more dearly loved than last year, my own little fellow—come to me now in the New Year, and forever—subdue me to thy fulness of soft, suffering Love—Love be in me as very substance—

Oh Sancta Trinitas![i][244] [. . .]

EC *After ten p.m.* Now I am alone in the Grot and my most Beloved alone in her river room—alone only to mortal seeming—But, oh, to miss that ruddy little form on the sofa, that watches with us for eight years—that loveliest and most[245] loving bond of old year with new year.

But he will be with his Minnie in her river room, for he is loved a thousand times more, and there is no shadow on our love and he never leaves us now any more than when he watched on his couch—Our Darling!

And 1907—though I write the seven with recoil—I feel it is a sacred number and I believe it will bless us—that the year will be as an octave of a feast. It will carry far into the surprises of a benison; it will be newer than any year it commissions to us.

Yet I do not feel we shall lease Paragon; rather that from that centre there will be exploits demanded as to spirits of the maze.

I feel our Chow will be our guardian in some special ways and our illumination be to us amazing . . . But he will guard us.

Our Art will amplify—it will take on sweetness with its strength that it may be more beloved. It will mount in might that we may magnify[246] our religion by our amplitude as Artists.[247] [. . .]

11:30 p.m.

I feel my Love and I are only beginning to love as we shall—thoughts in thoughts—hearts drawn along together into far depths of attraction and peace.

i "Oh Holy Trinity!"

Glad are the Dead tonight—they have lived and will live so far reachingly with us.

The Holy Trinity bless my Love and bless Chow—I kiss the dear little nose and bless the ruddy head of my deliverance!

O Chow, O little Love! The Trinity bless me and make me worthy of my great Love and my Little Love—And the [248] Trinity inspire and enlarge our Art to the true exaltation of Religion as the Fosterer not destroyer of splendid things![249]

Works and Days, Jan.–Sept. 1907

EC *January 12th.*

This day, no longer kept as my birthday, is dedicated to the dear mother who bore me and in her weakness from pain asked the Doctor "Has she a good head?"

I do not forget that Nativity, and as Michael says "It was the winter wild" when I was born.

So I think of the radiance of spirit that glorified Mother—her remoteness from the world, with rich interest in what really was living and moving in the world—her friendship growing and at last for me like the fine flowers of arbutus among the nocturnal berries—the grace that made me fire her last months with revelation between us of immortality—her embrace of passionate white flowers as her spirit left the body and sealed its love on mine.

I am a prayer for her: that eternal light may shine on her that she may know her God, as she did not in this life, no longer as a bare unity but a threefold power of creative blessedness.[250]

EC *Oscar Stories.*

The kind warden of Reading Gaol thought he might turn his chances to good account—so questioned Oscar as to what he should think of various authors.

"Well, Sir, there's Dickens?[251] [W]hat should one think of him?"

"As he's safely dead, you can think what you like."

"And John Strange Winter[i]—is he any good, Sir?"

"A charming lady—He is a charming lady. I prefer to talk to her rather than read her books."

"And would you tell me about Marie Corelli?"[ii]

i Nom de plume for novelist Henrietta Eliza Vaughan Stannard (1856–1911).
ii Nom de plume for novelist Mary Mackay (1855–1924).

At last Oscar turned "I could bear it no more—I approached him—'Of course there is nothing against her moral character—nothing in the world, you understand that: but as to her books she ought to be standing here in gaol where I am—and I should be out where she is!'"

Will Rothenstein, seeing Oscar in Paris after his imprisonment, told him of the Artists.

"They live in a good house now, and collect—are great buyers."

"You don't mean it. I can't imagine it."

"Yes—they live in luxury now."

"I can't imagine it—in luxury, you say. Luxury? Do you mean to say they have *fresh* eggs?"[252]

EC *Looking back a year.*

In the afternoon we three—the little Earthly trinity of lovers—went for our last walk—the wide air seemed to give joy to the frenzy, to make it Bacchic—so guiding the blind rush along we descended from the road to the towing path and Chow exulted with a closed kind of exaltation among the ivies of the wall.

Someone passing said "What a lovely Chow!," and I almost fell down dead with the sorrow of the praise.[253]

EC And I go out, for the first time for so many years, to face a strange experience without Michael. It is terrible—I reach for the door much as I should fancy one would reach the bottom of the sea if one fell into its depth.

A black figure turned toward the window—a priest! Think of what detestation the word has been to my ancestry—the anathemas of Charles Bradley[i]—My Mother's pride in them!

I bowed. "It is good of you to have come so soon, Father." "I had not other engagement, so I came at once."—"It was good of you to come."

And we sit down at the Table. "Now tell me how I can enter the Church. I know nothing." The horror of that moment!

Far worse than meeting Fay after a quarrel. It seems as if Eternal Reality had deluded me . . . This man rigid, on his guard, the eyes like cells—I see the bristle of hair in the glorious light, and with a cursing revolt I murmured to my soul[254] *The Seminary*!

Then I master my revolt by a strong despair. The gentle voice says with youthful intonation, "I cannot let you in without delay, as you wish. There

i Cooper's grandfather (Bradley's father) was a follower of the political and religious radical Zion Ward.

must be some delay—the Bishop is very severe about converts—and I must know if you really understand what you are undertaking."

Then he asks questions and is astonished at my answers. I feel like a St. Catharine of Alexandria, as the occult principles of the Mystery of the Faith are poured from my lips at the stroke of his questions.[255]

EC Michael feels that he must be puzzled and startled by my first interview with him—and comes up from her garden to speak with him first—to tell him we are old inhabitants, that she has "maternal" care for me! is delighted I should join the Church.

Michael's bounty[256] of vital human warmth and wisdom—she confides my health to him—has so wrought on Goss he receives me with quiet eyes filled with a kindness I have not met in any eyes for long years.

There is little talk this time. He promises, a few questions being asked, to see the Bishop and so avoid troublesome questions that a filled-in-form would require. Sometimes across tide of ancestry sweeps me—into foam of spirit for a while—I sail on—the foam is beyond me, though the calm sea rocks.[257]

EC *After her first Confession and assigned penance.*

Then Michael and I side by side give praise . . . and I bless my Guardian Angel, my Flame of Love, for what he has accomplished.

We bear the return—the missing of him in his dance of Love. Then off with a telegram to Ireland: "Henry first. At four this afternoon. Joy!"[258]

EC *Monday, April 29th.*

We have to leave our friends—the time is up and Scottish hospitality keeps strict time . . .

After Low Mass Fr. Gray sends his server to bring Michael into the sacristy.[i]

Kneeling on, I hear the wasp-hiss of his voice (so it sounds afar—wasps at apples) and the bumble-bee sound of Michael's. They come as through walls and swish and boom about the High Altar. Every now and then a server or the Priest's servant opens the door and I catch the blue and purple of Michael's[259] hat and scarf against a block of "soutane."

i Father John Gray (1866–1934), English poet perhaps best known for the volume *Silverpoints* (1893), which included sixteen original poems and translations of poems by Verlaine, Mallarmé, Rimbaud, and Baudelaire. Gray converted to Catholicism in 1895 and was the lover of poet Marc-André Raffalovich.

She speaks the saddest convictions of herself—questionings in the ear of choirboys or carpenters.

Fr. Gray standing before her beretta in hand. She is to go to him for instruction at four. He says "Go home and have a little lunch and a smoke, and then begin again"—he is anxious.[260]

EC *On Father Gray.*

"He is invariably kind, admirably sensible [. . .]. Divine in confidence in the Heavenly Love—a sweet, human gift and a poet. And he has assured me by the authority of every bishop I need never say a Rosary. He is so hearty and good.

"We looked at his books . . . 'Hardy is vile . . .' I took out his *Jude the Obscure*, clean cut out the inside, filled it with tobacco—sent this to a friend. Also with the *Well-Beloved*; more cutting out of the inside and tobacco packing . . . friend confounded to see on every headline *The Well-Beloved* and then tobacco!"[261]

EC Michael had said she did not wish for the Church to be closed—to her like making it stoop from its universality . . . But the Church *is* locked. I hear people wrestle with the door and exclaim.

I only hear the strophe and antistrophe of the "Te Deum"[i] as a hum, being so far away—but I call on my Flame of Love to come and dance his sunshine dance of the ecstasy of love and welcome—His work of love accomplished, his "Minnie" received in the Church of the Eternal Living Symbols from which our Delight is with us, our Whym Chow, ever with us!

Together we dance as at Paragon door, he and I who had waited for her so often in the old days. Warm and passionate as then the dance of joy, but now like the swinging of the golden thurible of the Archangel—gold, gold, aromatic . . . O Eastern wonder of love and power—little Whym Chow![262]

EC How much easier to take the absolute vow to idealism than to vow yourself to create beauty for God!

The Artist is always in the middle region; he can make no absolute vow to heaven or Earth—only the conditional vow of temperate and lovely poise between the eternal and the transient, the symbols and the senses, the spirit and the flesh . . . O, God, we are thy creators of beauty, *Miserere nobis*![ii]

i The hymn "Te Deum laudamus," or "We Praise Thee, Oh God."
ii "Have mercy on us."

Then the nuns file out, holding candles, moving on draped feet—their faces crucified in mouth and eyes, but in their restless womanhood peace[263] and permanence and stability and aim that reach one as a rich taste to one's thirst.[264]

EC *Thursday, September 17th, 1907.*

O loveliest day! Autumn in grace!

And we forget our lunch watching the bathers in the Tank[i]—so illuminating to joy is the nude in comic play with the elements. . . .

What substance in the world like flesh—so full of light is it, that light dawns there momentarily instead of daily as in the world—

And such regnant life in the motion of human limbs. The letter M with a knoll on one acclivity and all those obtuse and acute angles a plasticity of fluent rose!

One man mounted the highest diving-board and lightning zigzagged with his slender body as he dived. One lad was carried screaming and thrown into the water to swim (which he did)—then he flew away and was thrown like a poor dog into the water[265] again—after we heard him screaming in the bathing-shelter.

Brutality! I boiled with anger—It was a violation of a nature; it might be the ruin of the child's character and health—poor little flash of screaming nakedness—the awful sea behind a human captor clutching in the service of the Sea.

After, at the women's tank—such lack of the express and admirable if I had believed in the vote for the sex I should have drowned my belief and the vote forever. Yet, though the actions were diffusive, the plunges hysterical, though the forms were winged by the ideality of a purpose, yet there was, and there ever is, a curious beauty—some spell—about a woman's body in the sea (in any water).

It is the spell that has entered the world of imaginative beauty as Siren, sea nymph, mermaiden; and springs from the suavity of curves that do not express but trouble—a sea quality—and from the sinuous hair wet and sinuous as the tide round rock gullies; still more from the hands and the fingertips that arch and vibrate fitfully like waves. Women persuade the sea; men dominate it.

Then[266] the sanctity of a woman's breast, that must be hidden, puts her at a special disadvantage in her role as a bather with the almost nude man in his role.

Beyond the Bathers a guard marine of seabirds at rest—white, noiseless—

i That is, swimming pool.

in their position a touch of the absolute quality we revere in the horse guards of Parliament St.

Such sea! Broody cerulean and the rocks seeming as if beheld in paint.[267]

EC At the bathing tank the number of men and boys is doubled—the feats, the poses of incarnate and ductile light, the music of nudity!

Two naked men and a clothed one pull in a boat by one rope—most Shannonian!—it is as life and death were bound together: the clothes, non-conducting to rhythm and emotion; every sinew and ripple and angle and plane of the flesh distractingly harmonic, sheet-lightninglike in vibration, but beyond the life of lightning in contrivance of purpose.[268]

Works and Days, Sept.–Dec. 1907

EC *Father Goscannon's[i] visit to Paragon.*

As I shake hands, he says in a sweet low voice *Welcome* and goes round to greet Michael, sitting down in Chow's chair by her side and eating strawberry jam.

This *Welcome!*—I never thought to hear that word in Richmond. Never since Whymmie danced in the hall has welcome reached us—all my life I shall remember the broken seal of rock from which my heart leapt, like the leaping of a freed river, as this young priest said *Welcome.*

Sweet Goscannon! A very little of my love for Chow touched him as he sat in Chow's chair. And with the pathetic symbol of the seminary, he pretends he is shocked to find us eating jam; and as Michael, the docile, pauses as if convicted, he laughs "But you see I am eating it myself."

His joy over his faith in Ireland is an innocent brightness that is lovely to see. Michael bids goodbye at the tea table and we go into the Sun Room for a long talk. Strange! I can talk from my very self to Goscannon—apart from the Church, we have not our interest for interchange—our eyes[269] see the world differently in every aspect—he misconceives me, and I probably no more understand him than I should understand a giraffe.

Sometimes it is frightening to think how as a priest I have trusted him; and his Catholic head and his Catholic feelings are all the time excentric from my nature—yet I am drawn toward him and can trust myself to him and can *speak* to him in the way I am "silent" to Bernard or the Painter.

Yes, he sits in the Sun Room, a gentle and austere intruder, with boyish laugh, and sweet eyes that seem to belay to another animal kingdom than any

i "Goscannon" or "Goss" was Michael Field's nickname for Father Gerald Fitzgibbon.

eyes I have known that darken and grow bright with alien impulses, and yet, fixed on mine, do not startle into flight my secrets or my ideas. The cause of this singular understanding in the midst of opposition is, I think, his mysticism that opens to him so much of what I am saying; also the simplicity in him that reaches the Faun in me—and also my absolute faith in the inviolability of what I say to him as my confessor.

There too there is the beautiful fact between us that [270] he received me into the Church, into Redemption—he knows my sins with absolution over them, as sunk in a pure lake—he knows my temptations and has pity for my struggle to be good as well as bracing sternness if the good will has turned from its virtue.

Yet he is so quaint if he tries to talk about books or architecture. His idea of perfect art is Pugin.[i] In the Missal and Breviary his sense of quality is flawless . . . but Pugin!

And when he thinks I am not looking he slides his almond-shaped eyes toward Fay's designs with puzzled timidity, he who can administer the Sacraments and judge the actions and deeds of men and women so unhesitatingly.

It is strange—it is supernatural—but I have real affection for him; and his *Welcome*, so unexpected, will always remain with me, as the radiated faces of the beautiful Father and Mother in the home-doorway always remain with me, in the lonely world.[271]

EC *Writing to Berenson.*

Dear Bernard—yes, dearest Bernard,

To have met and made friends with a mind attuned to the large things and the secret things of one's own—what joy it has been through the years, a sort of perfection in kind not "earthly." That bond cannot be broken: it was *in principio* and therefore is *in fine.*[ii] You are right there.

But you go on to say you cannot believe "that an ocean has suddenly flown between my past and present."

Dear Bernard, but you must believe it, for it is true! The ocean of God's love that like the sea has been "shut up with doors."[272] [. . .]

It is not only that I apprehended the symbols now, but humbly and with *Askesis*[iii] I have begun the practice of the great art of life. You have

---

i Augustus Pugin (1812–52), English architect of the Gothic revival.
ii "It was in the beginning and therefore is in the end."
iii With great religious discipline.

always admired the rigorous way we lived to the idea of beauty, putting by all that was inexpressive, crowded, unbecoming to its kingdom.

Well, so it is now with life—so every hour is under ideal claim and what is simple, what is axial in the spin of life I am training to set my hours to; and this effort is sustained[273] by the communication of my spirit with the Divine through a will and heart broken into these living symbols my mind alone had adored.

The Catholic faith is to me the only organic canon of the art of life, the one initiation, the one discipline.[274]

EC *Christmas Eve.*

And beloved Michael is suffering terribly from a "thorn in the flesh"—a not dangerous but distractingly painful one.

Oh, the sharp-edged Christmas! And we are fasting. And the dead we love so profoundly press round this altered Christmas Eve; old scenes, old motives of joy; radiant faces full of feast not fast—the strangeness almost made one *déroutée*[i] in one's humanity.

We have a quick drive into Richmond for last gifts—I could laugh with a mouth like a cave at the[275] shops glutted with turkeys and blood-covered sheep, and boxes of fatted sugarplums and lustreless greens, and mistletoe of tortured agonizing little rings and pearls withering into age.

I pile eucalyptus and trumpet lilies on the Sun Room table, and golden-berried holly from the only golden-berried tree in the Park on the bowl of Leeds Ware: mistletoe and lilies of the valley on each mantelpiece and the "bough" in the grot—*voilà tout.*[ii][276]

EC *St. Stephen's Day.*

I love this feast—It is the Church's day for Whym Chow. She praises a sacrifice *in ipso*,[iii] not[277] voluntary—one that must be to fulfil the divine destiny, one made by the innocent the very dear.

O flower of the martyrs, O our rose, our Whym Chow, our victim by whom we have been saved to life!

I made my whole Mass in thanksgiving for what this little creature died to make manifest in us and his power of love is still by far the most powerful energy in the growth of the spiritual life, teaching us unfalteringly the terrible claims and perfections of love unto death.[278]

i "Baffled."
ii "That is all."
iii "In him."

EC *On New Year's Eve.*

Then the awful struggle with mortal pride before the Life-confession could be made, the doubts, the distrust of the Instruments of the Church—these strange half-inhuman priests. Then the plunge into the River of the Water of Life that was to sever one from all one had been . . . The jar between Michael and me at the broken confidence, the ragged unity at first[279] exacted by the conditions of initiation—the demon strife against change in oneself and another, and in all one's days![280]

EC *What will the next year hold?*

Whymmie will be very much with us, especially at the moments of discovery, and his alertness will often give[281] the cue to our emotion one of our beloved ones in the other life will be allowed greatly to influence us, but we ourselves shall not so much influence where we would as where we make no effort—

I am not at all sure if we shall find ourselves at Paragon, rather much moved in it, than actually moving from it, I opine—no more. I feel as if the surprises were around people—the preparation in places and moods of the soul.

There is something beautiful about the year—its sense of leading on, of slopes, of caprice, greenness—the stream getting more turbulent—the issues of the acclivities and descents more strenuous causes of labour.[282] [. . .]

O Whymmie, golden in rest by us—always near and now on the couch for my kisses. O little saviour on Earth—your work, your work! We are Catholics; we know the real presence—it is with us—and you *angele faciei* of us!

The dead in light or in the noble[283] fires of love bless us through God's heart with His will.

Pater Caritas.
Filius gratia.
Spiritus Sanctus Communicatio.
O Beata Trinitas!
Sancte Spiritus![i]—Oh, 1908!

Breath of flame and of fresh wind establish the days of it! So thy Church was established!

Veni![ii][284]

i "Father's Love," "Son of Grace," "The Communication of the Holy Spirit," "Oh Blessed Trinity!," "Holy Spirit!"
ii "Come!"

CHAPTER 5

The Long Denouement

1908–14

THE LAST HALF DECADE of Michael Field's lives saw a growing disconnection between the women's focused devotion to the Catholic Church and the worldly demands of secular modernism. As Michael Field adapted to their newfound Catholic faith, they also grappled with institutions of Catholicism that regulated dimensions of their lived experience in new ways. The demands of Catholicism challenged Michael Field's sense of daily and annual temporality; their gender identities both as women and as a male author; their kindred relations, whether as a married couple or as spinster aunt and niece; and their sense of private discourse, realized in different ways in the confessional than in the diary and vice versa. Finally, their Catholicism functioned as a wedge between the two, as Edith Cooper had perhaps intended. After Cooper's death, Bradley wrote: "How we loved one another then [. . .], the year before we entered the Catholic Church. [. . .] Out with thy tablets, truth: we have never loved each other since, as then."

Even as Michael Field recoiled from the filth and noise of modernity, they remained consistent in their representation of "Michael" and "Henry" in *Works and Days*. Just as they had always used strong male figures—Browning, "the Father," Bernard Berenson, Charles Ricketts, Whym Chow—to negotiate their intimate partnership, they now triangulate through the Church itself and through clerics, including Father John Gray and the pseudonymous Father Goscannon. As critics Frederick Scott Roden and Ruth Vanita have further noted, Michael Field's new Catholic trinitarianism—Father, Son, and Holy Spirit—bears close resemblance to their long investment in triune relationships. Michael Field's representation of Mary, Mother of God, opens only the latest chapter in their worshipping of women, including Sappho and the Beloved Mother-One: each a muse and an inspiration, as a focus for female desire, both subject and object of devotion.

Michael Field's final years were a time of loss and retrospection. The death of Swinburne silenced one more important Victorian voice, while the sad deaths of Amy Cooper Ryan in Dublin, and of the old basset hound Musico in Paragon, isolated the women even further. We see here Michael Field using *Works and Days* as a vehicle for retrospection: flipping back through the book to find that they had not written of a family conflict that they remembered bitterly; explaining to their friend, the priest and poet Father Gray, that they used the diary to calibrate their relationship to such literary phenomena as aestheticism. Throughout this ominous period, Michael Field run the film of their lives backward, recognizing in each other sparks of their Victorian prime, regretting their cruelty to Amy and indifference toward Musico, and motoring swiftly through familiar landscapes where they encounter ghosts of their former selves.

Works and Days concludes when Michael Field, as such, died: Cooper in 1913, Bradley nine months later, in 1914. The pain, fear, and sadness of her decline lives at the center of Cooper's narrative during the period following her diagnosis of colon cancer in January 1911. Bradley's narrative tracks closely to Cooper's during this two-year period and includes details of Cooper's care and the friends and family following her progress.

What Bradley's narrative omits, however, is a secret of her own. Bradley, too, had cancer, diagnosed a few months in advance of Cooper's death. Only after Cooper had died did Bradley reveal the fact of her breast cancer to the pages of *Works and Days*—in the form of direct address to Cooper, as if to tell the diary was to tell her lover. In the days following Cooper's funeral, Bradley experienced frightening hemorrhagic bleeding. She was cared for by a nun, not by a lover, and in this sad and frightening time she mourned not only the loss of Cooper but the distance that had grown up between the women since Whym Chow's death and their embrace of Catholicism. Death, it seemed to Bradley, only made literal the separation of Michael and Field.

"Michael Field" persisted, though, in a number of ways, including the publication, posthumous to Cooper, of the elegiac volume *Whym Chow, Flame of Love*. As the voice of Michael Field grew steadily quieter and finally silent, a new king was crowned in England and a new pope elected in Rome. The Triangle Shirtwaist Factory burned on what is now the campus of New York University, and the *Titanic* sank after striking a glacier that decades later would find itself cooking in warming seas. In the months between the deaths of Cooper and Bradley, James Joyce initiated the serial publication of *A Portrait of the Artist as a Young Man* and published *Dubliners*, and Wyndham Lewis published the first of two issues of the vorticist literary magazine *BLAST*. A suffragette named Mary Wood attacked John Singer Sargent's portrait of Henry James with a meat cleaver. And in the warm summer of 1914, days before Katharine Bradley wrote her final entry in *Works and Days*, the Great War, which would ultimately claim the lives of twenty million soldiers and civilians, erupted across Europe. This first "modern" war changed the political landscape of Europe. It altered forever the social and artistic conditions that shaped the experience of artists such as Michael Field. When Lytton Strachey published *Eminent Victorians* in 1918, the Victorians seemed very remote to the postwar present, as well as smug, simple, and self-satisfied.

On this threshold of all that was new, Bradley concluded *Works and Days*, writing: "God take my offering." One month later, Leonard and Virginia Woolf, a couple unknown to Michael Field (as far as we know) but closely linked to the poet by many tangled threads, moved to the Richmond suburb, minutes' walk from 1, Paragon. The "Woolves" eventually established the Hogarth Press in a Richmond house opposite the former home of Ricketts, Shannon, their Persian kitten, their gee-gee carpet, and their Sheffield jug named Fatty. Of the hundreds of volumes that poured forth from that house were T. S. Eliot's *The Waste Land*; and *Jacob's Room, The Common Reader*, and *The Waves*, all by Woolf herself. Hogarth publications also included James Strachey's 1953 English translation of *The Complete Psychological Works of Sigmund Freud*, the next chapter of work begun in earnest in the artistic circle of the poet Michael Field.

Works and Days, 1908

EC *Recording a letter she sent to Swinburne, enclosed with Michael Field's newly published volume "Wild Honey from Various Thyme."*

Dear Mr. Swinburne,

I am tempted to ask your acceptance of my honey book with deep affection—the affection of the aging poet for the Poet crowned with age—I offer it to you.

Of course, to us now there is no English-breathing poet save yourself. I, wistful for a reader, am glad you stay with us.

Michael Field.[1]

EC *Recalling a visit by a priest she calls here "Jewel."*

Before beginning [. . .] he says, "I have to congratulate you, Miss Bradley."

"On what, Father?" Michael's voice shows some disturbance as of earthquake from the other side of the world.

"On what we have all read in the paper."

"Oh, if you are going to congratulate, my fellow must come in."

So I step back into the Sun Room from the Grot and bow. "I thank the Father for any congratulation he is thinking of giving us."

Then "Jewel" speaks with fine courtesy and reticence of how he was drawn to read by the strange name *Michael Field* and then the names of the ladies, and that they had resided at Bristol—"I know then and I told . . ." (he mentions Goss).

"It is a great honour."

"No, no, father—we are just your children."

The Church approves and adds, "But it is a great gift to have."

"Jewel" says he soon found out we were learned and had poetic minds. We took the Breviary in such a different way from others.[2]

EC The news of Michael Field falls like Samson's pillar on the priests . . . Dear Goscannon! I am sure it is worse than his fall on the ice. We feel somehow as if a wrong had been done to him—in the confessional one ought to discover one's creature, though it is so dank! Is it a lynx or a 'pard? It is not really so: for to be a poet is not mortal sin, though pretty nigh![3]

EC *Wednesday, January 29th.*

Goss comes late. He is cloudy and guarded and talks of the *Initatio* and *Summa*[i] with eyes that "deny themselves."

I feel I must break this mood by direct speech about *Michael Field*—but it costs! He is so unaccountably distant.

At first, I might be in the Confessional—with toneless voice he asks questions that tend toward learning if *we* have spread the news to make an effect—at least, that is the inference I draw rather angrily. . . . Then he softens and becomes humanely interested, it seems from his voice; for the room has grown quite dark in the sudden way spring darkens, even over a silver river.

I say I regret it is known, but that in some ways I am glad he, as my confessor, knows, for it "will help him to understand some things I feel he has somewhat misunderstood, and also to understand how hard it is for a poet with his freedom of impulse to submit to the control and discipline of the Church."[4]

---

i The Catholic sacrament of initiation and the theological teachings of the Catholic Church, respectively.

EC *Saturday.*

A Miss G. has been sent to call on us by Fr. Sam, as several other women have been sent by Goss—Dear me! They run over one's experience like water off oilskin.

They have usually nothing central, when they are not mothers: they do not seem, unless they renounce the world, to make religion central. They never seem able to take things in except as appearance which they solidify into personal interests—not even into facts with the dignity, because inter-dependence of facts.

Women weary me—I am thankful when they are gone to forget them; and yet this should not be so, and if I found women at all like our Lady, I should adore them, as I adore the real Aphrodite beauty of women.

Miss G.—poor Miss G. A weariness! No desire for any future toward her—no relish that is the fresh prophecy of desire.[5]

EC We[6] [have] been warming our fatigue into bliss by the fire and this comes from Fr. Gray—

My dear Michael,

Certainly, the treasure of the world is increased by the content of the Honey Book. It was on my pen to write this long ago—but I did not care to make a solemn statement of the kind offhand. I cannot pretend to survey the past and the future, in the manner of the literary critic. I can however say of a given work what I now say of *Wild Honey*. It has the pulse and warmth of life. The magic of poetry has been achieved.

I can say of "Morning Rains" that it never was before and never will be again—but is, just as I know beyond proof that the organism is unique. Here is the swish and sob of the rain, the thrill and sob of the bird's voice, the gurglings mingling.

I may worry at *dewdrops* and yet be sure that I am wrong and the lyric right—it echoes in "through" and no doubt is justified in other ways. Had you lights? Had you *all* lights? We had.

John Gray.[7]

EC *March 13th.*

Nearly a month silent!

Our household has broken up—Mrs. Drew gave an account of her health—more from a wildness that was tired of control. She was a pleasant blustering presence, like a wind, as unstable and without any lingering when she went—a thing that ceased like a wind.

Old Music feels quiet now [that] she does not crumple his ears or ask him a very gale of questions: yet she parted from the old dog as if he were a feather and not a dog. But the hard blue sky of this cheery wind will be missed by Michael, who was not teased by it as I.

Alas, we have not held our maids to their duty and the little Lar of Paragon has a grimy face under his bits of box-tree garland.[8]

EC And on the Couch and up and down the stairs and by the inn door—always beside us is our bright Whym Chow: all the sun on the couch falls on him, and when we are happy, we are happy[9] among us three.

An inn was always the right place for Whymmie—the stagnancy of the lodging-house being as a disease to him and his beloved ones.

How good we can take him with us now into the very presence of the God to whom he has been allowed to lead us—our guardian angel of the little Torch, our Flame of Love—Whym Chow.[10]

EC *Tuesday*—

An emotion of spring through the air! A letter from Fay, intimate, reeling in that "make up" he loves when he assumes fancy dress ("Dressing up is a blight," Fr. Gray comments).

A brilliant picture of Peter Pan Barrie.[i][11]

EC Michael speaking of how she has found in herself a certain contempt for woman.

"I thank thee I am not as other women—unable to recognise beauty, etc.," concludes with the words "it is detestable."

Quiet as a seal pressed deep comes from the other side of the "grille"—*Yes.*[12]

EC I have left my white Year Book for the Divine Office—

My time has been learning to work in chains.[13]

EC *While Father John Gray is sprinkling Paragon with holy water.*

So from room to room in the sunlight, the spray of the rosemary lighting about caressingly; the stalwart figure of the little Father (John Gray of *Silverpoints*) with pictorial cleanness of colour in its appearance (a priest of an illuminated Missal or a cassocked angel from an early "Nativity" fresco)—John Gray leading the Catholic Michael and Field upstairs and downstairs and into the rooms of the house that is "Circumspice!" to Ricketts of "the *Dial.*"

---

i J. M. Barrie (1860–1937), Scottish novelist and playwright who published *Peter Pan* as a play in 1904 and as a novel in 1911.

What meeting of the spiritual streams and influences from the past in this illuminated bit of present! One is dizzy.[14] [. . .]

"Michael, we must walk," says the Father with sturdy resolution. And as soon as they are out of the house he makes confession of the old days—their reckless destruction of health by exotic habits—their low company; their idle hours at the foreign office—their long nights of vain pleasure (Michael gathers in the hearts of the world and the devil, not in sin—a conversing with sin, not so much sinning). A good Doctor, seeing death sure in two years, if such life were continued, broke the spell and got the fair young wreck to eat meat at each meal and take sleep in nature's way.[15] [. . .]

Not actually did the Famous say what drove him finally out of the world, but it was about the time of Oscar's imprisonment.

Once, when John Gray was walking out in Rome with his fellow seminarists, he passed a large form planted as if to waylay him—there was complete silence—but mockery dangled it. He never saw Oscar again.

Michael Field of *Callirrhoë*, etc., etc., John Gray of *Silverpoints*—in conversation of deep intimacy pace up and down the highland of Richmond Park—a convert to Rome and a Roman priest—Well, well!

As Michael says, "What greater miracle is needed than for you and they to be here and what we are?"[16]

Works and Days, 1909

EC *In Dublin.*

A wise word of Michael's—

When I am grim and in the dark, I say to myself, "My dark shall be *bulbous*; my pains shall be the pains of the lily writhing to make lily out of its onion-like materials!" [. . .]

Sunday.

A snow gale has been blowing. John yesterday read for hours from Dickens, that nightmare literature of a humanitarian age. He read till I was mad with depression and disgust.[17]

EC Now it is Sunday again—we were to have crossed yesterday.

But early in the week we heard that our cook Jane has been very ill, nursed by Josephine[i] and advised by Goscannon who was fetched to give counsel, that the illness should be kept from us till Jane was better and that then Josephine should write and tell all.

---

i Josephine Emily Woodger (1889–1984), Michael Field's housemaid.

We bow to the bold course—as we have been saved either a week of anxiety or a precipitate return—but that a priest should direct the affairs of Katharine Bradley and Edith Cooper's house in their absence is enough to start all the ancestors pointing skinny fingers till the air bristles and tingles with reproaches.

Poor maids![18]

EC *With Father Vincent.*[i]

We talk of the Aesthetic movement—where it had ideal elements, where it was perilous, especially to me—how Michael's youth came while Ruskin and the Pre-Raphaelites, with all their mistakes, had not drawn Beauty along the paths of shame—mine came, when Beauty was often being used to make sin an end in itself, a triumph.

I speak of the bitterness I used to feel against Oscar, when[19] though living Beauty, he could so degrade and ruin her, that her power in England was discredited—England only just waking from a long habitude toward her.

"It is so I hate the Modernists" breaks in Vincent. "They have discredited such precious things." Vincent would have talked on and on of the literary movement of the last century.

He asks "Would it be uncongenial to write of it as you now see it? That would be apostolic work." I tell him of the white *Works and Days* and how in that it is all lived through and naturally reflected on as we change, without bitterness and with pity.

"I am glad you don't fall foul of it—that would do no good." Vincent is intently interested in what I tell him of the White Book—But I will have him turn to *obedience*.

He realises at once how difficult it is for a poet, who is used to inspiration and its sudden conditions, to receive the bond of obedience as a grace. But the difficulty I feel is not of essential obedience, so much as the galling and fret of the trivial obedience of discipline. The fact that I am living in difficult self-control, since I have been a Catholic,[20] is a sign of the highest obedience—yet I am fretted by the voluntary obedience of now and then obeying another's will to get command of the power of true resignation.[21]

EC "Swinburne is dead," writes Michael to Fay. "I am glad. Watts-Dunton[ii] was as a napkin bound about his head. Now he is loosed. And when the throat has been well-cleared in Purgatory, what song!"

---

i Father Vincent McNabb (1868–1943), an Irish priest of the Dominican order who sought ecumenical conversation and social justice.

ii Watts-Dunton, the poet and critic who moved Swinburne into his home to help him recover from alcoholism, and who also perhaps stifled Swinburne's erotic writings.

Michael will soon be the most venerable of poets—Browning, Tennyson, Arnold, Swinburne have all been smitten down in her sight.[22]

EC On Wednesday, Oct. 6th, just as we are going to read Vespers a telegram comes from Amy that Cousin David is dead, struck [23] down when preaching on Tuesday night at Greenwich.

Oh, we are stunned—and all the past so vivid and so terrible in the new light in which religion beholds it.

Zermatt!

Cousin David had promised of himself to bring Father—the time came we telegraphed for him to join us on the boat. He never came and it was a wonder we got anyone to bring what the forest had given up. The only excuse offered after was that the curate was away and there would be no one to give confession on Sunday. And this on a Thursday (with agencies in town to supply at a telegram's notice). I do not comment on all this *now*.

But for ten whole years I never forgave it—ten whole years I allowed the sun to go down on my unabated wrath. The years, I see now in the light that burns the soul steadily in Purgatory!

I pray for his soul.

I pray Christ to forgive me.

I say the *De Profundis* and the *misera*[i] for him and for myself.

When I turn to the Year Book of 1897[24] that I may obliterate any passages of hate or violent anger—lo, nothing of the incident is mentioned!

In the vast pure sorrow, it is as if it had never been. *Deo Gratias*. The beginning of a decade of unforgivingness and no word of it defames that tragic year.

Again, *Deo Gratias*! And for me, *Miserere Mei, Deo*![ii][25]

Works and Days, 1910

EC It is now January 30th and my only sister, my little Pussy, is dead and buried. And the January warfare has had its victim.

It began with a scrawl from our Little One written on Friday, Jan. 14th, and reaching us on Saturday that she had got "influ" and fever.[26] [. . .]

On Monday, after Matins, I run upstairs for the Irish letters—one from John, not from Amy!

"My heart has been very, very sore because my Ewe Lamb has been very, very ill." He speaks of her high fever—up to 105.

---

i Catholic prayers for the dead.
ii "Thanks be to God," and "God have mercy on me," respectively.

She takes aspirin and the temperature falls to 101.4. She says, "it is like going from Geneva to Mt. Blanc."

Johnnie says she is very weak and inclined to cry—that morphia has eased her pains, but not brought sleep. "Don't be anxious how I don't telegraph. I will keep you informed of all changes good or bad."[27] [. . .]

Then that rap with the very knucklebones of fate on the door—a telegram.

"Doctor consultation this morning. Bad case influenza but hopeful."

Michael telegraphs—she will come. Reply "Better wait few days learning result—new treatment—nurse in charge and house congested."

Michael intends to leave me at home. She spends the afternoon at the Workhouse. I go to learn trains to Dublin—in the street I notice I knock against people. I am moving like a little wave of the wild sea in the harbour.

I pray for my Pussy hard at the altars. Outside I tell "Jewel"; and I begin to pack at home in the quiet, cold Paragon, full of frost light.

But that last telegram stays the packing. It is revealed to Michael we must keep together.

I am in an agony of anxiety over Little One, of terror at the thought of the journey, of confidence in my intercession by day and in the night watches before our Image of the Young Mother of Sorrows—Fay's blessed Madonna.

To this Michael telegraphs "Will wait provided I have wire morning and evening. Auntie Want to come to Pussy."[28] [. . .]

Tuesday, January 18th.

Telegram at 9.50.

"Not much change but I am fearful. Would like you to come without much hurry."

After much intercession and in a strong morning light we distrust this telegram as due to Johnnie's intense excitability and reply we will await doctor's bulletin.

At 1.45, that rattle of Fate's knucklebones—and the sun stands still in the little world of my heart—a telegram.

"Await letter. Amy and nurse disapproved my telegram of invitation to you. Doctor forbids conversation. I would like you established in quiet hotel about Friday."

And we have a letter.

"Should things go ill with us and the worst thereafter, you will both be wanted[29] over here. Whereas if we are only in for a battle with nature your presence will not help. Indeed, I dare not tell Little One of your telegram. It would distress her so, not merely because of the question of room, but because of the long journey which we fervently hope to be not necessary."

And Johnnie says the consultant found nothing wrong with Little One—
only that she has a bad influenza with unusually high temperature. He asks
our prayers day and night. And he writes, "I will not keep you in the dark if
danger comes. It is entirely a question of *food and sleep*. If we can win on
these all will be well . . . cheer up and pray hard!" Poor John. Today is his
birthday—what a mockery in this struggle.

Wednesday, January 19th.

Telegram at 10.44.

"Most dear love from Amy after good night: temperature better, but woe-
fully weak. I think crisis possibly coming."

Flocks of little birds sing in my heart with joy and at their liberation . . .
There is no song like that of the many little birds in my heart.

And Johnnie's letter says, "Sister Padua says I'm a pessimist and a man,
both of which I presume, unfit me to judge!"[30]

The Consultant said at the College, "that she would or should recover."

The only new item is that our Doctor says that she has a touch of pneu-
monia. This of course would account for the high temperature.

A night nurse is to be established with her—she is not to be allowed to talk
much or receive visits.

Johnnie continues, "It is an awful thing to be banished from the only
companion one has in the world. Last night I listened to her fitful sleep and
fed her and kept the fire. Now it must be done by a stranger. But the brave
little thing is resigned to it.

She sends you all her heart's love but sees that she must sacrifice everything to get well. Heaven bless you in this awful time . . . I am but a lump of
suspended animation."[31]

Telegram: Going into town cheerful temperature over 102.[32]

EC *In Dublin.*

The hours settle into days—the days of old centuries.

Never was there such measure of time weighed out to us. A meal is an
event, led up to by history—the slow patient gravelling that real history is.
And how strange when the only place for cheer is the stomach, as its exhaustion takes a morsel toward life! The only other cheer being the nurse's occasional murmur of hope. [. . .]

At last the doctor: He leans against the mantelpiece by me, his head
against the wood; he is dejected. We shall know tomorrow for certain. There
is perspiration, but no fall of[33] temperature.

We can bear no more the separation, especially as Pussy has asked if Michael is come and has not been reassured. We cannot bear it—that she should think us cold or faithless to her in her mortal strife—the pain is on the core of love, and we simply demand it should end. And the doctor makes no demur. Where is his hope?

Michael goes first—and the Little One smiles. "Michael, who is very happy, is come to Little One, who is very happy." "Oh, very happy." "Yes, very happy. It is our secret." [. . .]

Then I am sent for. O Little One!—She indeed, the characteristic Little One, but so pale with a harassed pallor—the nostrils sharp and breathing a breath—whizzing and sounding like flight on flight of warlike arrows—the little mouth shut firm—the round [34] brow and fine eyebrows noble, and just creased with trouble: The eyes deeply intent and clouded with fever . . .

It is impious to feel as I do. Panic at a loved one. But, with words of "Little Pussy, Hennie is come—it is Hennie come to the darling," I reach the range of her attention, penetrate that absorbed brooding over the dreadful arrow flight . . . Then a smile . . . The lips curve deprecatingly sweet, and the eyes are filled with the charm of those whose light is the light of the city of God.

Recognition is there, passionate love is there, that knows nothing of how or why the beloved is apparent but receives the apparition with golden *Laudes*.[i][35]

EC I kiss the dear round brow—it is damp and the dampness touches like night dew. I murmur love to her, but she does not hear, I am sure.

Then the nurse comes up from tea and turns me out! "We have something to do for the patient." Emily remains, as she has always done, being herself a nurse.[ii] And Johnnie is allowed in quietness quiet entrance and exit.

We are treated as enemies—the wrath that tightens my heart![36]

EC I know we are in the drawing room, when Emily comes in to say there is a change and we are all sent for.

I go upstairs to see death—rather dying—it is cold round my heart. A forsaken egg in a nest is my heart . . .

Johnnie is close, kneeling close, and in a lovely voice, the very honey of love in the clefts of the awful fastness—he is murmuring little hymns, very tender little hymns, and prayers to St. Joseph, and Aves, and Our Father[iii]—

---

i That is, with joyous acclaim.

ii Emily Fortey (1866–1946), a British Catholic feminist, politician, and accomplished chemist, a later-in-life friend to Michael Field, and beneficiary of their wills.

iii A prayer to St. Joseph for safe passage; the "Hail Mary" prayer asking the Virgin Mother for intercession with God; and the "Our Father" prayer of praise and gratitude to God.

the simple supreme prayers, and then simple little prayers made childishly beautiful by his voice.

On the other side of the bed, Emily is emphatic, probably hoping to reach beyond deafness; but she besets the air with "Jesus, Mary, Joseph." I should be frightened to die to an air so beset. And she says with devout stridency some of the prayers for the departing.

The nurse makes Little One drink—I hide my face.

Then she says to me "You should leave the room now and leave them together." I could murder the woman—making hatred rise in me at this solemn [37] moment of love. But I only say "I remain. He wishes it." (Why, Johnnie had even arranged how Auntie was to hold her hand to the last, and I to be where I could see her eyes to the last.)

And Johnnie's flow of honey keeps on and becomes more beautiful as he tells her he will be a priest and say masses for her. "You would like me to be a priest, dearie, and say masses for 'oo?" And he gently stoops the crucifix to her lips—he tells us hers reached forth a little way. "And I'll always be true to you, dearie, till I come to lie with you!"

And he murmurs on of parting and of meeting and of love and God's love. "And we will only think of how we love each other—not of anything we have to forgive—for I know everything is forgiven, is it not, dearie?"

To all this honey breath the dying breath whistles through the nostrils, and Pussy's little "um"—her sign of assent or attention all her life through—becomes a mournful little moan with the abruptness of the agony in it—something of a bird's timeless sob. The heart and soul is desperate that this is the only response. The half-draped eyes have [38] a look of thick substance about them and seem to be fixed on the Crucifix.

The nurse keeps feeling her, and then to my infinite revolt the hireling fingers span her brow and fix in her temples . . . I could have screamed with hatred . . . and she gives the professional hint, "You should send for a priest." [39] [. . .]

The nurse professionally whispers across to the Father, "I think you should read the Plenary Indulgence"[i]—fast and unstumbling the Priest reads on.

Then I hear in John's soft honey hum. "Is she gone?" "She passed during the [40] absolution." [. . .]

O profound penance of death—this tininess of humiliation! I am looking on the universal penance—ashes of the rose!—Little One's corpse.[41]

---

i A prayer to release one from punishments owed by sin.

EC I cannot touch the beloved—she has a look "That threatens the profane"—so still, so holy—so absolutely unimportant to mortal conditions—so
august in record of the spiritual use she has made of them.

Little Pussy! It has been a hard battle for 'oo! Pray for the "Old Cub"—pray
for "Hennie-boy"! Her names for me shake me into human seeming—I can
cry warm again, as I felt I never should.[42]

EC Dazed and controlled, I send off a batch of telegrams to many Fathers and
convents for prayers. Dazed and controlled we eat in the clear atmosphere bits
of fowl and drink cups of coffee. Dazed and controlled we undress.

Fervently we pray—soul to soul for her, our beloved, our faithful.

And before we can tell ourselves that Michael has no babe of the left
breast on Earth—that I have no only sister, we are dead asleep—asleep with
tomorrow in us; with waking and with the warm, suspended response to
time and the things of time, and to the revelation of eternal things in
time.[43] [...]

Our harshness to Little One—the way we failed to appreciate her—the
cruel things in our intercourse—our "modernism" of conduct—the red
wounds we had made in that reticent spirit—the pride and selfishness that
had struck the wounds.[44]

EC Pussy's face and chest lie lower in death—the high places are made plain;
and under the beautiful hands there is a sweep that lifts them up and falls
again.

And the expression is more of a peace that cannot help itself—a doom, not
a merit. And the eyes have no look of the sleep; and more incomprehensibly
affrighting it is to say, "Little One, Little One!" [...] I throw a last kiss—a kiss
from the roots of the heart, and leave my[45] Pussy, a stage deeper in death,
but with brows of very life and the hands of a saint fallen over the large crucifix. Then we have to return to the hotel and eat cold fowl and drink coffee,
and again plunge down into sleep.[46] [...]

In the grimness of the afternoon something orders me to secure Little
Pussy's will.

Emily acts like an angel or minister of grace, and all she wills Johnnie
does. The good Bridget knows where the paper is, and I have it and read it
again.

I know Johnnie is slow in business and that we must face the will with
him in England.—since my estate, being undivided from Little Pussy's, goes
into probate too, and all my income is tied up.[47] [...]

Then a passionate need strikes me to collect and carry away our letters—

always sent to her who is now in a coffin, under seal. Emily gains the permission and Bridget helps—our letters! They fill every crevice of the tables, bureau, drawers—they are packed "as precious things in deposit . . ." "She so valued them, she could not part from them," says faithful Bridget. "They were treasures."

And we had begged her to destroy them, as we did her dear, daily letters—only keeping those in which the very Amy herself spoke in her incomparable special way. This flood of letters seems a reproach to us! She never turned it off—she loved it round her to float her love—our sweet!

Then I gather together all[48] Michael Field's books we had given to her for her particular and own use and for her eye alone.

At last, all trace of us is coffined in hatboxes, as she herself in the last shell upstairs. I am resting from this cruel labour, and the fever of its pursuit, when Michael, who has just seen Little One, yields to my wish to see her, when I hear she looks beautiful.

I had never seen an open coffin before . . . It is shocking beyond speech—a shriek in the night and natural expression, but I am never natural, and I do not shriek. The noble figure on the deathbed has been taken and put in a box like a preserved fruit, and there is a fancy white round it. The lack of expansion is the want that convinces one of death in those that might be asleep—but the ample lines of the bed and pillow, the width of the light traversing the unconfined limbs, the illusion of motion, all make some sense of largeness round the sleepers of the deathbed: it is gone from the sleepers of the coffin.

They are little things[49] put in boxes. And from the moment she was coffined the hideous sense of the naught she was to be, in the body, till the last day, fell over Little One.

The face was no longer meant to meet eyes at all—and the slope from the chest to the knees was a slope for no sun to see or rest upon. The peace was inveterate to grimness. Still the firm lips—still the round brow and dark eyebrows with their little eddy of nervousness—but all, no more to be seen than Medusa—and not even, like her, in water. No element for them but Earth—Earth—Earth![50]

EC There is but one freedom—we are moving away from the dead for a little while—from the weight of the doom and punishment of Death on the creature we have loved as our only own Little One. We have grown used to Time as a giant—the huge stretch of its parts . . . So it seems natural to reach Euston,[i] near midnight.

---

i A major railway terminus in London.

We take a room—have human coffee, and even go beyond ordinary humanity and startle the waiter by demanding crisp celery—and reach our beds before twelve o'clock. A fathom-drop into sleep! But before that we have made up our minds to get up just after five—catch the workman's train to Richmond and go to Mass at our own vineyard.

Up in the dark . . . we went with the night porter in the hall, or in the smoke [51] room where there is a cinder fire—and endless cinders of cigars and cigarettes and empty glasses, and the corpse look of dead time.

Then the streets that seem shod with frost to meet the shod feet of the grand dray horses—so wide the streets of London; silent as if they belonged to Palmyra.[i] In the workmen's train we go to sleep, a guard having in pity brought us hot water cans for our feet. Only just do we get out at Richmond in time, and I give two half sovereigns to the guard for sixpences.

The honest guard brings them back. No cab! So, we leave our luggage, and determinedly walk up to the vineyard in the flawless frost.

Strange and more dreamlike to enter. No one we know there![52]

EC I am deeply tired and sleep at home. This afternoon we have been reading in last year's *Works and Days* of our last summer and how I felt the last parting with Little One and the magic spell of doom round her.

They are building a huge skating rink right across the Sun Room windows—and the motorcars and buses of the holidays begin to rumble past the Grotto. Our ears and eyes "offer" their pain, and no longer does beauty rise up in madness at her wrongs—she quietly notes them as worth offering, because they are wrongs it takes great quality to prepare for morning and evening sacrifice to Him who is beauty—and all beautiful.[53]

EC I dreamt I saw Pussy in her hat and long coat, showing me pansies, that grew aerially and hung down like orchids—very large they were and she was proud of their purples and gloams.

Then she disappeared and I knew she was dead, and I moaned till I was waked. All day I have felt flat—the day has felt flat.[54]

EC *Friday.*

There is Bank panic—addition and subtraction done on the rack of terror . . . but things not as bad as they appeared.

So we go out for a walk—buy some Marechal Niel[ii] roses—honey gold with

---

i A major city in ancient Syria, destroyed during the Roman Empire.

ii Strongly scented climbing roses that need a warm climate or greenhouse to flourish—certainly a luxury item in the London suburbs.

edges of fresh-washed silver and the most deliciously "select" perfume. Then we cross the churchyard and walk in the stiff soil of a nursery garden where ornamental apple trees are sharing their red buds, hard as little stones, and precious as if the stones were rubies.[55]

EC Dear old, old Music!

When I kissed the faint "fair Star" on his brow I fancied I should not kiss it again—this star, as stars are where they must vanish. He has been a beautiful form—a sensuous languor, an affectionate gourmand, a devoted, harmonic mass, and dangle of ears, and serious orb eyes—and sudden humour, when little legs were flung out and big body tossed with glee.

And for thirteen years! When he is gone *nothing* of the old days will lie with us—God will have detached from us all we loved and lived with. The old dog has been so clinging to Michael lately, swelled with disease or lank for death, he has,[56] as he varied in size, never varied in the aim to reach her and be near her. And I had no envy, for she has been so good to him, shown him such patience in his troublesome aging. Poor old Music!

That we must all come to tragedy in our bodies, all be cut from breath! one wonders that comedy could ever be heaved up—gay—from this mountain of dolour.

Perhaps that little leap up of comedy is the supernatural in nature. For the supernatural is always happy in the midst of manifold affliction.[57]

KB Music died deep in the night of Ascension Day.[i]

He died on his bundie; he was found dead. So dear to me, so very forgiving! I had preferred another to him all my life.

"Homo habet . . . sentire cum animalibus"[ii]

Music:

Faithful and affectionate hound.

May 1910.[58]

EC During Thursday night, the 12th, our darling old *Musico* died in his sleep.

We had prayed St. Joseph to let him die swiftly and naturally when his hour came. How sweetly and completely that prayer of many months has been answered!

i The fortieth day after Christ's Resurrection, and thus the day Christ ascended to heaven.

ii "Man must . . . feel with animals," a paraphrase of a passage from a homily (on Mark 16:14–20) by St. Gregory the Great: "Habet . . . sentire cum animalibus," suggesting that humans have emotion in common with animals.

The vet came, because the maids heard the sweet lean old dog make a strange sound—a reviving drought was given, and the maids left him asleep on his "bundie" and on his "bundie" just as he had been sleeping they found him dead.

Now indeed we are reft of all our old life! But that Michael has *not* to return to his pathetic welcome with the[59] knowledge he *must* be condemned to death is a favour for which I lift thanksgiving. To the end he followed the maids about, even lying the day before death in an attic sunbeam to be close to their room. And he enjoyed his meat to the end.

Our Basset—our friend, our care, our jest for thirteen years—from Zermatt to the little grave in Mortlake Cemetery! And Pussy always loved him with the real affection that laughs tenderly. She called him the "Merciful Mouse" (After B. Jones' *Merciful Knight*[i]) because he looked so distinguished and mild, and was called "the Muse" as short for Musico.

I am glad the noble companion lives in Fay's Jewel, and will be carried like the badge of an Order on my breast as long as I wear ornaments. I go through the thirteen years of his life and our lives—Fay teaching him to eat buns at the door; Shannon praising him; Holmes burlesquing him; Whymmie allowing his love, as a king; Pussy tapping his star! Then I see him going as a mourner to Whymmie's grave, almost dying to go after him—falling into age and disease (how joyous it is now that we were mostly patient!),[60] growing more ripe and tender in love as he wasted or swelled in body.

What joy he showed in our return to bury our Little One—the single note of gladness possible to bear: when on April 15th I kissed the shadowy star on his dear, spent old skull, and said goodbye, I had a fear it was the last goodbye.

And as we drove off, my tears fell—he stood in withered beauty and grandeur below the steps of the front-door . . . It was *Vale!*[ii]

Whym Chow must rescue his quaint and faithful spirit—for he loved; and Love has always its supernatural life.

He is buried in the Dogs' Cemetery at Molesworth, Huntingdon—our noble hunting Basset. I tried to get him a grave in a green field near us—but Bex could get no grant of a spot. So there was nothing but the distant cemetery.

Being so noble he had to be buried nobly—and the little Garden, dedicated to Whym, could not open for another grave.

---

i *The Merciful Knight* (1863), a painting by Sir Edward Burne-Jones (1833–98).
ii "Goodbye!"

Dear Basset—the old, old dog—St. Joseph have you still in his pitying care, he who watched God in the midst of the mystery of the Animals round the Crib, who led the Ass along the way to Egypt![61]

EC For his little tombstone this—

Homo habet . . . sentire cum animalibus

Musico

Faithful and affectionate hound

May 1910[62]

EC John, making trouble that broods over our brains—that scarcely the Holy Host in its validity of silence can lay to rest.

It is an atmosphere of threats, of impossible conditions, of the most offensive calumny. I am in a coil—by the ambiguities of the will, that Pussy promised should be made legal and then failed to have legally drawn out; I am at once executrix and trustee; for one part gives everything to John and the next puts Father Morey *in Trust* with me, Michael and John as trustees to the Spooners, who are final[63] heirs.

John wants all legal expenses to be laid on the Trust estate, which the lawyer says is illegal—he refuses to give up the money in deposit of Amy's estate, plunging the estate into debt to meet government demands, and finally, with what is religious mania turns and sends me because Amy, forsooth, has left a pagan will, and no charities.

So he would like to demand £500 of the Trust estate for Catholic purposes. Amy and I made our wills mutually to benefit she, John; I, Michael; and it was only in sheer justice to the solemn promise we had given to our own Father that when we each established *a Trust*, we left the capital, as he wished it left—to the needy in his own family.

I do not know where I am? So many winds of contention blow round me, I cannot tell which is the wind from Heaven. The only hope of settlement will be, I fear, an application to the Court to construe the will—and legally settle at once, what I have wasted nearly half a year in trying to get settled by mutual consent.[64] [. . .]

The Darling's presence was not peaceful—she had no open conflict; but we know in home life, as in politics, this is almost a condition of strife as this deadly will business has proved it. She, like me, was nervous and had grievances—a condition that does not in any way give absolute peace to others or to oneself. That she was in deep peace with our dear Lord above the storms, where her soul lit its lighthouse, I am sure; but round the little tower of her life there was struggle, and elements of discord. Indeed she, like me, had a nervous cowardliness that has nothing of the peace of God in it.

"In simple truth," as Michael writes to Fr. Vincent, "she was to her father and to Henry and to me for a bit of a cure—a little fatal and ill starred. You, Father, may supernaturally have looked down into her nature and seen how the divine love penetrated the fast-closed little cell of her Danae heart."[65]

EC Another day we face the glaring thunder sun, and among the motors of Inferno, and the brutal butcher manners of the men at the turnstiles, we go to the Japanese Exhibition[i] . . . Nightmare! The White City of Cement—[66] the water roaring under exotic domes, under the sky of London—the native and the exotic in a mongrel unity—such is an exhibition like this—a monstrosity only fit for the motorists.[67]

EC *June 18th, Saturday.*

Fay comes and Michael sends word "she would be very glad to see Mr. Ricketts in the garden."

He is charmed with the invitation and finds her plying the hose.

She is in a hat with a bold dash of white hydrangeas in it—she is full of the summer, as a hayfield is full of living hues and vitality; and then she is doing such cool work.

He takes the hose from her and soon the little plastic hand is directing the fountains from flower to flower, while Michael gleams through a trellis just beyond the peril of a *douche*. Pliantly, steadily he waters—[68]and we hear the cook chopping herbs in the kitchen.[69] [. . .]

Dinner is approved—especially youngest[70] peas and a mushroom savory. By mistake Josephine puts the stone cream before me, and before Michael a plain isinglass blancmange. Fay's glance is delicious . . . He confesses afterward that the isinglass made him think of the little sister who had no breasts. And Josephine, who is going to be confirmed tomorrow at Westminster Cathedral, hears this jesting!

The visit is full of laughter . . . I can't recall the causes . . . Fay is bantering Michael on *chers péres*[ii] as he alone can—with "no offence in't—no office 'n the world." And he pretends to be in dire dudgeon because he only inspired and did not write the *Times* Articles on the Japs . . . we mistook! O bitterness!

---

i The Japan-British Exhibition ran in London from May to October 1910, serving to signal the consolidation of Japan's colonial power in Asia, and to enhance trade with Britain.
    ii "Dear fathers."

His articles in the *Morning Post* are triumphs of journalism—he wants to do everything true to the right way of doing it . . . so he wants his journalism to be excellent. [. . .]

After dinner Michael and Fay sit and smoke and laugh as if they belonged to a younger world.[71] I am just inside the room and can watch . . . Really Michael is wonderful this summer evening. She has not taken off the hat, only put on a black blouse, with early last century tuckings of white net, round a fold set low on the shoulders, and her Victorian arms atwinkle as she lifts the cigarette. And she is warm and her eyes vivid; and laughter purls along and then breaks out recklessly from her voice. There are nankeen-coloured ramblers in wild rose near her and lilies very sturdy; and with the sagacity of a woman and the readiness of the child she glows and ripples and laughs free.

I watch one of the old scenes, when Whymmie was with us. Suddenly our dogless little Paragon, that has been visited with so much tribulation and care, itself goes back to its young days. I shall ever remember those two—with their lovely giggles of June; and the charm of Michael's gay cheeks, gay arms, gay laughter—and of Fay's pale shining convulsions of merriment—his hands rubbed, his face hidden or just[72] revealing the titters in the midst of his little Greek beard.

EC Another evening Tommy comes and Mrs. Tommy—they are full of loving simplicity.

The old times are with us. In the garden Tommy lays rambler roses on Marie's hair—just as a centaur would crown a centauress.

How he belongs to the world of incarnate elements—aboriginal forces and sensuousness in combination. He is quaint, froward, robustious and lusty—with the laughter at times of carnal strength, as when a fresh child grabs flaccid and wild for weariness.

It seems as if Whym Chow must become visible—our ever-present invisible Flame of Love—when Tommy proposes to read some sonnets.[73]

KB I have no dog.

The long ears—of Music, are not for my soothing. He is in his grave, near Leicester!

So there are three graves, and we look forth on no spot in life where the sun shines.[74]

EC Late on Saturday night we receive the terms suggested by Johnnie's lawyer. All is as I had planned it to be in early May—except that Johnnie wants the little Bradley property, still not standing in Pussy's name. We wish him to have it—Pussy thought it hers absolutely and I therefore thought it would be his. I appeal to the Spooners—knowing they are of grand stuff, that the £664 of Bradley Estate should be ceded and they should inherit, as Amy wished, all[75] the Cooper estate.[i]

And we hear there is every chance of a settlement. *Laus tibi, Christi!*[ii] We have our own wills about—we are just babes in legal woods. O language, what crimes you commit!

I take Michael to "make an oath" as I express a "Declaration on oath." The commissioner looks at Michael. "Widow or married woman?" Michael silently thinks this is strange—which is she? *One* she must be, yet she does not seem to answer to either. How can it be? "Spinster?" at last suggests the distracted commissioner, and Michael grasps deliverance with alert eyes. I simply take her up an entry outside and we sway drunkenly with laughter.[76]

EC When all the masterpieces are waxed, Fay stays on almost till eleven, talking about the virtues and vices of the age to which we all really belong— that of Swinburne and Pater and Rossetti.

We both agree we love to reread Swinburne—he is as silly often as a young colt in the grass—but what a sense of life! One laughs with it and becomes young, with young feet. Fay is afraid to reread Rossetti lest he should be cold to him, and that would break his heart. He has found himself cold to Pater's *Renaissance*—the aestheticism is not there an impulse but a cult.[77]

EC *New Year's Eve.*

Soon, soon will the year be gone by in which Little Pussy had any part. The stroke of midnight divides us sharply from her in time—O Little One, pray for us! Be indeed our intercessor!

We must not feel time—pray for us and all is eternal. May our dead bless us—the complete circle of our own dead.[78]

Works and Days, 1911

EC I am going back, though I write in the present, after a fortnight the greatest in experience of my life.

---

i The Spooners were cousins of Cooper's via the Cooper line; they were not directly related to Bradley. This decision keeps the Bradley and Cooper assets separate.

ii That is, "Praise to you, Christ."

February 6, 1911. [. . .]

I had not been well and had told the Doctor of certain symptoms he had examined into—and then had been silent about.

On the Friday he had asked me if I were thinner . . . He comes on this Monday and asks for Michael. As she is at the Vineyard he comes in and talks burly cheerfulness to me.

But I face him, tell him we are Catholics and must face reality and conjure him on this ground to tell me the truth.

"You think I am suffering from something serious?"—"Well, as you have put it to me in the way you have, I am bound to say I do." "With Cancer?"—"I believe so. It is my opinion." "And it will be fatal"—"Yes."

All this length of short time I feel like a marble temple in ruined and [79] immovable cold. Yet a breath slips round the cold—of God's will. I am immovable, but there is motion from the high sky about me.

And I learn more and more about this internal cancer, about its terrible indecisions and every way of its horror and disgrace. I am undone before my own face as death undoes one after he has covered one's face from earthly life.

There can be no removal—only a hideous operation of alleviation from what has to come. And I am to see a specialist tomorrow and learn his opinion. The Doctor, generally Scottish-kind and fond of me, is hard and speaks untemperately. Hard he is as an executioner, and he goes soon.

It was like this when the Vet left me with the news Whym was struck with meningitis—only then the tears came with a whole firmament's descent.

Now I am too cold for abundant weeping—drifts of bitter rain—then I think of the terrible doom, and then of my beloved, who has again to enter the door of little Paragon, and hear of death to the creature of her love.

A ring—she comes and her voice is of Dominican and Apostolic joys[i]— she has got an old convert, who had grown [80] negligent in his religious duties, to ask for the cleansing of penance . . . I cannot speak—she sees my speechlessness as an awful vision, far beyond anything heard, and her questions [illeg.] it.

To tell her, "The doctor says I have cancer"! To see her grow deadly fixed— and then the fixity break up in a moaning of negation. The dove moans over a nestful, the dove moans with springtime in labour, the dove affirms the pangs of living—the moan I hear is—"no, no"—it is of the abrogation of life, it is the moan of agony that we must be severed—we, who are flesh of one flesh in our imaginations—bone of one bone in our common life.

i Pertaining to the salvation of souls.

While she moans, I realise how infinitely distant from the love I have for her, are all, even the tenderest of other loves. I wonder the blow lets her heart go on beating—the moans come between its crannies. O my little love! I am cold no more—the fear of death made me cold—but the thought of losing my life on earth with my beloved brings warmth, and tears more like those I poured over Whymmie.

At last we eat, and made a comedy of life's attempt at nutrition.[81] [. . .]

We return to weep and weep and weep against each other—We are close, close—and the storm of parting breaks over us in deluges, through which we pray and kiss and then sever, only to unite in reading the divine office,[i] and in plans to dominate this sorrow, and to bring to the measure of faith and hope and divine love.

We will have a dog. We always told our little hound we should have to have another. We cannot gain any ring of cheer unless we all speak to a dog.

How I look at my Michael, and see in her our life of joy and sweetness—the violence of love one has for her quick smile, for the dapple on her brow of grief over her Hennie-boy.

As the world appears hostile—the face of the dearest becomes tenderer than could have ever been imagined. A transfiguration of the divinest union—that is glory of every look, that is a parting look of love's.

Oh, my little master!

But I forget . . . I send in the afternoon for Goscannon, with special urgency. He comes at five—the candles are lighted as I enter. He says briefly but[82] with interest "Well, what is it?"

My throat tangles—at last I untangle it enough to say, "I have had a great shock." I do not see so much as feel a dense anxiety settle over my confessor, and I sob out the terrible doom—everything I know—everything that tonelessly he asks to know.

"I did not imagine your desire to see me had anything to do with you or I would have come at once"—His words ooze out like thick blood from a wound. His parchment colour recalls me to pity for him—and the nerves that have been so broken. He shelters himself under hope—the way my sight was spared last year.

No, no! I cannot bear hope—it weakens me—

So he shelters me with his trust that I shall have peace at the end. He is sure I shall be blessed and have peace.

In his sorrow he is like a boy—or like an animal with delectable eyes. His man's sorrow has none of the expressions of completeness belonging to ma-

---

i That is, the Liturgy of the Hours, a collation of psalms, hymns, and readings that comprises the public prayer of the Catholic Church.

ternity—yet the holy self-control and priestly remoteness make the face in its sweet pain[83] venerable.

He blesses me lingeringly—then I call Michael—who finds him still more blank and boyish—only able to say the words of the beloved in agony "if it is possible may this cup pass from me. Nevertheless, not my will but thine be done."

It is so strange, after the passage of only one year, to lie down at night again, as if the nightfall were not the end of the day, but the end of sorrow.

And to walk to a consultation with a specialist, Darcey Power[i] at 11.30. [. . .]

For all the while I was speaking of my doom to Goss, yesterday, I had firmly maintained it was a just and merciful temporal punishment for my great, flagrant sinning.

I knew I deserved it; and there was wonderful love shown me by the blessed one in this act of laying on my shoulders the cross of penance I was too weak to lift upon them.

The way from Addison Rd. to Chandos Street seems beyond count in miles. The surgeon's house has comfort and a measure of comeliness. We are before our time and before our time we are seen.[84]

This is a grace for which we raise *Deo Gratias*. I like the humane hand of the surgeon. He seats us, asks me about my sufferings—where and what they are, and in three minutes has announced, "You are an artist or a writer?"

In that place!—on the edge of humiliation, everything said about one's disease a jagged nail driven through one's pride. Swift indeed is the investigation—the touch smooth and supple and judicial.

"That is soon done," he says, "now while you are arranging things, I will talk to your Aunt." They go—and I know his opinion, and clutching tighter the little crucifix I have hidden in my fist all the while, I say to that dread knowledge, "Thy will be done—*Fiat Voluntas Tua.*"[ii]

They return—Michael so quietly preparing—but I am prepared, and I hear that he finds cancer; that it is so placed it cannot be removed without the gravest danger; that it can be staved by a detestable operation, that would alleviate the offensiveness and pangs of the end . . .

We speak of God's will—the kind face is glad any fable supports us. Looking into my eyes, as we part over the fee, he says, "I am *very sorry* for you." We are left to consider if I shall undergo the light operation that alleviates. Home, home.[85]

i Sir D'Arcy Power (1855–1941), renowned surgeon and medical author.
ii "Thy will be done."

KB *From letter to Painter.*

Dear Painter,

I am writing to you a week *after the shock*. Henry told me—yesterday Monday week—at once, suddenly, letting me in at the door—the doctor had seen her while I was out.

   We have got used to it now as the several hills get used to their clever sides. And Henry is of course the first to dash a little verdure among the blackened slopes.[86]

EC *Tuesday, February 14th.*

At Mass I am moved to give up the operation and on my return home to seek the cutting I made ten years ago, about violet leaves as a cure.[i]

I open the drawer of the commode in the Grot and there it is! Then I confess that, when John offered Lourdes water and Michael neglected the idea, a pang had seized me, which made me know I wanted to use the curative water, on the chance of it having an aim of mercy toward me. Michael at once hopes with me and will try to start the violet leaves and the Lourdes water tomorrow.[87]

EC *Transcribing a letter Mary Berenson wrote to KB.*

I find Bernard *so crushed* by dear Field's news that it is as if the sun had gone out of the sky, and he left in darkness. He cannot see to write just yet, but it seemed to me I must let you have some word from me. He feels as if he could bear it, perhaps in a way welcome it, if it were *himself*, but oh, not for her, the truest, finest spirit he knows.

   Dear Michael I cannot say more or other than that we are heartbroken, and yet uplifted by Field's wonderful way of meeting it—Mary.[88]

EC *Having welcomed a new dog, an Irish Wolfhound they name Ferrer and nickname Elk.*

So May goes on! Elk wins on us with his dusky wickedness—he is a devastator; his wolf-eyes are flat in expression, as if to shine out of twilight in his victims—but he is gentle, for a wolf, and is in a form we can caress.[89]

He eats pens, he plays skittles with the coal, digs holes in the garden path—he consumes a shank bone with his invincible set of swordlike teeth.

I have had a great deal more pain—it is strong irritation and ache. [. . .]

---

i The history of violets as a cure for cancer reaches back centuries; they are associated with soothing qualities, pain relief, and healing inflammation.

When the pain is very bad, Michael takes me in her arms, and the vital warmth of her being is of such power the pain goes to sleep.[90]

EC *Coronation Day, June 2.*

For we have leisure today to talk; and we recall the Jubilee just before Midsummer Day in 1897, when Durdans was deep in maize-yellow stocks and old-fashioned roses round the flags and the old father in his beauty and fatality was already[91] marked for his mysterious death. We recall the last Coronation when Whym was with us, brilliant and inseparable. We speak of this spring, so marvelous, threatened and yet dedicated—we wonder, one moment, if it may be that we shall look back together on its holy sorrow.

My Loved and I are so close and fresh to each other—we must cry a little. What we are to each other!—we mean to each other earthly life; and into the next we are bound to run on together in our different natures along one channel of a love that cannot sever or dispart.

My little Love—and she has a most glowing sanguine rose, new from Kate Reily,[i] in her large black hat, and a scarf of dove-coloured gray.[92]

KB *It is September 28th, Wednesday, our Ember Day.*

I sit alone at breakfast looking out on to a stormy sea. To be alone, to look out on that stormy sea, and to believe that this afternoon Henry will be anointed! [. . .] I have seen Henry bear extremity of pain, so that she cried out to me, "Master, Master!" with the look in her eyes of a dumb animal. I have watched her face and waste. Gracious renewals come with the Rottingdean doctor. She is eased of her pain—with supernatural force she is arming for the journey—for the great one—but, subject to God's pleasure.[93]

EC Michael is sure a motor would be grateful to me for my journey. So at two o'clock a motor clacks grandly at the gate of little Paragon and we are off, as if we belonged to our age.

The swift sliding is attractive and the largeness and change of outlook. The air sweeps us shrewdly . . . we are on the top of Reigate Hill! Oh, my dear ones! I see the dear Father's majestic toiling form—and little Pussy by me—and Whymmie in golden youth pulling at his leash, and Dickie trotting, and Music lumping gloriously along—All gone from sight yet seen so clearly!

I did not think of it that we should descend in beautiful Reigate and say a *Confiteor*[ii] for our past life as we pass through it—so familiar after thirteen years' absence, so precious, so tragic, so remote.[94]

---

i A noted English dressmaker, née Harriet Reily and later Harriet Griffiths, with showrooms on Dover Street in Mayfair and in New York.

ii A Catholic prayer confessing sin and appealing for absolution.

EC A car and a gentleman chauffeur has been ordered overnight [. . .]. By nine we start into the dazzling, awful east wind—the radiance of the earth, the wide look of a Sunday morning—how we enjoy the drive till the wind closes down over the sunshine as we reach London—nobly empty: such grand heights of houses, such visitors contained by brick and stone; such atmosphere up slopes and down valleys of masonry!

All still almost as if moral. "And river run down in the Vale of Cheapside." We pass De Vere Gardens; we pass Pater's[95] London house, and Miss Vickers' old Kensington house . . . Many are the dead; and they were faithful and good to us. May they rest in peace.[96]

EC *Last night of the old year.*

To think of all the love I have had—my Loved lavishing on me love that must not be faced, if we dwell with thoughts of parting—love of a tenderness that grows terrible as the soft cover of the nest bird's[97] breast when the silence has fallen of the hawk's approach.

Such tender gifts—gray Ferrer, the wolf dog to play with; the large green silk quilt of eiderdown to cover me on the Sun Room floor; the eighteenth-century satinwood case to hold our books—the flowers and grapes in a crowd. [. . .] How I have been divinely loved! [. . .] Then there is the good Doctor at Rottingdean, who saved my life with[98] Trypy-Trypin-Trypyre-Tryp-Tryp-Tryp—my defender from the worst of the malady—Trypsin.[i] Then all the months of alleviation our Lady of Lourdes[ii] gave me by use of the violet juice and the violet leaves; and the alleviation she still gives me. All honour and glory to her tender help!

It was so true in the prophecy of last year that we should not receive great impressions of beauty—we have not had them from nature. But from flowers—"in boundless prodigality,"[iii] I have had joys of loveliness and freshness that have fought the outraging things of one's dire disease.[99]

EC When I think of my "Woe"—it is strange how lighthearted I become—one's breath becomes clear light as when one is very happy in childhood; and I do feel that this intensity does not turn away for the Earth, but toward it.

I wonder if loved and I are to be saved to each other, as poets here in the world, and allowed to sing mortally what Love has brought us from his highest—Immortality! I wonder if my sickness is to be arrested or only made a

---

i An enzyme used in the treatment of colorectal cancer to inhibit tumor growth and metastasization.

ii Prayer for a healing miracle.

iii A quotation from Wordsworth's Napoleonic poem "Dion," written in 1816 and published in 1820.

more perfect discipline. I feel it is to be used in the action—for the year is an action.[100]

EC The year is bold and will make us bold—it will reveal ourselves to our own imaginations.

Myrtle—ah, it has shadows very dark, but they are fragrant, and flowers as white and dim as milk, but they are worn by brides—and berries very curt in what they express of frontage, but they do not fall; they endure on the wiry stems triumphant.

And this is the Myrtle Year![i]

And this is the year of union with the Heavenly Love.

The attitude of my being is an humble confidence—even the grind of pain does not make the whir of dread in any corner of my soul.

O beloved, O loved Lover—thy ring our fetter forever, what should we fear.

It is getting near to twelve o'clock. I have just called my Michael from the silver Grot to come to the river bedroom where, in bed,[101] I am writing, as the damp, slow night grows more resonant, because time changes its guise behind the dusk.

I look at Whymmie's candle and see the eyes of love there—eyes that can light the fragrant shadows of the myrtle year as no other torches could— Whymmie—*Amoris Lumen*[ii]—the very guardian angel of this year's auguries.

May the holy dead, whom we love more and more, pray for us—the sweet, wild father; the mother, who gave to her circle of loving ones the glow of eyes to which mysteries were being revealed—the Little Pussy, who smiled at death—who has so helped me in my prayers that I might have life, I who have been brought almost through death to vital 1912.

More than ever before this year is for twain—for my loved and her Hennie! Dear Lord, who died for us, make us live for thee and in thee! I dare not write what thy ring names us—resting in each other's love may we love wholly in thee.[102] Do what thou will with us, we shall be in thee together and not alone—forever thine and thy twain in thee!

Welcome 1912!

Let us sing *IO*,[iii] as the Angels of the Incarnation sing it in the halls of Heaven. We know our song is a marriage song—and we throw our scapulars of St. Dominic over our faces[iv]—for our secret is beyond all singing.[103]

i Myrtle, a symbol of love, luck, and prosperity.

ii "The Light of Love."

iii A Latin expression of joy.

iv St. Dominic was the patron of divine mercy; the Dominican scapular, a shield, breastplate, or white woolen apron associated with the Blessed Virgin Mary.

Works and Days, 1912

EC In the river room we have a long talk and by evening all is well—the devil gone out and our one thought how we can make our Vow as solemn as possible.

I carefully write out Michael's profession and the vow for each of us in its legal form with spaces for signing our names and writing in the dates of day and month and year.[i] We try to arrange the disorderly books for tertiaries so as to have some fair order in beautiful St. Dominic's ceremony, the stupid books dislocute.

Then we go to bed. I have forgotten to say that on Thursday afternoon Michael went forth and found two firm old rings—mine chased, hers wrought, in gold—for our marriages at the altar.

One sees these things, one fondles them; but it is impossible for human thought for a while—a long, long while—to compass them—to it slides from them and finds itself far away or in hiding.

Thursday, January 4th. The day of our spousals with Christ, side by side.[104]

KB And I lay down all my trouble—My beloved little Amy is with Him whom she has touched so close—in his altars whom she has fondled in his poor. He has died for her; she has caught some drops of the precious blood.

Should I not write of that quiet wedding day? And of the bliss that moved in me silent as light. Father Prior and I, when we were together in the little gold-room spoke off and away—of other things.

I read to him "Thanatos"[ii]—to show him how hard it was to me to face the death of decrepitude and disease . . .

Before Fay's portrait, I said "There now, I love that face because it is loveable—not in Christ, not for His sake."

He responded, "It is quite correct to love what is loveable."

Then I said how Henry had chilled me, warning me that in the formalities of a Catholic deathbed—she might not be able to express herself to me. She was thinking of having the "Salve" very correct—and the prayers for the dying.[iii] Her words had turned me to stone—If she could think of the Salve when

i The religious profession and vow represented a formal entrance into the consecrated life, and in the Dominican tradition, the commitment to a life of prayer, study, and ministry. Michael Field wore rings to mark their standing as brides of Christ.

ii The Greek god of death. Michael Field published "Thanatos, Thy Praise I Sing," in their 1908 volume *Underneath the Bough.*

iii The "Salve" or "Salve Regina" is a prayer for intercession by the Blessed Virgin Mary. The prayers for the dying, known then as Last Rites or Extreme Unction and now as the Sacrament

she was dying from me, I [105] felt how the walls of ice would thicken between me and her spirit. [106]

EC In the early morning we found there was no salt to season my Brand's extract,[i] and devotedly Michael went down after it. She unshuttered the second staircase window, stepped back and fell as into a dark abyss, a shattered heap. She was amazed she could at last get up, and I was amazed at her stricken, rocking form as she came back.

One hand, the right, was injured. She refused brandy, rocked herself through the first pain, was helped in dressing and in the night of the Beloved went to Holy Mass and Holy Communion.

The hand had swollen dark, but she also went with me to the Canon of the Sung Mass and to the lifting of our Blessed Lord before his people on "Laetare" Sunday.[ii] She looked brilliant [107] in her new Konstin taffeta coat [iii] and her black Kate Reily hat, approved and slightly altered by Ricketts—the black adorned by a central bunch of sharp pansies, forget-me-nots, and a rosebud of intensity. [108]

EC The terrible curse that has fallen on the Petersham Road of two lines and motor buses, rivalling each other in their constant and noisome traffic, had overcome our patience during the afternoon, when I tried a little drive. The air was heavy. [109] The stench of the oil was all the freshness I got. We tried to turn away—and got a tiny space of relief in a pilgrimage to the river through byways.

But the sadness of this ruined world of Richmond and the personal misery suggested that we might have to leave the beloved Paragon, for the sake of health and sanity. Where—how? [110]

EC *Arundel.*

The Vicarage—"Parsonage," the Church calls it. July 6th. Sat.

Just one month since I have written anything in the White Book. Well, of June I must write what remains in mind during the days of quiet depth of

---

of Anointing the Sick, are meant to extend peace and grace to a dying person, and to unite that person with Christ through the Passion of suffering.

i Chicken bouillon designed for easy digestion by invalids.

ii Celebrated on the fourth Sunday during Lent. On Laetare Sunday ("Laetare" means "Rejoice"), Lenten solemnities are momentarily suspended to give parishioners hope before entering the dark days of Good Friday and Holy Saturday. Catholic Church altars are often dressed in pink roses, and the priests lay aside purple vestments for rose-colored ones.

iii A long, fashionable coat.

quietness we got under this roof Mary Berenson has offered us as a gift of old friendship.[111]

EC After the horrible machine clamour of the motor buses—the hot, the contemporaneous pursuit then made of one's soul, how sweet the coolness of pure air, the universality of all the access of it makes toward one's acquaintance sweet, sweet its discretion; its desirous solitude, adorned for one, clean for one as if for an expected guest.[112]

EC I am too weak to talk long—mostly [Berenson] talks to Michael, while I watch the face that launched all the ships in the harbour of my passion years ago and sent them voyaging among dreams and sorrows.[113]

EC Little Olivia[i] is brought for me to see as B.B. says she is Chinese. She is wrinkled deep with the wrinkles not of the end, but of the beginning—the lines of doom, not of the last, but of the first, of alpha not omega.

The habitants of Ford Place made themselves fairy godparents to her the night before—Logan wished her "The habit of reading"—her Gram (Mary) "An abstract interest." Logan asks me what I would wish her. I force back my cowardice "What is the best thing of which to me now—true Religion." "Well, you have wished her the best thing, Religion," Logan says with a rose red, emphatic smile on the abstract face.[114]

EC Trouble with my beloved Michael, who feels when I am under the indifference of disease that I am wholly severed from her, fears such severance for our souls when we are parted. I say how this sense of apartness is not with me—since we were made brides of the Heavenly Bridegroom together, I have felt the break in our old love the Church caused (causing us to have to issue [*Poems of*] *Adoration* and *Mystic Trees* apart from each other)[ii] was cementing in *Christo*. But Michael does not seem to feel this, nor does she trust my love enough—my soul sits (one must be trusted) as my heart sits and its love must be trusted. Still, it comes to this that those I love and who love me accuse me of being cold in response (I so fond of creatures!) and even a priest

i Barbara Strachey (1912–99), daughter of Oliver and Ray Costelloe Strachey; granddaughter of Mary Berenson.

ii Though *Poems of Adoration* and *Mystic Trees* were published under the name Michael Field, the former was a book by Cooper and the latter by Bradley. Here we see Michael Field responding to the pressure brought by the Church to rationalize both their authorship and their relationship.

has confirmed their complaint. So, there must be wrong in me and I am sure it is my carnal sin of pride.[115]

EC *August 16th, the Return to Paragon.*

There is delay around the luggage. At last, we are off [. . .] and we sweep through our beeches, saluting them in a heart-felt joy. As we sweep along the country lanes we become aware that we are going very fast. Graver is told not to drive so rapidly.[116] I drop my bag and in moving a wrap to recover it, I find I am desperately palpitating, and that my chest is filled with pain and my lungs slow to accept air. I am in great suffering. Michael gives me some Koka Wine.[i] I say the glorious mysteries[ii]—so struck that God and his holiest creature both ascend to heaven to descend in heavenly influence.

We have agreed to stay at Burford Bridge Hotel, where so many years ago we were the guests of Meredith. We nearly miss it; but our swift motor, guided by a countryman, is soon at the door.

I feel such effort crippling my heart I do not think of receiving help from the chauffeur but extended my hand to a vast creature in linen—the luggage man. He has arms that look like trolleys and kind broad blue eyes in the midst of ruddy flesh. As I trust myself to his arm and hand, I feel darkness coming over me—a horror of great darkness lying on my chest, pain itself in the throe of suffocation. One step more and I shall burst into death. The man encourages—just through the door . . . a chair! I sink on it in terrible strain. The German waiters stare. Michael has to go for the brandy and neat it is given me.[117]

At last, a waiter brings some hot water and dumps it down. The proprietor will not allow us any quiet room or any aid . . . The inhumanity fires Michael. Gradually the thundercloud of pain withdraws a little from the chest and breath labours less like a galley slave. I murmur after some tea to help against the splitting headache.

A lady student of medicine comes from the window and proffers help—a prescription for the heart. She is timid in humanity and yet humane, and I bless her in this hostel of barbarity. At last she finds my pulse will allow of an attempt to get back to the motor, and I am wellnigh carried by the blessed luggage man. The lady medical student follows with an air cushion we have left in our strife. She tells the driver of the car on no account to drive it above twelve miles an hour. It is a pleasure to tip the luggage man and smile grate-

i A beverage combining wine and cocaine.
ii That is, to pray a Rosary.

fully in his kindly face—also to smile recognition of kindness to the lady student.

Michael wonders how we shall get me into Paragon. She speaks[118] of her arm . . . I say Jane's would be better because she is taller and has a wiry hand to hold up with.

I have smiled on the luggage man and the lady student, I have chosen to be aided by Jane, I have been in the vestibule—almost in the throne room of death—Michael tears a piece out of her hair. I shall always see the bright silvery threads of her passion float torn to the floor of the car reproach me, bringing Father Vincent to my heart and conscience.

I think the sense of Love's anger at the brutal Inn-people, when there was the strife of mortality in my chest, had made me indifferent to her desperate suffering. If we had to part—Thanksgiving in the highest that we lovers were spared to each other!

The gentle swing of the motor at twelve miles an hour brings some alleviation to my chest, and more quickly than I thought familiar Surbiton[i] grows up along our route—Petersham . . . Paragon. Michael and Jane get brandy and hot water for me to have before I am got out of the car and I am soon in the tiny silver Grot, hearing the motor buses pass yet charmed by the dearness, all the sweet of home.[119] I am fed and helped with all tenderness and it is enough to sit in my big Queen Ann chair under my crucifix and be quiet, as if in nature at the benignant time of sundown. Yet there is great sorrow too—my beloved, shattered by strain and shock, weakened by the Friday's abstinence. And for the first time we do not eat together when we return to Paragon.[120] [. . .]

I go to bed. The buses seem fewer and there is a whir of life after the quiet of Arundel that sometimes filled me with the obliterating stillness of the grave.

Ferrer comes to lie by the bedside. Yesterday night they did not let him come to me at first. Then a gray wolf-thing jumped and sidled at the same time round me—a stranger, till I say, just on the edge of my voice,

"My wicked dog Ferrer
   I now have a terror
   I brought him in error,
   My wicked dog Ferrer.
   Da derra, derra,
   Da derra, derra,

i A suburb southwest of London, on the Thames, about five miles from Paragon in the Petersham Road, Richmond.

Da derra, derra,
  I brought him in Error—
My wicked dog Ferrer!"[121]

EC *August 21st.*
On Wednesday Michael has a long morning with "Keefy" and visits Fr. George.

While she is away little Dr. Duncan comes and gives me leave to get up. I ask him what I may do and what I may not with regard to my heart—I may not lift anything from the ground and I must not do anything quickly. "In cases like yours of terrible pain in the chest and throat" . . . "angina pectoris"?[i] I ask calmly. "Yes"—Duncan responds. "It is angina pectoris?" I ask: "Yes!" I again feel a doom of terrible name fasten[122] on me, Michael away—the doctor and I face to face, and I shall have to tell my beloved—this is hard to accept.

The doom I accept tearless and willing—only with a little wonder in my voiceless repetition to myself of "angina pectoris"—"angina."

I think of my Beloved, coming back again to a blow of torturing magnitude for the one who loves and watches. "Angina"—the voice of solitude grinds out. I get up and my dear returns joyous from last preparations for the Catholic marriage.

It is hard to be responsive, while the voice of solitude grinds out "angina pectoris." She looks so brilliant and so tired. It is only an hour and a half after lunch that at last she asks for all the doctor said, and gradually I try to prepare my tongue and her brain for the two cruel words.

But no preparation will save tongue or mind the sheerness. The blow falls—my beloved reels with anguish—a quiet martyrdom that as yet is far from being raised to the altar of God, but is sure to reach sanctification—I feel how sure. We have been warned[123] by our abject failure in the supernatural life at Burford Bridge.

We wait on our bridegroom to make this trial less shaming. As we wait on him, he gives us the honour of courage and peace. Michael goes up to the vineyard, and sending Goss does not tell him.

An unspeakable love comes forth from this sorrow between love and me—unspeakable and therefore in the world of our souls unfathomable. We are close as if moved together by miracle. Blessed be "angina pectoris" and the broken solitude and the accepted union in another sorrow for Michael and me together![124]

---

i Severe chest pain caused by insufficient blood supply to the heart.

Sometime later, Edith Cooper learned that she did not suffer from angina pectoris.

EC *Thursday, September 5th.*

Oh, how ill, how witheringly deathly I feel, as the winds sweep from sea and land. Yet Lishman thinks I may last another winter, for though the weakness of my heart is deplorable, I am actually gaining rather than losing flesh.

Somehow my good Doctor depresses me. He has been trying local application of the burning trypsin—in vain, as I knew; and he has let the rheumatism gain ground, which always means intense suffering.

He seems heavily sad and moody—since I gave him *Poems of Adoration.* He greeted me as "My good and gifted patient." Perhaps he wants to talk poetry—while I want to talk trypsin and salicylate.[125]

EC *Monday, September 9th, 1912.*

When I wake on Monday, I find as usual my Love has placed *The Following of Christ* on my bed on an *Academy.* I wash my face, "do" my hair—nor can I fail to see how spent the outlines, how faded the fabric—how my appearance, even where still asserting some quality of distinction, belongs to illness, or better still, to patience and pain united by the Holy Faith, that with the soul mould also the face lost to its natural attractions.

Such a spent, bleached face—well, well! Returning to bed, I lift the *Following of Christ*, and in the *Academy* underneath my eye falls on the signature Michael Field under Two Poems, reproduced from twenty-five years ago!

And the first poem—"No beauty born of pride my Lady hath." Oh, my Beloved, my Lover of all those years ago! And the poem has been put for my eyes! The joy of that firm and lovely praise—the jet of that worship through my heart—the sweetness of[126] reading of my beauty, when young, and a glorious love longed to make it known to the world poets live in and sing to.

I stagger as I glow. . . . And St. Thomas à Kempis makes intercession— "Grant me that I may die to all things that be in the world, and for thee to be despised and to be as a man unknown in this world."[i]

My voice is not alone with his voice—it goes on alone down its cloistral vistas.

I am warm, beating with life in the wrap of that adorable poem, a love song that exalted me to the ages . . . And Michael comes in from mass.

Tremulously I speak of what she has left for my eyes—she does not under-

---

i Dutch medieval cleric (1380–1481) who published *The Imitation of Christ*, a devotional volume emphasizing inner spirituality.

stand. It is a beautiful coincidence: indeed, she would not have left me to see again that dear poem by myself—it is too poignant.

We weep together—the strength of twenty-five years in our weeping, and the anxiety of day by day in its pressure of tenderness.[127]

KB O little love, but God has been very gracious to us—delivering us out of this noisome pit!

I write on the Feast of St. John Evangelist.[i] Henry is having mass said in my intention in honour of my intercessor[ii] by Fr. Prior and Fr. Green. Perhaps, bye and bye, we may recall some of the spaces. At once I will make record of Christmas Eve.

Dr. Lishman came in the afternoon.

In the evening I read to her the ode to the nativity—"the stars that bend one way their precious influence"—appeared to us this year the supreme verse.[iii] There we parted for rest, and the gathering of strength. At 11.30 we met—and I read to her bits from the Divine office and the Mass. She sang to me "Adeste Fidelis."

At midnight we read the Canon of the Mass.[iv][128] [. . .]

I carried up my Christmas dinner to that sacred corner. Henry delighted me by eating some spots of turkey, and two currants of the pudding.

—I thought of community and the Priest eating Paragon pudding. I tried to think only of the day, and all that was going on in Heaven. We were too busy with history for memories. For the evening Henry had the maids up, said to them all the divine ineptitudes over their Christmas Cards. We all played "Old Maids" at cards, and the room rang with our laughter as we paid our forfeits.[129]

KB *Last night of 1912.*

The wilderness shall rejoice, cruel the desert shall be glad and blossom as the rose.

It will be a high adventure—this year of 1913.

I am writing alone in the silver Grot—a green cloth covers Henry's choicest satinwood table. For weeks I have been taking Henry's writing-room—while the Sim-room lies in thick cloud beside me.

i Celebrated on December 27 in honor of St. John the Evangelist, author of the Gospel of John, the three Epistles of John, and the book of Revelation, and the disciple most beloved of Jesus.

ii For Cooper, the Blessed Virgin Mary.

iii John Milton wrote the ode "On the Morning of Christ's Nativity" in 1629.

iv The most solemn and central part of the Catholic Mass.

Slowly the abandoned rooms have been forsaken, the little dining room where she saw the first fire lit, the tiny gold room where the tits are no longer fed, the Sun Room—the grace of the fashion of it has perished; and in a way my bedroom and hers have ceased.

In moments of crisis, my altars have been overturned—I have given up the need—the north room and the south—the ancient altar to the trinity has been cast down—to give place to the new sacramental shrine—[130]everything has been destroyed or whirled about: from the ruins two fresh abodes have been reared.

My silver grot where I dwell with my crucifix—my Familiar—Painter's Sphinx on my table, my little couch, and my doves—

It is my liberal cell—

Above, and within sound of the silver voice is an upper chamber where there is still glory and delight—there is my captive prisoned to her couch. An electric bell has been fixed today that connects with her room. The new life begins from this evening. We are totally detached from the earth—not a root clings as far as we know. In the coming year we cannot travel.[131] [. . .]

Officially this night I abandon my quality of nurse. I take off my white apron. I become again her master and her lover. Very nearly I am worn down to the imbecile by my stupid and senseless devotion. Sick nursing, as I have been taught it by the Church, and by the sensual and devilish spirit of the age, is wrong. Had I carried it out to its excess—I should have established Henry in self-absorption, and the narrow tyrannies of the sickroom. I gave up my quality as nurse—I offer up my "nursing" as a child offers up a broken teacup to her mother—*broken*. I have failed—as a nurse—thank God I have failed.[132]

Works and Days, 1913

EC *Tuesday.*

In preparing for my Confession, I realise how deep in us Sloth is! It takes the form of a nervous sense of impossibility. It kept mother for years from the seaside and from changes and drives that would have enhanced her life. It has such hold on "the Puss," Francis says she cannot be got to go beyond her bit of town garden. She could have gone out *for years*, yet sloth, of the invidious kind that attacks us and our kin, has kept her, as it seemed a hopeless prisoner.

I am pursued by the dread of what I should *do*, by the sense things can never be done or compassed—and Michael is the same, leaving the things, if they are to be done, to others to do them.

This *Sloth* has[133] been our Curse, and Richmond has increased it and developed it with the years—till even the illumination of the Faith has only just touched it and made it apparent. Our only way of fighting it is to appeal to all the champagne-like qualities of the Holy Ghost to lighten us and fill us with the "bittersweet" of its irrepressible energy.[134]

EC *Monday, March 1st.*

Fay comes to lunch. He brings a sheet of decadent French journalism—all the colour reproductions of the theatre painted from a palate Satan has mixed. In and out of the infamies, Nijinsky and Korsavina[i] are shown in their attitudes and with their gestures of astonishing beauty; and the simplicity of what is beautiful shines forth from Hell—"grace must still look so."

I shall never forget the dumb incipiency of sex shown in Nijinsky's faun[ii]—the noble bluntness of ignorance guided by instinct—the sudden ice of panic—the abandon of a young animal to the sweets of wonder and caress.[135]

KB Henry has had a week of intense suffering from dropsy[iii]—her body defaming and being parceled off wild provinces of pain. Waking I have seen a bowed, hoary head—Alone the thoughts of a dearer head, so bowed, so hoary, has kept me from reproaching God. The days have been days of heavy sleep, the nights of breathlessness and sleep and woe.

Relief is sought in "tapping."[iv] I can scarcely write the abhorred word. Henry calls it—"the dispersion of the Jews."

Our lives have changed. I have had to face the necessity of daily making my hands surgically clean—in view of a possible wound on the leg. I felt at first the infinite fidget of the ritual would forever ruin me—then I yielded; I am being supernaturally helped.[136]

EC *May 6th, Tuesday.* [. . .]

The day is dismal round its large leaves, that have never been children of the spring (no dance in them, no play of golden sap with the sun this year!)—but it is a day that brings to my Love and me a great swell of pleasure.

We are singing at night the Novena of the Holy Ghost[v] and we are being raised and sustained by it. A sense of the old Michaelian life comes on us. The

i Vaslav Nijinsky (1889–1950) and Tamara Platonovna Karsavina (1885–1978), ballet dancers.

ii Nijinsky choreographed a ballet called *The Afternoon of a Faun* for the Ballets Russes, set to music by Claude Debussy and based on the symbolist poem *L'Après-midi d'un faune* (1865–67) by Stéphane Mallarmé.

iii Swelling or edema.

iv Bloodletting.

v A prayer for light, strength, and love.

little black leather strap, that is to bind our Catholic books *Adoration* and *Mystic Trees* together, arrives done nightly.

So at night we read from the enchained books dual poems on the same subjects—

My "Real Presence"
Michael's [. . .]
My "Virgo Potens"
Michael's "Midsummer Night's Dream"
My "Columba Mea"
Michael's "In Die Obitus"
My "Holy Cross"
Michael's "The Captain Jewel"
My "Qui Renovat Juventutem Meam"
Michael's "Gather, Gather!"
My "To Notre Dame de Boulogne"
Michael's "Praises"

Before we began our criticism of each volume by this dual reading, in its alternations[137] poem by poem of our treatment of the same theme, we read "In Christo" by me and "To see him in His Place" by Michael.

It is strange to find that, although each book as a whole is so different from its *strapfellow*, each poem has a family stamp in the character of its being.[i] The kind of imagination, the emotional quality, the shaping of the subject may all be different in Michael's religious work and mine—but the cast of likeness is in the blood of it, persistent in each part, though obscured in the whole by difference.[138]

EC (I have been trying to write at midnight in this White Book. I must beware of the attempt—I grow light-headed and commit all the above errors of sense and control.)[139]

EC *13, Well Walk, Hampstead*
　　Masefield's House[ii]
It is Sat. night—July 5th, and we started from Paragon on Thursday July 3rd. So strange I am allowed to creep into another summer holiday.

---

　i Cooper chooses her work here primarily from *Poems of Adoration*; Bradley from *Mystic Trees*. Cooper claims the poem "Qui Renovat Juventutem Meam," published in *Mystic Trees*, as one of her own. Through the trope of the strap, and the "family stamp," the poets reclaim these unusually distinct volumes on behalf of Michael Field.

　ii The home of poet John Masefield (1878–1967) in Hampstead, a northern suburb of London associated with good climate and healing spa waters. Sturge Moore helped to arrange for Michael Field to stay in Masefield's house during Cooper's convalescence.

A light van packs up our sofas, little tables, with blankets, pillows etc.

Then very slowly I am dressed, and I assume the feminine skirt and corset, to the astonishment of my body, and the tremulous overconfidence of my desire.

I rise up from my easy chair. My sunroom has been pulled about and is no more fair to part with. Old tradition comes to my support and greatly brave I move the satinwood chairs and a little satinwood half-table to make delicious light against the wall where my nursing-couch has stood till this morning. I hang in its place Shannon's little silverpoint of myself, and I nip dead flowers from the vase. Then I sink back, the tradition of Paragon gratified.[140] [. . .]

I have bidden *au revoir* to Chow's loved grave, to the rosy garden, to the Sun Room—my rest gown is put on me; the new carrying seat appears with the bland young chauffeur, and Mary Dwain's father, to carry me out to the motor.

When I get to the front doorsteps I feel as if the faintness of death comes round me—a whiteness like the fall of snow settles I know on my face . . . I see it on the others' faces. I am got into the motor and neat brandy stems the faintness of the heart's action.

There is such quick rally! Poor, pretty Mrs. Peek,[i] in pink dressing-gown, looks out at us as if from a New Year's card, and I have force to greet her.

How the air and the sliding vision of the world, its crowds, its shops, its open light, its emphasis without delay—how they delight me as we glide! We cross Thames at Hammersmith: the reaches seem to bring me waving ripples of goodbye for Richmond.

Along Kensington where so often the feet of our life trod—Church Street—Bayswater . . . at last, we've nearly turned into Amy Bell's own home street, Porchester Terrace, when I see the window of the Florest Piper and the window is full of carnations and loveliest flowers, and blue hydrangeas.

As we turn into Porchester Terrace,[141] I sigh. "And I have been longing for blue hydrangeas all the spring"—"You shall have them now"—the declaration of Michael on love's warpath! And she stops the motor and has it reversed at a corner and driven back to conquer those hydrangeas of blue vagueness for me. O Michael, beloved and blessed among lovers: after, in a quiet road, we rest from the adventure. [. . .]

The "lie" of the earth begins to grow more and more diagonal. We realise we are climbing northward . . . it is very steep—then the chauffeur speaks to a "Bobby"—we turn . . . There are many trees down the picturesque

i Elizabeth Georgina Peek (1856–1917) lived with her husband at 7, Riverdale Terrace, near 1, Paragon, for many years.

road—a well—we stop dead . . . Tommy Sturge Moore's house is shown me.[142] [. . .]

EC We have to part with our Gray Wolf, our Ferrer. Michael had fetched him on Sat. afternoon by taxi. Looking round her, she felt Paragon was as a framed picture—its present hold gone—its ideality made by a frame, spacious and cold. [. . .]

She was glad to bear the wolf off to friendly Hampstead. So strange to me to see him there, as usual all over hairs, yet so shiftily beautiful. I begin to suspect him of a "nosing"[143] holiday mood—he looks so wild, so Scandinavian. Anxiety as to his safe abiding with us reaches me—and as I am quite out of nerve with the terrible pain I have had to bear unremittingly, I feel the dear man is scarcely a boon or blessing. On Sunday morning, after sleep that is beloved as a respite, I wake to find May and Jane up the garden and cries for "Ferrer" breaking the still air of the Sabbath. Excited painfully at last I hear his distant bark. He is traced as a truant over the fences even to the fourth garden from here. The doors have to be assaulted with anti-Sabbatic knocks and at last Jane finds him uninjured—shy with freedom, fearful of punishment.

All day long his golden eyes are full of garden wall designs, of current aim after the illimitable. It is found that the whole Masefield property is a temptation to his fleet curiosity. Marie Sturge Moore brings the children in to see our wolf dog. He goes for them and growls after their legs. He must go back. He has had an aristocratic weekend; but he must return and leave our[144] rooms, shrunk from a certain poignant humanity a dog brings to the senses and heart.

Lack of his waving tail and his fall, like a flail's on the ground, and his appeal to the food-giving essence of love!—why, we shall be lost . . . To return to this morning, we are lost when Michael and Jane take him to the station, and Jane takes him back to his Paragon, where he lays down outside the garden door (his favourite summer couch) and seems thankful that vast temptations and the weariness of constraint are both withdrawn.

Dear Ferrer!—His docility a quaintness like a brick learned under the whip, a sudden wriggling bound—his silver legs stray as servants' wings—one of them laid on the knee of the mistress who is feeding, with a small caress or bump. And what uncertain eyes that would wish to be trustworthy and noble but are racially as uncanny as a wild wolf's eyes. How I miss him, having seen in Masefield's drawing-room, an iron-gray effectiveness, an interest filling the air—*heard*, as all domestic interest must be, whether it be roused by animal or child.[145]

EC *August 10th.*

Oh, how long a time no word has strayed into White Book! Not since I was suddenly "punctured" by Dr. Lishman and put to captivity, my toes in a bath—day and night. This was about the middle of July.

All went well—after the next morning's touch of collapse. But the sour coldness of the summer has united with North London air to give me rheumatism that has attacked my malady with the very desolation of pain. Some days and two nights have surpassed any suffering I have yet had to bear. And pain never leaves me—"She is so constant to me and so kind."[146]

EC *Thursday night and Friday morning.*

I am writing in the hope that my pain may drop with slumber. I am so unraveled—dear Lord, I want knitting up; I want the gentleness of closed eyes in conditions of desert heat and cruelty! Have mercy!

These last days at Hampstead have almost lost dirigibility—they have been such turmoil of anguish and sleeplessness. As Michael says, in words that limn a poem, the waves of suffering and desperation are so high up, so high and vast, that God and hope in Him and even love to one's own familiar Love are but as a few tiny stars on the edge of the enormous crests that threaten to submerge—stars and all else.[147]

EC I am moved to read Michael's poems to me. "Old Ivories"—"The Dear temptations of her face" with "Atthis, my darling" of *Long Ago* added—the loveliest nocturne of Love[148] ever created *Palimpsest*—to say by heart "A girl, Her smile a deep-wave pearl."

I am moved to show [Francis] my triumph and joy in this lovely praise and in showing him my so often-shaded mood before my glory I also let my Beloved realise what her poet's gift has been to me—her poet-lover's gift.

Think of it! She has often read these lovely poems to me; she has not heard them, tender but high-voiced, from my lips. It is Paradise between us. When we're together eternally our spirits will be interpenetrated with our love and our art under the benison of the Vision of God.[149] [. . .] I have felt culminating illness in me all day: the malady is as a stone chest on my hip; the ulcers tingle and declare their sharp-pointed agony, and internal bleeding breaks out, a strong attack of the whole night bringing relief from the crisis of pain the journey prepared for.[150]

KB It is Francis' last night—How spend it?

I find I am listening to Henry's voice. Hennie reading my love poems to her, aloud to Francis. Of course, I have never listened to them before—She reads—the famous sonnet "A window full of ancient things" . . . and also "Atthis" . . . and others.[i]

For a little while I am in Paradise. It is infinitely soft between us. Warm buds open. I feel at least I have "merited" with these years of passionate love.

And Francis, who has loved me so well—listens to the singing amid the boughs that is not for him—listens as he would listen to a nightingale overhead.

This is an intense moment. A moment not of memory—but of creation.[151]

EC *October 27th.*

It is the early morning of my own Love's birthday. How dear she is to me—how the sweetness and clench of love grow pain and joy as I look at her, touch her, and receive her little wreath of kisses in my withered hair.

We have had the bond of our art, precious, precious: we have had the bond of race, with the delicious adventure of the stranger co-nature introduced by the beloved father. We have had the bond of life, deep set in the years . . . and now we have the bond of the faith and the bond—different from any other bond—of threatened death. For Lishman thinks very badly of the strain on Michael's heart—her days have been a series of shock on shock—her days are precarious and the beloved, vital face has to envisage the loss of such passionately-loved beauty of earth and sky as has fed its reckless gratitude and magnificence of reception. She has to face withdrawal from common human life so full of in-[152]citement to her.

Above all she has to face the possibility of dying before I die. [. . .]

Michael has been *all life* to me: and now there are moments when she brushed my doomed earthly being with the flat and tragic preserve of nearness to death. No, no! This bond is too sharp to realise . . . But we are growing infinitely tender to each other.[153]

EC *November 25th*—

To think how long it is since I wrote a word in the White Book!

I have been very ill, very drowsy with the worst dreaded of my enemies— the dropsy, and with the needs of a very active heart.

I realised yesterday, when Dr. Lishman had been and had rejoiced to find my brain so much brighter than when he punctured and felt the intellectual need of each stab for me, how[154] [. . .] my real deepest physical sorrow is the dropsy.

i Michael Field published the "famous sonnet" "Old Ivories" in their 1908 volume *Wild Honey from Various Thyme*, and "Atthis, my darling" in *Long Ago* (1889).

I was speaking to Josephine of Dr. Lishman's joy when suddenly I heard a sound like that of a dove that fights against choking corn. I had to realise it came from my throat and that other spasms were there to choke me, till I let their strange noises grind themselves out. But I do not think our dear Lord will let me drowse into death when it comes. I have been allowed to offer poppy to Him that I may keep my brain and will clear: He will remember and drive away habitude at the end.

My Love and I are growing closer and closer in spirit. She comes down every night in a fleece of silver-blue with twisted golden cord—strange softnesses of pain and charm on her face and coming from under her hair ... and she reads to me "Lord Clifford" and "Dion" and "The Affliction of Margaret" and "Ruth" and other wonderful, deathless gems Old Wordsworth wrought— or else Odes in which Keats dethrones every poet.

Sometimes she has read one of Thomas Hardy's stories in "A Changed Man"[i]—stories full of arresting genius in spite of their monotony[155] of inception and the reckless way he will drop circumstance into any nest like a cuckoo. One does not hear of God and fate is very dry—still the work is a master's.

It came to me to go back to our old library Mudie's—the Times Book Club is for young and strong. We are getting many books—a French book on Synge, Jackson's *Eighteen Nineties*[ii]—a mirror that shows nothing of us but a name four times repeated with others we don't assort with.

It is curious how angry Fay and Tommy are at the neglect of their position in the nineties. Oh, all little fishes, we've been used to this kind of suppression in our days. We have always seen the same treatment meted out to Fay and mostly to Tommy.[156]

EC Again, we pray we may love God with all our heart and mind. Sometimes we have to give that mind wholly to him—as we give Him the heart to do what he likes with. We must remember we don't give to dictate but to delight. The dry sacrament of thanksgiving precedes in this precious death the blood-

---

i A collection of stories Hardy published in 1913.

ii Mudie's Lending Library offered public access to works of fiction and nonfiction on a subscription basis between 1842 and the 1930s. The Times Book Club associated with Cole's Circulating Library offered access to books in the early decades of the twentieth century. The French book on the Irish playwright John Synge (1871–1909) was likely *John Millington Synge and the Irish Theatre* (1913) by Maurice Bourgeois. Holbrook Jackson's *The Eighteen Nineties: A Review of Art and Ideas at the Close of the Nineteenth Century* (1913) did indeed give short shift to Michael Field.

weaknesses + merely mortal atmosph
of dereliction that God Himself endured
+ when dying

+ Christmas. Eve. 1913.
        O Hennie, Hennie, but a little blue
nun has been with me in the Inner-room,
dressing a wound in my breast - Cancer.
O Hennie, my Blue Bird, my Beloved - &
this woe was shown to me in the octave
of Corpus Christi -
        I have been a bad nurse. this little
extra opening & have been able to make clean
for thee -
        two days after thou wentest - bleeding
came - God's quiet sign that I must
open my secret.
        But I write of Christmas Eve. Last
night-eve - I could not go to the Mid-night Mass
to-night I go alone - And is it my last midnight
Mass?
        They gave some adeste fideles - and the
Nativity Ode - then we loved best the hush
Of the Stars" bending our way their precious in
- fluence"
        To-night it is the line
    "When such music sweet
        their hearts terns disposed
    as never was by mortal finger toucht

    - Was it that hue exhalation of the senses
    in its disembodied thanks? does the
    smile trembling at the rapture
        Christ stuff Hennie in little blue

drenched[157] weaknesses and merely mortal strength of dereliction that God Himself endured when dying

Edith Cooper did not complete this sentence before her death on December 13, 1913.

KB *Christmas Eve 1913.*

O Hennie, Hennie, but a little blue nun has been with me in the river room dressing a wound in my breast cancer. O Hennie, my blue Bird, my Beloved—and this woe was shown to me in the octave of Corpus Christi—

I have been a bad nurse—this little extra offering I have been able to make clean for thee.

Two days after thou wert gone—bleeding came—God's quiet sign that I must open my secret.

But I write of Christmas Eve. Last night eve—I could not go to the Midnight Mass; tonight I go alone. And it is my last Midnight Mass!

She gave to me "Adeste Fidelis"—and the Nativity Ode—then we loved best the lines of the stars—"touching one with their precious influence."[158] [. . .]

My Beloved—Twelve months ago what a year of suffering was before her! And now she is her crisp, delicious, gay and gamesome Ariel spirit of old. I saw her like this the Sunday after she was punctured—[. . .]

O Verbum Dei—she is loved by thee new! Her confessor hopes believing, she is among the Angelic host tonight. My beloved, my beloved![159] [. . .]

And then, Hennie My Beloved, the kindles to all the beauty thou hast builded for us in Paragon—to thy flowers, the soft colouring, the charm.

The Blue nurse returns.

I order her tea in the Sun Room.

Her lips savour the names of our rooms—the Sun Room, the River Room, the Gold Room, the little Gold Room, and thus, though she is come to dress a deadly wound I have given her delight[.] [. . .] She has had a gay Christmas Day. [. . .]

My two black marks were with me at the Midnight Mass. And "Adeste Fidelis" was sung. O little Hennie, my most loved—I give myself in service to thee—to grow sweeter to thee, every day.[160]

KB *New Year's Eve.*

How incredible is life—

O little Henry how incredible! I have received the Painter's visit—Is it all a dream that through the years I was loved!

I feared to pain the Painter with the news of my malady. I thought he would mind. Gradually my eyes are being opened to the fact that people mind very little—It is strange and wonderful!

I have made ground with the Painter; he has got to see that of the two courses, silence concerning the dead, and being natural, and alluding to them naturally, the latter is best. [. . .]

In further talk he said the reason Henry and I did not always perfect agree was just this—*Aunt and Niece*.

O Painter!

I will not write more till the time.[161]

Eleven-thirty

I have been praying—praying the Verbum Dei[i] but I may sing glorious sunset songs, with her and for her, and to her. My great hope in God shall be that I may do this—

Henry, my beloved, I am with thee again, and beside thee in our work.

I cannot pray for thee, as thou wert a distant thing—thou dost not remain half thy time with me in Paragon, as Proserpine[ii] in hell, but half thy self—is restored to me and in secret Henry and Michael are one.

Sing with me, through me, O My Beloved!

I have the comfortable feeling of the mermaid tavern about thee, Henry. "Souls of poets dead and gone"—Beloved dwell in the Paragon, its gentle mistress and queen. Be again my little, sweet, fine Henry[iii]—be my Ariel.[iv]

Time is beating up towards another year. Hennie, it begins without thee, will it close without thee?

Lovely, make me loveable!

What of this new year? What will come to me? Incomparable blessings I feel sure.

Pray for me, my beloved. Draw very nigh me; so soon we shall both be dead. What action this[162] is—why fear I to become?

It will be the Bridegroom Year—His—altogether His.

Michael will become the Michael, as the emerald is emerald. There will be great joy!

I do not turn to kiss and embrace my beloved. She is close beside me,

---

i Praying the Word of God.

ii Proserpine, the Roman goddess of spring, was abducted to the underworld by Pluto. Though she escaped, she was forced to return to the underworld for half of each year. Her return each year caused spring to blossom; her departure caused winter.

iii From John Keats, "Lines on the Mermaid Tavern" (1820). Bradley imagines Cooper's soul communing with those of other writers who gathered at the Mermaid Tavern, near St. Paul's Cathedral, in the Elizabethan era.

iv Ariel, the magical spirit in Shakespeare's *Tempest* (1611), is bound to servitude to Prospero until Prospero frees him in the play's final act.

praying for me. The new year, or the fragment of it given me will be greatly blessed.[163] [...]

Friday even.

Henry, how my heart cries after thee—but in this book, I retrospect.

I write of 1913.

Well, loved, there was the kink in 1913—We did not hope. Beloved; there was not the nightingale at last.

Beloved, come back, sing over me, sing with me. Sing some of the marvelous songs with me.

Beloved.

End of 1913.[164]

Works and Days, 1914

KB *New Year's Day.*

But the charge, since I write from my rapture

"Queen Dawn shall find us on one bed."[i]

Henry! To work for thee, to defend thee, my one Love! to write with thee. O Verbum Dei.[165]

KB *Her Birthday Eve. Saturday, January 11th.*

O little Hennie, pray that tomorrow thou mayest give sign that we are together, longing, praying for, loving one another.

Little Hennie, to whom I have been so loveless—Oh Hennie that we had loved one another more![166]

KB *January 27th.* I have been preparing the Chow Book—Hennie's from M.S.—not my beautiful parchment—for mad-Pissarro. How we loved one another[167] then [...], the year before we entered the Catholic Church.

Out with thy tablets, truth: we have never loved each other since, as then—As she was dying she spoke to Fr. Barret of meeting him in heaven, and I hear she spoke to Jane wondrously—as Jennie deserved—of her gratitude to her nurse ... O little Hennie, how I have borne the utmost of pain! The priests, the Church's set words, the rocking infinitudes of life and death. Might we not have rocked awhile on them together?

How you loved me little Hennie in Chow! Break up the crusts! Show me how you love me now.

---

i From Michael Field's poem "Atthis, my darling."

We have loved so that all men have marveled, and yet—the Church sev-ered us.[168]

KB *Ash Wednesday* [. . .]

And now to the great task of giving up my will—giving the jewels to Painter, with him determining their last resting place and his costs—

And trying to reconcile myself to *Works and Days* being with Tommy. To the Verbum Dei, I commend it.

Faith, faith, faith![169]

KB *In conversation with Father Gray on Easter Monday.*

I open up my grief at the Church's action—first speaking of the Loved as among the Angels; then after a few weeks, in Purgatory.

I tell him how this has checked me—and use the simile of Henry landing in Australia—and engaging the kangaroos, and Henry still tossing on an un-known sea.

Michael, he says, you must accept this paradox. He always thinks of a dead friend as with God. The awful thing is for it to become possible to God to have His desire and be able to admit man into his presence. Father Gray makes me feel how awful God's task is.

Yes: what I feel about Henry's being gone—is *Aridity*: it happens.[i]

He commands me to be sure that whatever suffering is before me, suffi-cient grace will be with me to meet that suffering.[170]

KB *Yesterday, April 23rd.* Mrs. Pissarro with Chow things; and we drove into the glorious park. Today she will bring me the Chow cover—radiant, as his fur.[ii] [171]

KB I begin again—when? how?

August 25th

Incredible!

I begin again, writing in a Park Farm parlour, and my beloved Father Vincent is Prior of Hawkesyard, and the Pope is dead,[iii] and Europe seething in blood.

---

i   Bradley refers to her poem "Aridity" in *Mystic Trees*: the poet addresses her bereft soul, waiting quietly for word from the lost loved one.

ii   The "Chow cover" was a presentation box for *Whym Chow, Flame of Love*; it comprises the remarkable russet suede of the book's binding, absent its title tab. The box is now part of the Mark Samuels Lasner Collection at the University of Delaware.

iii   On August 20, 1914, Pope Pius X died, prompting a papal enclave that resulted in the election of Pope Benedict XV.

On August 5th England declared war.[i]

That night I returned from Liphook. There's a little book Chow bound, and next fills in some details between now and the operation.

It is my duty now to write in the big year book of the big events.[172]

KB Peace—no moment of it has yet been won.

The war news is that the advance of the Germans has been majestic and terrible. The Germans are close on Paris. Fr. Prior would not care if Paris were burned down like Moscow. He is confident of the ultimate issue.[173]

KB *Paragon Cottage. Thank God. September 18th.*

All night Sister Carmel says I lay smiling; this morning I was saved the cruel torture of being carried and tossed, wheeled into church, receiving the immense charity—though so much shamed of myself—I must offer the Mass in Thanksgiving.

And I am striving now to write a bit. The Fathers are in retreat which makes it so hard for me. They are merciful and charitable.

God take my offering.[174]

Katharine Harris Bradley died on September 26, 1914, six days after she wrote this final entry on the pages of "Works and Days." She spent her final days in "Paragon Cottage," in Hawkesyard Priory, Staffordshire, under the care of Father Vincent McNabb.

i The beginning of the Great War, which extended until November 11, 1918.

love God!

We have been here a month; & have greatly learnt & profited

I must be true to my little Ones to the end And I must be true to my own soul

Suppose God wishes me to leave all these Holy actual Dominicans, & to find my rest at Wincanton convent

St Theresa, I call on you to help. Oh my Beloved come & comfort me

My intercessors stand round & must bless me!

Paragon Cottage. Thank God. Sept 18th

All night Sister Carmel says I lay smiling this morning I was saved the cruel torture of being carried & tossed, wheeled into church, receiving the immense charity — though so much ashamed of myself — I must offer the Mass in thanksgiving. And I am striving now to write a bit. The Fathers are in retreat which makes it so hard for me. They are merciful & charitable

God take my offering!

PUBLISHED WORKS BY
KATHARINE BRADLEY AND EDITH COOPER

By Katharine Bradley as "Arran Leigh": *The New Minnesinger and Other Poems* (1875).
By Katharine Bradley and Edith Cooper as "Arran and Isla Leigh": *Bellerophôn* (1881).
By Katharine Bradley and Edith Cooper as "Michael Field":

Plays

Callirrhoë; and Fair Rosamund (1884)
The Father's Tragedy, William Rufus, and Loyalty or Love? (1885)
Brutus Ultor (1886)
Canute the Great: The Cup of Water (1887)
The Tragic Mary (1890)
Stephania: A Trialogue (1892)
A Question of Memory (1893)
Attila, My Attila! (1896)
Fair Rosamund (2nd ed., 1897)
The World at Auction (1898)
Anna Ruina (1899)
Noontide Branches: A Small Sylvan Drama Interspersed with Songs and Invocations (1899)
The Race of Leaves (1901)
Julia Domna (1903)

Poetry

Long Ago (1889)
Sight and Song (1892)
Underneath the Bough: A Book of Verses (1st ed., spring 1893; 2nd ed., autumn 1893; rev. ed., 1898)
Wild Honey from Various Thyme (1908)
Poems of Adoration (1912)
Mystic Trees (1913)
Whym Chow: Flame of Love (1914)

By Katharine Bradley and Edith Cooper, writing anonymously or as "the author of *Borgia*"

Borgia: A Period Play (1905)
Queen Mariamne (1908)
The Tragedy of Pardon and Diane (1911)
The Accuser, Tristan de Léonis, and A Messiah (1911)

Published posthumously

Dedicated: An Early Work of Michael Field (1914)
In the Name of Time (1919)
A Selection from the Poems of Michael Field, ed. T. Sturge Moore (1923)
The Wattlefold: Unpublished Poems, collected by Emily C. Fortey, preface by Vincent McNabb (1930)
Works and Days: From the Journal of Michael Field, edited by T. and D. C. Sturge Moore, preface by William Rothenstein (1933)

FURTHER READING

Bickle, Sharon, ed. *The Fowl and the Pussycat: Love Letters of Michael Field, 1876–1909*. Charlottesville: University of Virginia Press, 2008.

Bristow, Joseph. "Michael Field in Their Time and Ours." *Tulsa Studies in Women's Literature* 29, no. 1 (2010): 159–79.

Dellamora, Richard. *Masculine Desire: The Sexual Politics of Victorian Aestheticism*. Raleigh: University of North Carolina Press, 2011.

Denisoff, Dennis. *Decadent Ecology in British Literature and Art, 1860–1910*. Cambridge: Cambridge University Press, 2021.

Dever, Carolyn. *Chains of Love and Beauty: The Diary of Michael Field*. Princeton, NJ: Princeton University Press, 2022.

Donoghue, Emma. *We Are Michael Field*. Bath: Absolute Press, 1998.

Dytor, Frankie. "'The Eyes of an Intellectual Vampire': Michael Field, Vernon Lee and Female Masculinities in Late-Victorian Aestheticism." *Journal of Victorian Culture* 26 (2021): 582–95.

Ehnenn, Jill R. *Michael Field's Literary Poetics*. Edinburgh: Edinburgh University Press, 2023.

———. *Women's Literary Collaboration, Queerness, and Late-Victorian Culture*. Aldershot: Ashgate, 2008.

Evangelista, Stefano. *British Aestheticism and Ancient Greece: Hellenism, Reception, Gods in Exile*. Basingstoke: Palgrave Macmillan, 2009.

Fraser, Hilary. *Women Writing Art History in the Nineteenth Century: Looking Like a Woman*. Cambridge: Cambridge University Press, 2014.

Friedman, Dustin. *Before Queer Theory: Victorian Aestheticism and the Self*. Baltimore: Johns Hopkins University Press, 2019.

Huseby, Amy Kahrmann. "Queer Social Counting and the Generational Transitions of Michael Field." *Women's Writing* 26, no. 2 (Spring 2019): 199–213.

Laird, Holly. *Women Coauthors*. Urbana: University of Illinois Press, 2000.

Locard, Henri. "*Works and Days*: The Journals of 'Michael Field.'" *Journal of the Eighteen-Nineties Society* 10 (1979): 1–9.

Mahoney, Kristin. "Michael Field and Queer Community at the Fin de Siècle." *Victorian Review* 41 (2015): 35–40.

Marcus, Sharon. *Between Women: Friendship, Desire, and Marriage in Victorian England*. Princeton, NJ: Princeton University Press, 2007.

Maxwell, Catherine. *Scents and Sensibility: Perfume in Victorian Literary Culture*. Oxford: Oxford University Press, 2017.

Murray, Alex, and Sarah Parker, eds. *Michael Field: "For That Moment Only" and Other Prose Works*. Cambridge: Modern Humanities Research Council, 2022.

Parker, Sarah. *The Lesbian Muse and Poetic Identity, 1889–1930*. London: Pickering and Chatto, 2013.

Parker, Sarah, and Ana Parejo Vadillo, eds. *Michael Field: Decadent Moderns*. Athens: Ohio University Press, 2019.

Prins, Yopie. *Victorian Sappho*. Princeton, NJ: Princeton University Press, 1999.

Richardson, LeeAnne M. *The Forms of Michael Field*. Basingstoke: Palgrave Macmillan, 2002.

Roden, Frederick S. *Same-Sex Desire in Victorian Religious Culture*. Basingstoke: Palgrave Macmillan, 2002.

Stetz, Margaret D., and Cheryl A. Wilson, eds. *Michael Field and Their World*. High Wycombe: Rivendale Press, 2007.

Sturge Moore, Thomas, and D. C. Sturge Moore, eds. *Works and Days: From the Journal of Michael Field*. London: Murray, 1933.

Sturgeon, Mary. *Michael Field*. London: Harrap, 1922.

Thain, Marion. *"Michael Field": Poetry, Aestheticism and the Fin de Siècle*. Cambridge: Cambridge University Press, 2007.

Thain, Marion, and Ana Parejo Vadillo. *Michael Field, the Poet: Published and Manuscript Materials*. Peterborough, Ontario: Broadview Press, 2009.

Thomas, Kate. "'What Time We Kiss': Michael Field's Queer Temporalities." *GLQ: A Journal of Lesbian and Gay Studies* 13 (2007): 327–51.

Trebor, Ivor C. *Binary Star: Leaves from the Journal and Letters of Michael Field, 1846–1914*. London: De Blackland Press, 2006.

———. *The Michael Field Catalogue*. London: De Blackland Press, 1998.

Vadillo, Ana Parejo. *Women Poets and Urban Aestheticism: Passengers of Modernity*. Basingstoke: Palgrave Macmillan, 2005.

Vanita, Ruth. *Sappho and the Virgin Mary: Same-Sex Love and the English Literary Imagination*. New York: Columbia University Press, 1996.

Vicinus, Martha. *Intimate Friends: Women Who Loved Women, 1778–1928*. Chicago: University of Chicago Press, 2004.

White, Chris. "Flesh and Roses: Michael Field's Metaphors of Pleasure and Desire." *Women's Writing* 3 (1996): 47–62.

———. "'Poets and Lovers Evermore': Interpreting Female Love in the Poetry and Journals of Michael Field." *Textual Practice* 4 (1990): 197–212.

The following endnotes provide citations by year, page, and author for passages from *Works and Days* quoted in this volume.

1. Prehistory: The 1860s Diaries

1. 1867–68, 3v, KB.
2. 1867–68, 4r, KB.
3. 1867–68, 5v, KB.
4. 1867–68, 6r, KB.
5. 1867–68, 11r, KB.
6. 1867–68, 11v, KB.
7. 1867–68, 12r, KB.
8. 1867–68, 13v, KB.
9. 1867–68, 14r, KB.
10. 1867–68, 16v, KB.
11. 1867–68, 17r, KB.
12. 1867–68, 17v, KB.
13. 1867–68, 18r, KB.
14. 1867–68, 19v, KB.
15. 1867–69, 26r, KB.
16. 1867–68, 31v, KB.
17. 1867–68, 40r, KB.
18. 1867–68, 40v, KB.
19. 1867–68, 47v, KB.
20. 1867–68, 48r, KB.
21. 1867–68, 53r, KB.
22. 1867–68, 71v, KB.
23. 1867–68, 78v, KB.
24. 1867–68, 80r, KB.
25. 1867–68, 80v, KB.
26. 1867–68, 84r, KB.
27. 1867–68, 84v, KB.
28. 1867–68, 85r, KB.
29. 1867–68, 89r, KB.
30. 1867–68, 89v, KB.
31. 1867–68, 90r, KB.
32. 1867–68, 93r, KB.
33. 1867–68, 94r, KB.
34. 1868–69, 4r, KB.
35. 1868–69, 18r, KB.
36. 1868–69, 18v, KB.
37. 1868–69, 21r, KB.
38. 1868–69, 21v, KB.
39. 1868–69, 22r, KB.
40. 1868–69, 22v, KB.
41. 1868–69, 23r, KB.
42. 1868–69, 23v, KB.
43. 1868–69, 24r, KB.
44. 1868–69, 24v, KB.
45. 1868–69, 25r, KB.
46. 1868–69, 25v, KB.
47. 1868–69, 35r, KB.
48. 1868–69, 47v, KB.
49. 1868–69, 48r, KB.

2. Ambition and Desire: 1888–93

1. 1888–89, 1r, KB.
2. 1888–89, 3r, KB.
3. 1888–89, 4r, KB.
4. 1888–89, 5r, KB.
5. 1888–89, 6v, EC.
6. 1888–89, 8v, EC.
7. 1888–89, 13r, KB.
8. 1888–89, 40r, EC.
9. 1888–89, 41r, EC.
10. 1888–89, 59r, KB.
11. 1888–89, 59v, KB.
12. 1888–89, 64r, KB.
13. 1888–89, 65r, KB.
14. 1888–89, 66r, KB.
15. 1888–89, 67r, KB.
16. 1888–89, 67v, EC.
17. 1888–89, 70r, KB.
18. 1888–89, 73r, EC.
19. 1888–89, 73v, EC.
20. 1888–89, 74r, EC.
21. 1888–89, 74v, EC.
22. 1888–89, 74v, EC.
23. 1888–89, 75r, EC.
24. 1888–89, 77v, EC.

25. 1888–89, 80r, KB.
26. 1888–89, 85r, KB.
27. 1888–89, 86r, KB.
28. 1888–89, 90v, KB.
29. 1888–89, 92r, EC.
30. 1888–89, 92v, EC.
31. 1888–89, 93v, EC.
32. 1888–89, 97r, EC.
33. 1888–89, 97v, EC.
34. 1888–89, 98r, EC.
35. 1888–89, 98v, EC; EC, transcription of KB letter.
36. 1888–89, 99r, EC.
37. 1888–89, 99v, EC.
38. 1888–89, 101v, EC.
39. 1888–89, 102r, EC.
40. 1888–89, 102v, EC.
41. 1888–89, 103v, EC.
42. 1888–89, 104r, EC.
43. 1888–89, 113r, EC.
44. 1888–89, 119r, EC.
45. 1888–89, 120v, EC.
46. 1888–89, 121r, EC.
47. 1888–89, 121v, KB, EC.
48. 1888–89, 122r, EC.
49. 1888–89, 124v, KB.
50. 1890, 1r, EC.
51. 1890, 1v, EC.
52. 1890, 2r, EC.
53. 1890, 2v, EC.
54. 1890, 3r, EC.
55. 1890, 3v, EC.
56. 1890, 4r, EC.
57. 1890, 11r, EC.
58. 1890, 18r, EC.
59. 1890, 18v, EC.
60. 1890, 19v, EC.
61. 1890, 25v, EC.
62. 1890, 26r, EC.
63. 1890, 26v, EC.
64. 1890, 32v, EC.
65. 1890, 35r, EC.
66. 1890, 35v, EC.
67. 1890, 44v, KB.
68. 1890, 94r, KB.
69. 1890, 95r, KB.
70. 1890, 96r, KB.
71. 1890, 97r, KB.
72. 1890, 98r, KB.
73. 1890, 102v, EC.
74. 1890, 103r, EC.
75. 1890, 103v, EC.

76. 1890, 104v, KB, transcribing Johnson review.
77. 1890, 105r, KB, transcribing Johnson review; EC.
78. 1890, 105v, EC.
79. 1890, 106r, EC.
80. 1890, 109r, EC.
81. 1890, 126r, KB, EC.
82. 1891, 19r, KB.
83. 1891, 19v, KB.
84. 1891, 24r, KB, EC.
85. 1891, 29r, KB.
86. 1891, 42r, EC.
87. 1891, 42v, EC.
88. 1891, 43r, EC.
89. 1891, 43v, EC.
90. 1891, 47r, EC.
91. 1891, 47v, EC.
92. 1891, 53r, EC.
93. 1891, 54r, EC.
94. 1891, 54v, EC.
95. 1891, 58v, EC.
96. 1891, 59r, EC.
97. 1891, 65v, EC.
98. 1891, 66r, EC.
99. 1891, 67v, EC.
100. 1891, 89v, EC.
101. 1891, 90r, EC.
102. 1891, 90v, EC.
103. 1891, 91r, EC.
104. 1891, 91v, EC.
105. 1891, 92v, EC.
106. 1891, 93r, EC.
107. 1891, 93v, EC.
108. 1891, 94r, EC.
109. 1891, 94v, EC.
110. 1891, 95r, EC.
111. 1891, 95v, EC.
112. 1891, 96r, EC, attributed to KB.
113. 1891, 96v, EC, attributed to KB.
114. 1891, 97r, EC.
115. 1891, 97v, EC.
116. 1891, 98r, EC, attributed to KB.
117. 1891, 98v, EC.
118. 1891, 99r, EC.
119. 1891, 105v, EC, attributed to KB; EC.
120. 1891, 106r, EC, attributed to KB; EC.

121. 1891, 106v, EC, attributed to KB.
122. 1891, 107v, EC, attributed to KB.
123. 1891, 108r, EC, attributed to KB.
124. 1891, 108v, EC, attributed to KB, and EC, as dictated to KB and transcribed by EC.
125. 1891, 109r, EC.
126. 1891, 109v, EC.
127. 1891, 111v, EC.
128. 1891, 112r, EC.
129. 1891, 113r, EC.
130. 1891, 113v, EC.
131. 1891, 114r, EC.
132. 1891, 114v, EC.
133. 1891, 128r, EC.
134. 1891, 142v, EC.
135. 1891, 143r, EC.
136. 1891, 146r, EC.
137. 1891, 161v, EC.
138. 1892, 12r, EC.
139. 1892, 12v, EC.
140. 1892, 13r, EC.
141. 1892, 30r, EC.
142. 1892, 45r, EC.
143. 1892, 46r, EC.
144. 1892, 49v, EC.
145. 1892, 53r, EC.
146. 1892, 58v, EC.
147. 1892, 59v, EC.
148. 1892, 60r, EC; KB letter transcribed by EC.
149. 1892, 60v, EC; KB letter transcribed by EC.
150. 1892, 60v, EC.
151. 1892, 62v, EC.
152. 1892, 66r, KB.
153. 1892, 68r, EC.
154. 1892, 68v, EC.
155. 1892, 71r, KB.
156. 1892, 75v, EC.
157. 1892, 76r, EC.
158. 1892, 76v, EC.
159. 1892, 77r, EC.
160. 1892, 77v, EC.
161. 1892, 78v, EC.
162. 1892, 79r, EC.
163. 1892, 81r, EC.
164. 1892, 81v, EC.
165. 1892, 82v, EC.

166. 1892, 86r, EC.
167. 1892, 86v, EC.
168. 1892, 87r, EC.
169. 1892, 89r, EC.
170. 1892, 89v, EC.
171. 1892, 90v, KB.
172. 1892, 97v, EC.
173. 1892, 98r, EC.
174. 1892, 99v, EC.
175. 1892, 105v, EC, attributed to KB.
176. 1892, 106r, EC.
177. 1892, 106v, EC.
178. 1892, 107v, EC.
179. 1892, 108r, EC.
180. 1892, 108v, EC.
181. 1892, 110r, EC.
182. 1892, 110v, EC.
183. 1892, 111r, EC.
184. 1892, 111v, EC.
185. 1892, 112r, EC.
186. 1892, 112v, EC.
187. 1892, 113r, EC.
188. 1892, 114v, EC.
189. 1892, 115r, EC.
190. 1892, 115v, EC.
191. 1892, 116r, EC.
192. 1892, 116v, EC.
193. 1892, 117r, EC.
194. 1892, 118r, EC.
195. 1892, 120r, EC.
196. 1892, 120v, EC.
197. 1892, 121v, EC.
198. 1892, 122r, EC.

199. 1892, 122v, EC.
200. 1892, 123r, EC.
201. 1892, 123v, EC.
202. 1892, 124v, EC.
203. 1892, 124v, EC.
204. 1892, 126r, EC.
205. 1892, 126v, EC.
206. 1892, 127v, EC.
207. 1892, 129v, EC.
208. 1892, 130r, EC.
209. 1892, 130v, EC.
210. 1892, 131r, EC.
211. 1892, 132r, KB.
212. 1892, 134r, KB, EC.
213. 1892, 135v, KB.
214. 1892, 136r, KB.
215. 1892, 136v, KB.
216. 1892, 139r, KB.
217. 1892, 139v, KB.
218. 1892, 140r, KB.
219. 1892, 141r, KB.
220. 1892, 156r, EC.
221. 1892, 157r, EC.
222. 1893, 3r, EC.
223. 1893, 6r, EC.
224. 1893, 7r, EC.
225. 1893, 12r, EC.
226. 1893, 12v, EC.
227. 1893, 18r, EC.
228. 1893, 19r, EC.
229. 1893, 19v, EC.
230. 1893, 20r, EC.
231. 1893, 20v, EC.
232. 1893, 21r, EC.

233. 1893, 45v, KB.
234. 1893, 47v, KB .
235. 1893, 49v, KB.
236. 1893, 53r, EC, KB.
237. 1893, 53v, KB.
238. 1893, 54v, KB.
239. 1893, 55r, EC.
240. 1893, 55v, KB.
241. 1893, 73r, KB.
242. 1893, 74r, EC.
243. 1893, 74v, EC.
244. 1893, 79v, EC.
245. 1893, 80r, EC.
246. 1893, 84r, EC.
247. 1893, 86v, EC.
248. 1893, 87r, EC.
249. 1893, 87v, EC.
250. 1893, 88r, EC.
251. 1893, 88v, EC.
252. 1893, 89r, EC.
253. 1893, 89v, EC.
254. 1893, 90r, EC.
255. 1893, 90v, EC.
256. 1893, 91r, EC.
257. 1893, 91v, EC.
258. 1893, 92v, EC.
259. 1893, 95r, EC, clipping.
260. 1893, 99v, EC.
261. 1893, 100r, EC.
262. 1893, 103r, EC.
263. 1893, 103v, EC.
264. 1893, 104r, EC.
265. 1893, 104v, EC.
266. 1893, 105r, EC.

3. Domestic Negotiations: 1894–99

1. 1894, 3r, KB.
2. 1894, 3v, KB.
3. 1894, 4r, KB.
4. 1894, 9r, EC.
5. 1894, 9v, EC.
6. 1894, 10r, EC.
7. 1894, 11r, EC.
8. 1894, 23v, EC.
9. 1894, 24v, EC.
10. 1894, 37v, EC, KB, EC.
11. 1894, 38r, EC.
12. 1894, 44v, EC.
13. 1894, 45v, EC.
14. 1894, 46r, EC.

15. 1894, 47r, EC.
16. 1894, 50r, EC.
17. 1894, 61r, EC.
18. 1894, 73v, EC.
19. 1894, 74r, EC.
20. 1894, 74v, EC.
21. 1894, 75r, EC.
22. 1894, 77r, EC.
23. 1894, 77v, EC.
24. 1894, 79v, EC.
25. 1894, 80r, EC.
26. 1894, 81r, EC.
27. 1894, 82r, EC.
28. 1894, 90v, EC.
29. 1894, 94r, EC.

30. 1894, 94v, EC, attributed to KB.
31. 1894, 106r, EC.
32. 1894, 121v, EC.
33. 1894, 133r, KB.
34. 1894, 143v, EC.
35. 1895, vol. 1, 4r, KB.
36. 1895, vol. 1, 4v, KB.
37. 1895, vol. 1, 6v, EC.
38. 1895, vol. 1, 10v, EC.
39. 1895, vol. 1, 12v, EC.
40. 1895, vol. 1, 13r, EC.
41. 1895, vol. 1, 13v, EC.
42. 1895, vol. 1, 14v, EC.
43. 1895, vol. 1, 15r, EC.

44. 1895, vol. 1, 47r, EC.
45. 1895, vol. 1, 47v, EC.
46. 1895, vol. 1, 48r, EC.
47. 1895, vol. 1, 52r, EC.
48. 1895, vol. 1, 57v, EC.
49. 1895, vol. 1, 58r, EC.
50. 1895, vol. 1, 61r, EC.
51. 1895, vol. 1, 62v, EC.
52. 1895, vol. 1, 63v, EC.
53. 1895, vol. 1, 63v, EC.
54. 1895, vol. 1, 65v, EC.
55. 1895, vol. 1, 66r, EC.
56. 1895, vol. 1, 67r, EC.
57. 1895, vol. 1, 67v, EC.
58. 1895, vol. 1, 68r, EC.
59. 1895, vol. 1, 78v, EC.
60. 1895, vol. 1, 82r, EC.
61. 1895, vol. 1, 111r, KB.
62. 1895, vol. 1, 151r, EC.
63. 1895, vol. 1, 168r, EC.
64. 1895, vol. 2, 4r, EC.
65. 1895, vol. 2, 7r, EC.
66. 1895, vol. 2, 20r, EC.
67. 1895, vol. 2, 20v, EC.
68. 1895, vol. 2, 21r, EC.
69. 1895, vol. 2, 21v, EC.
70. 1895, vol. 2, 22v, KB.
71. 1895, vol. 2, 24v, EC.
72. 1895, vol. 2, 25r, EC.
73. 1895, vol. 2, 26v, KB.
74. 1895, vol. 2, 28r, EC.
75. 1895, vol. 2, 37r, EC.
76. 1895, vol. 2, 37v, EC.
77. 1895, vol. 2, 38v, EC.
78. 1895, vol. 2, 54r, EC.
79. 1895, vol. 2, 54v, EC.
80. 1896, 10r, EC.
81. 1896, 10v, EC.
82. 1896, 18r, EC.
83. 1896, 19v, EC.
84. 1896, 20r, EC.
85. 1896, 23r, EC.
86. 1896, 23v, EC.
87. 1896, 25r, EC.
88. 1896, 45v, EC.
89. 1896, 48v, EC.
90. 1896, 50v, EC.
91. 1896, 54v, EC.
92. 1896, 87v, KB.
93. 1896, 90v, EC.
94. 1896, 91r, EC.
95. 1896, 99v, EC.
96. 1896, 196v, EC.
97. 1896, 197r, EC.
98. 1897, 3v, EC.
99. 1897, 4r, EC.
100. 1897, 5v, KB.
101. 1897, 7r, KB.
102. 1897, 21r, EC.
103. 1897, 22r, EC.
104. 1897, 76r, EC, attributed to KB.
105. 1897, 76v, EC, attributed to KB.
106. 1897, 77r, KB, attributed to EC; EC.
107. 1897, 78v, EC.
108. 1897, 79r, EC.
109. 1897, 82v, KB.
110. 1897, 83v, EC.
111. 1897, 84r, EC.
112. 1897, 84v, EC.
113. 1897, 85r, EC.
114. 1897, 87r, EC.
115. 1897, 87v, EC.
116. 1897, 88r, EC.
117. 1897, 96r, EC.
118. 1897, 96v, EC.
119. 1897, 97r, EC.
120. 1897, 99r, EC.
121. 1897, 105v, EC.
122. 1897, 130v, KB, clippings.
123. 1897, 131v, KB, clippings.
124. 1897, 133r, KB.
125. 1897, 135r, EC.
126. 1897, 135v, EC.
127. 1897, 137r, EC.
128. 1897, 137v, EC.
129. 1897, 138v, EC.
130. 1897, 140v, EC.
131. 1897, 145v, EC.
132. 1897, 159r, EC.
133. 1897, 159v, EC.
134. 1897, 161r, KB.
135. 1897, 164r, EC.
136. 1897, 164v, EC.
137. 1897, 165r, EC.
138. 1897, 165v, EC.
139. 1898, 8v, KB.
140. 1898, 11r, KB.
141. 1898, 11v, KB.
142. 1898, 12r, KB.
143. 1898, 12v, KB.
144. 1898, 14v, EC.
145. 1898, 15r, EC.
146. 1898, 15v, EC.
147. 1898, 16r, EC.
148. 1898, 16v, EC.
149. 1898, 17r, EC.
150. 1898, 18r, EC.
151. 1898, 18v, EC.
152. 1898, 19r, EC.
153. 1898, 21r, EC.
154. 1898, 25v, EC.
155. 1898, 26r, EC.
156. 1898, 29r, KB.
157. 1898, 29v, KB.
158. 1898, 34v, KB.
159. 1898, 39v, EC.
160. 1898, 64r, EC.
161. 1898, 92v, EC.
162. 1898, 93r, EC.
163. 1898, 97v, EC.
164. 1898, 98r, EC.
165. 1898, 100v, EC.
166. 1898, 101r, EC.
167. 1898, 127r, EC.
168. 1898, 130r, EC.
169. 1898, 130v, EC.
170. 1898, 131r, EC.
171. 1898, 136v, EC.
172. 1898, 137v, EC.
173. 1898, 138r, EC, KB.
174. 1898, 138v, EC.
175. 1898, 139r, KB.
176. 1898, 141v, EC.
177. 1898, 142r, EC.
178. 1898, 142v, EC.
179. 1899, 3r, EC.
180. 1899, 3v, EC.
181. 1899, 4v, KB, EC; EC, transcription of letter from Ricketts.
182. 1899, 5r, EC, transcription of letter from Ricketts.
183. 1899, 6v, KB.
184. 1899, 11r, KB.
185. 1899, 13r, EC.
186. 1899, 13v, KB.
187. 1899, 14r, KB; EC, transcription of letter from Shannon.
188. 1899, 14r, EC, transcription of letter from Shannon.
189. 1899, 15r, EC,

transcription of letter
from Shannon.
190. 1899, 16r, EC.
191. 1899, 16v, EC.
192. 1899, 17r, EC.
193. 1899, 17v, EC.
194. 1899, 19r, EC.
195. 1899, 19v, EC.
196. 1899, 23r, EC.
197. 1899, 23v, EC.
198. 1899, 28r, KB.
199. 1899, 28v, EC.
200. 1899, 29r, EC.
201. 1899, 29v, EC; EC,
transcription of letter
from Shannon.
202. 1899, 35r, EC.
203. 1899, 35v, EC,
transcription of letter
from Ricketts.
204. 1899, 36r, EC,
transcription of letter
from Ricketts.
205. 1899, 36v, EC; EC,
transcription of letter
from Shannon; EC.

206. 1899, 43v, EC.
207. 1899, 44r, EC.
208. 1899, 44v, EC.
209. 1899, 45r, EC.
210. 1899, 45v, EC.
211. 1899, 49r, EC.
212. 1899, 49v, EC.
213. 1899, 50r, EC.
214. 1899, 50v, EC.
215. 1899, 51r, EC.
216. 1899, 55v, EC.
217. 1899, 58r, EC.
218. 1899, 58v, EC.
219. 1899, 59r, EC.
220. 1899, 59v, EC.
221. 1899, 60r, EC.
222. 1899, 60v, EC.
223. 1899, 61r, EC.
224. 1899, 70r, EC.
225. 1899, 70v, KB.
226. 1899, 71r, KB.
227. 1899, 71v, EC.
228. 1899, 76v, EC.
229. 1899, 79r, EC.
230. 1899, 79v, EC.

231. 1899, 80r, EC.
232. 1899, 80v, EC.
233. 1899, 81v, EC.
234. 1899, 82r, EC.
235. 1899, 82v, EC.
236. 1899, 83r, EC.
237. 1899, 89v, EC.
238. 1899, 96v, EC.
239. 1899, 101r, EC.
240. 1899, 104r, KB.
241. 1899, 106v, EC.
242. 1899, 107r, EC.
243. 1899, 107v, EC.
244. 1899, 109r, KB.
245. 1899, 130r, KB.
246. 1899, 139r, EC.
247. 1899, 141r, EC.
248. 1899, 141v, EC.
249. 1899, 142r, EC.
250. 1899, 142v, EC.
251. 1899, 143r, EC.
252. 1899, 144r, EC.
253. 1899, 144v, EC.
254. 1899, 145r, EC.
255. 1899, 145v, EC.

4. Crash: 1900–1907

1. 1900, 6r, EC; EC
transcribing letter from
KB; EC.
2. 1900, 6v, EC.
3. 1900, 7r, EC.
4. 1900, 7v, EC.
5. 1900, 9r, EC.
6. 1900, 9v, EC.
7. 1900, 10r, EC.
8. 1900, 10v, KB.
9. 1900, 11r, KB.
10. 1900, 46r, EC,
recounted from KB.
11. 1900, 47r, EC.
12. 1900, 57v, EC.
13. 1900, 58r, EC.
14. 1900, 60r, KB.
15. 1900, 69r, KB.
16. 1900, 74r, EC.
17. 1900, 89v, EC.
18. 1900, 90r, EC.
19. 1900, 92r, EC.
20. 1900, 112v, KB, EC.

21. 1900, 113r, EC.
22. 1900, 134r, KB.
23. 1900, 148r, EC.
24. 1900, 148v, EC.
25. 1900, 152v, EC.
26. 1900, 162r, EC.
27. 1900, 162v, EC.
28. 1900, 163r, EC,
recounted from KB.
29. 1900, 163v, EC.
30. 1900, 165r, EC.
31. 1900, 165v, EC.
32. 1900, 166r, EC.
33. 1900, 166v, EC.
34. 1900, 167r, EC.
35. 1900, 167v, EC.
36. 1900, 180v, EC.
37. 1900, 183r, EC.
38. 1900, 183v, EC.
39. 1900, 184r, EC.
40. 1900, 185r, EC.
41. 1901, 4v, EC.
42. 1901, 5r, EC.

43. 1901, 5v, EC.
44. 1901, 17r, KB.
45. 1901, 17v, KB.
46. 1901, 19r, EC.
47. 1901, 22r, EC.
48. 1901, 45v, KB.
49. 1901, 46r, KB.
50. 1901, 46v, EC.
51. 1901, 46r, EC.
52. 1901, 84r, EC.
53. 1901, 84v, EC.
54. 1901, 85r, EC.
55. 1901, 85v, EC.
56. 1901, 86r, EC.
57. 1901, 86v, EC.
58. 1901, 87r, EC.
59. 1901, 87v, EC.
60. 1901, 88r, EC.
61. 1901, 88v, EC.
62. 1902, 4v, EC.
63. 1902, 7v, KB.
64. 1902, 8v, EC.
65. 1902, 9r, EC.

66. 1902, 21v, KB.
67. 1902, 43v, EC.
68. 1902, 44r, EC.
69. 1902, 54v, EC.
70. 1902, 84v, EC.
71. 1902, 85r, EC.
72. 1902, 85v, EC.
73. 1902, 86r, EC.
74. 1902, 89v, EC.
75. 1902, 90r, EC.
76. 1902, 139v, EC.
77. 1902, 140r, EC.
78. 1902, 147v, EC.
79. 1902, 148r, EC.
80. 1902, 148v, EC.
81. 1902, 149r, EC.
82. 1902, 150v, EC.
83. 1902, 151r, EC.
84. 1902, 155v, EC.
85. 1902, 156r, KB.
86. 1902, 156v, KB.
87. 1902, 158r, KB.
88. 1902, 173r, KB.
89. 1902, 188v, EC.
90. 1902, 189r, EC.
91. 1902, 190r, EC.
92. 1903, 20r, EC.
93. 1903, 20v, EC.
94. 1903, 21r, EC.
95. 1903, 21v, EC.
96. 1903, 22v, KB.
97. 1903, 27v, EC.
98. 1903, 52r, EC.
99. 1903, 52v, EC.
100. 1903, 53r, EC.
101. 1903, 60r, KB.
102. 1903, 63r, EC.
103. 1903, 65r, EC.
104. 1903, 65v, EC.
105. 1903, 68v, EC.
106. 1903, 71r, KB; KB, transcribing letter from Yeats.
107. 1903, 87r, EC.
108. 1903, 88v, EC.
109. 1903, 91r, EC.
110. 1903, 91v, EC.
111. 1903, 92r, EC; EC, transcribing letter from Yeats.
112. 1903, 92v, EC; EC, transcribing letter from Yeats; EC,

transcribing KB letter to Yeats.
113. 1903, 93r, KB.
114. 1903, 108v, EC.
115. 1903, 109r, EC.
116. 1903, 110r, EC.
117. 1903, 110v, EC.
118. 1903, 111r, EC.
119. 1903, 111v, EC.
120. 1903, 114v, EC.
121. 1903, 115r, EC.
122. 1903, 120v, EC.
123. 1903, 121r, EC.
124. 1903, 121v, EC.
125. 1903, 130v, EC.
126. 1903, 131r, EC.
127. 1903, 136r, EC.
128. 1903, 136v, EC.
129. 1903, 137r, EC.
130. 1903, 138r, EC.
131. 1903, 166v, EC.
132. 1903, 167r, EC.
133. 1903, 167v, EC.
134. 1903, 172v, EC.
135. 1903, 185v, EC.
136. 1903, 186r, EC.
137. 1903, 186v, EC.
138. 1903, 199v, EC.
139. 1903, 200r, EC.
140. 1903, 213v, KB, EC.
141. 1903, 214r, EC.
142. 1904, 4r, KB.
143. 1904, 9r, EC.
144. 1904, 24r, EC.
145. 1904, 28r, EC.
146. 1904, 29v, EC.
147. 1904, 60v, KB.
148. 1904, 61r, KB.
149. 1904, 67r, KB.
150. 1904, 67v, EC.
151. 1904, 93v, EC.
152. 1904, 94r, EC; EC, transcription of KB letter.
153. 1904, 104r, EC.
154. 1904, 143r, KB.
155. 1904, 146r, EC.
156. 1904, 183v, EC.
157. 1904, 184r, EC.
158. 1905, 8r, KB.
159. 1905, 11v, EC.
160. 1905, 12r, EC.
161. 1905, 17v, EC.

162. 1905, 28r, EC.
163. 1905, 30v, EC.
164. 1905, 31r, EC.
165. 1905, 32v, EC.
166. 1905, 33v, EC; EC. transcription of letter from Ricketts to Bradley.
167. 1905, 41v, KB, transcription of her own letter to Tommy Sturge Moore.
168. 1905, 57v, EC.
169. 1905, 92r, EC.
170. 1905, 108v, EC.
171. 1905, 111r, KB, EC.
172. 1905, 111v, EC.
173. 1905, 116v, EC.
174. 1905, 117r, EC.
175. 1905, 120r, KB.
176. 1905, 120v, KB.
177. 1905, 122v, KB.
178. 1905, 123r, KB.
179. 1905, 124v, KB.
180. 1905, 125r, KB.
181. 1905, 125v, KB.
182. 1905, 126r, KB.
183. 1905, 127r, KB.
184. 1905, 146v, EC.
185. 1905, 147r, EC.
186. 1905, 149r, EC.
187. 1905, 150r, EC.
188. 1906, 4v, EC.
189. 1906, 5r, EC.
190. 1906, 8v, EC.
191. 1906, 9v, EC.
192. 1906, 10v, EC.
193. 1906, 14v, KB, EC.
194. 1906, 15r, EC.
195. 1906, 15v, EC.
196. 1906, 16r, EC.
197. 1906, 16v, KB.
198. 1906, 17r, EC.
199. 1906, 17v, EC.
200. 1906, 18r, EC.
201. 1906, 18v, EC.
202. 1906, 19r, EC.
203. 1906, 19v, EC.
204. 1906, 20r, EC.
205. 1906, 20v, EC.
206. 1906, 21r, EC.
207. 1906, 21v, EC.
208. 1906, 22r, EC.

209. 1906, 22v, EC.
210. 1906, 24r, EC.
211. 1906, 25v, EC.
212. 1906, 26r, EC, transcription of KB letter.
213. 1906, 35r, EC.
214. 1906, 37v, EC.
215. 1906, 38r, EC.
216. 1906, 38v, KB.
217. 1906, 39r, EC.
218. 1906, 41v, KB.
219. 1906, 42r, KB.
220. 1906, 46v, EC.
221. 1906, 47r, EC.
222. 1906, 50r, EC.
223. 1906, 50v, EC.
224. 1906, 52r, EC.
225. 1906, 52v, EC.
226. 1906, 54v, EC.
227. 1906, 59r, EC.
228. 1906, 57r, EC, transcription of KB letter.
229. 1906, 59v, EC.
230. 1906, 61v, EC.
231. 1906, 90v, KB.
232. 1906, 100r, KB.

233. 1906, 111r, EC.
234. 1906, 126r, EC.
235. 1906, 148v, EC.
236. 1906, 154v, EC.
237. 1906, 168v, KB.
238. 1906, 195v, EC
239. 1906, 196r, EC.
240. 1906, 202r, EC.
241. 1906, 218v, EC.
242. 1906, 233v, EC.
243. 1906, 234v, EC.
244. 1906, 235r, KB.
245. 1906, 235v, EC.
246. 1906, 236r, EC.
247. 1906, 236v, EC.
248. 1906, 237v, EC.
249. 1906, 238r, EC.
250. 1907, vol. 1, 8v, EC.
251. 1907, vol. 1, 10r, EC.
252. 1907, vol. 1, 10v, EC.
253. 1907, vol. 1, 28r, EC.
254. 1907, vol. 1, 58v, EC.
255. 1907, vol. 1, 59r, EC.
256. 1907, vol. 1, 63r, EC.
257. 1907, vol. 1, 63v, EC.
258. 1907, vol. 1, 80v, EC.
259. 1907, vol. 1, 90r, EC.
260. 1907, vol. 1, 90v, EC.

261. 1907, vol. 1, 100v, EC, transcribing a letter from KB to Amy Ryan; "Hardy is vile" interpolation is by Fr. Gray.
262. 1907, vol. 1, 104r, EC.
263. 1907, vol. 1, 118r, EC.
264. 1907, vol. 1, 118v, EC.
265. 1907, vol. 1, 207v, EC.
266. 1907, vol. 1, 208r, EC.
267. 1907, vol. 1, 208v, EC.
268. 1907, vol. 1, 210v, EC.
269. 1907, vol. 2, 7r, EC.
270. 1907, vol. 2, 7v, EC.
271. 1907, vol. 2, 8r, EC.
272. 1907, vol. 2, 56v, EC.
273. 1907, vol. 2, 57r, EC.
274. 1907, vol. 2, 57v, EC.
275. 1907, vol. 2, 63v, EC.
276. 1907, vol. 2, 64r, EC.
277. 1907, vol. 2, 67v, EC.
278. 1907, vol. 2, 68r, EC.
279. 1907, vol. 2, 69v, EC.
280. 1907, vol. 2, 70r, EC.
281. 1907, vol. 2, 71v, EC.
282. 1907, vol. 2, 72r, EC.
283. 1907, vol. 2, 72v, EC.
284. 1907, vol. 2, 73r, EC.

5. The Long Denouement: 1908–14

1. 1908, 1v, EC.
2. 1908, 15v, EC.
3. 1908, 18v, EC.
4. 1908, 20v, EC.
5. 1908, 29r, EC.
6. 1908, 32r, EC; EC, transcribing a letter from Fr. Gray.
7. 1908, 32v, EC.
8. 1908, 47r, EC.
9. 1908, 53v, EC.
10. 1908, 54r, EC.
11. 1908, 68r, EC.
12. 1908, 106v, EC.
13. 1908, 195r, EC.
14. 1908, 201v, EC.
15. 1908, 202r, EC.
16. 1908, 202v, EC.
17. 1909, 13v, EC.
18. 1909, 16r, EC.
19. 1909, 27v, EC.

20. 1909, 28r, EC.
21. 1909, 28v, EC.
22. 1909, 74r, EC, transcription of KB letter.
23. 1909, 169r, EC.
24. 1909, 169v, EC.
25. 1909, 170r, EC.
26. 1910, 7r, EC.
27. 1910, 7v, EC.
28. 1910, 8r, EC.
29. 1910, 8v, EC.
30. 1910, 9r, EC.
31. 1910, 9v, EC.
32. 1910, 11v, telegram.
33. 1910, 17r, EC.
34. 1910, 17v, EC.
35. 1910, 18r, EC.
36. 1910, 25r, EC.
37. 1910, 25v, EC.
38. 1910, 26r, EC.
39. 1910, 26v, EC.

40. 1910, 27r, EC.
41. 1910, 27v, EC.
42. 1910, 29v, EC.
43. 1910, 31r, EC.
44. 1910, 31v, EC.
45. 1910, 37r, EC.
46. 1910, 37v, EC.
47. 1910, 38r, EC.
48. 1910, 38v, EC.
49. 1910, 39r, EC.
50. 1910, 39v, EC.
51. 1910, 42v, EC.
52. 1910, 43r, EC.
53. 1910, 57r, EC.
54. 1910, 68v, EC.
55. 1910, 70r, EC.
56. 1910, 76v, EC.
57. 1910, 77r, EC.
58. 1910, 89v, KB.
59. 1910, 92v, EC.
60. 1910, 93r, EC.

61. 1910, 93v, EC.
62. 1910, 99v, EC.
63. 1910, 100r, EC.
64. 1910, 101r, EC.
65. 1910, 102r, EC; EC, transcription of KB letter.
66. 1910, 104r, EC.
67. 1910, 104v, EC.
68. 1910, 106v, EC.
69. 1910, 107r, EC.
70. 1910, 107v, EC.
71. 1910, 108r, EC.
72. 1910, 108v, EC.
73. 1910, 109r, EC.
74. 1910, 110r, EC.
75. 1910, 111v, EC.
76. 1910, 112v, EC.
77. 1910, 155v, EC.
78. 1910, 234v, EC.
79. 1911, 18r, EC.
80. 1911, 18v, EC.
81. 1911, 19r, EC.
82. 1911, 20r, EC.
83. 1911, 20v, EC.
84. 1911, 21r, EC.
85. 1911, 21v, EC.
86. 1911, 22r, KB, transcription of letter to Ricketts.
87. 1911, 40r, EC.
88. 1911, 54r, EC, transcription of M. Berenson letter to KB.
89. 1911, 85r, EC.
90. 1911, 85v, EC.
91. 1911, 94v, EC.
92. 1911, 95r, EC.
93. 1911, 124v, KB.
94. 1911, 128r, EC.

95. 1911, 146r, EC.
96. 1911, 146v, EC.
97. 1911, 162r, EC.
98. 1911, 162v, EC.
99. 1911, 163r, EC.
100. 1911, 164v, EC.
101. 1911, 165r, EC.
102. 1911, 165v, EC.
103. 1911, 166r, EC.
104. 1912, 6r, EC.
105. 1912, 14v, KB.
106. 1912, 15r, KB.
107. 1912, 24r, EC.
108. 1912, 24v, EC.
109. 1912, 56v, EC.
110. 1912, 57r, EC.
111. 1912, 60r, EC.
112. 1912, 63v, EC.
113. 1912, 73r, EC.
114. 1912, 84v, EC.
115. 1912, 100v, EC.
116. 1912, 104v, EC.
117. 1912, 105r, EC.
118. 1912, 105v, EC.
119. 1912, 106r, EC.
120. 1912, 106v, EC.
121. 1912, 107r, EC.
122. 1912, 109r, EC.
123. 1912, 109v, EC.
124. 1912, 110r, EC.
125. 1912, 114v, EC.
126. 1912, 116r, EC.
127. 1912, 116v, EC.
128. 1912, 137r, KB.
129. 1912, 137v, KB.
130. 1912, 139r, KB.
131. 1912, 139v, KB.
132. 1912, 140r, KB.
133. 1913, 8r, EC.
134. 1913, 8v, EC.

135. 1913, 29r, EC.
136. 1913, 30v, KB.
137. 1913, 39r, EC.
138. 1913, 39v, EC.
139. 1913, 48v, EC.
140. 1913, 60r, EC.
141. 1913, 61r, EC.
142. 1913, 61v, EC.
143. 1913, 62r, EC.
144. 1913, 62v, EC.
145. 1913, 63r, EC.
146. 1913, 72r, EC.
147. 1913, 85r, EC.
148. 1913, 89v, EC.
149. 1913, 90r, EC.
150. 1913, 90v, EC.
151. 1913, 91r, KB.
152. 1913, 93v, EC.
153. 1913, 94r, EC.
154. 1913, 94v, EC.
155. 1913, 95r, EC.
156. 1913, 95v, EC.
157. 1913, 97r, EC.
158. 1913, 97v, EC, KB.
159. 1913, 98r, KB.
160. 1913, 98v, KB.
161. 1913, 99v, KB.
162. 1913, 100r, KB.
163. 1913, 100v, KB.
164. 1913, 101r, KB.
165. 1914, 3r, KB.
166. 1914, 4v, KB.
167. 1914, 7r, KB.
168. 1914, 7v, KB.
169. 1914, 15r, KB.
170. 1914, 29r, KB.
171. 1914, 31v, KB.
172. 1914, 34r, KB.
173. 1914, 35v, KB.
174. 1914, 37v, KB.

INDEX

Abbreviations: EC = Edith Cooper; KB = Katharine Bradley; MF = Michael Field

Addleshaw, Percy, 119
aesthetic movement, 7, 8, 272, 278, 292
Alvary, Max, 132
Anna Ruina (MF), 161, 167, 195, 201
Anstruther-Thomson, Clementina, 138
Anthony Derivian (MF), 149
Archer, William, 11, 33–34, 119, 120, 130
"Aridity" (MF), 320
Arnold, Matthew, 13, 32, 34–35, 279
Attila, My Attila! (MF), 142–43, 144, 145, 236
Austen, Jane, 13, 58
Austin, Alfred, 107n

Baker, Rosa, 47, 54
Barlow, Thomas, 210
Barrie, J. M., 276
Baudelaire, Charles, 13, 49n, 84, 97
Beardsley, Aubrey, 123, 128n, 129
beauty, 8, 43, 80, 139–40, 210, 265–66, 269, 309; Wilde and, 278
Beethoven, Ludwig van, 209, 225
Bell, Amy, 38, 41, 43–44, 55, 64, 81, 108, 109, 126, 131, 132, 145, 311; on Berenson, 208; her maid Florence, 255
Bell, Ernest, 65
Bellerophôn (MF), 3
Bellini, Giovanni, 78
Berenson, Bernard, 13, 34, 60, 63, 73, 74, 90, 107–8, 114, 120–21, 126–27, 133, 139–41, 142, 143, 147–48, 186n, 200, 296; "*Be contemporaneous*" command by, 92, 104, 113, 186; EC's obsession with, 33, 65–67, 78, 95, 98, 102, 104, 126–27, 128, 134–37, 145, 146, 196, 208, 216, 231, 267–69, 302; lim-

erick about, 239; MF humiliated by, 10, 33, 34, 91–105; nicknames for, xviii, 4; photo of, 59; religion and, 66–67; sexuality and, 140; in 20th century, 196, 203, 208, 211, 212–16, 218, 228, 231–32, 233, 236, 246
Berenson, Mary Costelloe, 63, 65–67, 73–74, 78, 107–8, 113, 120, 124–25, 133, 134, 136, 140, 142, 143, 147, 186; during Paris visit from MF, 90–104; limerick about, 239; married life with Berenson, 124, 194, 196, 203, 208, 212–15, 216, 228–30, 231n, 242, 246, 254, 255, 302; on Whym Chow's death, 296
Bernhardt, Sarah, 13, 130–32
Bickle, Sharon, 4, 15
Blake, William, 39, 41, 47, 48, 62, 179
Boccaccio, Giovanni, 137
Borgia (MF), 241
Botticelli, Sandro, 60, 93, 112
Braddon, Mary Elizabeth, 7
Bradley, Charles (father), 5, 55, 64, 85, 263
Bradley, David, 279
Bradley, Emma Harris, 3, 5, 6, 17, 19–26, 28, 55, 168, 289–90
Bradley, Francis, 86, 148, 190, 196, 200, 243, 308, 313–14
Bradley, Katharine Harris: "Arran Leigh" pen name of, 3; background of, 3–4, 5–6; early diaries of, 3, 5–6, 17–31; nicknames for, xviii, 4; sickness and death of, 272, 317–18, 321
Braun, Adolphe, 80
Bridges, Robert, 107

Brontë sisters, 7, 13, 58, 141

Brooks, Mary Louisa, 85–86

Browning, Elizabeth Barrett, 13, 37, 51n, 185

Browning, Robert, 3, 4, 10, 11, 14, 35–38, 39, 41, 42–43, 44, 48; death of, 13, 32, 33, 49–52, 279; later references to, 53, 74, 83, 93, 114, 128, 139n, 141, 145, 147, 233, 238

Browning, Robert Wiedemann Barrett ("Pen"), 35, 42–43

Browning, Sarianna, 8, 39, 41, 42–43

Brutus Ultor (MF), 46

Bunting, Percy, 52

Bunyan, John, 20

Burke, James, 94, 96–97, 125

Burne-Jones, Edward, 124, 288

"But, if our love is dying, let it die" (MF), 259

Caine, Hall, 116, 118

Callirrhoë (MF), 3, 62, 277

Campion, Thomas, 41

Canute the Great (MF), 138

Carducci, Giosuè, 139

Carloman (aka *In the Name of Time*; MF), 47, 81–82, 121, 145

Carlyle, Thomas, 89

Carroll, Lewis, 124

Catharine of Alexandria, 253, 264

Catholicism, MF and, 9, 197, 263–66, 267–70, 271, 273–78, 300–302, 319–20

Clelia Guidascarpe (MF), 47

Clough, Blanche Athena, 79

Cobbe, Frances Power, 237

Collins, Wilkie, 7, 22n, 34

Columbus, Christopher, 174

Combes, Miss, 185

Confucius, 163

Coombe, Helen, 230, 232

Cooper, Edith Emma: background of, 3–4, 17; Dresden illness of, 33, 69–77, 84, 211; early life of, 23, 24–25; limericks by, 239; nicknames for, xviii, 4, 33; on 19th century's end, 194; sickness and death of, 272, 293–98, 303–17 passim; ultimate references to, 317–20. *See also under* Berenson, Bernard

Cooper, Emma Harris Bradley, 3, 4, 7, 10, 23, 24, 32; decline, death, and burial of, 38–41, 43–49, 50; later references to, 52, 55, 61–62, 70, 75, 77, 80, 89–90, 94, 100, 111, 128, 147, 152–53, 166, 185, 247, 262, 268, 308

Cooper, James Robert, 3, 21–22, 23, 24, 44, 45, 46, 70, 89, 111–12, 117, 120, 143, 149;

death of, 122–23, 124, 150, 152–62, 164–65, 188; memories of, 174, 185, 187, 210–11, 216, 247, 254, 268, 279, 289; socialism and, 34, 110; as woodworker, 47, 166

Cooper, John, 20, 202, 209

Corelli, Marie, 262–63

Correggio, 94, 133

Costa, Giovanni, 90

Costelloe, Frank, 65–66, 124, 136

Costelloe, Mary. *See* Berenson, Mary Costelloe

Cowden Clarke, Mary, 20

Cowper, William, 198, 257

Craik, Dinah, 20

Crane, Walter, 217n

Creswick, Mrs. Charles, 116, 117

Croquis (aka *For That Moment* Only; MF), 120, 127, 145

Cruttwell, Maude Alice Wilson, 137–38, 140

Daniell, James Livett, 180

Dante Alighieri, 72, 218

"Dear temptations of her face, The" (MF), 313

death, EC on, 142, 180, 241

Deirdre (MF), 18, 195–96, 225, 227–28

Dellamora, Richard, 8

Dickens, Charles, 7, 10, 22n, 63, 167, 190n, 262, 277

Dickinson, Goldsworthy Lowes, 230–31

Doone, Neville, 116, 118

Dossi, Dosso, 63

doves, 8, 181, 240

Duffy, Carol Ann, 107n

Dumas, Alexandre, 132

du Maurier, George, 218n

Duncan, Dr., 305

Dürer, Albrecht, 73n

Duse, Eleonora, 13, 132

Edison, Thomas, 124

Edward II, 234

Edward VII, 272

Egerton, George, 129

Elgin Marbles, 62, 117, 132

Eliot, George, 7, 13, 42

Elizabeth I, 234

Elliot, Jean (or Jane), 141

Ellis, Edith, 82–83

Ellis, Havelock, 9, 13, 33, 82–83, 220, 225

Ellis, Louisa Eleanor, 82, 84, 85, 112, 219–20

Equal Love (MF), 121

Fair Rosamund (MF), 3, 147, 150–51
Ferencz (MF), 47, 117
Ferrer (dog), 296, 304–5, 312
"Fifty Quatrains" (MF), 173
Fitzgibbon, Gerald, 4, 263–64, 267, 271, 274–
   75, 277–78, 294–95, 305
Flaubert, Gustave, 13, 91n, 103n, 108
Fleming, Albert, 115, 117, 143
Fortey, Emily, 282–85
Francis of Assisi, 230
Fry, Joan, 232–33
Fry, Roger, 13, 230, 232

Garnett, Richard, 169
Gaskell, Elizabeth, 7
Gautier, Théophile, 8
Gérente, Alfred, 6, 17–18, 27–31, 135, 237
Gérente, Mademoiselle, 17, 26, 28–31, 237
Gilbert, William, and Arthur Sullivan, 205
Giorgione, 80, 94
Goethe, Johann Wolfgang von, 20, 165
Goncourt brothers, 84
Gonne, Maud, 223
Goscannon, Father ("Goss"). *See* Fitzgibbon,
   Gerald
Gray, Effie, 42
Gray, John, 13, 214, 234, 264–65, 271, 272,
   275, 276–77, 320
Great War (World War I), 196, 272, 321
Gregory, Isabella Augusta, 225, 227, 232
Greiffenhagen, Maurice, 87–88
Grein, J. T., 33, 114, 118
Grove, William Henry, 42
Grundy, Sydney, 120

Halifax, John, 20
Hall, Alfred, 85–86
Hardy, Thomas, 144, 148, 265, 315
Harland, Henry, 133–34
Harris, Frank, 204
Harrison, Fredric, 89
Heaton, Ellen, 56
Hegel, Georg Wilhelm Friedrich, 148
Hesiod, 32n
Hesse, Nicolas-Auguste, 30n
Hewetson, J. T., 180, 181
Hogarth, William, 204
Hokusai, 186
Holland, Augusta, 235
Hollyer, Frederick, 52
Holmes, Charles, 151, 171, 205, 207, 288
homosexuality, 4–5, 8, 12, 18, 33, 34, 123
Horne, Herbert, 81, 98, 231

House Beautiful movement, 123
Hutton, Richard Holt, 109
Huysmans, Joris-Karl, 13, 84, 138

Ibsen, Henrik, 13, 34, 109, 110, 112, 119, 120,
   130, 179
Image, Janet McHale, 227
Image, Selwyn, 81
Irving, Isabel, 37
"It was deep April and the morn" (MF), 87

Jackson, Holbrook, 315
James, Henry, 148, 273
Japanese-British Exhibition, 290
Johnson, Lionel, 60–61
Joyce, James, 272
Julia Domna (MF), 170

Karsavina, Tamara, 309
Keats, John, 13, 114, 165, 209, 218, 315;
   "Lamia" by, 102, 127; unattributed quota-
   tions from, 162, 232, 235, 318
Keegan, Mary, 116, 118
Kipling, Rudyard, 13, 195, 220–21, 230
Klafsky, Katharina, 132

Lane, John, 125, 146n
Lee, Vernon, 13, 137–38
Lees, Edith. *See* Ellis, Edith
Le Gallienne, Mildred Lee, 88
Le Gallienne, Richard, 88, 142–43
Leonardo da Vinci, 11, 94, 101n, 126
Leppington, Blanche, 65
Lewis, Wyndham, 272
Lishman, Dr., 306, 313, 314–15
Little, William John Knox, 42
Long Ago (MF), 3, 32, 33, 37, 39, 40, 47, 54,
   79, 88n, 170n: "Atthis, my darling" in,
   313–14, 319
Lotto, Lorenzo, 131
Lowell, James Russell, 96
Lucian of Samosata, 143
"Lumber-Room, A" (MF), 52
Lumière brothers, 124

MacColl, Dugald Sutherland, 207
Mallarmé, Stéphane, 84
"Mandie," 96–97
Manet, Édouard, 98, 103
Mantegna, Andrea, 93, 166
Marbury, Elizabeth, 128
Marcus, Sharon, 4–5
marriage, views on, 83, 228, 231, 243

Martini, Simone, 94
Masefield, John, 310, 312
massacre game, 229–30
Mathews, Charles Elkin, 78–79, 84, 91, 143, 146n
McNabb, Vincent, 278, 290, 300, 304, 307, 320–21
Meinhold, Johannes Wilhelm, 151
Meredith, George, 13, 33, 47n, 66, 83–84, 109, 144, 148; encounters with, 52–54, 85, 88–89, 144–45, 303; on *Long Ago*, 40; *Modern Love* by, 82, 83
Meredith, Marie Eveleen, 85, 88–89
Michelangelo, 47
Mill, John Stuart, 18
Millais, John Everett, 42, 124
Millet, Jean-François, 81, 113
Milton, John, 49, 192, 259–60, 307
Miss Toplady (decorating shop), 186–87, 198, 224, 235
modernity and modernism, 11, 16, 34, 99, 100–101, 111, 112–13, 119, 121, 122, 127, 149, 192, 195, 271, 278, 284; KB's condem- nation of progress and, 196, 200, 210, 258; KB on "moralities" in, 106
Moore, George, 13, 33, 61, 62, 91, 214, 218, 231
Moore, Miss, 224
"Morning-Rains" (MF), 275
Morrellian method, 95n, 101
Morris, William, 124; bed by, 170; carpet by, 186; wallpapers by, 65, 79, 184
Moulton, Louise Chandler, 56–57, 60, 203
Musico (dog), 123, 156, 160, 162, 164–65, 166, 167–68, 173–74, 178, 180–81, 189–90, 191–92, 199, 202, 211, 213, 221, 251, 276; death and memories of, 272, 287–89, 291, 297
Musset, Alfred de, 36, 80
Mystic Trees (MF), 302, 310

New Minnesinger and Other Poems, The (KB), 3
New Woman movement, 7–8
Nietzsche, Friedrich, 13, 124, 145, 149, 196, 203–4, 208, 219
Nijinsky, Vaslav, 309
"No beauty born of pride my Lady hath" (MF), 306–7
nudity, EC on, 103, 266–67
Nutt, Alfred, 201

Obrist, Hermann, 134
"Old Ivories" (MF), 313–14
Old Wine in New Bottles (MF), 98–99

Paris Morgue, 10, 34, 56, 62, 96, 99–101, 102
Pater, Hester, 8, 49, 79
Pater, Walter, 13, 33, 49, 57, 58, 65, 82, 91, 109; death of, 124; encounters with, 42–43, 79; evaluations and memories of, 136, 171, 189, 292, 298
Paul the Apostle, 198, 255
Pease, Dora, 168
Peek, Elizabeth Georgina, 311
Pennell, Joseph, 207
Petrarch, Francesco, 31
Phillimore, John Swinnerton, 168
Pindar, 214
Pinero, Arthur Wing, 120, 125
Pissarro, Lucien, 197, 253–54, 255, 319
Plato, 58, 127
Plowden, Edith Ramsey Chichele, 220
Poe, Edgar Allan, 84
Poems of Adoration (MF), 302, 306, 310
Poldi Pezzoli, Gian Giacomo, 214
Potter, Beatrix, 33, 68
Potter, Paul M., 143
Power, D'Arcy, 295
Pugin, Augustus, 268
Purcell, Henry, 51–52

Question of Memory, A (MF), 33–34, 47n, 113–21, 125–26, 128, 131, 211, 216

Raffalovich, Marc-André, 264n
Redon, Odilon, 78–79
Reily, Kate, 297, 301
Renan, Ernest, 222
Reyer, Ernest, 103
Reynolds, Russell, 115
"Rhythm" (MF), 133
Ricketts, Charles de Sousy, 4, 125, 129–30, 147, 167–74, 189, 195, 197–201, 204–7, 209, 213–14, 217–20, 222–228 passim, 231, 233, 239–42, 246, 253, 259, 263, 267–68, 276, 288, 290–92, 296, 300, 309, 315, 317–18, 320; background of, 170; *Dial* and, 151, 276; limericks about, 239; *L'Oiseau bleu* brooch by, 198–99, 213, 233; Paragon house and, 123, 175–86; photo of, 126; "Sabbatai" ring by, 236; on Wilde, 234–35, 236, 241
Robins, Elizabeth, 13, 129, 130
Robinson, Ralph W., 164, 166, 255
Roden, Frederick Scott, 271
Ross, Robert, 205–6, 236
Rossetti, Christina, 13, 124, 141

Rossetti, Dante Gabriel, 35, 56, 68, 88, 101, 170, 199, 292

Rothenstein, William, 125, 147, 170, 205, 206, 224, 263

Rubens, Peter Paul, 71

Ruskin, John, 7, 56, 124, 278; death of, 196, 200; *The Eagle's Nest*, 40; KB and, 3, 13, 196, 200; Whistler and, 125n

Russell, Frank, 229

Ryan, Amy Katharine Cooper, 3, 5, 18, 20, 23, 24–25, 37, 47, 70, 82, 111–12, 117, 127, 188; engagement and wedding of, 123, 162, 168, 169, 173, 174, 181, 183, 186, 190–91, 193, 216; father's death and, 149, 152, 158; later references to, 192, 198, 209, 242, 254, 279, 288–89, 292, 297, 299, 300; sickness and death of, 272, 279–86

Ryan, John, 167–68, 173, 183, 190–91, 193, 279–84, 289, 291–92, 296

Sand, George, 58

Santayana, George, 13, 214, 228–30

Sappho, 3, 33, 35, 79, 141, 243n, 271

Sardou, Victorien, 131

Sargent, John Singer, 84, 272–73

Schreiner, Olive, 13, 33, 82n, 112

Second Boer War, 196, 197–98

Sellar, Robert, 168

servants: Alice, 40, 47, 63, 67, 80; Crofts, 190; Delia, 150; Ellen, 174; Eva, 161; Jane, 277, 304, 312, 319; Josephine Emily Woodger, 277, 290, 315; Kate Crisp, 166; Kate Dufter, 213; Lillias, 202, 213, 218; Lizzie, 190; Lygel, 150; Mary, 20, 24, 25; May, 312; Mrs. Drew, 275–76; Mrs. Riches, 252; Sarah, 48, 174, 190

Seton, Emma Elizabeth, 60

sexuality, 140–42, 144. *See also* homosexuality

Shakespeare, William, 20, 34, 61, 87, 107. Works of: *Antony and Cleopatra*, 131, 244; *As You Like It*, 151, 228–29; *Hamlet*, 158, 214, 241, 249; *King Lear*, 102, 132, 244; *Macbeth*, 309; *Measure for Measure*, 119; *Othello*, 53, 132, 141, 172; *Romeo and Juliet*, 185; *The Tempest*, 317, 318

Shannon, Charles, 123, 125–26, 130, 147, 168–74, 189, 195, 197–201, 204–7, 209, 211, 213–14, 217–20, 231, 233–36, 263, 267, 288, 311; limerick about, 239; Paragon house and, 123, 175–86; photo of, 126; reaction to Wilde's death by, 206

Sharp, William, 53–54

Shaw, George Bernard, 130, 168

Shelley, Percy Bysshe, 13, 107, 117, 129

"She Mingled Me Rue and Roses" (MF), 46

Siddall, Elizabeth, 56n

Sight and Song (MF), 78–79, 81, 84, 89–90, 91, 101, 104, 125

Smiles, Samuel, 42

Smith, Logan Pearsall, 78, 136, 168, 228, 302

socialism, 34, 66, 110

Song Book (MF), 41, 47, 49

Sophocles, 152–53, 155

Spencer, Herbert, 33, 54, 64, 68

Spenser, Edmund, 129, 181

Spinoza, Baruch, 120

Spooner cousins, 289, 292

Stephania (MF), 78, 90, 91, 109, 193

Stevenson, Robert Louis, 124

Strachey, Barbara, 302

Strachey, Lytton, 272

Sturge, Caroline, 211–12

Sturge, Marie Henriette, 226–27, 228, 237, 251–52, 291, 312

Sturge Moore, Thomas, 212, 224, 237–38, 242, 243–44, 250, 291, 310n, 312; Berenson on, 232; critical neglect of, 315; as executor/editor, 5, 15, 186, 195, 226, 320; marriage of, 196, 226–27, 228, 245–46; Yeats and, 217–19, 221–23

Sudermann, Hermann, 227

suffrage movement, 7, 12, 18, 266

Swanwick, Anna, 37

Swinburne, Algernon, 107, 169, 234, 272, 273, 278–79, 292

Symonds, John Addington, 82n, 125n

Symons, Arthur, 94, 98, 103, 125, 225

Synge, John Millington, 315

Tennyson, Alfred, Lord, 34, 65; death of, 107, 279; *Idylls of the King*, 83; *In Memoriam*, 30–31, 52; "The Lady of Shalott," 156; *Queen Mary*, 47

Terry, Ellen, 37, 235

Thackeray, William Makepeace, 7, 58, 135

"Thanatos, Thy Praise I Sing" (MF), 300

Thomas à Kempis, 306

Todhunter, John, 118, 119

Tolstoy, Leo, 13, 112; EC on *Anna Karenina*, 34, 108–9

Tragedy of Pardon and Diane, The (MF), 244

Tragic Mary, The (MF), 60–61, 68, 93, 125, 221, 254

"Train of Queens, A" (MF), 173

Tree, Herbert Beerbohm, 61, 63

Tristan de Léonis, 222, 225, 238, 241
Tura, Cosimo, 78
Turner, J.M.W., 84, 113
Turner, Reginald, 205–6

Underneath the Bough (MF), 113
University Club for Ladies, 79, 82
University of Oxford, 171–72, 229, 258

Vanita, Ruth, 271
Verlaine, Paul, 13, 78, 84, 146
Verrocchio, Andrea del, 169
Vickers, Miss, 216–17
Victoria, Queen, 18, 124, 192, 202; death of, 196, 209–10
Virgil, 129
Viti, Timoteo, 166

Wagner, Richard, 71, 73, 132–33, 151, 209
Wallace, Alfred Russel, 120
Watson, William, 107
Watteau, Jean-Antoine, 81, 84n
Watts, George Frederic, 42, 112, 235
Watts, Isaac, 78
Watts-Dunton, Theodore, 57, 278
Weingartner, Felix, 225
Whistler, James Abbott McNeil, 125, 147, 207
White, George Stuart, 198
Whitman, Walt, 13, 34, 39, 40, 43, 84, 230
Whym Chow (dog), 4, 12, 122, 123; early years of, 162–69, 173, 174–75, 176, 179, 180–82, 185, 187, 189, 191–92, 194; Kipling's rabbit and, 195, 220–21; later years of, 195, 202, 212, 213, 216, 217, 229, 245–46; sickness, death, and memories of, 197, 246–65, 267, 269–70, 276, 288, 291, 293–94, 297, 299, 311
Whym Chow, Flame of Love (MF), 197, 254, 255–56, 272, 319, 320–21
Whymper, Edward, 160, 164, 226
Wilde, Constance Lloyd, 67, 205, 206–7
Wilde, Oscar, 7, 8, 13, 33, 124, 130, 147, 204,
224, 262–63, 278; death of, 196, 205–8; encounters with, 10, 34, 57–58, 60, 67–68, 90, 119; letter from, 127–28; persecution of, 4, 12, 123, 139, 145, 151, 217, 277; Ricketts on, 234–35, 236, 241. Works of: "The Ballad of Reading Gaol," 166–67, 250; *The Critic as Artist*, 57n; *De Profundis*, 196, 241–42, 257, 259; *A House of Pomegranates*, 68, 78; *An Ideal Husband*, 135–36; *The Importance of Being Earnest*, 200; *Lady Windemere's Fan*, 34; *The Picture of Dorian Gray*, 34, 84n; "Roses and Rue," 46n; *Salomé*, 34; *A Woman of No Importance*, 34
Wild Honey from Various Thyme (MF), 259, 273, 275, 314n
William Rufus (MF), 61, 138
Winter, John Strange, 262
womanhood, views on, 18, 66, 89, 142–43, 185, 222–23, 237, 238, 246, 266, 275, 276
Woolf, Leonard and Virginia, 173
Wordsworth, William, 13, 74, 144, 165, 243, 298, 315; "Ode: Intimations of Mortality" by, 44, 45, 55, 141
Works and Days: composition of, 6–7, 9–10, 16, 32; history in, 11; intentions for, 5; novelistic aspects of, 6–8, 10, 13, 17; poems in, 12–13, 87, 239, 245, 259; scholarship on, 15; structure of, 8–9, 15; title of, 32
World at Auction, The (MF), 142, 145, 163
Worthington, Mary Grace Thomas, 224

"Yea, we had been one soul, and we divide" (MF), v, 245
Yeats, William Butler, 13, 18, 47n, 209, 222, 223, 232; *Deirdre* and, 195–96, 225–26, 227–28; encounter with, 195, 217–18, 221
Yellow Book, The, 123, 125, 128–29, 133–34

Zola, Émile, 84
Zorn, Anders, 103